D0151852

Meramec Library
St. Louis Community College
11333 Big Bend Blvd.
Kirkwood, MO 63122-5799
314-984-7797

Ancient Canaan and Israel

New Perspectives

St. Louis Community College
at Meramec
LIBRARY

ABC-CLIO's
Understanding Ancient Civilizations

The Ancient Maya
The Ancient Greeks
The Aztecs
The Romans
Ancient Canaan and Israel

Forthcoming

The Ancient Celts
The Ancient Egyptians
Ancient Mesopotamia
The Incas

St. Louis Community College
at Meramec
LIBRARY

Ancient
Canaan
and Israel

New Perspectives

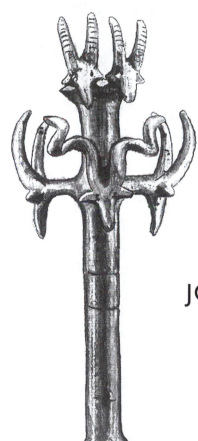

JONATHAN M. GOLDEN

A B C ⬖ C L I O

Santa Barbara, California
Denver, Colorado   Oxford, England

Copyright © 2004 by Jonathan M. Golden

All rights reserved. No part of this publication may be reproduced, stored in a retrieval system, or transmitted, in any form or by any means, electronic, mechanical, photocopying, recording, or otherwise, except for the inclusion of brief quotations in a review, without prior permission in writing from the publishers.

Library of Congress Cataloging-in-Publication Data
Golden, Joseph, 1928–
  Ancient Canaan and Israel : new perspectives / Jonathan M. Golden.
    p. cm. — (Understanding ancient civilizations)
  Includes bibliographical references and index.
    ISBN 1-57607-897-3 (hardcover : alk. paper) — ISBN 1-57607-898-1 (e-book)
1. Jews—History—1200–953 B.C. 2. Jews—History—953–586 B.C. 3. Jews—Politics and government—To 70 A.D. 4. Jews—Social life and customs. 5. Canaanites—History. 6. Palestine—History—To 70 A.D. I. Title. II. Series.
DS121.55.G57 2004
933—dc22
                                                            2004009633

08 07 06 05 04 10 9 8 7 6 5 4 3 2 1

This book is also available on the World Wide Web as an e-book.
Visit abc-clio.com for details.

ABC-CLIO, Inc.
130 Cremona Drive, P.O. Box 1911
Santa Barbara, California 93116-1911

This book is printed on acid-free paper.
Manufactured in the United States of America.

For my parents, Dorie and Carl Golden,
who taught me a love of learning

Contents

Maps

Series Editor's Preface

In recent years, there has been a significant and steady increase of academic and popular interest in the study of past civilizations. This is due in part to a surge in coverage of the archaeological profession in popular film and television, both in documentaries and dramas, and to the extensive journalistic reporting of spectacular new finds from all parts of the world. Yet, because archaeologists and other scholars have tended to approach their study of ancient peoples and civilizations exclusively from their own disciplinary perspectives and for their professional colleagues, there has long been a lack of general factual and other research resources available for the nonspecialist. The Understanding Ancient Civilizations series is intended to fill that need.

Volumes in the series are principally designed to introduce the general reader, student, and nonspecialist to the study of specific ancient civilizations. Each volume is devoted to a particular archaeological culture (for example, the ancient Maya of southern Mexico and adjacent Guatemala) or cultural region (for example, Israel and Canaan) and seeks to achieve, with careful selectivity and astute critical assessment of the literature, an expression of a particular civilization and an appreciation of its achievements.

The keynote of the Understanding Ancient Civilizations series is to provide, in a uniform format, an interpretation of each civilization that will express its culture and place in the world as well as the qualities and background that make it unique. Series titles include volumes on the archaeology and prehistory of the ancient civilizations of Egypt, Greece, Rome, and Mesopotamia, as well as the achievements of the Celts, Aztecs, and Inca, among others. Still more books are in the planning stage.

I was particularly fortunate in having Kevin Downing from ABC-CLIO contact me in search of an editor for a series about archaeology. It is a simple statement of the truth that there would be no series without him. I am also lucky to have Simon Mason, Kevin's successor from ABC-CLIO, continue to push the production of the series. Given the scale of the project and the schedule for production, he deserves more than a sincere thank you.

JOHN WEEKS

Preface

The invitation to write this book came from my colleague, former employer, and longtime friend, John Weeks. Weeks cornered me in his office in the Museum Library at the University of Pennsylvania Museum, where I had worked evenings and weekends for more than seven years, insisting I agree. Though daunting, the prospect of writing a volume covering some 4,000 years of ancient history in the southern Levant was simply too enticing to turn down. Several outstanding books on the archaeology of the region had been published during the 1990s—most notably Ami Mazar's *Archaeology of the Land of the Bible* (1990), Amnon Ben-Tor's edited volume *The Archaeology of Ancient Israel* (1992), and Thomas E. Levy's edited *Archaeology of Society in the Holy Land* (1995; 3d ed. 2003)—but the new millennium called for a new synthesis. Indeed, new excavations have continued to produce a windfall of archaeological finds related to the ancient peoples of the southern Levant, while major shifts in the field's theoretical underpinnings have been forcing academics and others to reconsider the interpretation of older discoveries.

The book that follows was not easy to write. The very premise of an Israelite archaeology is one that has become increasingly controversial in recent decades. Past generations of scholars took for granted a great deal in terms of accepting the biblical narrative concerning the Israelites as relatively accurate, if not precise. But this approach has been seriously challenged to the point where no scholar can afford to ignore the issue. And if the wave of exploration of "the Holy Land" that began two centuries ago was largely an effort to prove the historicity of the Hebrew Bible, many subsequent discoveries have made portions of the Bible rather difficult to accept as fact. Where then is the point of departure for the archaeologist who wants to discuss evidence relating to ethnicity?

It is also a sober reality of archaeology that the past does not exist in some form of hermetically sealed vacuum, but rather is actively created and perceived of in the present. Thus, current political situations also play a role in the way the past is received in the present, and this is particularly true of the southern Levant, where modern land disputes sometimes involve the interpretation of archaeological remains.

Modern politics, for instance, are played out in the site nomenclature, which also relates to some broader issues concerning linguistics and terminology that should be mentioned here. This book, for purposes of consistency, generally uses the word *Tel* (for example, Tel Beit Yerah), as opposed to *Khirbet* (Khirbet Kerak), for site names, simply because the former terminology is more commonly used in the literature. Many of the people, places, and things described in this book are named in modern Hebrew, Arabic, or one of several different ancient languages. These words of course are transliterated here into English, and thus multiple spellings are often acceptable; for example, the coastal site of the Philistines, Ashqelon, may be spelled with either a *q* or a *k* (Ashkelon), though the former is consistently used throughout this book. Similarly, the *tz* sound and *z* are generally interchangeable, as are, in some instances, the *b* and *v*.

The ancient history of the southern Levant, the central region of the "Bible Lands," has for a long time captured the public imagination and continues to do so today, in part because it allows many Christians, Jews, and Muslims throughout the world to point to some tangible relationship between fact and faith, science and scripture. To be sure, some of the discoveries made at archaeological sites throughout the region, including ancient texts, do more to document the historical value of portions of the Hebrew Bible than to discredit them (though, as would be expected, the later in time the portion of the Bible, the more likely it reflects some historical reality). The purpose of this book is neither to confirm nor to deny, but to present a representation of life—economic, social, political, and religious—in ancient Canaan and Israel, and to do so as accurately as the current archaeological and textual evidence will allow.

Jonathan M. Golden

Acknowledgments

I would like to thank the many people, including mentors, professional colleagues, and friends, who provided help and support in the completion of this book. To begin, I would like to thank those who read and commented on drafts of the text. First and foremost, I thank Catherine Pasquale, who read and commented on every chapter. Aaron Brody, Isaac S. D. Sassoon, Steven Golden, Seymour Gitin, Whitney Paplailiou, and Yfat Thearani all read various portions of the book, offering insights, comments, and constructive criticism. Other people who were helpful in providing ideas include Herbert Huffmon, Yorke Rowan, Morag Kersel, Serge Avery, and Thomas E. Levy.

I also wish to acknowledge the counsel provided by my legal "Dream Team," Robert Strent, Rebecca Houlding, and Jonathan Weiss, as well as Michael Weiss, who accompanied me on a whirlwind tour of Israel in June 2003. I would like to thank members of Kibbutz Ein Harod, and David Motin in particular, for hospitality during my most recent visit to Israel. The staff at the Nelson Glueck School of Biblical Archaeology, Hebrew Union College–Jewish Institute of Religion (HUC-JIR), were also helpful, especially David Ilan, Hanni Hirsch, Rachel Ben-Dor, Malka Hershkovitz, Adi Kafri, and Avram Biran. Images were provided by Margie Burton and Emerson Grossmith; Kerry Moore helped with research on museum collections and university programs.

There are a number of people at ABC-CLIO whom I would like to thank by name, including John Weeks, Kevin Downing, Simon Mason, Michelle Trader, and Sharon Daugherty, all of whom were extremely patient with a sometimes scattered author, from the initial signing of the contract to the submission of the final illustrations.

I would also like to thank Oriana Kopec, Gabriella Frisoli, Brian Gardner, and the rest of the staff in the faculty computer lab at Drew University, as well as Alan Canditotti for technical computer support. Very special thanks must be extended to Julie Hanlon, who helped with this project in a number of ways, especially in the preparation of illustrations, and without whom several key deadlines may have been in jeopardy. Finally, I would like to thank my mother and father, Dorie and Carl Golden, for their constant support and encouragement.

Jonathan M. Golden

Chronology

Year B.C.E.	Levant	Syria-Anatolia	S. Mesopotamia	Egypt	Historical Materials and Events
5800	Wadi Rabah (Local Halaf)	Halaf	Early Ubaid		
4700–3500	Chalcolithic	Ubaid	Late Ubaid	Nagada Culture / Buto-Maadi Culture	
3500–3050	Early Bronze Age 1	Khabur–Tel Brak / Uruk Expansion	Early Uruk / Late Uruk / Jemdet Nasr	Narmer / Dynasties 1–2	c. 3050 B.C.E. Narmer Palette
3050–2200	Early Bronze Age 2–3	c. 2400 B.C.E. Spread of Hurrians / c. 2500 B.C.E. Alaça Höyük	Early Dynastic 1–3 / c. 2800 B.C.E. Royal Tombs of Ur / c. 2300 B.C.E. Sargon (I)	Old Kingdom Dynasties 3–6 / Saqqarra; Giza Pyramids	Pyramid Texts / 2234 B.C.E. Akkadian Empire begins / Ebla Archive Naram Sin takes Ebla
2200–2000	Intermediate Bronze Age (EB4/MB1)	Ebla / Mari	c. 2200 Ur-Nammu "Third Dynasty, Ur" / Dynasty of Isin	First Intermediate Period / 2181–2040 B.C.E. Dynasties 7–10	Elam takes Ur
2000–1800	Middle Bronze Age 1	Kanesh / Assur	2025–1863 Dynasty of Larsa (Amorite) / c. 2000–1600 B.C.E. Old Babylonian Pd.	Middle Kingdom / 2040–1782 B.C.E. Dynasties 11–12	c. 1900–1800 B.C.E. Execration Texts / c. 1900–1750 B.C.E. Kanesh Archive / c. 1800–1750 B.C.E. Mari Archive
1800–1550	Middle Bronze Age 2–3	1775–1762 B.C.E. Zimrilim	c. 1815–1775 B.C.E. Shamshi-Adad / c. 1790–1750 B.C.E. Hammurabi	1782–1570 B.C.E. Hyksos in Delta / 1550–1525 B.C.E. Second Intermediate Period (D13–17)	c. 1760 B.C.E. Babylon takes Mari / c. 1630 B.C.E. Hittites take Alalakh / c. 1600 B.C.E. Hittites sack Babylon / Alalakh Archive
1550–1200	Late Bronze Age	c. 1650–1200 B.C.E. Old Hittite Period; Hittite capital at Hattusas (Boghazköy) / c. 1380–1340 B.C.E. (or 1350–1315 B.C.E.) Suppiluliumas I	1500–1365 B.C.E. Mitanni conquest / c. 1375–1150 B.C.E. Kassite Dynasty	1550–1070 B.C.E. New Kingdom Dynasties 18–20 / 1351–1334 B.C.E. Akhenaten (Amenhotep IV)	c. 1550 B.C.E. Expulsion of the Hyksos by Ahmose (1550–1525 B.C.E.) / c. 1457 B.C.E. Thutmose III defeats the King of Qadesh in the Battle of Megiddo

Year B.C.E.	Levant	Syria-Anatolia	S. Mesopotamia	Egypt	Historical Materials and Events
		c. 1365–1330 B.C.E. Tushratta		1279–1213 B.C.E. Rameses II	c. 1365–1335 B.C.E. Amarna Letters
		c. 1275–1250 B.C.E. Hattusili III			c. 1279 B.C.E. Battle of Qadesh
1200–1000	Iron Age 1		1100 B.C.E. King Tiglath-Pileser	1213–1203 B.C.E. Merenptah	
1000–586	Iron Age 2	c. 830–600 B.C.E. Urartu Kingdom	911–600 B.C.E. Neo Assyrian Empire	Third Intermediate Period	c. 875 B.C.E. Reliefs at palace at Nimrud
			883–859 B.C.E. Assurnasirpal II	1070–525 B.C.E. Dynasties 21–26	722 B.C.E. Samaria falls to the Assyrians
			612–539 B.C.E. Neo-Babylonian Empire		586 B.C.E. Jerusalem falls to Babylonians

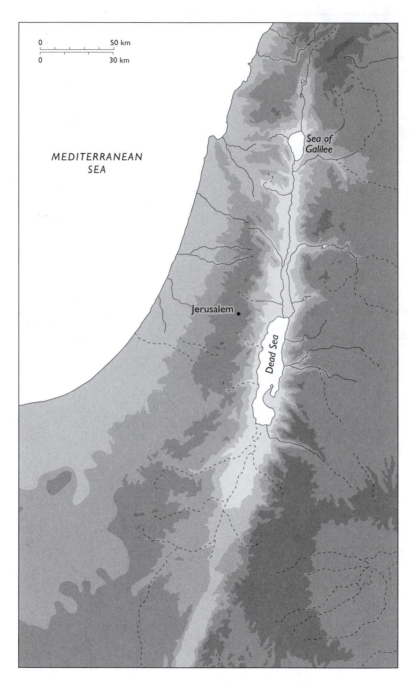

Southern Levant

PART I

Introduction

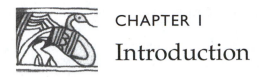

CHAPTER 1

Introduction

CULTURAL HISTORY OF ANCIENT ISRAEL: AN OVERVIEW

The southern Levant has been more or less continuously occupied for more than a million years. As a corridor between Africa and Eurasia, it served as both a passageway and a home to some of the first humans to leave Africa. And as a thin strip of fertile land in what is otherwise largely an arid zone, it hosted some of the world's earliest farming communities during the late prehistoric period known as the Neolithic, and perhaps even earlier.[1] Therefore, from the fifth millennium B.C.E. onward, any historical study concerning the Middle East, and the southern Levant in particular, must take into account the cultural ecology of the region. The motif of the desert and the sown, echoed in the biblical tradition, clearly reflects the overriding concern with the complementary role played by pastoral nomadism and transhumance, on the one hand, and intensive agriculture and urbanism, on the other.

General trends in settlement patterns over time reflect a cycle characterized by the development of urban systems and their subsequent breakdown, only to emerge anew. Close examination of long-term trends in settlement in the region, for instance, has revealed a pattern of alternating demographic expansion and decline. In fact, it is possible to identify three main waves of settlement during the third and second millennia B.C.E., the first being the Early Bronze Age (EBA), ending with its collapse at the end of the third millennium B.C.E. After several centuries characterized by rural settlement and transhumance, there began a second "urban revolution" early in the second millennium, but by the end of the millennium the broader "pan-Eastern Mediterranean" system collapsed rather suddenly, and a period of rapid social change ensued. But by the beginning of the first millennium there was a return to denser settlement and urban renewal representing a third peak in a cyclical history (Finkelstein 1999). Each of the cultural groups and periods discussed in this volume generally correspond with one or more of these phases.

Pre- and Proto-Canaanite Cultures

Prehistoric cultures may be identified only to the extent that their distinct traditions and ways of doing things are reflected in their material culture. For example, the widespread use of a common iconographic system reflects the sharing of ideas and beliefs, but it is virtually impossible to identify a specific people by their pottery styles alone. Thus, it is possible to speak about certain commonly recognizable culture complexes, but more specific terms such as

3

"Canaanite" cannot be supported with any historical accuracy until at least the Middle Bronze Age.

The survey presented here begins with the Chalcolithic period (c. 4700–3500 B.C.E.), meaning, literally, the "copper-stone" age, from the Greek words for copper, *chalkos*, and stone, *lithos*. This period followed on the heels of Neolithic times (8500–4700 B.C.E.), or the "new stone" age. By the mid-fifth millennium

1.1 Decorated metal vessel from the Nahal Mishmar hoard (Drawing by J. Golden, adapted from Bar-Adon 1980)

B.C.E., a variety of new cultural practices began to appear, and new, larger farming villages were established in many parts of the southern Levant, including, for the first time, in the Negev. Archaeological discoveries from this period suggest there were at least two distinct phases of the Chalcolithic period separated by the local inception of copper technology at the end of the fifth millennium (c. 4200 B.C.E.). The rise of metallurgy was, in fact, part of a much broader suite of changes related to economic organization that entailed, among other things, specialized craft production and long-distance trade. Seminomadic communities relying on the specialized production of pastoral goods, especially dairy products, were first established at this time, setting a precedent in subsistence practice that would remain much the same for millennia. As prosperity rose, some people, probably certain lineage groups, emerged as "elites"—members of society with greater wealth and status.

The Chalcolithic cultural system, however, seems to have broken down by the mid-fourth millennium B.C.E. for reasons that remain unclear. In the Early Bronze Age (c. 3500–2200 B.C.E.), people were at first living in small- to medium-sized farming villages, but later in the period the first cities appeared on the Levantine landscape. The people of these cities, sometimes called the "Proto-Canaanites," established regular contacts with neighboring peoples, namely the Egyptians to the south and the Syro-Mesopotamians to the north, establishing a trend that would continue through the Iron Age. The end of this era is marked by the abandonment of cities and the dispersal of populations into smaller farming communities and seminomadic tribes during the period known as the Intermediate Bronze Age (IBA, 2200–2000 B.C.E.; also the EB 4–MB 1). Specialized craft production continued, and trade routes remained active, but the southern Levant as a whole experienced a period of relative economic decline.

The Canaanites

Middle Bronze Age.　The Middle Bronze Age (MBA, c. 2000–1550 B.C.E.) represents the "golden age" of the Canaanite culture. Urbanism again took hold in the region, and the countryside was divided into a series of city-states characterized by a site hierarchy system, with regional centers and large gateway communities surrounded by subregional centers and numerous small villages. During the Middle Bronze Age, settlement expanded onto the coastal plain, particularly the northern portion, where there was rapid population growth. A chain of new settlements was also founded on the Sharon Plain. Virtually all of the major cities, and even some smaller centers, were surrounded by massive earthworks, also known as earthen ramparts, still visible today in the characteristic sloping mound form of most tell sites. Inside these ramparts, cities with public buildings (such as temples and palaces) and distinct neighborhoods rapidly grew.

The Canaanites of the Middle Bronze Age had an especially rich and varied material culture. One of the great developments of the period was the widespread use of true tin bronze technology. This new material allowed the Canaanite metalsmiths to greatly expand the repertoire of weapons and tools available (making, for example, the duckbill axe), and it quickly became the medium of choice for fashioning images of Canaanite deities. The copper and tin used to make bronze, along with a range of other raw materials and finished goods, traveled through vast "international" trade networks that were just beginning to emerge. Kinship relations probably continued to play an important role in social and political organization, particularly where ties between the urbanites and the substantial mobile population were concerned. Most people living in or near the cities, however, probably gave their allegiance to the king of their city-state, especially as the region entered the historical era. Texts from contemporary sites in Syria (such as Mari), for example, refer directly to the king of Hazor, the great city of the north. Hazor was truly outstanding in terms of both its sheer size and the overall scale of urban development, and its architectural design and layout recall that of Syrian cities. Indeed, many aspects of Canaanite material culture reflect a Syrian influence, and it is generally assumed that the emergence of this new culture is attributable in part to influences from the north, which came through both lively trade relations and waves of migration. Although the Syrian influence was particularly pronounced in the north, peoples from southern Canaan had penetrated

1.2 Hazor, lower city from the south (Photo courtesy of BiblePlaces.com)

into the territory of a weakened Egypt, in time becoming the dominant force in the eastern Delta. But the ascendance of this people, known historically as the Hyksos, would not last long.

Late Bronze Age. The Canaanites remained in Syro-Palestine during the sixteenth through the thirteenth centuries B.C.E., the period known as the Late Bronze Age (LBA, c. 1550–1200 B.C.E.), but they were no longer alone. The shame of having any part of their country dominated by a foreign people was the rallying point for political reunification in Egypt, giving rise to the New Kingdom. Following the celebrated "Expulsion of the Hyksos" under the Egyptian pharaoh Ahmose (r. 1550–1525 B.C.E.), the pharaohs, most notably Thutmose III (r. 1479–1425 B.C.E.), led a series of brutal military campaigns into Canaan toward the end of the fifteenth century B.C.E. For much of the ensuing Late Bronze Age, the Canaanites lived as subjects in Egyptian vassal states. The strength of Egyptian domination, however, varied considerably in different parts of the land. Although Egypt maintained important strongholds in the south of Canaan, its strength in the north was curtailed by the growing power of the Hurrians (Mitanni). It is also unclear to what extent the Egyptian presence influenced the daily lives of the Canaanites.

One of the most striking features of the Late Bronze Age was the rise of "internationalism," which had begun during the Middle Bronze Age but reached new heights in the mid-second millennium. Vast exchange networks, channeling both luxury items, such as wine, and industrial goods, such as timber and metals, were in operation throughout the eastern Mediterranean. The material culture of Late Bronze Age Canaan, in addition to texts found in this and adjacent regions, indicates regular commercial interaction with people of Cyprus and the Aegean. It also reflects the infiltration of such people, along with Egyptians and Hurrians, into various parts of the southern Levant. By the end of the thirteenth century B.C.E., however, this network collapsed. The end of the Late Bronze Age was characterized by political instability, profound social change, and the displacement of peoples throughout the eastern Mediterranean. It was precisely these factors that set the stage for the rise of new cultures and new kingdoms during the Iron Age.

Iron Age Cultures

The Iron Age (1200–586 B.C.E.) roughly corresponds with the post-Exodus era described in the Hebrew Bible when peoples such as the Israelites, Philistines, and Phoenicians, among others, inhabited the southern Levant. Although the Bible and inscriptions dating to the period are vital to the study of the Iron Age, the task of sorting out fact and legend is not an easy one. Understanding the story of the "emergence of Israel," which begins at the end of the thirteenth century B.C.E. and culminates in about 1000 B.C.E. with the establishment of the United Monarchy, has proven particularly problematic for archaeologists and historians. Evidence from both excavations and archaeological surveys suggests a process whereby pastoral tribes already inhabiting Canaan grew in number and began to settle down. In time, they built impressive cities in the

Shephelah, inland valleys, and highlands, the latter being the region with which the Israelites are traditionally associated. The Hebrew Bible describes political unification, development of a complex state, and a centralized monarchy. The archaeological record from the southern Levant often does not concur with the biblical account. It is always difficult to identify specific events involving specific individuals in the archaeological record, however, and it is important always to keep in mind the old archaeological adage: Pots don't equal people.

Some of the great achievements of the Israelite culture include innovations in engineering and design, with the construction of monumental architectural works in their great highland cities. The larger cities typically were protected by massive city walls with multitiered gates. There can be no doubt that such great architectural works would have brought prestige to the city, but they also reflect the pervasive level of conflict that prevailed at the time. These cities included grand palaces with extensive storage facilities and other royal buildings. The existence of a social hierarchy with a noble class is evident in the elaborate rock-cut tombs that surround Jerusalem, as well as in the *bullae,* clay envelopes stamped with inscriptions bearing names with various important titles.

A different people altogether, the Philistines, lived on the southern coast during the Iron Age. Again, it is not always simple to identify an individual people by their archaeological remains alone, yet the material culture of the coast is generally quite distinct from that of the inland and highland peoples. These coastal people had their cultural roots in Cyprus and the Aegean, but it was not long before they developed a unique culture of their own, establishing a series of large settlements along the coast and inland. The Hebrew Bible tells of five cities, the Philistine Pentapolis, though archaeologists have yet to positively identify all five. Of course, those great conquerors of Israel and Philistia—the Neo-Assyrians and Neo-Babylonians—later in the Iron Age also had an extensive impact on the lives of people in the region.

SUMMARY OF RESOURCES

Monographs and Journals

There are several journals dedicated exclusively to the archaeology of the southern Levant, including *Annual of the American Schools of Oriental Research; Annual of the Nelson Glueck School of Biblical Archaeology Jerusalem; Àtiqot; Australian Journal of Biblical Studies; Biblical Archaeologist; Biblical Archaeology Review; Bulletin of the American Schools of Oriental Research; Edah Ve'Lashon; Eretz-Israel; Israel Exploration Journal; Journal of the American Oriental Society; Levant; Mitekufat Haeven; Near East Archaeological Society Bulletin; Paléorient; Palestine Exploration Quarterly; Qedem; Syria;* and *Tarbiz.*

There are also a number of more generalized periodicals that often feature articles on topics related to southern Levantine archaeology. These include the *American Journal of Archaeology; Ancient Art: The Magazine of Antiquities and Archaeology; Antiquity; Archaeology; Archaeomaterials; Bulletin of the Institute of Archaeology* (University of London); *Cambridge Archaeological Journal; Current An-*

thropology; Discovery (Peabody Museum of Natural History, Yale University); *Expedition; International Journal of Nautical Archaeology; Ioudaios Review; Iraq; Israel Museum Journal; Jerusalem Studies in Hebrew Literature; Jewish Quarterly Review; Journal of Ancient Civilizations; Journal of Archaeological Science; Journal of Biblical Studies; Journal of Hebrew Scriptures; Journal of Mediterranean Archaeology; Journal of Near Eastern Studies; Journal of Northwest Semitic Languages; Journal of Semitic Studies; Massorot (Studies in Language Traditions); Michmanim: The Bulletin of the Reubin and Edith Hecht Museum* (Haifa University); *Oxford Journal of Archaeology; Radiocarbon;* and the *Royal Ontario Museum Archaeological Newsletter.*

A number of academic publishing houses put out books related to the archaeology of the southern Levant, including Addison-Wesley; Archaeological Institute of America; Biblical Archaeology Society; British Archaeological Reports; British Museum Publications; Cambridge University Press; Council for British Research in the Levant; Deutsches Bargbau-Musum, Bochum; Eisenbrauns; Emery and Claire Yass Publications in Archaeology, Sonia and Marco Nadler Institute of Archaeology, Tel Aviv University; Institute for Jewish Studies, Hebrew University; Institute of Archaeology, University of California, Los Angeles; Israel Antiquities Authority, Jerusalem; Magnes Press, Hebrew University; Museum Applied Science Center for Archaeology; Oriental Institute, University of Chicago; Prehistory Press; Sheffield Academic Press; Shelby White–Leon Levy Program for Archaeological Publications, Harvard University; University of California Press, Berkeley and Los Angeles; University of Pennsylvania Museum of Archaeology and Anthropology, University Museum Publications; and Yale University Press.

Major Museum and Library Collections

A number of museums and other institutions in North America own significant collections pertaining to southern Levantine archaeology. Harvard University has several libraries with relevant collections, including the Andover-Harvard Theological Library, the Aranne Library, the Humanities Reading Room, and the Harvard Semitic Museum (http://www.fas.harvard.edu/~semitic/). Other institutions include the Hebrew Union College–Jewish Institute of Religion Museum (New York) and the Jewish Museum, also in New York (http://www.thejewishmuseum.org), as well as the J. Paul Getty Museum in Los Angeles (http://www.getty.edu/museum). Johns Hopkins University hosts the Milton S. Eisenhower Library and the Johns Hopkins Archaeological Museum. Other institutions include the Horn Archaeological Museum at Andrews University; the Kelsey Museum of Archaeology at the University of Michigan (www.lsa.umich.edu/kelsey/); the Metropolitan Museum of Art (www.metmuseum.org); and the Oriental Institute Museum at the University of Chicago (http://oi.uchicago.edu/OI/MUS/OI Museum.html). The University of Pennsylvania hosts the Museum of Archaeology and Anthropology, the University of Pennsylvania Center for Judaic Studies Library, the University of Pennsylvania Museum Library, and the Museum Applied Science Center for Archaeology. There are several important institutions affiliated with the Skirball Foundation of Hebrew Union College–Jewish Institute of Religion (HUC-

JIR), including the Skirball Museum (Cincinnati), the Skirball Cultural Center (Los Angeles), and HUC-JIR in Jerusalem. Yale University has the Library of the American Oriental Society and the Semitic Reference Library, Peabody Museum of Natural History (http://www.peabody.yale.edu/). In Canada, there is the Royal Ontario Museum in Toronto, which has a Near Eastern and Asian Civilizations Department.

There are many important institutions in England, including the British Museum with its Department of Ancient Near East (www.thebritishmuseum.ac.uk); the University of Cambridge with the Museum of Archaeology and Anthropology (http://museum-server.archanth.cam.ac.uk/), the CMEIS Library, and the Centre of Middle Eastern and Islamic Studies; and the Manchester Museum at the University of Manchester (http://museum.man.ac.uk/). The University of Oxford (http://www.ashmol.ox.ac.uk/) has the Oxford Middle East Centre Library, the Ashmolean Museum of Art and Archaeology, and the Ashmolean/Sackler Library, including the Griffith Institute Library. Elsewhere in Europe there is the Louvre in Paris (http://www.louvre.fr/louvrea.htm); the Museum of Antiquities, Institute of the Near East, in Leiden; and the National Museum of Antiquities, Leiden (http://www.rmo.nl/new/home.html).

Institutions in Israel include the Ben-Gurion Research Center, Ben-Gurion University of the Negev; the University of Beirut Museum; the American University of Beirut; the Bible Lands Museum, Jerusalem (http://www.blmj.org); Eretz Israel Museum, Tel Aviv (http://www.eimuseum.co.il/english/main.html); the Reuben and Edith Hecht Museum at Haifa University (http://research.haifa.ac.il/~hecht/); the Israel Antiquities Authority, Jerusalem; the Israel Museum, Jerusalem (www.imj.org.il/); the Archaeological Museum at Kibbutz Ein Dor (http://www.geocities.com/Athens/3603/indexfr.html); the Library of Archaeology and Ancient Near East Civilizations at the Hebrew University of Jerusalem; the Rockefeller Archaeological Museum, Jerusalem (http://www.imj.org.il/eng/branches/rockefeller/index.html); and the Tower of David Museum, Jerusalem (http://jeru.huji.ac.il/info_museum.htm). The Hebrew Union College–Jewish Institute of Religion (Jerusalem) has a Museum of Biblical Archaeology in addition to the S. Zalman and Ayala Abramov Library. Tel Aviv University has the Mehlmann Library of Jewish Studies and the Library of the Department of Archaeology. In Jordan, there is the Amman Archaeological Museum.

Museum and University Research Programs

There are many research programs related to the study of the southern Levant in the United States, including Arizona State University, with a Jewish Studies Program in its Department of Religious Studies (http://www.asu.edu/clas/jewishstudies/); the University of California–Los Angeles, which, in addition to its Department of Near Eastern Languages and Cultures, has the Center for Jewish Studies; the University of California–San Diego, with its Archaeological Research Laboratory; the University of Chicago, which has a Department of Near Eastern Languages and Civilizations (http://humanities.uchicago.edu/depts/nelc/index.html) as well as the Oriental Institute (http://oi.uchicago.

edu/OI/MUS/OI Museum.html); and the Detroit Institute of Arts, which has a Department of Ancient Art (www.dia.org).

Harvard University has the Department of Near East Languages and Civilizations (http://www.fas.harvard.edu/~nelc/), the Center for Middle Eastern Studies, and the Shelby White–Leon Levy Program for Archaeological Publications. The Hebrew Union College has programs at its various campus locations, including the School of Graduate Studies in Cincinnati and the F. Magnin School of Graduate Studies in Los Angeles, as well as one in Jerusalem. The Jewish Museum, New York, offers a master's degree program in Jewish Art and Material Culture, and Johns Hopkins University has a Department of Near Eastern Studies (http://www.jhu.edu/~neareast/).

The University of Michigan has a Department of Near Eastern Studies as well as the Jean and Samuel Frankel Center for Judaic Studies. The University of Pennsylvania has the Department of Jewish Studies, the Center for Ancient Studies, and the Center for Judaic Studies, with a fellowship program, and Yale University has a Department of Near Eastern Languages and Civilization (http://www.yale.edu/nelc). In Canada, there is the University of Lethbridge's Religious Studies Department and the University of Toronto's Department of Near and Middle Eastern Civilizations.

There are a number of important institutions in the U.K., including the University of Cambridge, which has a Department of Archaeology (http://www.arch.cam.ac.uk/), a Department of Oriental Studies (http://www.oriental.cam.ac.uk/), and the Centre of Middle Eastern and Islamic Studies (http://www.cmeis.cam.ac.uk/). The University of Manchester has a School of Art History and Archaeology and a Department of Middle Eastern Studies, and the University of Oxford has the Department of Oriental Studies (http://www.ox.ac.uk/) with a Near and Middle Eastern Studies Program (http://www.orinst.ox.ac.uk/nme/index.html). The University of Sheffield has a Department of Archaeology and Prehistory (http://www.shef.ac.uk/uni/academic/A-C/ap/index.html) and a Department of Biblical Studies (http://www.shef.ac.uk/uni/academic/A-C/biblst/index.html).

Additional programs in Europe include the University of Leiden in the Netherlands, which has a Department of Archaeology and hosts the Netherlands Institute for the Near East (http://www.leidenuniv.nl/nino/nino.html). In addition, the Pontifical Biblical Institute is located in Rome (http://www.pib.urbe.it/).

In Australia, there is the University of Sydney School of Archaeology and the Nicholson Museum (http://www.usyd.edu.au/nicholson/). In 1998, the British School of Archaeology in Jerusalem and the British Institute at Amman for Archaeology and History combined to form the Council for British Research in the Levant (CBRL). The Kenyon Institute, which provides CBRL facilities in Jerusalem, was launched in 2003 (http://www.britac.ac.uk/institutes/cbrl/jeruindex.html). The Department of Bible and Near Eastern Studies and the Archaeology Division at Ben-Gurion University of the Negev hosts the Ben-Gurion Research Center (http://www.bgu.ac.il/bible/). Haifa University has the Zinman Institute of Archaeology (http://www.haifa.ac.il/), the

Reuben and Edith Hecht Museum (http://research.haifa.ac.il/~hecht/), and the Nelson Glueck School of Biblical Archaeology in Jerusalem. The Hebrew University of Jerusalem has a Department of Middle Eastern Studies and the Institute of Archaeology. Another important research institution is the Israel Antiquities Authority, with several different locations that house many of the artifacts found from sites around the country. Tel Aviv University hosts the Sonia and Marco Nadler Institute of Archaeology and also has departments in Archaeology and Near Eastern Civilizations, Middle Eastern and African History, and Jewish History (http://www.tau.ac.il/humanities/jewishhistory/). Two important institutions that support graduate student research are the W. F. Albright Institute of Archaeological Research and the British School of Archaeology, both in Jerusalem. The American University of Beirut has a Center for Arab and Middle Eastern Studies (http://wwwlb.aub.edu.lb/~webcames/index.html). The Council for British Research in the Levant is located in Amman (http://www.britac.ac.uk/institutes/cbrl/who%20we%20are.htm).

For a list of research institutions with links to various websites, visit http://archaeology.about.com/library/atlas/blisrael.htm#University%20Programs.

NOTES

1. The people of the Natufian period (10,500–8500 B.C.E.) practiced what is sometimes called "intensive gathering," that is, selecting certain plant strains, setting the stage for the domestication of wheat, barley, and other foods during the Neolithic period (Vallas 2003; Bar-Yosef 2003).

PART 2

Canaanite and Israelite Civilization

CHAPTER 2

Environment and Ecology

Unto a good land and a large, unto a land flowing with milk and honey; unto the place
of the Canaanites, and the Hittites, and the Amorites, and the Perizzites, and the Hivites,
and the Jebusites.
  —Exodus 3:8

The Levant, situated on the eastern shores of the Mediterranean Sea, is a beautiful land. Although relatively small in terms of geographic area, it is great in ecological diversity. Its physical landscape has played into the cultural history of the peoples inhabiting the region for millennia. It includes modern Turkey, Syria, and Lebanon; however, the core area of the peoples mentioned in the passage from Exodus was to the south—the southern Levant—the lands of modern-day Israel, the Sinai, and Transjordan. The traditional term "Syro-Palestine" refers to the same region, as does "Canaan," so oft used in the Hebrew Bible. The latter term, however, must be understood in a general sense, for while the name Canaan was already in use by the Middle Bronze Age (Rainey 2001), and it appears numerous times in the Bible, the precise parameters of the area referred to as "Canaan" in the Bible are not known.

The southern Levant is delimited to the north by the Litani River, to the east by the Jordan Rift Valley, to the south by the Gulf of Aqaba, and to the west by the Mediterranean Sea and the Sinai Desert. It straddles northern Africa and Asia, effectively creating a corridor between two continents. From as early as the Lower Paleolithic age, its location has been a critical factor in the story of human settlement in this region, for some of the earliest species of humans to venture out of Africa lurked in the caves of the Carmel and Galilee.

Descriptions of the region derived from historical sources generally paint a picture of lush lands abundant in a variety of food resources. For instance, there are multiple references in the Bible, especially the first few books known as the Torah, to foods produced in Canaan, particularly the oft-mentioned trilogy of "thy corn [or wheat/barley], thy wine and thy oil" (e.g., Deut. 14:23). The "Tale of Sinuhe," an Egyptian text dating to the time of the Middle Bronze Age, also conveys a sense of Canaanite ecology. It recounts the story of an expatriate who sojourns among the tribes of Canaan-Syria. Marrying the daughter of one of the local tribal leaders, Sinuhe is given a plot of land, which he describes in some detail, saying, "It was a good land called Yaa. Figs were in it and grapes. It had more wine than water. Abundant was its honey, plentiful its oil. All kinds of fruit were on its trees. Barley was there and emmer, and no end

2.1 The northern coastal plain, the road between Tel Aviv and Haifa (Photo courtesy of Zev Radovan, Land of the Bible Picture Archive)

of cattle of all kinds . . . as well as desert game and milk dishes of all kinds" (Lichtheim 1973, 226–227).

Another important facet of the region's culture history is its central position in relation to the much broader world of the Mediterranean and Near East. From the Early Bronze Age on, it is safe to say that all of the various cultural groups that would inhabit the southern Levant were influenced by the great states that emerged to the southwest and to the north-northeast, namely Egypt, Syria, and Mesopotamia. As ethnicity became increasingly important (or at least more visible to archaeologists), the human mosaic became ever more complex, reaching its zenith in the Iron Age as the land was divided into Philistia, Phoenicia, the Kingdoms of Judah and Israel, Edom, Amon, and Moab, among others. These cultures and their respective careers in this landscape were shaped, in part, by their physical environment.

THE PHYSICAL LANDSCAPE

The region of ancient Canaan and Israel is largely contiguous with a better portion of the modern state of Israel, which is generally defined to the south and west by coastlines: the Red Sea, the Gulf of Aqaba, and the Mediterranean Sea. In ancient times, the eastern boundary for the region was generally de-

2.2 The fertile highlands of the Galilee (J. Golden)

fined by the Jordan Valley. To the north, the region is delimited by the high-lands of southern Syria and Lebanon. Although the northern region and the highland zones are well watered, much of the southern Levant lies in or at the margins of semiarid land where even minor climatic shifts can have a signifi-cant and immediate impact on subsistence. For the purposes of examining the climate, geology, and topography of the region, it may be divided into ten eco-logical subzones: Upper Galilee, Lower Galilee, Huleh Valley, Jordan Valley, Jezreel Valley, Samaria, Judean foothills, northern coastal plain, southern coastal plain, northern Negev.

Climate

The general climate of the southern Levant during ancient times was not un-like that of present times, though there has, of course, been variability over time. Paleo-environmental evidence such as lake pollen cores suggests a series of dry phases broken up by times of increased humidity. In the region today, winters (November through March) are generally short and cool with a high concentration of rainfall. Summers tend to be long, hot, and dry. There is great variability in rainfall patterns between the subregions in the present climatic regime, and this seems to have been the case in the past. For example, while parts of the southern Negev receive as little as 50 mm (about 2 in.) of annual rainfall, the semiarid northern Negev receives 200 mm (about 8 in.), the Judean mountains receive 600 mm (about 24 in.), and the Galilee and Golan regions as much as 1,000 mm (about 40 in.).

Average temperatures also vary significantly throughout the broader region. At the southern extent of the Jordan Valley (for example, near Eilat), temperatures go no lower than 10°C (50°F), with a mean temperature of 18°C (64.4°F) in the winter, often reaching a blistering 40+°C (104+°F) in the summer months, with a mean temperature of 33°C (91.4°F). The highland regions, such as the area around Jerusalem, tend to be considerably cooler, with temperatures ranging from 9–30°C (48.2–86°F) and a mean temperature of 24°C (75.2°F) in summer and 10°C (50°F) in the winter.

Topography

Again, variability is the rule in the southern Levant, not only in terms of climate across the region, but in terms of topography as well (Danin 2003; Goldberg 2003; Zohary 1992). Together, the combination of these factors has resulted in the creation of distinct ecological niches with unique microclimates.

The coastal plain, which includes the eastern shore of the Mediterranean Sea and the interior dune systems, stretches roughly 300 km (185 mi.) from just south of Tel el-Ajjul (just north of the 31st latitude) up to Tyre (just north of the 33rd latitude) along the eastern shore of the Mediterranean Sea. The plain is roughly 20 km (12 mi.) wide on average, though it widens somewhat in the south. The southern portion of the coastal plain features large, trough-shaped valleys covered with fertile alluvial soils that were important subsistence areas in the past, though sandy plains generally cover the remainder of the region. Along the north Mediterranean coast, the hard, calcareous *kurkar* sandstone forms ridges that create small inland swamps. The southern end of this zone, which articulates with the northern Negev, receives below 150 mm (6 in.) of rainfall annually, while the northern portion of the coast receives more than 500 mm (20 in.). There is virtually no plain on the coast immediately south of the Haifa port, as the mountains practically border the sea. The coastline is dotted with a series of natural coves at places such as Jaffa, Dor, and Atlit. Like the south, the northern portion of the coastal plain is traversed by perennial *wadis*, or dry seasonal riverbeds, sometimes called *nahals*.

To the east of the coastal plain is the low foothill zone commonly known as the Shephelah, a narrow strip of foothills between the coastal plain and the Judean mountains. It is generally regarded as a transitional zone, with elevations of less than 100 m (328 ft.) above sea level in the west that rise to more than 400 m (1,300 ft.) in the east. Rainfall patterns are similar to those of the coastal plain, varying from south to north. In the southern Shephelah, alluvial sediments consisting mainly of Holocene gravels are typical. The wide valleys (for example, the Soreq Valley) that transect the Shephelah contain fertile gray to grayish-white Mediterranean *rendzina* soils.

The central highland region, or central hill country, as it is often called, includes the small mountain system stretching from south of Jerusalem north toward the Galilee region. Several broad valleys, such as the Beth Shean and the

Jezreel Valleys, transect the highland region, serving as major conduits for movement between the interior and coast throughout the history of the region.

Moving eastward, the hills rapidly rise into the dramatic Judean Mountains, which reach some 1,000 m (3,280 ft.) above sea level. Bordering the hill country to the east is the Judean Desert, a semiarid region characterized by dramatic topographic features. The area surrounding the Sea of Galilee (also known as Lake Kinneret and Lake Tiberius), to the north of the Jordan Valley, is commonly referred to as the Galilee. This area receives the highest amount of rainfall and is one of the more fertile regions in the southern Levant. Small hills and broad valleys characterize the Lower Galilee, while the Upper Galilee has sharper contours with steep hills and deep river channels. The Kinneret Valley surrounds the Sea of Galilee, and the Huleh Valley was the site of a small lake with extensive swamps until recent times.

The northern extent of the southern Levant includes the mountainous region known as the Golan, as well as broad valleys such as the Dan and Huleh Valleys, which form rich plains well watered by both rainfall and springs such as the Banias spring. This northern region is heavily influenced by volcanic activity, with hard *dalwe* basalt bedrock covered by brown Mediterranean soils. Weather conditions vary within the central Golan, and thus the general texture and size of basalt outcrops is variable. Throughout antiquity and especially in earlier times, basalt was used as a material for building homes and other structures, as well as a medium for tools and art. The highland regions, including the Galilee area and the Judean Mountains, are overlain with *terra rosa* (silica-rich soils made red by a high iron content) on top of hard limestone, and these more humid regions in general are associated with colluvial soils. The plains and low plateaus of the north are covered with a continuous band of rich, dark red loams, called *hamra* soil.

The Jordan Rift Valley is a relatively flat plain bordered by the Judean and Transjordanian mountain systems to the east and west. Running north-south from the Red Sea to the Galilee, it is actually part of the much broader African rift system. In the area just south of the Galilee, the rift broadens to the west. Near the center and lowest point of the Rift Valley (398 meters [1,300 ft.] below sea level) is the Dead Sea, or Lissan Basin, the lowest continental depression on Earth. The Dead Sea lies just east of the Rift Valley in Jordan, where the Transjordanian plateau and mountain system begins; this zone also articulates with the Eastern Desert of Jordan. The Dead Sea region is famous for its salt deposits and other natural resources deriving from mineral springs (Fig. 2.3).

The geology and topography of the Negev Desert vary considerably from north to south, with broad plains and valleys in the north and more rugged, steep terrain in the south. The Negev climate varies from arid to semiarid, with an average annual rainfall of 200 mm (about 8 in.) in the north, approximately 100 mm (4 in.) in the central Negev, and as little as 50 mm (2 in.) in the south. Heavy loess deposits containing silt and clay characterize the geology of the northern Negev. The southern Negev has virtually no arable land, with arable soils generally limited to the plateaus. This region, however, is rich in mineral

2.3 The Dead Sea region is famous for its salt deposits and other natural resources deriving from mineral springs. (Photo courtesy of Zev Radovan, Land of the Bible Picture Archive)

2.4 A lone gazelle grazes in Timna Park in the southern Negev. (J. Golden)

resources such as the copper-bearing deposits of Timna, an offshoot of the Wadi-Aravah system.

Of course, topography is dynamic, with certain transformations in the landscape occurring over time. For instance, on the coastal plain, the relatively high water table and shifting sand dunes have probably altered the landscape significantly over time (Goldberg 2003). Other factors contributing to these localized topographical transformations include tectonic activity, especially around the Jordan Rift Valley, and shifts in seasonal drainage systems, resulting largely from variations in rainfall.

Climatic conditions also varied in the past, as demonstrated by paleolimnological evidence that suggests shifting Dead Sea levels, as well as by pollen cores from Lake Huleh and Kinneret that indicate lake expansion and a moist phase during the Early Bronze Age (in about 3340

2.5 Olive trees thrive in the Judean foothills. (J. Golden)

B.C.E.). Geomorphological evidence from the wadis also indicates variations in waterflow with occasional flooding due to variations in rainfall, particularly in the southern portion of the region (Rosen 1986; Goldberg 1986).

Plant and Animal Populations

For purposes of describing the flora and fauna of the southern Levant, the region may be divided into four major climatic zones: Mediterranean humid zone; Irano-Turanian semiarid zone; Saharo-Arabian arid desert zone; and Sudanian tropical desert zone. The Mediterranean humid zone in the north receives an average annual rainfall fluctuating between 350 and 1,000 mm (about 14–40 in.) and is generally characterized by denser vegetation than the more southern regions.

Dense forests of oak, pistachio, and carob covered the highland area in antiquity (Liphschitz et al. 1989); today, cypress and olive trees thrive in the Judean foothills (Fig. 2.5). The discovery of olive pits and grape pips indicate that these and other fruits were cultivated in the area (Zohary 1992). Generally speaking, the Mediterranean region, particularly the fertile inland valleys, which receive greater rainfall, was the wheat-growing area, while barley was the main crop in the semiarid zones.

2.6 Grove of date palms in the Jordan Valley (Photo courtesy of Zev Radovan, Land of the Bible Picture Archive)

The Irano-Turanian semiarid zone is a 30 km–wide band lying between the Mediterranean zone and the arid desert zone to the south. It receives about 150–350 mm (6–14 in.) of rainfall per annum. The Saharo-Arabian arid desert zone receives less than 125 mm (about 5 in.) and as little as 25 mm (about 1 in.) of rainfall annually and has limited vegetation. The Sudanian tropical desert zones are small oases with pockets of relatively dense vegetation (for example, date palms) created by natural springs such as the one at Jericho. The Negev is best characterized as a semiarid transitional zone with regard to climate, temperature, and wildlife. Low desert brush and the occasional acacia, tamarisk, or sycamore tree flourish in and around wadi systems, but generally speaking there is little vegetation. It is a very different story in the well-watered Judean Mountains, which were heavily wooded with kermes oak and terebinth trees at various points in antiquity. Cereals such as barley grow wild in the area today (Zohary 1992; Danin 2003).

In antiquity, southern Levantine wildlife included wild goats, sheep, and cattle along with equids, aurochs, and hedgehogs, though these species mainly inhabited the northern regions. The more lush microenvironments also supported aquatic birds and marine fish. Fallow and roe deer also appeared on the northern coast on occasion, while their cousins, the gazelle, roamed the south, joined in the southern and central regions by the ibex, fox, and wild boar.

2.7 Sheep and goats grazing in the Galilee (J. Golden)

SHIFTING PATTERNS OF LAND USE

The Negev

The southernmost portion of the southern Levant is generally a desert region ranging from arid to semiarid. During the Natufian and Neolithic periods, this area was exploited by small groups of hunters following herds of gazelle and gathering the sparse resources available. During the Chalcolithic period, the northern Negev was host to a great cultural fluorescence with occupation of some sites continuing into the Early Bronze Age. Human activity continued in the region throughout the Bronze and Iron Ages, though this environment seemed unable to support more than two or three real population centers. Beyond this, occupation of this "marginal" environment was somewhat limited.

The Shephelah and Southern Coastal Plain

To the north, the Negev transitions into the southern Shephelah, and to the west into the coastal plain, and the western portion of the northern Negev articulates with the southern foothill zone. Each of these three subregions supported large populations and political centers at one time or another. The southern coastal plain from the Early Bronze Age on was consistently the scene of urban centers oriented toward a maritime economy. A number of sites that would continue to play a role for a millennium thereafter were first established during the Middle Bronze Age, when the coastal population was booming. Beginning in the Late Bronze Age, the southern coastal plain saw the arrival of newcomers referred to collectively as the "Sea Peoples." By the Iron Age, this group had evolved into a new culture known as the Philistines, and this region is generally referred to as Philistia. The southern Shephelah hosted Chalcolithic and Early Bronze Age peoples, and later, during the Middle and Late Bronze Ages, people known as the Canaanites. The region was probably populated by a mixture of Canaanite and Israelite peoples in the following Iron Age.

Central Highlands

The earliest wave of settlement in the central highlands was during the Early Bronze Age. Numerous cemeteries representing a sizable mobile population were in use during the Intermediate Bronze Age in the central highlands. A number of important Canaanite settlements were established during the Middle Bronze Age, continuing through the Late Bronze Age. By the second part of the Iron Age (Iron 2), and perhaps earlier, the central highlands would become the heartland of Israelite culture. By the mid-Iron 2, the southern highlands were part of the Judean Kingdom, while the northern foothill zone was the site of the Kingdom of Israel; at various points in time, the south was more likely to have hosted significant pastoral populations.

Two specific ecological problems for the central hill country were the amount of arable land and the water supply. People solved the first problem by cutting terraces into the slopes beginning in the early second millennium B.C.E. and possibly earlier (Fig. 2.8). The problem of water supply was solved in several ways, most notably through the use of cisterns, which probably began around the same time as the terraces.

2.8 Almond trees grow on agricultural terraces cut into the hillside in northern Israel, near Bel Voir. (J. Golden)

Central Jordan Valley

The Jordan Valley was the scene of human occupation from the earliest times, exploited by Natufian and Neolithic peoples. There were also some important Chalcolithic settlements north of the Dead Sea. The northern portion of the central Jordan Valley south of the Galilee was heavily populated around the middle of the Early Bronze Age, with several important settlements in the same area during the Middle and Late Bronze Ages. This region appears to have been less important during the Iron Age as settlement shifted into the hills on both sides of the valley.

The Inland Valleys

The Beth Shean and Jezreel Valleys represent two subregions similar to each other and to parts of the Jordan Valley, though unique in the rest of the land. Both regions saw settlement during the Chalcolithic period and had considerable populations for most of the Bronze and Iron Ages. Two cities in particular, Beth Shean and Megiddo (Jezreel), were the centers of sizable political entities, fueled by command of trade routes and strong staple production; indeed, this was the "breadbasket" of the southern Levant.

2.9 The flat, broad expanse of the Jezreel Valley (Photo courtesy of Zev Radovan, Land of the Bible Picture Archive)

Central-Northern Coastal Plain

During the late Neolithic (Wadi Rabah) and Chalcolithic periods, there were both settlements and burial sites on the central coastal plain. Canaanite peo-

ples occupied this region during the Early Bronze Age, with some signs of settlement during the Intermediate Bronze Age as well. There appears to have
been a population explosion during the Middle Bronze Age on the central-
northern coastal plain, which was still heavily populated during the Late
Bronze Age. The northern coastal region was also home to Canaanites, though
there appears to have been some turnover during the Middle Bronze and Iron
Ages in terms of ethnic groups. During the Middle and Late Bronze Ages,
Amoritic-speaking peoples occupied the region. But by the Iron Age, the
northern coastal region represented the southern extent of Phoenicia, with
Phoenician settlement centered further north in what is today Lebanon.

The Northern Valleys

The northern extension of the Jordan Valley, the Dan Valley, was inhabited
during the Neolithic period and Early Bronze Age, though there does not appear to have been significant Chalcolithic occupation. Canaanites settled in the
Dan Valley during the Middle and Late Bronze Ages, followed by Israelites in
the Iron Age. The Huleh Valley in the far north of what is today Israel was part
of a distinct political entity dominated by Hazor during most of the Bronze
Age. During the Middle and Late Bronze Ages, there was a growing Hurrian
presence in the northern regions.

Transjordan

Settlement in Transjordan was relatively sparse prior to the thirteenth century
B.C.E. This region can be divided into three distinct zones—Ammon, Moab,
and Edom, from north to south—based on textual evidence referring to what
were probably tribal kingdoms.

Environment and Culture

The southern Levantine landscape comprises a large number of small "micro-
ecological niches," with a great amount of diversity for a relatively small region. This great ecological diversity has factored into the history of human
land use in interesting ways, promoting specialization in adaptive strategies.
For example, certain regions were always dominated by pastoral groups,
while other regions relied on agriculture—with further specialization in certain types of crops. In many cases, people would have found it more prudent
to practice a multiresource strategy, combining agriculture and pastoralism. It
also promoted the development of distinct subcultures; thus, for instance,
kingdoms and smaller political entities were often situated within narrowly
defined areas (for example, Judah), and ethnic groups often seem to have clus-
tered in similarly defined regions (for example, Philistia).

   Over the millennia, the inhabitants of the southern Levant exploited the various parts of the region differently, and dramatic shifts in settlement patterns
occurred. During the Early Bronze Age, for instance, settlement moved away
from the more arid regions inhabited during the Chalcolithic period and into
the foothills. This, of course, is the place where grapes and olives thrive, and
these two early "cash crops" would play a vital role in these ancient

economies. As a result, numerous changes in the cultural ecology of the southern Levant occurred over the course of some nine millennia.

SUGGESTED READING

Danin, A. 2003. "Man and the Natural Environment." In *The Archaeology of Society in the Holy Land,* 3d ed., edited by T. E. Levy, 24–37. New York: Facts on File.

Frumkin, A. 1997. "Middle Holocene Environmental Change." In *Late Quaternary Chronology and Paleoclimates of the Eastern Mediterranean,* edited by O. Bar Yosef and R. Kra, 314–331. Madison, WI: Prehistory Press.

Goldberg, P., and A. Rosen. 1987. "Early Holociene Paleoenvironments of Israel." In *Shiqmim I,* edited by T. Levy, 35–43. Oxford: British Archaeological Reports.

Rosen, A. 1995. "The Social Response to Environmental Change in Early Bronze Age Canaan." *Journal of Anthropological Archaeology* 14: 26–46.

van Zeist, W., and S. Bottema. 1982. "Vegetational History of the Eastern Mediterranean and the Near East during the Last 20,000 Years." In *Paleoclimates, Paleoenvironments and Human Communities in the Eastern Mediterranean Region in Later Prehistory,* edited by J. Bintliff and W. van Zeist, 277–324. Oxford: British Archaeological Reports.

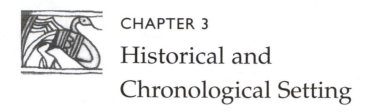

CHAPTER 3

Historical and Chronological Setting

MAJOR EVENTS IN THE HISTORY OF SYRO-PALESTINIAN CULTURES

Much of the Levantine chronology has been reconstructed with the aid of historical data from both within and outside the region itself. For example, the beginning of the Late Bronze Age generally coincides with the reunification of Egypt and the establishment of the Eighteenth Dynasty by Ahmose in 1550 B.C.E. Thutmose III's forays (1470 B.C.E.) provide a guideline for dividing the Late Bronze Age into LB1 (1550–1400 B.C.E.) and LB2 (1400–1200 B.C.E.), while LB2 is generally subdivided into LB2a (1400–c. 1300 B.C.E.) and LB2b (c. 1300–1200 B.C.E.), which corresponds with the Egyptian Nineteenth Dynasty. It should be noted, however, that these dates are not always certain, and for some, the historicity of certain entries, especially the reigns of David and Solomon, are altogether questionable.

4700	Chalcolithic period begins
3500	Early Bronze Age begins
2200	Early Bronze Age societies collapse, Intermediate Bronze Age begins
2000	Middle Bronze Age begins and city-states emerge throughout Canaan
1900–1800	Egyptian "Execration Texts"
1756	Mari destroyed by Hammurabi (Middle Chronology)
1550	Late Bronze Age begins
1541	Expulsion of the Hyksos, Ahmose's campaigns
1470	Thutmose III's military incursions
1457	Battle of Megiddo, Canaan becomes vassal state of Egypt
1365–1335	The Amarna Letters
1279	Rameses II (r. 1279/1278–1213) ascends throne of Egypt
1274	Battle of Qadesh
1225–1187	Wars between Egypt and the Sea Peoples
1200	Iron Age begins
1050	Philistines defeat Israelites at Aphek
1000–961	Reign of David
961–922	Reign of Solomon
923	Campaign of Egyptian Pharaoh Sishak

922	Collapse of the United Monarchy; Rehoboam rules Judah and Jeroboam establishes the northern Kingdom of Israel
923	Campaign of Egyptian Pharaoh Sishak
853	Coalition of kings of Syro-Palestine, including Ahab, hold off Shalmanezzer III and the Assyrians in the battle of Qarqar
732	Tigath-Pileser III conquers the Galilee and exiles much of its population
727–698	Reign of Hezekiah
722	Sebastia destroyed at the hands of the Assyrians
701	Conquest of Lachish by Sennacherib
586	Defeat of Judah and destruction of Jerusalem by Nebuchadnezzar

MAJOR TECHNIQUES IN CHRONOLOGY BUILDING

Ceramic Seriation

Working at the Egyptian sites of Nagada and Ballas in the 1880s, the archaeologist William Flinders Petrie developed a method of sequence dating called seriation that would become the most important chronological tool available to archaeologists. This system was based on the principle that styles of pottery changed over time and that through careful observation of these changes it was possible to reconstruct chronologies. Petrie's use of this system was generally limited to his study of material from cemeteries, which, while spanning substantial amounts of time, did not display the effect of superposition of mul-

3.1 Exposed layers at Tel Ashqelon demonstrating law of superposition, where each successive layer represents a subsequent phase of occupation (J. Golden)

tiple layers characteristic of the Near Eastern tell sites (see Fig. 3.1). As a result of the presence of Levantine pottery in some of the Egyptian graves, Petrie was also aware of early contact between the peoples of Egypt and those of the southern Levant.

Petrie was a pioneer in terms of his understanding of the significance of ancient tells for what they were: artificial mounds created over time by successive layers of occupation. Petrie had visited Heinrich Schlieman's excavations at Hissarlik in northwestern Turkey (1871–1890), where he learned the principles of stratigraphy and how the sequence of deposition of material culture

3.2   The archaeologist Sir Flinders Petrie (1853–1942) arranges some of the pottery he found in Southern Palestine, which was part of an ancient pottery and bronze work exhibition at University College, London (ca. 1930). (Hulton-Deutsch Collection/Corbis)

represented changes in time, with the earliest material at the bottom and the most recent at the top. Thus, asked to conduct research in southern Palestine, Petrie was intrigued by the possibility of being able to employ his methods of pottery analysis to a stratified tell site and to further test the chronological links between the Levantine cultures and the Egyptians.

Ceramic analysis would remain the most important methodological tool for archaeologists working in the region. During the mid-twentieth century, William Foxwell Albright mastered this method and made an art of identifying the different pottery styles and understanding how they represented different time periods. G. Ernest Wright played a vital role in establishing the tradition of on-site "pottery reading" during the 1950s to 1970s, and Ruth Amiran would later codify the ceramic chronology for the region in *Ancient Pottery of the Holy Land* (Amiran 1969). In recent years, petrographic analysis, the microscopic study of ceramic fabric, including types of clays and inclusions, has become an important part of the archaeologist's tool kit, with researchers such as Yuval Goren and Naomi Porat leading the way.

Historical Data

One of the first and still most reliable means for reconstructing chronologies for ancient Palestine is the use of historical data—texts both from the region itself and from outside of it. One of the most important of these is the Egyptian King List, for it is possible to coordinate the known years for the reigns of Egyptian kings with events in Palestine, especially when there was direct interaction between the two. There are numerous documents written in a variety of languages that contribute to chronology building, too many, in fact, to name individually. However, several major groups of texts, such as the archives from Mari and Ebla and the Amarna Letters, stand out. Collectively, these sources are often referred to as "extra-biblical" texts. Of course, this method does not apply to the prehistoric periods.

Both the biblical and the extra-biblical traditions are relevant and interesting in relation to each other. In addition, they draw the attention of a large public. Archaeologists have benefited greatly from the biblical texts, as they have from the archives of Amarna, Ebla, Ugarit, and Mari and from thousands of other texts from within and outside of Syro-Palestine. A majority of these documents, however, concern religious and political figures and thus may be less concerned with historical accuracy than with making some point. It is thus incumbent upon the archaeologist to treat *all* of them with some degree of circumspection, just as any good historian seeks to qualify his or her sources. Furthermore, where outside sources are concerned, significant problems arise when these do not fit smoothly with local chronologies, and in some cases they have internal inconsistencies of their own. Again, the archaeologist must beware. In fact, one of the great debates in Syro-Palestinian archaeology concerns the high-mid-low chronologies (see Chapter 11). Although this issue remains unresolved, this book generally follows the middle chronology, if for no other reason than to limit the damage should the high or low prove more accurate at some point in the future. For the purposes of periodization, I have generally rounded off dates by centuries in recognition of the fact that there is uncertainty regarding some of these dates and to streamline the chronology in order to focus on broad trends.

Radiocarbon Dating

The impact of radiocarbon dating, the method of determining the age of organic materials based on the rate of decay of carbon-14 developed by Willard Frank Libby in the 1950s, was immediately felt in the archaeology of Syro-Palestine. Some of the chronological configurations as proposed by Petrie, Albright, and Nelson Glueck were seriously challenged by this new, less subjective method of dating archaeological remains. Colin Renfrew (1971) pointed out that more profound than the dating and redating of individual artifacts was the fact that major models for the archaeology of the Old World—for example, explaining the spread of technologies throughout the Near East—would need to be reconsidered. Other forms of radiometric dating are not applicable to the time period under consideration.

Metal Age Terminology

Despite the wealth of knowledge about specific cultural groups such as the Canaanites, Israelites, and Philistines, the metal age terminology provides the basis for the generally accepted chronology of the ancient southern Levant. A closer look, however, reveals that although the actual division of periods and subphases holds up fairly well, the metal age terminology is in some cases misleading. For instance, the first few hundred years of the Chalcolithic period (the Copper Age) are without copper, while true bronze does not gain widespread use until after the Early Bronze Age. This system is also problematic in that there are long periods of overlap between the times when various metals were current (see Chapter 9), particularly when we extend our purview beyond just the southern Levant. Nonetheless, the metal age terms are generally perceived as more neutral than those based on the culture history of specific peoples, and in truth, they are probably less likely to encounter some fundamental challenge.

A BRIEF HISTORY OF DISCOVERY

The history of exploration and archaeological research in the southern Levant is filled with colorful characters and dazzling discoveries. It is also the story of great shifts in both the methodological and theoretical orientation of research, most notably the move toward a more secular archaeology, which still makes use of the biblical texts, but is less beholden to them. In discussing the history of archaeological research in the region, Amihai Mazar (1990) outlined three distinct periods. The first was the era prior to World War I, best characterized as romantic in terms of its relationship with the past. The second phase, which falls between the two world wars, generally conceived of archaeology as a method for documenting, and later testing, the historical veracity of the Bible. The third phase, the time after the founding of the modern state of Israel, has taken many new turns and expanded our understanding of the past by employing ethnographic and experimental data as well as developed social theory. Throughout these three periods, a host of characters made up the history of the Western discovery of ancient Palestine.

Napoleon Bonaparte

It is perhaps somewhat fitting that a survey of the history of the Western (re)discovery of Palestine should begin with one of the last of the European imperialists, Napoleon Bonaparte (1769–1821). At the end of the eighteenth century, most of the "superpowers" of the day, including the British, the Russians, the Americans, and, of course, the Ottomans, had interests in the Middle East. Napoleon was one of the first Europeans to demonstrate an active interest in not only the modern geopolitics of the region but in its ancient history as well. Napoleon had conceived of a French colony centered in Egypt from which he could revive the ancient glories of the country's past, drawing parallels to his own empire. Thus, in addition to the apparatus of war, Napoleon brought with him a team of scholars, including some of France's most prominent scientists, engineers, and naturalists as well as Orientalists and antiquarians (Silberman 1982). Their charge was to survey virtually every aspect of present-day Egypt and to propose a plan for restoration. Napoleon also had plans for Palestine, and though these were cut short with his defeat at Acre in 1799, his work in Egypt indirectly made a great impact on the rediscovery of Syro-Palestine.

Perhaps the most important singular discovery made by Napoleon's Scientific and Artistic Commission was the Rosetta Stone, which would ultimately prove to be the key to deciphering Egyptian hieroglyphics. It was also recognized early on that this relic had great significance for the emerging field of Biblical Archaeology, as it was for the first time possible—via associations with datable artifacts from Egypt—to provide some "absolute" chronological framework for the archaeological remains found in Palestine.

John Burkhardt

Upon the defeat of Napoleon, the British gained ascendancy in the region and soon initiated their own exploration of Palestine. Travel to the region during the eighteenth century was generally limited to military personnel, traders, and "Holy Land pilgrims" (Silberman 2003), but by the turn of the century things would begin to change. One of the first among the "British explorers" was Edward Daniel Clarke, a Cambridge scholar who surveyed the region seeking the tangible remains of biblical history, pledging "not to peer through the spectacles of priests," but to be more objective (Clarke 1817). In 1804, a British organization, the Palestine Association, was established with a charter that was explicitly secular in nature, its stated aim being the gathering of information on the geography, people, climate, and history of Palestine. John Burkhardt (1784–1817), a Swiss scholar trained in Oriental studies at Cambridge, was to represent the association in its early exploration of the region. In 1812, Burkhardt, motivated not only by scholarly interest but also by personal ambition to outdo the French, set out in earnest.

Launching into Palestine from Syria, Burkhardt assumed a false identity, donning a disguise and going by the name "Sheikh Ibrahim." Investigating the remote wadis south of the Dead Sea in about 1810–1812, Burkhardt "discovered"—or rather, became the first European in recent times to encounter—the ancient site of Petra. Petra had been the capital of the Nabatean desert kingdom from the third century B.C.E. to the first century C.E.

Lady Hester Lucy Stanhope

One of the great characters of this era was Lady Hester Lucy Stanhope (1776–1839), who set out for the Middle East in 1810 in the spirit of adventure. A chance meeting with Burkhardt in Nazareth, in addition to the "prophecy" of a committed inmate at Bedlam, convinced Stanhope that it was her destiny to explore the Holy Land (Silberman 1982). Stanhope, like her contemporaries, was interested primarily in hunting for treasure, though not for the same reasons as other British antiquarians, who aspired to fill the museums back in Europe. Rather, Stanhope conceived of her efforts as an opportunity to develop relations between Britain and the Ottoman Sultanate. A visit to a Franciscan monastery in Tripoli brought into her possession an ancient document that described a fantastic treasure buried beneath the ruins of the ancient city of Ashqelon on the Mediterranean coast of Palestine. Stanhope arrived at Ashqelon and commenced investigation of the site, enlisting the labor of hundreds of local workers. The highlight of her discoveries was a headless statue of a Roman emperor, and though for her this was a disappointment, the sculpture was, technically speaking, "the first archaeological artifact ever discovered in Palestine" (Silberman 1982).

Edward Robinson

Edward Robinson (1794–1863) was arguably the first westerner to apply scholarly rigor to the exploration of Palestine. A trained seminarian with skills in ancient Hebrew and other languages, Robinson was the foremost authority on the historical geography of Palestine of his time. This time, though, was marked by a rise in liberalism and skepticism toward the Bible in both Europe and the United States (Silberman 1982). Influenced by his father, a Puritan minister, and Rev. Moses Stuart, his mentor at Andover, Robinson made it his purpose to demonstrate the literal accuracy of the Bible.

Robinson began by studying the accounts of travelers and missionaries in order to reconstruct a biblical geography, and with a series of publications he established his reputation as an authority on such matters without even once traveling to the Middle East. When Robinson met the American missionary Eli Smith, the two conceived of a field study where they could document the veracity of the Bible by identifying the sites mentioned in the text. Robinson's expertise in biblical scholarship, coupled with Smith's command of Arabic, made the two a formidable pair, for they surmised that many of the Arab villages in Palestine (for example, el-Jib) retained the ancient Hebrew in their names (in this case, Gibeon). It is interesting to note that more than a century later, when the Levantine map was being redrawn by Zionists, a similar logic was employed. For instance, the Negev Names Committee translated Harabat Umm Dumma as Dimona, the city mentioned in Joshua (15:22), thus "reinstating" the ancient moniker (Benvenisti 2000).

In 1837, Robinson and Smith met up in Cairo, from whence they embarked upon their historic expedition through Palestine. Together the two identified more than 100 sites mentioned in the Bible. The results of this research were reported in Robinson's landmark work *Biblical Researches in Palestine, Mount Sinai, and Arabia Petraea* (1841), which, published simultaneously in the United States, England, and Germany, had an immediate impact on the field, becoming a standard for biblical students and researchers as well as European and American travelers (Moscrop 2000).

The Palestine Exploration Fund

The work of Robinson and Smith stimulated even greater interest in the field and a number of new research projects were initiated in the region during the latter part of the nineteenth century. For instance, in 1847 Lt. William F. Lynch, an American, began exploration of the area between the Sea of Galilee and the Dead Sea, searching for the biblical cities of Sodom and Gomorrah. One of Lynch's great contributions was his publication of reports on the fauna, flora, and geology of the region, in addition to detailed drawings and maps (Moscrop 2000).[1] He also added an element of adventure to the field with his personal account of the expedition, which included encounters with "fierce Bedouin, and the rugged landscape," fueling public interest (Silberman 1982, 62).

From 1864 to 1865, Charles W. Wilson, a retired major general of the Royal Engineers, conducted excavations and surveys in Jerusalem on behalf of several different government agencies, including the War Office. Wilson's expertise in topographical studies helped him produce accurate maps of ancient Jerusalem, thereby encouraging further research, and in 1865, the Palestine Exploration Fund (PEF) of London was established. Wilson was hired and immediately dispatched back to Palestine. For years to come, the PEF would support surveys in the region and excavations at a number of major sites. Although the PEF was interested in the prospect of making discoveries that supported the biblical accounts, the organization also espoused a scientific approach (Watson 1915).

After some years, the PEF ran into financial problems, but its leaders then became even more anxious to continue exploration in the region in the hopes of producing the sort of spectacular find that would help secure funds. In 1867, another officer of the Royal Engineers, Charles Warren, was sent to Jerusalem to study what structural remains could be discerned beneath the modern city. Though his method of cutting deep shafts made it difficult to assign accurate dates to his discoveries, his practice of carefully recording his findings and his work on the early topography of Jerusalem were important steps away from the days of pure plunder and toward those of more serious investigation (Silberman 2003; Chapman 1990).

In the meantime, Lord Horatio Kitchener, the distinguished British field marshal famous for his triumphs in the Sudan, was ready to join the game.

From 1872 to 1878, Kitchener, with his partner, Captain Claude Reigner Conder, conducted extensive geographical surveys, recording some 10,000 sites in an area of 6,000 square miles. Conder and Kitchener went on to produce several volumes on their research as well as extensive maps of the region.

Charles Clermont-Ganneau and the Moabite Inscription

The Frenchman Charles Clermont-Ganneau (1846–1923) began work in the region in 1873. He is best known for several remarkable finds, including the Gezer boundary marker and his identification of the site as biblical Gezer. He also discovered the famed Moabite Stone, which recounts the ninth-century-B.C.E. victories of King Mesha of Moab against Israel.

The great tradition of historical geography continued to be an important part of biblical scholarship with the work of G. A. Smith and A. P. Stanley toward the end of the century. Smith (1894) in the preface of *The Historical Geography of the Holy Land*, presaged the coming of archaeological investigation in the region, stating that the geographers had all but exhausted the potential for studying the surface of Palestine while pointing to the "great future for it under-ground."

Archaeology and the Military

By the beginning of the twentieth century, the efforts of the PEF had become entwined with the goals of the imperialist British government. The British turned their attention toward the Negev, the biblical "Wilderness of Zin," a region that represented a potentially key point in the growing conflict between the British and Ottomans. One of the most famous surveys in Near Eastern archaeology was that conducted by Leonard Woolley (excavator of the Mesopotamian City of Ur) and T. E. Lawrence (also known as Lawrence of Arabia). Woolley and Lawrence succeeded in identifying and documenting several important Nabatean cities while collecting information for military reconnaissance (Silberman 1982), though the PEF was not forthcoming about these efforts (Moscrop 2000). The convergence of military and scholarly interests is perhaps best represented by the fact that in 1914 Woolley and Lawrence's report was received by both the War Office and the Palestine Exploration Fund in London. Meanwhile, a PEF Quarterly Statement of 1915 touted the utility of "surveying, map-making, and all that contributes to a better knowledge of a country, its resources, and its people," saying that such projects were "of enormous practical importance" and generally of help to the war effort.

William Flinders Petrie and the Beginning of Scientific Archaeology

The PEF recognized that Warren's work in Jerusalem had been hindered by the confines of the modern city and disputes over property. In response, its leaders turned their attention to the excavation of a tell site, where there would be more room to operate. They were also seeking a new talent to direct these excavations and settled on an archaeologist well known for his work in Egypt, Sir William Matthew Flinders Petrie (1853–1942).

During his tenure in Egypt, Petrie established a reputation for his austere lifestyle on the dig as well as for his hands-on style, often reexamining the dig heaps and training the local workers himself (Hoffman 1979). Petrie recognized that the incidentals—potsherds and mud walls—were just as important, and often more informative, than the great temples and artifacts displayed in museums. Above all, Petrie can be credited with having introduced the practice of systematic and controlled archaeological excavations. He refined his method of ceramic seriation while in Palestine and was able to establish firm chronological links between the Levantine cultures and the Egyptians.

Petrie conducted several surveys in southern Palestine and, with the American scholar Frederick J. Bliss, commenced his first excavations in the region Tel el-Hesi in 1890. Employing his meticulous methods of excavation and analysis, he was able to establish a sequence for pottery forms, many of which he recognized from his research in Egypt. In many ways, Petrie moved Palestinian archaeology beyond the more limited realm of purely biblical studies and into the much broader framework of the ancient Near East (Silberman 1982, 149).

Petrie's attitude and approach to his research stood in sharp contrast to that of his predecessors as well as that of many of his contemporaries and would ultimately revolutionize the field. But as Paul Lapp had explained, "While excavations from that time on in Palestine were more than treasure hunts, they frequently left much to be desired for the scientific standards of their day, and some of them were strongly oriented toward biblical trove" (1969, 67).

Assuming that he had found the biblical town of Lachish at Tel el-Hesi, Petrie's sponsors at the PEF were pleased. But after the close of his first excavation season at Tel el-Hesi, Petrie was ready to return to Egypt. It would be three more decades before he would revisit Palestine as an excavator.

Frederick J. Bliss and the Tel el-Hesi Excavations

The PEF, seeing the great potential for serious archaeological research in the region, continued to retain the services of Bliss (1859–1937). Traveling first to Egypt in 1891 to observe Petrie's excavation methods at Medum, Bliss returned to Palestine and began his own work at Tel el-Hesi. One of the most exciting finds from Bliss's expedition was the first example of a cuneiform tablet, including a reference to Lachish, to be discovered in Palestine. Despite a number of outstanding discoveries, future excavators found some of Bliss's work at Tel el-Hesi (1891–1894) lacking in terms of methodology.[2] For instance, Bliss took the unconventional approach of cutting a giant, wedge-shaped trench and used arbitrary "layers," which resulted in additional challenges when it came to sorting the material into distinct phases of occupation. Bliss, however, did build on the stratigraphic concepts that Petrie had introduced to the region. The results of his four seasons at Tel el-Hesi were published in his book *A Mound of Many Cities* (1894), where he described the nature and structure of the tell for the first time (Mazar 1990).

Soon thereafter, Bliss teamed up with the young Irish archaeologist R. A. S. Macalister to conduct what is recognized as the first regional archaeology project. Massive amounts of artifacts were retrieved and recorded in a systematic fashion during these excavations in the Shephelah, and for the first time archaeologists managed to produce a complete chronological sequence spanning from the Bronze Age to the time of the Crusades.

R. A. S. Macalister at Gezer

By the turn of the century, Bliss and Macalister (1870–1950) had split, and the latter went on to lead a major long-term excavation at Tel el-Jazar (Gezer) on behalf of the PEF (1902–1909). One of the great finds of this expedition was the large inscribed stone commonly known as the "Gezer Calendar." Macalister published his findings, which are notable for their extensive documentation of ceramic finds, in three volumes entitled *Excavations at Gezer* (1912).

Like Bliss's work at Tel el-Hesi, however, Macalister's methodology at Gezer has been questioned (Laughlin 1999). Indeed, it was probably a case of trying to excavate too much without enough attention to provenience and stratigraphy. Macalister identified but eight of the strata at Gezer where subsequent archaeologists found twenty-six. Bliss, in his determination to dig up the entire mound in search of a royal archive, probably lacked the resources and experience necessary to organize the work and process the finds from such an ambitious undertaking. William G. Dever, who would revisit the site in the 1970s, referred to the earlier publications on Gezer as "vast treasure houses of intriguing, but often useless information" (1980, 42).

Around this time, a German team directed by Gottlieb Schumacher and Carl Watzinger excavated at Megiddo (1903–1905). Excavations would resume at Megiddo, under the direction of Clarence Fischer, P. L. O. Guy, and Gordon Loud, between 1925 and 1939 as one of the largest projects in the region.

3.3   The W. F. Albright Institute of Archaelogical Research (Photo courtesy of Sy Gitin)

The Founding of the Albright Institute

By the turn of the century, the Americans were prepared to sponsor exploration in Palestine as well. To facilitate this goal, several American institutions formed a consortium and founded the American Schools of Oriental Research, a landmark both literally, with the school based in a villa just north of the Old City's Damascus Gate in Jerusalem, and figuratively, with the establishment of a great tradition in Syro-Palestinian archaeology. The school, now named the W. F. Albright Institute of Archaeological Research, continues to thrive today under the leadership of Seymour Gitin.

George Andrew Reisner at Samaria

The first major American excavations in Palestine were carried out at Sebastia under the direction of George Andrew Reisner (1867–1942), known for his work in Egypt, in association with Harvard University and the newly established Semitic Museum. Beginning in 1908, this was conceived as a project in science, not in theology, and for this reason the job fell to Reisner, an experienced excavator without the "biblical baggage" (Silberman 1982).

3.4   Remains of ancient Tel-Sabastia and the modern Israeli settlement of Shavi Shomron in Samaria, an Israeli designation for a part of the Occupied West Bank, Israel. (Richard T. Nowitz/ Corbis)

Sebastia, located about 35 kilometers (22 miles) north of Jerusalem, was thought to be the site where Herod had built the city of Sebastia atop the ruins of Samaria, the ancient capital of the northern Kingdom of Israel, and thus held the prospect of discovering the great city built by King Omri and his son Ahab. Applying the principles of stratigraphy to his field methodology, Reisner had developed a technique while working in Egypt whereby the different layers were peeled off individually as distinct strata. He also employed a system of recording information on each artifact, including its precise location, and keeping a registry of artifacts as well as photo records, daily written logs, and architectural plans. The publication of Reisner's excavation reports on Samaria (1924), however, was delayed by the outbreak of World War I.

William Foxwell Albright and the "Golden Age" of Biblical Archaeology

In the years between the two world wars, W. F. Albright (1891–1971) would emerge as the region's foremost archaeologist. During what is often referred to as the "Golden Age of Biblical Archaeology," Albright worked tirelessly to produce more than 1,000 publications, the better part of which was concerned with the relationship between archaeology and biblical scholarship. Albright's agenda was formulated partly in reaction to the work of scholars such as Julius Wellhausen, who asserted that the biblical accounts contained little if any information of true historical value. Employing the methods of literary criticism, Wellhausen and others attempted to discredit the Bible's historical value by pointing to internal contradictions and inconsistencies within the text itself, meanwhile disregarding extra-biblical texts and archaeological finds that seemed to support the biblical narrative.

Albright, in addition to having expertise in Assyriology and biblical studies, was extremely diligent in his command of archaeological data and thus challenged many of the minimalist arguments. In fact, one of Albright's great contributions to the archaeology of the southern Levant was the emphasis he placed on mastering the material evidence. It was his visits to sites throughout the region, and his examination of pottery sherds from surface collections, that provided him with the background necessary for developing a new ceramic typology. Ultimately, he would also establish himself as a bona fide excavator with his work at Tel el-Ful (1922–1923), Bethel (1927), and Tel Beit Mirsim (1926–1932), and his field reports on these sites were quite thorough.

Albright conceived of Biblical Archaeology as relating to *all* of the lands mentioned in the Bible and set the standard for the comparative study of extra-biblical texts and material culture. In 1950, he declared, "Archaeological discoveries of the past generation have . . . [provided] that rapid accumulation of data supporting the substantial historicity of the patriarchal traditions" (Albright 1950, 3). Indeed, during the Golden Age of Biblical Archaeology, the discipline's prevailing paradigm was the doctrine of the "perfect match" between what spade and scripture had to say. Albright's scholarly résumé would ultimately include several stints as director of the American Schools for Oriental Research, a post as professor of Semitic languages at Johns Hopkins University, and the job of editor of the *Bulletin of the American Schools of Oriental Re-*

search (*BASOR*). Though more than half a century of subsequent research would call into question some of Albright's theories, he is still today regarded as one of the greatest scholars to work in the region and the founding father of serious Biblical Archaeology.

Nelson Glueck

Albright had also trained an entire generation of Biblical Archaeologists, one of his star students being Nelson Glueck (1900–1971). But it was also during Glueck's career that the "infallible" approach that Albright had propounded began to face serious challenges. Glueck's work was critical in its own right as he established the importance of archaeological survey and settlement pattern studies. During the 1930s and 1940s, Glueck embarked on a series of archaeological surveys in Transjordan, traveling alone either on foot or on horseback. He focused on Moab, Ammon, and Edom, mapping these regions and photographing various natural and manmade features while collecting pottery sherds and recording his finds. He was then able to synthesize his data, constructing maps of human settlement through time. Glueck's books, such as *Rivers in the Desert* (1959), had great popular appeal, and the charismatic young adventurer captured the public imagination, appearing on the cover of *Time* magazine in 1963. As P. R. S. Moorey explained, "In retrospect the years between the World Wars have come to be seen as the time when Biblical archaeology, particularly through men like Albright and Glueck, had an academic status and a self-confidence that it had not enjoyed before and was rarely to achieve again" (1992, 55). Indeed, as the use of radiocarbon dating emerged in the late 1950s, some of Glueck's assertions concerning chronology became problematic, and the myth of the "perfect match" would not last long.

G. Ernest Wright

G. E. Wright (1909–1974), one of Albright's most influential students, went on to lead the field in the early 1950s and 1960s (Laughlin 1999; King 1987). As his mentor in the 1930s, Albright had encouraged Wright to work on the first systematic pottery typology for the southern Levant, resulting in Wright's doctoral dissertation, entitled "The Pottery of Palestine from the Earliest Times to the End of the Early Bronze Age" (1937). In 1938, Wright founded the journal *Biblical Archaeologist* in an effort to appeal to both a popular and a scholarly audience.[3]

Wright directed excavations at the site of Tel Balata, also known as biblical Shechem, using this expedition as an opportunity to train future generations of American archaeologists. He emphasized the principles of stratigraphic excavation with refinements in technique that had been introduced by Kathleen Kenyon (a student of the great British archaeologist Sir Mortimer Wheeler) in her work at Samaria and Jericho. Yigael Yadin would later apply Wright's excavation methods and field school concept when he began his excavations at Hazor. In the tradition of Albright and Glueck, Wright made similarly bold statements about the historical veracity of the Bible as confirmed through archaeological research, but in the following decade weak links between the two began to appear (see Chapter 11). Some of the scholars who studied under

Wright at Harvard (for example, William Dever and Lawrence Stager) continue to lead the field today.

Paul Lapp and the Shift toward a Secular Archaeology

One of the first to suggest that there ought to be less theological emphasis and more of a secular orientation in Syro-Palestinian archaeology was Wright's own student, Paul Lapp. Lapp produced a relatively great amount of work in a career shortened by his premature death in 1970, including the large-scale excavations at Ta'anach near the Jezreel Valley and the Early Bronze Age cemetery at Bab edh-Dra. Yet one of his most significant contributions to the discipline was to offer constructive criticism. Lapp (1969) grappled with important issues about the implications that Biblical Archaeology had for religious faith and criticized the circular logic whereby archaeologists assign subjective dates to pottery types and then use these dates in turn to date the levels at other sites in which similar pottery is found.

ISRAELI ARCHAEOLOGY

Eliezer Sukenik

The roots of Israeli archaeology go back to the beginning of the Zionist movement and the founding of the Jewish Palestine Exploration Society back in 1914. One of the original "native" archaeologists was Eliezer Sukenik (1889–1953), known for his involvement with the discovery of the Dead Sea Scrolls. Sukenik, like most members of (pre-)Israeli archaeology's founding class of the 1920s and 1930s, was, in fact, trained abroad both academically (in ancient languages and biblical studies) and methodologically (by taking part in foreign excavations).

Yigael Yadin

Sukenik's son, Yigael Yadin (1917–1984), was one of Israel's most celebrated archaeologists. Yadin's legend as a national hero was greatly enhanced by his role as a general during the Israeli War of Independence when he used his knowledge of ancient roadways to military advantage. The Israeli tradition of Biblical Archaeology arrived with Yadin's excavations at Hazor from 1955–1958. Through the ages, Hazor was one of the most prominent sites in the southern Levant—it is mentioned numerous times in the biblical and extra-biblical texts—and Yadin saw the opportunity not only to procure evidence supporting the historicity of the biblical tradition but also to recover great treasures. His methodology involved the horizontal excavation of broad areas, thus exposing entire foundations of monumental structures, which could be recorded with impressive aerial photos. Like Wright at Shechem, Yadin also conceived of his excavations at Hazor as an opportunity to train an entire generation of Israeli archaeologists. In the 1960s, Yadin would excavate Masada, the desert fortress where zealots are said to have taken their lives rather than surrender to the Romans, thus contributing to the creation of a national symbol still used today (Silberman 1993, 1990).

Yohanon Aharoni and Benjamin Mazar

Another of these early Israeli archaeologists was Yohanon Aharoni (1919–1976), who conducted a site survey to study the problem of Israelite settlement in the Upper Galilee (Aharoni 1957). As a result, he and Yadin enjoyed a great scholarly rivalry that influenced both of their works. Aharoni's research was under the tutelage of Benjamin Mazar (1906–1995) of the Hebrew University, who, along with Moshe Dothan, encouraged interest in the archaeology of the Philistines with his excavations at Tel Qasile (1948–1951, 1956). Mazar would later go on to conduct important excavations in the Old City of Jerusalem, and his nephew Amihai Mazar is one of the leading Israeli archaeologists today.

LITERARY EVIDENCE FROM ANCIENT ISRAEL

The Biblical Tradition

A critical issue for the archaeology of the southern Levant concerns the relationship between archaeological evidence and the numerous textual sources. The Bible, in particular, poses a challenging problem in that it relays stories of people and places directly related to the region, but its veracity as a historical document is highly questionable. Nonetheless, the Bible is useful to archaeologists and historians for several reasons. First, there appear within the biblical narrative specific lists, many of which appear to derive from real historical documents grafted directly into the text. In addition, some of the events described in the Bible can be generally corroborated by some of the other textual sources, with the latter serving as a corrective with regard to the dating of these events (see Chapter 11 for an expanded discussion on these and related problems).

A great deal of what archaeologists know about ancient Canaan and Israel comes from sources discovered elsewhere in the ancient Near East—the extra-biblical texts. These include thousands of surviving documents from all over the ancient Near East, including Sumer, Babylonia, Assyria, Susa, and Nuzi as well as Ugarit, Ebla, Mari, and Egypt. The latter two, Mari in Syria and Amarna in Egypt, are famous for their vast archives of royal correspondence, a good portion of which directly concerns the peoples of the southern Levant.

In most cases, the extra-biblical texts can be more reliably dated to the time periods that they describe, and they generally corroborate with the archaeological evidence to a much greater degree than the Bible itself. In other words, if the various textual sources were to be ranked in terms of how their historical value is borne out by archaeological evidence, the Bible would probably be one of the less reliable. A number of scholars have argued that the books of Deuteronomy and 1 and 2 Chronicles should actually be regarded as fairly reliable where history is concerned, though others have remained more circumspect (Smith 2002). It has been pointed out that the sequence outlined in 2 Kings can be cross-checked with dates derived from Assyrian, Babylonian, and Egyptian sources, some of which can be further verified by astronomical data (Dever 1992a, 19).

NOTES

1. Many of Lynch's maps, however, have turned out to be somewhat inaccurate.

2. Philip J. King (1985, 24) has pointed out that although the British often ridicule Bliss's methodology, many American archaeologists are less critical.

3. The journal recently changed its name to *Near Eastern Archaeologist.*

SUGGESTED READING

Chapman, Rupert. 1990. "Pioneers of Biblical Archaeology." In *Archaeology and the Bible,* edited by J. Tubb and R. Chapman, 9–37. London: British Museum Publications.

Dever, William. 1980. "Archaeological Method in Israel: A Continuing Revolution." *Biblical Archaeology* 43: 40–48.

———. 1992. "The Chronology of Syria-Palestine in the Second Millennium B.C.E.: A Review of Current Issues." *Bulletin of the American Schools of Oriental Research* 288: 1–25.

King, Philip. 1987. "The Influence of G. Earnest Wright on the Archaeology of Palestine." In *Archaeology and Biblical Interpretation,* edited by L. Purdue, L. Tombs, and G. Johnson, 15–30. Atlanta: Scholars Press.

Lapp, Paul. 1969. *Biblical Archaeology and History.* New York: World Publishing.

Moscrop, J. 2000. *Measuring Jerusalem: The Palestine Exploration Fund and British Interest in the Holy Land.* London: Leicester University Press.

Silberman, Neil A. 1982. *Digging for God and Country: Exploration, Archeology, and the Secret Struggle for the Holy Land, 1799–1917.* New York: Knopf/Random House.

———. 1990. *Between Past and Present: Archaeology, Ideology, and Nationalism in the Modern Middle East.* New York: Anchor.

———. 1993. *Prophet from amongst You: The Life of Yigael Yadin, Soldier, Scholar, and Mythmaker of Modern Israel.* Reading, MA: Addison-Wesley.

Silberman, Neil A., and David Small, eds. 1997. *The Archaeology of Israel: Constructing the Past, Interpreting the Present.* Sheffield, England: Sheffield Academic Press.

CHAPTER 4

Origins, Growth, and Decline
of Levantine Cultures

W hen studying any culture area from a long-term perspective, it is necessary to consider a range of questions concerning continuity and change
among peoples and cultures over the course of time. The processes of change
can be generally attributed to the internal evolution of cultures, the movement
of peoples, the impact of external influences, or some combination of all three.
It is the charge of the archaeologist and historian, therefore, to offer the most
accurate picture of change that is possible based on what is usually a highly incomplete material record.

PREHISTORIC CULTURES: MAJOR DEVELOPMENTS
IN LATE PREHISTORY

Chalcolithic Period

The Chalcolithic period was marked by the local inception of copper technology, although many aspects of material culture remained much the same as in
the Neolithic (Wadi Rabah) period. There soon emerged a new culture, probably with several subregional variants, which departed in significant ways from
its Neolithic predecessors. Defining a cultural group in prehistory without
help from literary sources can be quite challenging for the archaeologist. Based
on patterns in material culture alone, however, it appears there were at least
two distinct cultural entities in the southern Levant during Chalcolithic times:
the Ghassulian and the Beer Sheva cultures. It is not clear, however, to what extent these were contemporary regional variants, as suggested by Isaac Gilead
(1989, 1994), successive cultures that changed over time, or some combination
of the two (Golden 1998).

One of the main challenges for Chalcolithic archaeology in the southern Levant concerns establishing temporal divisions for a period that has otherwise
been largely treated as monolithic. Various socioeconomic developments occurred during this phase, and it lasted for about 1,200 years. It is clear that further research on Chalcolithic subchronology is greatly needed. Based on research at sites in the northern Negev, for example, it has been suggested that
there were three phases in the architectural development of the region: (1) subterranean architecture built by original settlers; (2) semisubterranean structures rebuilt from this foundation; and (3) a final phase of surface occupation

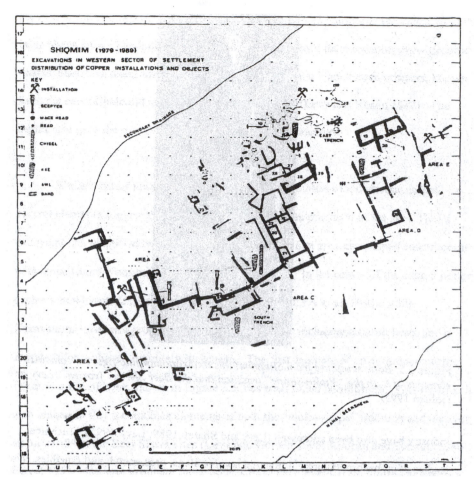

4.1   Plan of the Chalcolthic village of Shiqmim (Courtesy of T. E. Levy)

(Perrot 1955, 1984; Levy 1992). Others (Gilead, Rosen, and Fabian 1991; Gilead 1993) have disputed this reconstruction, however, and no consensus on a sub-chronology has emerged.

During the Chalcolithic period, significant transformations in socioeconomic life occurred. New, larger, more settled communities were established throughout the southern Levant, including the first large villages in the northern Negev desert. People lived in rectilinear stone and mud-brick structures, though several sites (for example, Shiqmim and Gilat) had buildings that either housed extended families or were used for public purposes (Levy 2003a). Although sheep- and goat herding had been practiced for centuries, if not millennia, it was during the fifth millennium B.C.E. that a symbiotic relationship between specialized pastoral groups and sedentary farming communities developed—an arrangement that persists in parts of the Middle East to this day. A shift in the focus of pastoral production occurred, often referred to as the "secondary products revolution" (Sherratt 1981; Levy 1992), where the production of dairy goods was emphasized. The accumulation of large herds by some individuals probably constituted one of the earliest forms of wealth.

With this development, accompanied by individual control over land for both grazing and farming, a sense of territoriality emerged.

Of course, the local advent of metal was significant, not only as a technological breakthrough but also as an indication of the development of trade, specialized craft production, and a luxury goods economy. The early smiths worked in designated production areas, as at Abu Matar, producing both utilitarian forms and intricate castings with symbolic meaning, and using both "pure" copper and complex metals (that is, natural alloys). All metal was relatively rare at this time, and great value must have been placed upon these items. The Chalcolithic period also saw the emergence of unique symbolic and artistic traditions in various media, including basalt, bone, and ivory (see Fig. 4.2). Wall paintings at Teleilat Ghassul strongly suggest the development of new ritual belief systems. The Chalcolithic ceramic assemblage, in addition to vessels for cooking, storage, and service, also had unique forms such as cornets, churns, and "V-shaped" bowls. Ritual items, particularly statuettes, were also created from ceramics, and the practice of burying infants in jars became widespread. Other changes in burial practices, specifically the first extramural cemeteries and the establishment of wealthy cave tombs, suggest important changes in social structure.

In summary, the Chalcolithic period in the southern Levant was a period of relatively rapid social change. During this time, we see the earliest evidence for a division of labor, with at least some level of coordination for differentiated economic activities, and the advent of new technologies that impacted society in significant ways. In particular, the local advent of metallurgy was a critical development as it was the beacon for an overall shift toward greater economic complexity in general. The presence of metal, including gold found at Nahal Qanah (Gopher and Tsuk 1996), coupled with wealthy burials in cave tombs situated throughout the region, point to the emergence of nascent forms of complex sociopolitical units, indications of modest social ranking, and perhaps warfare.

4.2 Ivory female figurine from Bir es-Safadi (Drawing by J. Golden; adapted from Jean Perrot. 1968. "Préhistoire Palestinienne." In *Supplément au Dictionaire de la Bible*, 286–466. Paris: Letouzey et Ané)

Early Bronze Age

A clear picture of the transition from the Chalcolithic period to the Early Bronze Age has been elusive to date. There is evidence for a certain degree of continuity with the preceding period, as some stylistic and technological fea-

4.3   View of the Valley of Jezreel from Tel Megiddo (Photo courtesy of Zev Radovan, Land of the Bible Picture Archive)

tures persist into the Early Bronze Age, but many of the hallmarks of Chalcolithic culture had already disappeared as new forms and styles in material culture began to appear. Ironically, the earliest phase of the Early Bronze Age actually precedes the local appearance of bronze, a technological development that does not occur until later in the period. Many of the important tell sites that would be occupied repeatedly in the following millennia owing to their desirable locations were first settled during the Early Bronze Age. Archaeological research has been limited by the fact that levels dating to this period often sit in the basal layers of sites, rendering the type of broad horizontal excavations necessary for exposing extensive architectural remains quite difficult, if not impossible.

The initial stages of the Early Bronze Age have been characterized as a period of cultural decline. Although there is probably some validity to this, by the end of the fourth millennium marked social and economic change had occurred (Kempinski 1992a; Esse 1989). The discovery of well over 300 habitation sites indicates a sharp increase in population accompanied by an overall shift in settlement to more fertile environments. Moving into the Levantine hills and highlands, the people of Early Bronze Age societies made significant advances in farming technology, bringing new territories under the plow. Economic development based primarily on staple surpluses allowed for specialized craft pro-

duction in areas such as ceramics and metallurgy. This shift toward settlement in the hill
country—the ideal habitat for the cultivation of
grapes and olives—was concomitant with the
birth of the Mediterranean economy. During
the first part of the Early Bronze Age (EB1,
3500–3050 B.C.E.), the city of Ai (Callaway 1978)
was the centerpiece of a great highland city-
state, comprising both sedentary and mobile
populations, and served as an administrative
center for the production and trade of horticultural goods such as wine, olive oil, and grapes.
These early cash crops were decidedly attrac-
tive to Egyptians and served as an engine that
drove lively associations between the two regions. This relationship intensified in the later
EB1 (EB1b), culminating in a sustained Egyptian presence in southern Canaan, as evidenced
by large amounts of Egyptian pottery, seal impressions, and architecture at a number of sites
(for example, En Besor). In turn, pottery forms
typical of the Palestinian Early Bronze Age,
such as wavy ledge-handled pots and Line
Group Painted Wares, have been found at sites
throughout Egypt, particularly in the Delta
(Kohler 1995; van den Brink 1992; Dreyer 1992,
see Fig. 4.4).

4.4   Levantine Line Group Painted Ware from
Abydos (Drawing by J. Golden; adapted from
Luc Watrin. 2002. "Tributes and the Rise of a
Predatory Power: Unraveling the Intrigue of EB I
Palestinian Jars Found by E. Amélineau at Abydos." In *Egyptian and Canaanite Interaction during
the Fourth–Third Millennium B.C.E.*, edited by E. van
den Brink and T. Levy, 450–463. London: Leicester University Press.)

Cities of the northern region, in contrast,
clearly reflected influences from the Syrian and
northern Mesopotamian cultural sphere. It has
been suggested, in fact, that the origins of Early
Bronze Age culture should be sought in the
north, perhaps as a result of population "spillover" associated with the collapse of the Uruk colonies of northern Syria (Amiran 1970; Portugali and
Gophna 1993).

One of the most outstanding developments of the Early Bronze Age was the
rise of urbanism in the southern Levant. Large, often fortified cities played
host to an increasing number of people integrated into an emerging urban
market system based upon an agricultural surplus and the specialized production and exchange of nonagricultural goods. At the beginning of the Early
Bronze Age, a relatively low level of political organization and integration
most likely existed, but by the third part of the Early Bronze Age (EB3,
2650–2200 B.C.E.), vast city-states with developed urban centers appeared
around the countryside. The EB3 city of Beit Yerah was surrounded by a large
glacis and had a central silo facility used to stockpile vast amounts of grain.

Exactly who the Early Bronze Age people were is difficult to determine, par-

4.5   Panel from the Narmer Palette depicting Asiatics (Drawing by J. Golden)

ticularly since there is very little historical data to assist in this regard. A certain level of uniformity in material culture and style is apparent throughout
the region, suggesting some form of common identity. At the same time, regional variants or subcultures can also be discerned. It has long been thought
that the famous Narmer Palette (Fig. 4.5), discovered at Hierakonpolis in

Egypt, depicts the region's inhabitants (Yadin 1955; Yeivin 1960). The men represented in bas-relief on the ceremonial palette wear beards and thick, shoulder-length hair or perhaps some form of headdress. It is difficult, however, to say whether these people represent the people of southern Palestine in general or a more specific group (for example, desert dwellers). In one register, an early hieroglyphic symbol used to denote a city appears above two naked men who seem to be fleeing. The city has bastions not unlike those found at the great northern Negev center Arad, which might indicate that these individuals hail from that region, if not the city itself. Regardless, it is clear that they are intended to be distinct from the Egyptian peoples—a fact underscored by virtue of their being naked, a sign associated with enslavement in Egyptian iconography. Scholars do sometimes refer to the people living in the southern Levant during the Early Bronze Age as Canaanites, though strictly speaking, this term cannot be applied with confidence until the Middle Bronze Age.

Intermediate Bronze Age

Toward the end of the Early Bronze Age, significant socioeconomic and political changes occurred, and the urban system collapsed. The ensuing phase was clearly distinct from both the urban culture of the Early Bronze Age and the cultural fluorescence to come during the Middle Bronze Age. Archaeologists now recognize this period as the Intermediate Bronze Age (IBA, also known as EB4). In terms of settlement patterns, there was a general shift toward rural areas as the cities, including Ai, Beit Yerah, Megiddo, Halif, and Yarmuth, were abruptly abandoned or destroyed. Thereafter, much of the population dispersed into the more marginal zones of the Jordan Valley, Transjordan, and Negev.

In contrast with the developed urbanism of the preceding Early Bronze Age and the succeeding Middle Bronze Age, this period is often depicted as one of cultural decline. It is no less accurate, however, to construe the Intermediate Bronze Age as a time when pastoral societies flourished, as there was a shift away from urbanism. In explaining this change from urban culture to more rural ways of life, several different theories have been proposed.

In the 1960s, it was generally held that incursions into Palestine by West Semitic "Amorite" tribes from Syria brought nomadic culture into the area. The Amorites, whose name derives from the Hebrew Bible, were a people who emerged on the northern fringe of the Syrian Desert in the area known as the Hamad. They also appear frequently as the "Amurru" in Akkadian cuneiform texts. The semiarid environment of the Hamad could not support large, centralized populations, and thus transhumance, with varying configurations of agro-pastoralism, was the general way of life. Precisely who the Amorites were is difficult to say with certainty (Gerstenblith 1983; Dever 1987), and David Ilan (1995) has warned that although it is not necessarily inaccurate to use this term to refer to groups entering Canaan, it is too ambiguous to have any real meaning.

The collapse of the urban culture of the Early Bronze Age has also been linked to events in Egypt and to a change in the relationship between the Egyptians and their counterparts in Palestine. With the demise of the Old Kingdom, Egypt experienced the first of several phases of political disunity; in this case, Dynasties 7–11 are known as the First Intermediate Period (c. 2300 B.C.E). One immediate effect of this was the disruption of trade networks involving Egypt and Byblos that had thrived for centuries.

It is generally believed that the destruction of cities at the end of the Early Bronze Age was perpetrated by raiding Egyptians at the end of Old Kingdom. This is based in part on textual evidence from Egypt, for example, an inscription from the tomb of Pepi I's general in Dashasheh, Uni, who claims to have defeated the land of the "sand dwellers." There is also a Fifth Dynasty depiction of the Egyptian siege of a fortified city in Asia. The city wall is represented with rounded, horseshoe-shaped towers that are, again, very similar to those found at Arad. (Arad was mostly abandoned by this time, but it is likely that this motif had become something of a catchall sign for "Asiatic city" in the Egyptian lexicon.) As for the motivation behind the Egyptian attacks, Mazar (1990) has suggested that these raids were designed to stem the flow of Asiatics into Egyptian lands.

Others have attributed the collapse of the Early Bronze Age culture to environmental factors, specifically a decline in rainfall accompanied by lower water-table levels. Unable to maintain the stores of staples, the cities began to experience urban flight as more people turned to the nomadic alternative. William Dever (1989) has proposed a more multifaceted approach, arguing that multiple factors related to ecology had a significant impact on economic and social organization. During periods of severe drought, nomadic peoples would have competed for access to water and pasture, with conflict spilling over into settled areas.

Arlene M. Rosen (1995) has pointed out that it was not simply environmental change in itself that caused this trend, but rather the human response to these changes. According to her, in addition to the drop in rainfall, there were also acute hydrological problems. During the earlier portion of the Early Bronze Age, there had been widespread alluvial activity leading to the growth of floodplains and floodwater farming, where overflowing waters from rain-filled wadis could be captured and used to the benefit of the farmer. But this trend later ceased and a regime of wadi incision began, where floods did not water the plain, thus rendering floodwater farming virtually impossible. In explaining the collapse, Rosen pointed to overall agricultural mismanagement and the impact of social factors, such as the emphasis on "luxury" crops by members of the elite class. This shift in focus away from staple goods led to agricultural overspecialization in less resilient crops, ultimately at the expense of the society's ability to maintain stores of food and hedge against leaner times; that is, those heavily vested in the cash-crop system were less able to adapt to the drier climate. To compound problems, the urban system, with its demanding elite, drew labor away from the subsistence agricultural sector for construction of various public structures. It was in the context of these internal problems that military campaigns were visited on the peoples of Palestine by the Egyptian kings of the Fifth and Sixth Dynasties, dealing these societies a fatal blow.

As there were few built-up settlements during the Intermediate Bronze Age, much of what is known about the period comes from the excavation of cemeteries such as those at Beth Shean, Gibeon, Lachish, Megiddo, and Tel el-Ajjul, as well as Tel Umm Hammad esh-Sharqiya and Khirbet Iskander in Transjordan. The characteristic burials from the period were rock-cut shaft tombs, hundreds of which have been excavated at Jericho (Kenyon 1979) and Jebel Qa'aqir (Dever 1987). At Khirbet Kirmil, more than 900 shaft tombs were excavated by archaeologists (though most had already been robbed at the time of their discovery), and at Dhahr Mirzbaneh near Jerusalem, some 1,100 tombs were surveyed (Dever 2003a; Finkelstein 1991). Israel Finkelstein (1991) has argued that these cemeteries were often used by mobile groups of herders, centered mainly in the Negev, who migrated into the central hills, where they camped and buried their dead. It is not clear from the mortuary evidence whether there were pronounced social gaps in the society. Although Talia Shay (1983) infers from burial practices at Jericho that the society was relatively egalitarian, others have argued that a social hierarchy is observable (Palumbo 1987; Dever 2003a).

Dever (1989b, 2003a) has pointed out that archaeologists were previously aware of a few scattered settlements, such as Beer Resisim, which may have been inhabited on a seasonal basis, and that most sites were typically characterized as ephemeral. Recent research, however, has revealed much more extensive settlement, particularly in Transjordan, where archaeologists have discovered villages that feature circular, semisubterranean houses (Palumbo 1987). Flat bowls were used for food service, while drinks were presented in goblets. Tall, wheel-made jars with flaring necks were also used, along with small vessels called *amphoriskoi*. Rooms were lit with four-spouted lamps.

It also appears that urban centers were not entirely absent, as Suzanne Richard (1990) has discovered at Khirbet Iskander, where a city wall has been excavated. A number of scholars (Dever 1995; LaBianca 1990; Richard 1990) have also argued that the focus on transhumance in the Intermediate Bronze Age has tended to obscure the fact that farming was still a vital activity during this time, as people practiced mixed economies and/or the exchange of pastoral and agricultural goods.

Models emphasizing internal factors and those focusing on external factors such as invasions and migrations do not necessarily exclude each other, however. Although it has been demonstrated that internal factors played a role in the collapse of the Early Bronze Age culture, and that indigenous peoples continued to thrive in parts of the region during the Intermediate Bronze Age, there is also evidence, in the way of pottery styles, architecture, burial customs, and weaponry, that an infiltration of new peoples into Canaan may have been a factor. The question of what brought about the reestablishment of urban societies during the Middle Bronze Age is once again answered through the assessment of a combination of both internal and external factors.

THE CANAANITES

Middle Bronze Age

Understanding the origins and early development of the Canaanite civilization is one of the most fascinating challenges addressed by the archaeology of the southern Levant. Though the term "Early Canaanite" has at times been ap-

4.6   MBA rampart systems give Near Eastern tell sites their characteristic shape (J. Golden)

plied to the Early Bronze Age (for example, Kenyon 1979; Albright 1973), it is the Middle Bronze Age that represents what may be called the "Golden Age" of Canaanite culture. Following the ruralization that occurred at the beginning of the second millennium during the Intermediate Bronze Age, a new urban culture began to take hold throughout the southern Levant.

The Middle Bronze Age landscape was divided into city-states with a site hierarchy involving large gateway communities and regional centers surrounded by subregional centers and numerous small villages. The coastal plain, particularly the northern portion, became a major settlement area characterized by rapid urban development, while a chain of new settlements appeared on the Sharon Plain. One of the hallmarks of the Canaanite culture was the construction of massive earthworks, also referred to as ramparts, or glacis systems, which surrounded virtually all of the major cities as well as a number of smaller centers. In fact, these ramparts are what give most tell sites their characteristic sloping form today. In the case of cities, the earthen ramparts enclosed areas of urban development that included public buildings such as temples and palaces as well as residential structures.

In addition to great architectural works, the Middle Bronze Age saw the first widespread use of true tin bronze in the region. Canaanite metalsmiths exploited this new technology in order to expand the repertoire of weapons and tools. The "duckbill axe" was a product of this latest expertise. Bronze was also used to craft images of Canaanite deities and heroes, while gold was used to make jewelry, often with anthropomorphic motifs. It is evident from these representations, as well as from the imagery found on seals and other media, that new symbolic and ideological systems had emerged. Kilns used for the production of pottery have been found at a number of sites, such as Tel el-Ajjul and Afula, where local buff ware and various types of juglets were produced. One distinctive type of pottery was the Tel el-Yehudiyeh Ware (Fig. 4.7), mainly juglets, memorable for the zoomorphic (including fish and birds) and anthropomorphic forms that it incorporated. Tel el-Yehudiyeh Ware was first

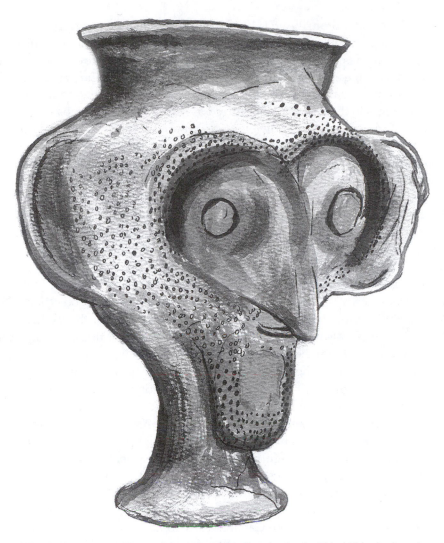

4.7   Anthropomorphic ceramic vessel from Jericho in the Tel el-Yehudiyeh style (Drawing by J. Golden; adapted from Amnon Ben-Tor. 1992. *The Archaeology of Ancient Israel*. New Haven, CT: Yale University Press, and the Israel Museum.)

identified at the site for which it is named in the eastern Delta of Egypt and suggests contact between the two regions. The appearance of these wares in Cyprus, as well as painted Cypriote jugs found in the southern Levant, also points to maritime trade. Overall, Canaanite material culture during the Middle Bronze Age displayed a rich and vivid decorative style and a dynamic iconographic system incorporating both local and imported ideas.

The Middle Bronze Age was also characterized by the emergence of large city-states where allegiance was most probably given to a king. The city dwellers maintained ties with a substantial transient population that inhabited the surrounding lands, and kinship continued to play a role in social and economic organization. Current understanding of the process of urbanization during the Middle Bronze Age is based, in part, upon a group of Egyptian inscriptions known collectively as the "Execration Texts." These texts, which list the proper names of foreign places and/or peoples considered hostile to Egypt, provide the equivalent of rough geopolitical maps of Canaan. Spanning a period of more than 100 years (Dynasty 12), the two separate groups of texts reflect changes in the region that occurred as semisedentary groups with tribal leaders of the earlier phase developed into a culture with multiple urban centers.

The city of Hazor (Yadin 1972) in the north was the most outstanding center in terms of the scale of urban development and sheer size (80 hectares). The architectural style and layout of Hazor recall some of the great Syrian cities and, along with general similarities in various facets of the material culture of the Canaanites, indicate a strong northern cultural influence. Textual sources such as the Mari Letters specifically mention Hazor as an important center that played a prominent role in a much broader cultural system. During this time, copper, tin, wine, and a host of other valuable goods traversed vast "international" trade networks in the form of both raw and finished goods (Ilan 2003; Maeir 2000). Although trade relations played a vital role in the exchange of ideas, new people also moved into the region during the Middle Bronze Age, probably coming down the coastal plain of Lebanon in waves of migration.

Canaanite culture of the eighteenth century B.C.E. was thriving at the very time that the land of Egypt was in disarray. The Second Intermediate Period in Egypt, marked by political instability, created a situation that invited the influx and ultimate ascendancy in the eastern Delta of Asiatic groups commonly known as the Hyksos. This name is based on the Egyptian term *hekau khasut*, which literally means "foreign rulers." These foreigners came to dominate much of Lower Egypt and established the Fifteenth Dynasty, which was roughly contemporaneous with the second part of the Middle Bronze Age (MB2, c. 1800–1650 B.C.E.). The prevalence of Levantine MB2 material culture suggests that the Hyksos were Canaanites who had migrated into the Delta and established the capital city of Avaris—the archaeological site known as Tel el-Dab'a and Zoan of the Bible.

The Egyptians, however, would regroup and manage to defeat the Hyksos at Avaris, ultimately driving them from the Delta altogether. Egyptian armies then pursued the Asiatics into southern Palestine, destroying the city of Sharuhen. Archaeologists have attempted to identify this ancient city, with most agreeing on Tel el-Ajjul, where evidence for mass burning and destruction has been observed; other scholars have argued for Tel el-Far'ah South. It is unclear what other cities fell victim to Egyptian aggression, but it is generally believed that the attack on Sharuhen, in particular, had a destabilizing effect on the region as a whole.

One other issue that concerns the Middle Bronze Age is the suggestion that this period represents the time of the patriarchs of Genesis (Albright 1973; see also Mazar 1990, 224–225). For instance, Albright associated the story of Abraham and his departure from the Mesopotamian city of Ur with the migration of the Amorites, a process believed to have occurred during the early Middle

Bronze Age, sometime between 2100 and 1800 B.C.E. Albright's student G. E. Wright (1961) argued that while it may be extremely difficult to identify archaeologically specific individuals mentioned in Genesis, archaeologists can draw parallels between the general cultural environment conveyed in the Bible and that inferred from archaeological evidence. In recent decades, however, the patriarchal tradition and the historical veracity of Genesis have faced great scrutiny.

The great Canaanite culture of the Middle Bronze Age began to collapse toward the end of the sixteenth century B.C.E. It would appear that the political systems of the period experienced great turbulence around this time, and a number of cities saw either a considerable decline in population or were abandoned altogether. Several possible explanations have been advanced, but it was probably a combination of internal economic strife and Egyptian aggression that brought about this degeneration. A number of cities in the south were destroyed by Egyptian armies, which sent shock waves throughout the rest of the countryside and in turn precipitated their downfall. Most likely, it was a number of interrelated factors that led to the demise of Middle Bronze Age culture.

Late Bronze Age

The Canaanites persevered in the fourteenth and thirteenth centuries B.C.E., but the people of Syro-Palestine had come under the political aegis of a powerful and expansionist Egypt (Weinstein 1981). The end of the Middle Bronze Age and onset of the period known as the Late Bronze Age (LBA) is traditionally marked by the military campaigns of Ahmose (1550–1525 B.C.E.) and Thutmose III (1479–1425 B.C.E.); during the centuries that followed, much of Canaan was a vassal state. In addition to the archaeological evidence, the Amarna Letters, an archive of 336 tablets discovered at the Egyptian New Kingdom capitol of Amarna in 1887, are an important source of information for this period. The letters, written mainly in Akkadian cuneiform, date to the fourteenth century B.C.E. and mention prominent cities in Canaan such as Megiddo and Lachish. Some seventy of the Amarna Letters are thought to have been written in the city of Byblos.

The collapse of the Middle Bronze Age was associated with an overall decrease in population, the abandonment of cities, and a dispersal of any peoples that stayed behind. The picture of settlement patterns during the Late Bronze Age, however, is not always clear. For instance, while a number of towns were apparently destroyed in the fourteenth century, prominent sites, such as Shechem and Jericho, may not have been abandoned until sometime during the thirteenth century B.C.E.

The disruption of trade networks and production systems resulted in widespread economic decline. Along with the internal problems that plagued the Canaanites toward the end of the Middle Bronze Age, it is probable that the destruction of Sharuhen at the hands of the Egyptians, in addition to the tax burden that had already been imposed, contributed to this cycle of economic decline. A significant portion of the population that fled the cities may have turned to various forms of transhuman alternatives. It is interesting that the

4.8   Egyptian relief from Tel Beth Shean (J. Golden)

term *Hapiru*, which appears in the Amarna Letters, was used as a pejorative to refer to the peoples inhabiting the margins between city-states, that is, the areas where nomadic peoples dominated.

Despite the apparent level of economic depression seen throughout much of the region, the Late Bronze Age was also marked by the occurrence of rare, ostentatious displays of great wealth and an increasing emphasis on the consumption of luxury goods. For instance, elaborate tombs with sumptuous grave goods were found at a number of sites. It is possible that the excessive expenditures on these wealthy burials created an eventual drain on limited resources.

The linguistic diversity in the region reflects the variety of people coming through this area. West Semitic was probably the primary language spoken throughout most of Canaan, but Egyptian would have also been spoken by those people under Egypt's direct control. Hurrian may have been the dominant language in parts of the north, but Akkadian was the lingua franca of the entire Near East at this time.

From a political point of view, a number of cities, such as Beth Shean, were under direct Egyptian control. "Anthropoid" coffins reflecting Egyptian influence have been found at Beth Shean; at Deir el-Balah, an important coastal Late Bronze Age site that was the last way station on the "Way of Horus"

(Dothan 1978); and at Tel Aphek, where an Egyptian "governor's residence" has been excavated. Overall, the distribution of evidence for the Egyptian presence (for example, burial customs) indicates that Egyptian influence was felt most strongly near the major lines of communication and less so in other parts of Canaan. Shlomo Bunimovitz has suggested that there was a certain degree of internal conflict within Canaan during the Late Bronze Age (2003, 322–323). Mazar (1990), however, sees a general lack of evidence for conflict in the region and has argued that the Egyptians may have prohibited Canaanites from building any form of fortifications.

The presence of local rulers can be inferred from the discovery of palace remains at various cities, for example the elaborate palace architecture of Megiddo. It is difficult to determine, though, to what extent some of these rulers were truly sovereign or under direct Egyptian governance. An interesting trend during the Late Bronze Age was the separation, at least in terms of urban layout, of the temple and administrative buildings, but it is not clear whether this reflects a deliberate break between these institutions themselves or was simply a matter of shifting urban design.

Many of the ceramic forms used during the Middle Bronze Age continued into the Late Bronze Age, which generally provides one line of evidence that much of the Canaanite population remained in the region. The Late Bronze Age pottery assemblage, however, is also marked by the appearance of a range of new imported forms, indicating that international trade was on the rise. For example, Bichrome Wares, named for their red and black painted decorations, often combined both local Canaanite and Cypriote forms and decorative motifs. Cypriote imports, such as Ring-Base Wares, appeared with increasing frequency in the late fifteenth century, followed by a rise in Mycenaean Wares in the fourteenth century.

New art forms also appeared during the Late Bronze Age, most notably the carved ivories, small relief sculptures that were in most cases pieces of decorative inlay. Some of the most outstanding examples of these ivories come from Megiddo. Bronze production was important during this time with much of the copper coming from Cyprus.

Trade, of course, played a major role in economic life, but the effect of international interaction was even more profound as maritime networks began to transform the cultural landscape in significant ways. For one thing, the coast saw the first appearance of the so-called "Sea Peoples," a fairly broad term that actually refers to several different groups of people who probably arrived from Cyprus and the Aegean. People from mainland Greece, commonly known as the Mycenaeans, also began to expand, moving into Crete sometime near the beginning of the Late Bronze Age, and ultimately developing far-reaching contacts. The well-known Mycenaean painted ceramics found their way throughout the eastern Mediterranean and inland into Egypt and the Levant. For the people of the Late Bronze Age world, this would have felt like an early version of globalization. During this period, the southern Levant played an important, if passive role in the balance of power in the Near East, serving as a buffer between the Egyptians and the Hittite Empire that loomed to the north.

The Fate of the Canaanites

The subject of what happened to the Canaanites at the end of the Late Bronze Age raises a set of questions that are just as intriguing as those concerning their initial appearance. Although the rise of the Canaanites appears to have been a relatively sudden phenomenon, their decline was more diffuse and gradual, making it even more difficult to comprehend from an archaeological perspective. The myth of the Israelite conquest leading to the complete displacement of the Canaanites is probably exactly that. The archaeological evidence indicates that the Canaanites did not simply disappear. For instance, at sites such as Megiddo and Tel es-Sa'idiyeh, there may have been somewhat of a Canaanite revival at the beginning of the Iron Age (c. twelfth century B.C.E.) (Tubb 2002). In addition, Canaanites made significant contributions to Iron

---

Destruction Levels

The biblical story of the Israelite conquest describes an army led by Joshua that moved throughout the land devastating Canaanite cities in its path. The story as described in the Hebrew Bible specifically mentions a number of cities by name, and in searching for evidence relating to this story, some archaeologists have pointed to destruction levels identified at these sites. More recently, a number of scholars (Dever 2001; Finkelstein 1999) have rejected this approach, questioning the essential premise—a renegade group's ability to vanquish successfully and with relative ease into a well-established population—as well as the facts. William Dever (1992a), for instance, has argued that there is not a single destruction layer dated to around 1200 B.C.E. that can be attributed with certainty to the Israelites.

In some cases, specific chronological problems impeach the "conquest evidence." For example, at Lachish, British excavators believed they had found evidence for the Israelite conquest when they dated a destruction level to 1220 B.C.E. However, more recent excavations have unearthed Egyptian scarabs dating to the time of the Ramesside pharaohs, lowering the date of the destruction to 1150 B.C.E. Similar chronological problems were encountered when comparing the destruction of Hazor as described in the Hebrew Bible (Joshua 11:1–15) with the archaeological evidence for a destruction layer at the site, now dated to around 1250 B.C.E., too early for the Israelites under Joshua. Considering evidence from both sites, though, it is not impossible that Joshua lived for 100 years. It is, however, highly improbable that he could have led Israelite troops against both Hazor in 1250 B.C.E. and Lachish in 1150 B.C.E.

Perhaps the most memorable event of the Israelite conquest was the destruction of Jericho, where Joshua famously brought down the walls with the mere blowing of a horn, having marched around the city for seven days. Excavating at Jericho in the 1930s, John Garstang (1948) believed he had uncov-

Age cultures. For instance, the Philistine culture probably represents some form of fusion between Aegean arrivals on the southern coast and indigenous Canaanites, with similar phenomena involving the Phoenician culture on the northern coast and Israelite culture in the interior. According to Finkelstein (1988), pastoral groups also inhabited the region at this time, as evidenced by cemeteries and open cult centers not in proximity to any settlement. (See sidebar, "Destruction Levels.")

The collapse of Late Bronze Age culture must also be seen in terms of events that took place in the broader context of the Near East and Aegean. At the same time that Egyptian power began to diminish, the empire of Egypt's rivals to the north, the Hittites, also began to collapse. The Mycenaean world, too, was disrupted as cities such as Pylos and the outer town of Mycenae itself experienced violence at this time. Two of the most important cities in northern

ered evidence for a violent destruction, thereby confirming the biblical account. However, subsequent excavations by Kathleen Kenyon (1979) turned up Mycenaean pottery within Garstang's destruction layer, setting a terminus of 1300 B.C.E. for the event, more than a century earlier than Joshua's campaign is thought to have occurred. As it turns out, Jericho may not have even been occupied during the end of the Late Bronze Age–early Iron 1. The same is true of Ai, where, despite its inclusion in the conquest related in the Hebrew Bible, there was no evidence for a Late Bronze Age occupation. Although there is evidence for the destruction of some sites at the end of the twelfth and during the eleventh century B.C.E., the Egyptians and Sea Peoples, who were present at the time, seem the more likely culprits.

In addition to the problem of datable destruction layers, a number of scholars have pointed to the evidence for cultural continuity, with little in the way of dramatic changes in material culture that might be expected with the sudden incursion of a new people. For instance, the Bull Site in northern Manasseh reflects an ongoing Canaanite influence on religious practices, and the same may be said for the linguistic evidence (Smith 2002). As an alternative to the tale of violent conquest, models suggesting a more peaceful infiltration (Alt 1925) and stressing social theory (Mendenhall 1973; Gottwald 1979) have been advanced.

Thus, considering the evidence for cultural continuity during the Late Bronze Age–Iron 1 transition, and the lack of evidence for securely dated destruction layers, the literal truth of the biblical narrative concerning the conquest becomes increasingly difficult to support. Indeed, Israel Finkelstein and Neil Asher Silberman have reviewed a good part of the archaeological evidence from this period and concluded that "the process we describe . . . is the opposite of what we have in the Bible: the emergence of early Israel was the outcome of the collapse of the Canaanite culture, not its cause. . . . There was no violent conquest of Canaan. The early Israelites were—irony of ironies—themselves originally Canaanites!" (2001, 118).

Syria, Ugarit and Alalakh, were destroyed, as was their counterpart in north-ern Canaan, Hazor. Although older theories posited large-scale invasions into the various regions in order to explain such widespread turmoil, more recently scholars have pointed to the effects of drought, famine, and other economic woes. Although there is no certain answer, it is clear that significant numbers of people moved about the Mediterranean at this time, many of them landing on the Levantine coast. A number of prominent Canaanite cities were de-stroyed toward the end of the Late Bronze Age, including Aphek, Beth Shemesh, Debir (Khirbet Rabud), Hazor, Lachish, and Megiddo. Ultimately, new cultural powers emerged in various parts of the southern Levant, and while the Canaanites survived on the coast and inland valleys, in time their culture was absorbed by that of the Philistines, Phoenicians, and Israelites.

PEOPLES OF THE IRON AGE

The transition from the Bronze Age to the Iron Age began late in the thir-teenth century B.C.E., though much of the first part of the Iron Age (Iron 1a) can be regarded as a transitional period. The collapse of Late Bronze Age Canaanite culture was a gradual process, part of which involved the emer-gence of a new, more diverse population in the southern Levant. Though most scholars date the beginning of the Iron Age to the end of the Nineteenth Dynasty in Egypt, it is important to note that the Egyptian influence in the southern Levant continued into the twelfth century. For instance, at Beth Shean, Building 1500, which probably served as an Egyptian administrative center, was destroyed late in the thirteenth century (Str. VII) but rebuilt in the same style at the beginning of the twelfth century (Str. VI). A lintel found in this building with a dedicatory inscription dating to the reign of Rameses III and a statue of that ruler most likely derive from the same phase (Mazar 1994). A range of artifacts from the northern cemetery, most notably anthro-poid coffins similar to those from Deir el-Balah, also attests to the presence of Egyptian officials. The continued Egyptian influence has also been noted at Tel Sera and Tel el-Far'ah South.

The Canaanite culture also continued to thrive in parts of the region. De-struction was visited upon the city of Megiddo at the end of the Late Bronze Age, but when the city was rebuilt, its Canaanite character was retained. The palace, temple, and a number of houses were restored, and important features of Canaanite culture, such as the red and black decorated pottery, bronzes, and jewelry, also reappeared. Some essential elements of Late Bronze Age Canaan-ite culture, however, were missing, most notably imported Aegean and Cypri-ote goods. This seems to represent the cessation of the great trade networks of the Late Bronze Age. In addition, some of the most important cities of the Canaanite world, such as Hazor and Lachish, remained in ruin for many years into the early Iron Age.

The beginning of the Iron Age roughly corresponds with the emergence in the region of several different cultures, namely the Philistines and the Is-raelites, among others. These peoples, as well as those from Transjordan, are known in the Bible. Although archaeologists cannot ignore the biblical tradition, as it is both relevant and useful to any reconstruction of this time period, it is critical to treat the biblical accounts with circumspection. They were written in many cases considerably after the time in which the events described therein are thought to have occurred and by people with a clear religious and nationalist agenda. If the goal is to draw the most accurate picture possible of the cultures in question, this must be taken into account.

People of the Hill Country

One of the liveliest debates in the archaeology of the southern Levant concerns the emergence of the Israelite culture, a phenomenon that may have begun as early as the end of the thirteenth century. The earliest reference to Israel as a people is found on the inscribed Egyptian stele of Merenptah (Stager 1982), which also mentions the cities of Ashqelon, Gezer, and Yenoam.

Although later historical texts of the Iron Age (Iron 2, 1000–586 B.C.E.) provide a reliable picture of the southern Levantine ethnoscape, it is difficult to say much about the identity of the peoples of the first part of the period (Iron 1, 1200–1000 B.C.E.). There is, however, one important indicator that a new, distinct cultural identity was in the works. When attempting to define an ethnic identity, one of the most important features that anthropologists consider is cuisine and the various practices surrounding food consumption. Traditions concerning the timing of certain feasts and decisions about which types of foods are prized and which are shunned often provide clues about the unique ecological history of a group.

Thus, it is significant that while pig bones appear at Iron 1 sites throughout the lowlands and Transjordan, as well as at highland sites of the preceding Bronze Age, in the faunal assemblages of the early Iron highland sites—the core area of the Proto-Israelites—the remains of pig were absent. It is reasonable to propose that this practice began with people exploiting the more arid areas that simply could not support pig husbandry (as in the northern Negev during the Chalcolithic period). In time, this may have translated into an avowed cultural prohibition against the consumption of pig, which at the same time served as a clear point of difference between distinct cultural groups, namely the Israelites and their neighbors.

Over the years, archaeologists have spent considerable energy attempting to investigate the veracity of the biblical accounts with regard to the origins of the Israelite people (Albright 1939; Aharoni 1957; Lapp 1967; Yadin 1979; Finkelstein 1988; Finkelstein and Silberman 2001). Yohanan Aharoni's (1957) pioneering application of the method of settlement survey in the Galilee region represented an important breakthrough in the study of Iron Age cultures. These surveys revealed that a number of unwalled settlements in the Upper Galilee during the early Iron Age were established in places where there had been no previous Late Bronze Age settlement. Based on this evidence, coupled with the redating of pottery from Hazor, Aharoni surmised that the peoples usually conceived of as the Israelites probably infiltrated the region in a relatively gradual and peaceful manner.

Based on more recent surveys in the central highlands, it appears there was a relatively dense concentration of sites in the northern hill country (also known as Menasseh) (Zertal 1988). More than 100 Iron 1 sites, many of them small villages of five or six *dunams* (1 dunam equals about 1,000 square meters), have also been observed in the hill country of Ephraim; several important sites in this region, including Shiloh (Finkelstein, Bunimovitz, and Lederman 1993) and Ai (Callaway 1980), have been excavated. The highland site of Tel en-Nasbeh provides one of the best examples for extensive architectural remains from this time (Zorn 2003).

The portion of Finkelstein's (1988, 1995) model concerning the cyclical nature of settlement in the southern Levant that has caused the most debate is that which concerns the Iron Age. Finkelstein (1988) argued that settlement patterns in the highlands during the Iron 1 represent yet another peak in this cycle, which culminates with the rise of territorial states in the Iron 2. According to this model, Israelite culture began with pastoral-nomadic tribes already indigenous to Canaan, which then coalesced politically and evolved into a developed urban society. Initially limited to the hill country, especially the eastern portion, this culture began spreading into the southwestern portion of the hill country, the Negev, and the Galilee later in the Iron 1. Evidence for regional variation in this early phase of the Iron Age, however, suggests that this could also represent the simultaneous settlement of distinct tribal groups that only later joined the "Israelite tribal coalition" (Mazar 1994, 287).

As for settlement layout, there are a number of instances where the general plan points to the pastoral roots of some Iron 1 people. At many sites, large open spaces were used to maintain herds, and at sites such as 'Izbet Sartah the layout of houses around the perimeter of a large open space is thought to recall the plan of a pastoral tent camp (Finkelstein 1986). The most common type of structure in the hill country during the Iron 1 was the pillared building, often in the form of three- and four-room pillared houses. Another plan typical of Iron 1 highland architecture was the arrangement of rows of broad rooms looking onto an open courtyard.

At several Iron Age settlements, evidence for communal or public works has been observed. For example, Israelite towns such as Ai, Giloh, 'Izbet Sartah, and Tel Masos were surrounded by large stone walls. In a few cases (for example, Shiloh), houses inside the settlement were built right up against the interior of the city wall. But monumental architecture from this period is relatively rare, and the frequency of small storage-pit silos at many Iron 1 sites indicates a general lack of centralized economic organization.

Overall, the pottery assemblage demonstrates continuity with the preceding Late Bronze Age. There was little in the way of decoration on pottery. Although incised and impressed decorations are occasionally found, painted decoration is virtually absent. There are some differences in ceramic styles that have allowed archaeologists to observe regional variation. For example, the *pithoi*, in particular the collared-rim variety, were the hallmark for Israelite settlement, though they are sometimes found outside the hill country at Tel Qasile and Tel Keisan.

In addition to links established via the ceramic assemblages, a certain level of continuity is implicit in the rapid revival of several cities destroyed during

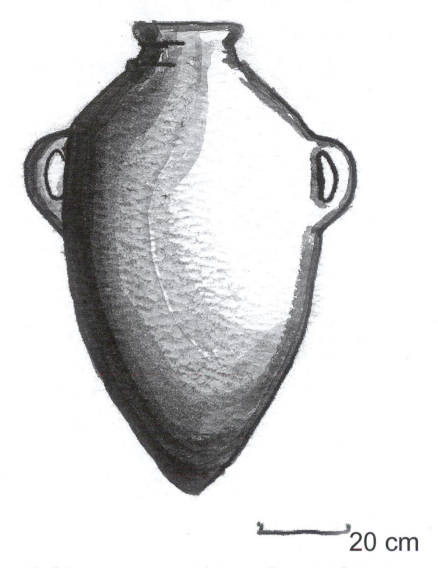

20 cm

4.9   Collared-rim store jar (*pithos*) from Iron I (Drawing by J. Golden; adapted from Adam Zertal. 1991. "Israel Enters Canaan." *Biblical Archaeology Review* 17: 28–49, and 75.)

the preceding Late Bronze Age. Some of the religious beliefs also seem to carry over. For example, the Bull Site in northern Samaria seems to reflect Canaanite influence (Mazar 1982). There are also indications—from the discovery of cult vessels decorated with animal heads, as well as the biblical accounts—that the Israelites established a cult center at Shiloh, the site of Canaanite worship during the Late Bronze Age (Finkelstein, Bunimovitz, and Lederman 1993). Despite evidence for continuity, significant changes can also be observed. Again, throughout most of the southern Levant, ceramic imports from Cyprus and the Aegean had all but vanished. By the end of the Iron 1, other changes become apparent.

THE ISRAELITES OF THE IRON 2

The emergence of the Israelite state is one of the most intriguing events in the history of the southern Levant. Although it is true that the biblical accounts of this event were codified some time after the events actually took place, and that the Bible almost certainly reflects a specific ideological agenda, there is nevertheless a wealth of archaeological evidence that demonstrates the historical reality of the Israelite state. According to Finkelstein: "The emergence of early Israel was . . . determined by a combination of long-term history and short-term circumstances, and by a balance between local developments and external influences. . . . The genuine exceptional event in the highlands of the southern Levant in the late second to early first millennium B.C.E. was not the 'Israelite Settlement' but the emergence of the United Monarchy—the unification of the entire region and most of the lowlands under one rule" (1995, 362).

Archaeologists' understanding of this period is also greatly enhanced by the sharp increase in the number of extra-biblical texts deriving from within Palestine during the Iron 2. This is especially true of *ostraca*, inscribed ceramic sherds, many of which bear early Hebrew writing (Naveh 1982). If for the Iron 1 it was necessary to restrict the discussion to speculation about Proto-Israelites, it is certainly possible to speak of a conscious Israelite identity and ideology by the time of the Iron 2 (Dever 2003b).

As the population of the hill country expanded, it gradually moved west. In the area between Ramallah and Jerusalem, for instance, the number of sites on the western slopes of the hills during the Iron 2 was roughly double that of the Iron 1, and the same is true of most of Samaria (Finkelstein 1995). Though the population during the Iron 1 was still largely agrarian, by the early Iron 2 there is evidence for significant demographic change. For instance, during the Iron Age 2a (c. mid-eleventh to tenth centuries B.C.E.), the population of the Judean hill country grew to almost twice that of the preceding period, and large cities began to appear (Ofer 1994). Some of the key Israelite cities found throughout the southern Levant include Dan, Gezer, Hazor, Jerusalem, and Lachish.

There currently exists a reasonable amount of survey data indicating considerable population growth in much of the southern Levant during the tenth to seventh centuries B.C.E. (Broshi and Finkelstein 1992). Finkelstein, however, has argued that despite the increase in population, there is little evidence for a state this early, asserting that some form of settlement hierarchy should be observable. Other scholars (Ofer 1994; Rainey 2001) also point to survey data and argue that indeed there was a hierarchy, with several primary sites, such as Tel Rumeida (Tel Hebron) and Ras et-Tawil, surrounded by smaller, second-order sites, such as Khirbet ez-Zawiyye on the plateau of the central range and Khirbet Attir in the southern portion of the central range.

The biblical account, corroborated with extra-biblical sources and securely dated historical data from outside the region (for example, Neo-Assyrian texts), points to the beginning of the ninth century B.C.E. as the time of the United Monarchy. This short-lived period was characterized by the establishment of a single Israelite kingdom united under the rule of King Saul, followed

4.10 Iron Age houses abutting the medieval walls that surround Jerusalem's Old City today (J. Golden)

by David and then Solomon. Though small in scale compared with the states of Egypt and Syro-Mesopotamia, the southern Levant in the Iron 2 period was a true nation-state with centralized political organization.

A direct and perfect fit between the biblical accounts and the archaeological evidence will never be found. Despite the difficulties in ascribing structures specifically to Solomon, there are some interesting parallels. For example, following the books of 1 and 2 Kings, Solomon was the master builder responsible for the construction of great temples at Gezer, Hazor, and Megiddo. However, extensive excavations and suites of radiocarbon dates from all three of these sites have revealed that these temples were first erected at least 100 years after Solomon is supposed to have lived. The problem is further complicated by the fact that investigation of Jerusalem's Iron Age occupation today is extremely difficult owing to some three millennia of continuous subsequent occupation as well as the current political climate. Nonetheless, the limited archaeological research that has been conducted has revealed the remains of wealthy houses dating to the Iron Age on the eastern slope of the City of David in Jerusalem. Also, the remains of a large city wall have been excavated in and around Jerusalem's Old City.

The period of the United Monarchy, however, was short-lived, and some seventy-five years after it was first established, tensions between peoples of the northern and southern highlands resurfaced. During the time of the Divided Monarchy, Jerusalem was the capital of the southern Judean Kingdom, while the northern Kingdom of Israel established Dan as its capital at first, and later on Samaria. Each of these cities had large-scale monumental and public architecture, including a distinct sacred precinct, a well-defended citadel or acropolis, and a fortified lower city. Important regional centers were also distributed about the countryside at sites such as Beer Sheva, Lachish, Gezer, Megiddo, Jezreel, Hazor, and Tel en-Nasbeh, all of which had large residential buildings or palaces. Public structures that characterized these centers include city walls of the casemate style (though the solid inset-offset design becomes more popular during the Iron 2); multiple city gates with multiple chambers (the number of which diminish in time from four to two); and palaces that functioned as administrative complexes, often located near the gates. Architectural features typical of the monumental style include palmette capitals and ashlar masonry, which appear to derive from Phoenicia.

Although direct evidence for the kings of the United Monarchy may be elusive, those of the Divided Monarchy are relatively well documented. Other examples of architecture from the Iron 2 include Hezekiah's tunnel, a water system that runs beneath Jerusalem, and royal/noble tombs of the tenth century in the surrounding Kidron Valley. In addition, an elaborate palace ascribed to the biblical King Ahab, inspired in part by Phoenician building traditions, has been excavated at Samaria (Crowfoot, Kenyon, and Sukenik 1942; Mazar 1990; Tappy 1992).

As for domestic life, most people still lived in four-room or courtyard-style houses, though some atypically large ones demonstrate disparities in wealth. Evidence for luxury living can also be seen in the remains of carved ivory inlays, dating to the ninth to eighth centuries B.C.E., which originally decorated the furniture of wealthy homes at important cities such as Samaria (Crowfoot and Crowfoot 1938; Barnett 1982).

Vessels used for serving food, such as bowls, jugs, and juglets, were treated with a red slip and burnish, while pottery used for cooking and storage typically had no surface treatment (Faust 2002b). This represents a change that occurred at the beginning of the Iron 2, as does the trend toward more uniform production, standardization of forms, and a reduction in regional variation (Aharoni 1982; Dever 1995c). It has been suggested that this pattern reflects not only a modification in economic organization, but social change on a broader level (Dever 2003b; Faust 2002b). During the eighth century, pottery was mass-produced (Zimhoni 1997), and by the end of the period jar handles often bore the royal *la-melekh* stamp, indicating official involvement with certain transactions.

Evidence for the development of a social hierarchy during the Iron 2, with noble genealogies playing an important role, can also be observed in the mortuary evidence. Monumental tombs that were used over several generations served to help keep these elite families intact, and it is also evident from the wealth of burial goods, including jewelry and imported commodities, that status and wealth were inherited (Bloch-Smith 1992; Dever 2003b). Foreign grave goods, including imported wares from Cyprus and scarabs from Egypt, also point to the revival of lively trade relations and outside influence during the Iron 2.

Philistine Culture

Another major cultural force in the southern Levant during the Iron Age was the Philistines, a group also known from the Bible. As an ethnic group, the Philistines probably coalesced through the integration of the second and third generation Sea Peoples and local coastal Canaanites. The initial presence of a new people on the coast was announced by the appearance of a new form of decorated pottery with clear affinities to ceramics from the Aegean known as Mycenaean IIIC. These ceramics spread throughout the Aegean and into Cyprus at the end of the thirteenth century and represent the expansion of sea-faring peoples who emanated from the Aegean, rapidly reaching much of the eastern Mediterranean. During the Late Bronze Age, Sea Peoples brought and continued to import pottery and other items originating in Cyprus and the Aegean. As Philistine culture evolved, however, these goods were increasingly manufactured locally yet retained the style of their imported prototypes. The

4.11 Philistine Bichrome Ware from Miqne-Ekron (Drawing by J. Golden; adapted from Trude Dothan and Moshe Dothan. 1992. *People of the Sea: In Search for the Philistines*. New York: Macmillan.)

most outstanding example of this phenomenon is the presence of Philistine Bichrome Wares.

The Philistine culture area is traditionally conceived of as limited to the coastal plain and Shephelah, especially in the south. The recent discovery of extensive Philistine cultural material, such as ceramics with red, black, and white geometric patterns as well as intricate inscriptions dating to the ninth and tenth centuries B.C.E. at a site near Tel Aviv (Kletter 2002), may push their cultural boundary further north. The fact that the artifacts discovered include cultic stands used in religious ceremonies suggests the presence of Philistine peoples and not just material goods that migrated north by happenstance. According to biblical tradition, there were five main cities making up the Philistine Pentapolis, yet only three of these—Ashqelon, Ekron, and Ashdod—have been both positively identified and excavated, while the identification of Gaza and Gath is still at issue. Many scholars now accept Tel es-Safi as ancient Gath, and it is all but certain that Gaza remains buried beneath the modern city by that name.

The Philistine economy was based in large part on command of maritime trade, with the establishment of great coastal cities such as Ashdod and Ashqelon. Lawrence Stager has established that the latter city was as large as 60 hectares. The fortification system of the Philistine city, built in about 1150 B.C.E., incorporated a mud-brick tower that was 34 feet long and 20 feet wide and a huge earthen rampart, or glacis (Stager 1991). Another important site dating to this period is Tel Qasile near the mouth of the Yarkon River.

The Philistine economy and culture, however, were not limited to maritime activities but included inland settlements and large-scale agricultural production as well. Nowhere is this better attested to than at the site of Tel Miqne–Ekron (Gitin and Dothan 1987). Tel Miqne, a huge Philistine city covering some 35 hectares during its third and final phase (seventh century B.C.E.), is located in the southern Shephelah near the modern Kibbutz Revadim. Unique circumstances, namely the lack of significant overburden from later occupation levels and years of dedication on the part of archaeologists, have made Tel Miqne the most extensively researched and informative site with regard to the Philistine culture of the Iron Age. The identification of Tel Miqne as biblical Ekron is based in part upon strong geographical parallels: its location in Joshua (15:10–20) between Beth Shemesh and Timna (Tel Batash), just south of the Nahal Sorek. With the discovery in 1996 of a royal Assyrian inscription referring to Ekron, this identification is all but certain (Gitin, Dothan, and Naveh 1997). During the seventh century B.C.E., Tel Miqne–Ekron (Str. IC-IB) hosted a large administrative center of the Neo-Assyrian Empire, and archaeologists have uncovered the remains of a massive commercial olive oil production industry dating to this time (Gitin and Dothan 1987; Gitin 1995). This important economic center most likely would have had a sphere of influence that extended further inland.

In the northern Shephelah, the site of Tel Batash has been identified as biblical Timna, based in part on its geographical location between Beth Shemesh and Ekron as described in Judges 14–16. Stratum V contained the remains of a Philistine settlement that may have been occupied for a considerable amount of time. At some point during the period, fortification walls were built, but it is not certain whether some perceived threat inspired this project. Of course, there were smaller, nonurban Philistine settlements as well. For example, Iron 1 levels at Tel Aphek have yielded Philistine pottery (Beck and Kochavi 1985) as well as a number of installations and pits, but no monumental architectural works.

Phoenician Culture

The heartland of the Phoenicians was located further north along the Mediterranean coast, outside of the core area of the southern Levant, but they played an important role in the political economies of the Iron Age. The name "Phoenician" comes from the Greek word for the peoples of the northern coastal region. They established great cities at Tyre and Sidon on the coast as well as several important sites in the Acre Valley, including Achzib, Tel Abu Hawam, and Tel Keisan. At the latter, archaeologists have excavated a residential quarter with pillared houses similar to those found at Tel Qasile, which probably reflects their common Aegean ancestry. The same is true of the ceramic assemblage, where jugs and globular flasks from the site, known as "Phoenician Bichrome," display a style of decoration with concentric circles in red and black as well as white painted designs on a burnished buff background, also sharing affinities with Aegean material.

After the crises in Canaan during the late twelfth century, the Canaanite culture saw somewhat of a revival in the eleventh century. The growing influence of the Sea Peoples probably played a role in this process, and not just on the coast. Cypriote pottery has been found at Beth Shean and Megiddo, the two great cities of the northern interior valleys. On the north coast, this phenomenon manifested in the Phoenician culture.

Like the Philistine economy to the south, the Phoenician economy was focused largely on maritime trade. Via port cities such as Sidon and Tyre, various materials made their way inland. The Phoenicians ruled the sea in their time, and their impact on the entire Mediterranean cannot be overestimated. This people also played a pivotal role in contributing to the evolution of the modern alphabet.

SUGGESTED READING

Albright, William F. 1973. "The Historical Framework of Palestinian Archaeology between 2100 and 1600 BC." *Bulletin of the American Schools of Oriental Research* 209: 12–18.

Ben-Tor, A., ed. 1992. *The Archaeology of Ancient Israel.* New Haven, CT: Yale University Press.

Broshi, Magen, and Israel Finkelstein. 1992. "Population of Palestine in Iron Age II." *Bulletin of the American Schools of Oriental Research* 287: 47–60.

Dever, William G. 1995. "Will the Real Israel Please Stand Up?: Archaeology and Israelite Historiography—Part I." *Bulletin of the American Schools of Oriental Research* 297: 61–80.

———. 1999. "Histories and Nonhistories of Ancient Israel." *Bulletin of the American Schools of Oriental Research* 316: 89–105.

Dothan, Trude, and Moshe Dothan. 1992. *People of the Sea: In Search for the Philistines.* New York: Macmillan.

Kenyon, Kathleen. 1979. *Archaeology of the Holy Land,* 4th ed. New York: W. W. Norton.

Levy, Thomas E., ed. 2003. "Plough and Pasture in the Early Economy of the Southern Levant," In *The Archaeology of Society in the Holy Land,* 3d ed., edited by T. E. Levy. New York: Facts on File.

Mazar, Amihai. 1990. *Archaeology of the Land of the Bible, 10,000–586 B.C.E.* New York: Doubleday.

Oren, Eliezer D., and Donald W. Jones, eds. 2000. *The Sea Peoples and Their World: A Reassessment.* University Museum Monograph, 108. Philadelphia: Museum of Archaeology and Anthropology, University of Pennsylvania.

Tubb, Jonathan N. 2002. *The Canaanites.* London: British Museum.

Yadin, Yigael. 1967. "The Rise and Fall of Hazor." In *Archaeological Discoveries in the Holy Land,* compiled by the Archaeological Institute of America, 57–66. New York: Crowell.

CHAPTER 5

Economics

Though each successive cultural group that has inhabited the southern Levant right up to the present has had its own way of drawing a living from the land, certain environmental patterns have persisted throughout. It is critical when considering the ecology of the region to take into account the various microenvironmental conditions that prevail within a relatively small area, a factor that may have encouraged the development of economic specialization. The most general ecological divisions in the southern Levant involve a set of broadly defined dichotomies: desert and sown; highland and lowland; north and south. Yet these have been exaggerated and overemphasized at times and, at least in some cases, are in need of reconsideration.

The first of these dichotomies, the desert and the sown, is significant in that it correlates with variation in economic adaptation and thus interregional interaction. Owen Lattimore (1940) had originally construed a perpetual conflict between the societies of the desert and the sown. A variation on this theme is the "dimorphic model" proposed by Michael B. Rowton (1976), which describes economies with two basic components: agriculturally based sedentism and pastoral nomadism. Decades of ethnographic research in the modern Middle East (this time period expands to well over a century should we include the rich body of "traveler's literature"), however, suggest that the situation was probably too complex to be construed as a simple dichotomy. More likely, there was a continuum of adaptational strategies—ranging from settled peoples maintaining small herds, to seminomadic peoples orbiting a single settlement, to camel herders living deep in the desert—all of which can be broadly subsumed under the general heading of transhumance. The desert and sown dualism, however, has taken on great cultural significance, which to this day plays a role in the political economies of the region and continues to be a recurrent theme in Middle Eastern scholarship.

The tension between desert and sown existed not only in spatial terms but within a temporal framework as well. Israel Finkelstein (1988, 2003) has advanced a model wherein the history of settlement during the third through the first millennia B.C.E. can be explained as a series of cycles where pastoral peoples settle down, become increasingly urban, and then revert to nomadic ways when the urban system undergoes some form of crisis.

The highland/lowland dichotomy became increasingly important from the Early Bronze Age on, shifting in relation to a range of factors, including variability in the demand for horticultural "luxury" goods, such as wine and olive oil, as well as changes in the environment, such as varying rainfall patterns.

The north-south division is more of a cultural and geopolitical division, but there are ecological aspects to this dichotomy as well.

CHALCOLITHIC PERIOD: THE ORIGINS OF ECONOMIC COMPLEXITY

The Chalcolithic period can be characterized as a time of great innovation and imagination, not only in the areas of art and architecture, but in cultural ecology, technology, and economic organization (Gilead 1988; Levy 2003b). During this time, people first settled in the semiarid regions of the northern Negev and lower Jordan Valley. There is evidence that the climate may have been more humid in 4000 b.c.e. than it is today, yet adaptation to these new and challenging ecological niches would still require ingenuity.

Farming remained the primary means of subsistence, and crops were much the same as those first domesticated during the Neolithic period. Barley, which can grow with as little as 200 mm (about 8 in.) of annual rainfall, was the main staple in the semiarid zones, and wheat was grown in the humid Mediterranean zone. A few new items, such as the olive, were added to the diet. In these more arid areas where dry farming was difficult, the Chalcolithic peoples implemented some of the earliest forms of water management systems. Analyses of phytoliths (silica skeletons from plants) conducted by Arlene Rosen (1995) indicate that at the small farming village of Shiqmim, floodwater farming and basin irrigation were employed in order to increase agricultural output (Levy 1996). At the same time, animal husbandry began to evolve into a specialized form of economic activity, with an increased emphasis on the production of dairy goods (for example, cheese and clarified butter) and wool. This development is commonly known as the "secondary products revolution" (Sherratt 1981; Levy 1983). The faunal assemblages (Grigson 2003; Levy

5.1   Clay-made churn for making cheese or butter was filled with milk and shaken while it was hanging by a rope. Chalcolithic Period; 4500–3150 b.c. (Photo courtesy of Zev Radovan, Land of the Bible Picture Archive)

et al. 1991) and large ceramic churns found at Chalcolithic sites (along with churns made of hide that do not survive) represent dairy production, and a vast number of spindle whorls indicate the spinning of wool.

Craft Specialization

This focus on the production of pastoral goods was part of a broader trend whereby a division of labor and craft specialization began to develop. Food production systems overall had become more efficient, allowing some people to engage in economic activities other than farming and herding. One of the key developments in the period—indeed, the one for which it is named—was the advent of metallurgy and the emergence of a local copper industry. The production of copper was a new technology that ultimately had a profound impact on society, both reflecting and producing changes in material existence, economic organization, and sociopolitical structure. From the Chalcolithic period, metals played a vital role in the economic history of the region as an item of import and export, of production and consumption, of display and concealment, of celebration and solemn dedication. Its value was based on its rarity and aesthetic appeal as well as on its strength, for the emphasis on maceheads (for example, at Nahal Mishmar) no doubt represents an association between metal and warfare.

There appears to have been two different copper industries during the Chalcolithic period. One industry focused on the production of tool-type items using pure copper and a technique of casting in open molds and hammering. The other used exotic, complex metals (copper with arsenic, antimony, and rarely, nickel) and the lost wax casting method to produce a range of more elaborate goods, many symbolically charged. Two primary sources for the "pure" copper are known in the southern Levant at Faynan and Timna, two different branches of the Wadi Arabah. Ores that probably derived from both these regions, along with crucibles, simple furnaces (Fig. 5.2), and prills of raw copper, have been found at workshops in villages such as Abu Matar (Perrot 1957; Golden forthcoming) and Shiqmim (Levy and Shalev 1989; Golden, Levy, and Hauptmann 2001). Donkeys, which were first domesticated during the Chalcolithic era (Ovadia 1992; Mairs 1997), were probably used to cart ore from the mines to the village workshops.

Information regarding the production of the complex metal castings has been elusive, though some new clues have recently emerged. A small piece of unworked copper with antimony from Bir es-Safadi has come to light (Golden forthcoming), while crucibles and prills from Abu Matar indicate the processing of complex metals (Shugar 2002). The fact that the complex metals were used exclusively for the manufacture of prestige goods (such as scepters) suggests that this second industry involved attached specialization where production was sponsored by some elite group or political figure (Costin 1991).

Another specialized craft was the production of groundstone and lithic goods. Working with hard stones such as basalt and limestone, craftspeople produced a variety of goods ranging from maceheads to elegantly sculpted stands commonly known as fenestrated incense burners, though their precise function remains uncertain. Studies in experimental archaeology suggest that flint tools, especially the adze, were probably used for working the basalt.

5.2 Reconstruction of a Chalcolithic copper-smelting installation from Abu Matar (Drawing by J. Golden)

Claire Epstein (1998), conducting research in the Golan close to sources of raw material, has reported three circular basalt pieces that may represent bowls in the process of manufacture on site that were never completed. It is also feasible that at least some of the basalt found at sites throughout the Chalcolithic landscape derived from the Golan (Amiran and Porat 1984), but petrographic analysis points to Transjordan as a source for artifacts found at the southern sites (Rosen 1993; Phillip and Williams-Thorpe 1993), and Epstein suggests that little of the local Golan basalt actually left the area. According to Yorke Rowan (1998), product design became increasingly stylized, and overall quality improved with time. Specialization in flint tool production is evident in the fan-shaped scrapers as well as "proto-Canaanean blades," both forms making use of a fine-grained material known as tabular flint (Rosen 1987; Rowan 1998). Tiny flakes and a blade core of very fine, translucent flint attest to the production of microblades, or micro-end scrapers, at Gilat.

Ceramic production also reached a level that would have required the skills of specialists. By the latter part of the Chalcolithic period, a class of pottery known as Cream Ware, notable for its fine quality and delicate design, emerged; one type from this group, the "V-shaped pot," was made on the slow wheel, or tournette (Commenge-Pellerin 1987, 1990). Ceramic sculptures, best known from Gilat, also attest to an advanced level of craftsmanship (Alon and Levy 1989).

Commercial Networks

The extent of exchange networks began to expand during the Chalcolithic period. According to Claire Epstein, the Golan Chalcolithic should be viewed "against the backdrop of wider geographical zones where influences from Mesopotamia and Anatolia were felt" (1998, 335). Contact during the Chalcolithic era between the Golan sites and Syro-Lebanese sites such as Byblos, Ugarit (Ras Shamra), and the Amuq sites is seen largely through affinities in pottery styles. The discovery of obsidian at Gilat indicates the movement of materials from Anatolia as far south as the northern Negev. Overall, most trade items probably moved "down-the-line" (Rosen 1984), that is, without a major overarching structure.

EARLY BRONZE AGE

At the beginning of the Early Bronze Age, people made a living in much the same way as during the Chalcolithic period: through a combination of farming with simple irrigation techniques and pastoralism. As time went on, Early Bronze Age farmers shifted toward a more intensive agriculture, emphasizing specialized production for trade. Economic organization became more complex, and an urban-based market system emerged, with an increase in the production of nonagricultural goods and growing interdependence among the various producers. Changes in settlement patterns, particularly the spread of settlers into the rich, well-watered soils of the Mediterranean zone, further encouraged specialized production, particularly of wine and oil. In fact, several Early Bronze Age cities achieved great prosperity based largely on their ability to produce surplus goods, with trade becoming a major factor in the Levantine economy.

The primary staples in the Early Bronze Age diet were cereals, mainly wheat and barley. The discovery of multiple hearths and bread molds (that is, a small bakery) at Halif Terrace indicates that people were making bread. Legumes such as peas, lentils, and chickpeas were also a vital part of the diet and may have been eaten with olive oil. People also began to engage in horticulture, and many of the fruits and berries that make up the typical diet of the region today, such as figs and pomegranates, were domesticated by the Early Bronze Age; berries, almonds, and walnuts grew wild, but people had begun to rely on domesticated varieties. In order to extend their shelf lives, dates, figs, and raisins were prepared as dried fruits (Zohary 1992). Gazelles, wild sheep, goats, and pigs were hunted on occasion, but they made up only a small part of the Early Bronze Age diet (Grigson 2003).

In the northern Negev and central Israel, emmer wheat was grown under irrigation conditions, and in the lowland valleys and coastal plain overflowing rivers were exploited for basic floodwater farming. Arlene Rosen (1995) has suggested that such innovations might have been employed in order to help create a hedge against drought. Another breakthrough in agrotechnology was the modification of the landscape via terracing in order to create beds for planting and to prevent soil erosion. At several sites (for example, Ai), runoff water was collected in reservoirs, foreshadowing the later tradition of using large cisterns (Callaway 1978). This particular type of agriculture could probably be practiced at the level of village subsistence with little or no management.

By the late EB1 (3500–3050 B.C.E.), the production of "cash crops" such as grapes and olives for wine and oil had become a priority, largely in response to the growing demand emanating from Egypt. Initially, the Early Bronze Age peoples not only grew the fruit but also processed the finished goods. Spouted vats used for separating oil were fairly common in the Golan at this time, and olive wood has been found in the Jordan Valley (for example, Shuna) and in the northern valleys (for example, Megiddo). Evidence for the cultivation of flax (linseed), used as a fiber to make clothes, has been found at a number of Early Bronze Age sites (such as Erani).

Pastoral production continued to play an important role in the local economies. There was a peak in the proportion of sheep and goats in Early Bronze Age faunal assemblages throughout the region, especially on the desert margins. Over time, sheep raised primarily for secondary products increased relative to goats, a pattern that may suggest a shift toward a market economy. Certainly, some specialization in secondary goods production was present, and, as during the Chalcolithic period, economic interdependence with farmers was inevitable. In addition to typical pastoral products such as dairy goods and wool, semisedentary peoples also dealt in other crafts, such as the production of beads from semiprecious stones, an opportunity presented by their movement between sources of raw material in remote areas and the cities. By the EB2, copper from the Sinai had become the key commodity in a trade ring involving Egypt and the cities of southern Canaan. The northern Negev city of Arad played a central role in this exchange network (Ilan and Sebbane 1989; Shalev 1994; Amiran et al. 1978).

By the EB2 (3050–2650 B.C.E.), the emphasis had shifted away from basic subsistence and toward agriculture with the intention of generating surplus goods. This surplus was vital to the new economy, especially in the urban centers where there was growing stress on economic specialization and the exchange of goods and services. At cities such as Arad and Ai, evidence for centralized storage facilities increased over the course of the Early Bronze Age (Amiran and Ilan 1996), indicating that their inhabitants maintained communal holdings, which in turn functioned as a staple surplus that could be used to support various artisans and craftspeople in some system of redistribution. This trend may have started as early as the late EB1, when a building at Beth Shean, which contained large amounts of wheat and chickpeas, was used for administrative purposes, perhaps for the storage and redistribution of food (Mazar 2002). Silos have been found in late EB1 strata at Small Tel Malhata (Amiran and Ilan 1993), Halif Terrace (Levy et al. 1997; Seger et al. 1990), and Khirbet et-Tuwal (Eisenberg 1998). By the EB2, centralized storage had reached a new level at the site of Beth Yerah, on the southern shore of the Sea of Galilee, where a large public building (30 x 40 m), incorporating nine circular silos (8 m in diameter), probably served as a central storage unit for a significant staple surplus (Maisler, Stekelis, and Avi-Yonah 1952; Mazar 1990; see Fig. 5.3). According to one estimate, the granary was capable of holding an estimated 1,400–1,700 tons of grain, an amount that could easily accommodate a population much greater than the 4,000–5,000 people estimated for the site (Mazar 1990).

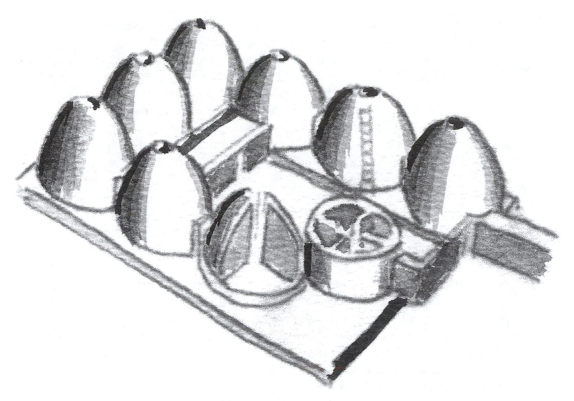

5.3   The EB3 granary at Beit Yerah (Drawing by J. Golden; adapted from Benjamin Maisler, Moshe Stekelis, and Michael Avi-Yonah. 1952. "The Excavations at Beit-Yerah (Khirbet el-Kerak), 1944–1946." *Israel Exploration Journal* 2: 165–173.)

Craft Specialization

A surplus of staple goods allowed further economic diversification and specialization to develop, especially in the areas of metallurgical and ceramic production (Esse 1989). Several lines of evidence point to increased specialization in ceramic production over the course of the Early Bronze Age. Though most vessels were still handmade through the end of the period, the use of the tournette, especially for manufacturing pot rims, increased early in the period (Dessel 1991; Yekutieli and Gophna 1994). Early Bronze Age potters learned to maintain greater control of firing conditions and, from a technical standpoint, produced what were on the whole superior ceramics. It appears that Egyptian and Canaanite potters may have shared some technological expertise with each other, as suggested by forms of "hybrid" pottery combining technical and stylistic elements typical of both ceramic traditions (Gophna 1992; Yekutieli and Gophna 1994). A new form of high-fired ceramics known as Metallic Ware peaked in popularity during the EB2. By the EB2–3, there was greater standardization in pottery types as ceramics were being mass-produced and the regional variation noted in earlier assemblages had declined.

As the sociopolitical systems that had driven the great metal traditions of the Chalcolithic period dissipated, the metal industry seems to have declined somewhat at first, at least in terms of the types of goods produced. Evidence for copper production early in the Early Bronze Age has been discovered at the site of Ashqelon-Afridar (Site E) (Golani and Segal 2002), Halif Terrace (Golden 2002c), and Tel es-Shuna (Baird and Philip 1994; Rehren, Hess, and Philip 1997). By the EB2, a large workshop producing standardized copper goods emerged at the northern Negev city of Arad (Ilan and Sebbane 1989). Several standard tool forms, such as chisels, were mass-produced by casting copper into open molds, a technique that has been observed throughout the region, which points to a widespread standard in technological knowledge. At Faynan, a large copper manufactory supplied "raw" copper to much of the broader region (Levy et al. 2002).

Standardization in production can also be observed in the Early Bronze Age lithic assemblage. This is especially true with regard to sickles and other farming implements. The "Canaanean blades," generally about 15 cm (about 6 in.) long and 3 cm (a little more than 1 in.) wide and trapezoidal in cross section, were made from a carefully selected, fine-grained flint found in the western Negev and Sinai. In most cases, the knapper retouched the back of the blade in order to remove both the bulb of percussion and striking platform, which appears to represent an appeal to aesthetics and not just function. A station for the production of Canaanean blades has been discovered at Megiddo (Rosen 1983; Kempinski 1989), and blade cores appear at several sites. During the Early Bronze Age, Canaanean blades had become the "standard sickle implement for most farming communities" (Rowan and Levy 1994, 173). Horticultural goods such as wine and olives also most likely entailed the work of specialists, especially as production intensified in response to the Egyptian demand for these commodities. Tel es-Sa'idiyeh, a large EB2 complex thought to be a palace, included an industrial wing with evidence for both olive oil and wine production, suggesting attached specialization (Tubb 2002).

The ranks of Early Bronze Age craftspeople also included those who specialized in the production of groundstone implements. At Halif Terrace, limestone maceheads found in various stages of completion demonstrate that they were produced on site, and the production of basalt vessels continued at sites in the north (Braun 1990). The proliferation of intricately designed stamp seals along with serekhs (royal insignia) inscribed on wine jars suggests that at least a delimited number of merchants and/or nobles controlled some trade activities of the day.

In the more arid zones, especially the southern Negev, pastoral nomads specialized in the production of secondary products as well as in some simple crafts and trade. Large stone enclosures in the eastern Lower Galilee and Golan (for example, Lawiyeh), probably used as pastoral camps and animal pens, indicate that pastoralism was also an important practice in the more well-watered areas as well. A connection between these pastoralists and people of the lowland cities in the Jezreel and Jordan Valleys is demonstrated by similarities in the pottery assemblage and cylinder-seal impressions discovered inside the camps (Ben-Tor 1978; Epstein 1993; Esse 1989). A significant portion of this mobile population, however, may have been swallowed up by cities as the process of urbanization took hold in the north (Kempinski 1978; Esse 1989).

5.4 Egyptian seal impression from Halif Terrace, late EBI (Photo courtesy of T. E. Levy)

Interregional Economics and Emerging Trade Networks

Economic organization at the regional level can be inferred from settlement data as well as from the archaeological evidence relating to economic activities. Each of the larger cities probably served as the economic center for their respective regions, at the same time participating in a much broader system of interregional economic interdependence. At the southern settlements of Arad, En Besor, and Halif, people were engaged in vigorous trade relations with Egypt during the late EB1. During the EB2, Arad emerged as the principal "gateway to the south," commanding an exchange network that involved much of the Sinai, but by the EB3 the city was abandoned. Megiddo in the north, and perhaps Lod (central) and Tel Sakan (Gaza Strip), also served as key commercial centers. Trade activity in this southern sphere declined altogether by the EB3 as the center of economic and political power shifted north. Beit Yerah was clearly one of the most important commercial centers during the EB2 but may have been overshadowed by the rise of centers such as Hazor and Beth Shean in the EB3.

It appears that some settlements thrived by positioning themselves as specialized production communities that could take advantage of ecological diversity and strategic location to manufacture specific commodities for export. Several sites located on the southern coast, such as Ashqelon and Tel Sakan, probably functioned as ports during the EB1 (Gophna 2002). During the EB2, it was northern cities such as Byblos that served this function as the exchange network and seafaring activities shifted northward (Stager 1992; Marcus 2002). Sites situated in the valleys and along wadi banks (such as Tel Erani) controlled conduits leading from the coastal plain up into the mountains. Settlements of the interior, such as Megiddo, also served as trade hubs, benefiting from their location along trade routes that traversed the broad inland valleys. By the EB2, small villages emerged near mineral deposits in the southern Sinai. At the mining town of Sheikh Awad, the ceramic assemblages and "Arad-house" style demonstrate a connection between Arad and the mining villages. At Tel es-Shuna, in the central Jordan Valley, metalworkers produced copper ingots (Baird and Philip 1994; Rehren, Hess, and Philip 1997), which could then be distributed via overland routes; copper was also processed at the coastal site of Ashqelon-Afridar, whose inhabitants had immediate access to the trade routes of the sea (Golani and Segal 2002). Some of this copper may have made its way into the tombs of early Egyptian kings (Golden 2002c).

Several settlements seem to have exploited their location near more than one ecological zone to advantage by focusing on the production and exchange of "cash crops" such as grapes and olives in addition to cereal cultivation. For example, Yarmuth, a large site located in the foothills of southern Shephelah, controlled agricultural activities in the nearby Haela and Sorek Valleys, at the same time producing horticultural goods for both immediate consumption and trade. Ai, the first city-state established in the highlands, was populated by both sedentary and transhumant peoples in EB1, ultimately developing into an administrative center for the production and trade of horticultural goods. By around 2300 B.C.E., however, internal crises, brought on perhaps by environmental change and the disintegration of exchange networks, appear to have affected most of the southern Levant, leading to the collapse of the Early Bronze urban culture.

Intermediate Bronze Age

Upon the decline of urbanism at the end of the Early Bronze Age, the region underwent a reverse process aptly termed "ruralization" (Dever 1992). During this transitional phase known as the Intermediate Bronze Age (IBA), much of the urban population dispersed into the more marginal zones of the Negev, the Jordan Valley, and Transjordan, while Ai, Beth Yerah, Yarmuth, and other urban centers of the EB3 were either destroyed or altogether abandoned. As a result, many people settled in smaller units, such as farmsteads and hamlets, while others moved into areas such as the central Negev highlands to subsist primarily as pastoral nomads.

Much of what we know about the Intermediate Bronze Age comes from the cemeteries of Beth Shean, Gibeon, Lachish, Megiddo, and Tel el-Ajjul as well as Tel Umm Hammad esh-Sharqiya and Khirbet Iskander in Transjordan; burials from this period have also been excavated at Tel Esur (Assawir) (Yannai 1997). Pastoral groups probably used these cemeteries as they migrated between the Negev, where they wintered, and the central hills, which were more hospitable in the summer months (Finkelstein 1991).

It may well be that ecological conditions were such that people could no longer afford to rely exclusively on specialized production, and a sort of economic despecialization ensued, with adaptive strategies becoming more varied. As the urban centers that supported specialized shops collapsed, people reverted to household production. During the Intermediate Bronze Age, a majority of people seem to have gravitated toward pastoralism as a reliable mode of production. Yet despite the emphasis on pastoralism, people would have implemented mixed strategies combining agriculture and horticulture, shifting from one strategy to the other as deemed necessary (Dever 2003a; LaBianca 1990; Richard 1990). Settlements such as Beer Resisim and Jebel Qa'aqir were probably inhabited on a seasonal basis; settlements from this period have also been discovered at Sha'ar ha-Golan, Efrat, and 'Emeq Refaim (Dever 2003a). At the latter site, archaeologists found stone houses situated near a riverbed along natural terraces that could have been used for farming. Interaction and exchange between the various people practicing different economic strategies was vital to these small-scale economies (Palumbo 1991).

One of the most significant developments during the Intermediate Bronze Age was the first appearance of true tin bronze. To date, the earliest examples of tin bronze in the area appear sometime around 2200–2000 B.C.E., which is roughly contemporaneous with its first appearance in Cyprus (Stech, Muhly, and Maddin 1985; Merkel and Dever 1989). Excavations at an Intermediate Bronze Age burial cave near Enan (north of Hazor), in fact, have produced a number of bronze artifacts with strong Cypriote parallels (Eisenberg 1985). The crescentic axe heads of the previous period evolved into fenestrated axes with a shaft hole during the Intermediate Bronze Age. Long, thin copper ingots were used for casting these items. It is possible that people migrating from the north brought this technology to the southern Levant. Metalworking may have been practiced by itinerant craftsmen, as suggested by a wall painting from Beni Hassan in Egypt (c. 1900 B.C.E.) depicting a group of traveling Semites that may have a pair of bellows strapped to their donkey.

The relative poverty of Intermediate Bronze Age society is betrayed by the dearth of expensive luxury goods in circulation at the time. One of the few examples of artistic work demonstrating fine craftsmanship from the period is the silver vessel from 'Ain Samiya, which was decorated with various mythical beings in repoussé, pointing to a Syrian origin. Trade with people of Syria continued (Mazar 1990), but formal interaction between the Levantine peoples and Egyptians, who faced economic problems of their own, altogether ceased; not a single artifact of certain Egyptian origin has been found in Intermediate Bronze Age Palestine (Dever 1992a). And as Egyptians lost their hold on the Sinai, pastoral peoples were quick to fill this void yet again (Clamer and Sass 1977; Dever 1985a; Oren and Yekutiele 1990).

MIDDLE BRONZE AGE

Subsistence

From the perspective of economic organization, it is the transition back to agriculture as the primary means of subsistence that marks the beginning of the Middle Bronze Age. The Canaanite culture of the period probably originated as a result of interaction between seminomadic peoples inhabiting this region during the Intermediate period and new peoples arriving from the north. Pastoralism was still the primary means of subsistence at first, and in fact, these herder societies had begun to realize a considerable measure of success (Cohen 1992). Herds were abundant at the time, as suggested by a reference to healthy livestock in Canaan in the "Tale of Sinuhe," a contemporary Egyptian text that offers an account of an Egyptian's sojourn among the seminomadic tribes of Canaan. At Dan and Hazor, faunal assemblages recovered from tombs suggest that goat and sheep, especially the latter, were essential to the Middle Bronze Age diet (Ussishkin 1992; Biran, Ilan, and Greenberg 1996). Evidence for consumption of meat has been observed at Hazor, Aphek, and Tel Dalit, where the high concentration of limb bones indicates an appetite for choice cuts. The exploitation of these animals for their meat as opposed to the more economical practice of producing secondary dairy goods among pastoral societies represents an extravagance. It is interesting to note how modern Bedouin societies indulge in meat as part of social feasting. It is possible, therefore, that these Middle Bronze Age faunal assemblages reflect a trend toward intensified social relations as tribal leaders vied for social prestige and access to and control of grazing land. In time, competition for grazing land may have developed into territorialism as sedentary agricultural communities began to emerge throughout the southern Levant.

There was a sharp increase in settlement on the coastal plain during the Middle Bronze Age, which by the middle of the period was heavily populated (Broshi and Gophna 1986; Finkelstein 1992b). The region's general lack of broad, open areas discouraged large pastoral movements, and the population in fertile areas such as the coastal plain was largely sedentary. The well-watered northern and inland valleys were even more densely populated (Broshi and Gophna 1986), and once more, agriculture became the basis of subsistence, with barley and wheat constituting the primary staple goods. Lentils, peas, and chickpeas also formed an important part of the Canaanite diet. The "Tale of Sinuhe" presents the picture of a fertile country where barley, grapes, olives, honey, and various herbs were plentiful.

As the emphasis on agriculture grew, hydraulic technologies were increasingly employed in order to boost production. Climatic conditions in areas such as the Huleh Valley were probably not sufficient for dry-farming, and feeding the growing population living in and around Hazor required the use of irrigation technology. Sealed, stone-built channels that diverted runoff water to exterior channels and moats were in use at cities such as Dan, Tel el-Ajjul, Tel Beit Mirsim, and Gezer. The stone-roofed canals found in the fields surrounding Hazor ran for several hundred meters in some instances. On the coastal plain and in lowland valleys, simple irrigation systems based on floodwater farming were probably employed. A unique tunnel system discovered at Tel el-Ajjul may have functioned as a water system. It has been recently proposed that the Warren Shaft of Jerusalem, traditionally recognized as one of the great waterworks of the Iron 2, may actually have been part of the broader fortification system at Jebus dating to the second part of the Middle Bronze Age (MB2, c. 1800–1650 B.C.E.) (Nur el-Din 2002), though this theory certainly requires further investigation.

By this time, undomesticated resources played only a minor role in the subsistence economy. Wild berries and nuts such as almonds and walnuts were still collected, while various species of deer and the occasional wild sheep, goat, or pig were hunted, probably on an opportunistic basis, in order to supplement the diet. In neighboring states, hunting was generally treated as a prestige activity associated with the lifestyles of the rich and famous; for example, the "hunting scene" was common in the royal iconography in kingdoms of Syro-Mesopotamia and Egypt.

Craft Specialization

As the Canaanite culture evolved, staple wealth amassed through agricultural endeavors was redirected toward sectors of the economy focused on nonagricultural production. Several different industries provide evidence for specialization. The potter's craft continued to thrive, with advances in technology evident in the quality of the wares produced. At stratified sites such as Tel Dan, improvements in the quality of pottery can be observed over time. The standardization of ceramics also suggests this was a specialized industry with shops concentrating on the mass-production of a limited range of types. Excavations at Tel el-Ajjul have uncovered a ceramic workshop with multiple kilns, and at Tel Michal multiple kilns were found along with wasters and ceramic slag reflecting repeated use of the kilns. At sites in the Tel Aviv area (Ramat Aviv, Tel Qasile, Ben-Nun Street), as many as fourteen kilns, mostly dating to the later MB2, have been identified. The kilns were constructed with an oval combustion chamber hewn directly into the kurkar sandstone that was lined with clay. A flue used to control temperature and atmosphere was located between pairs of radial supports at the base of the chamber. Kilns have also been discovered at Jerishe and Aphek. These ceramic workshops were usually located away from domestic areas, as at Qasile, where kilns were built along the city slopes. The distribution of kilns across Canaan indicates that although pottery styles and techniques may have originated in the larger cities, production also took place at the local level where families of potters manufactured ceramics (Kletter and Gorzalczany 2001, 102).

Evidence for metal workshops has also been found at a number of cities, including Nahariyah on the coast and Tel el-Hayyat in Transjordan (Falconer 1987; Magness-Gardiner and Falconer 1994). At Tel el-Ajjul (City II) and Tel el-Dab'a (Avaris), an impressive number of gold objects, including solid-gold toggle pins, and pendants made of gold, silver, and bronze leaf attest to great technical expertise, and the use of electrum, and in rare cases lead, point to a mastery of metalworking techniques. True tin bronze as a medium for making tools, weapons, and objects of art and worship was employed on a large scale for the first time, representing a major technological breakthrough. (See sidebar, "The Coming of Bronze," in Chapter 9.)

The archaeological record suggests that some craftspeople and/or shops were affiliated with a specific institution, that is, "attached specialists." For instance, at both Nahariyah and Tel el-Hayyat, it appears that craft industries were associated with a goddess cult (Dothan 1965; Falconer 1987). At both of these sites, molds used to cast images of a horned goddess were discovered in the vicinity of a temple, suggesting that the religious establishment either commissioned large amounts of work or maintained in-house workshops. Contemporary texts from Mesopotamia and Syria demonstrate that there was a direct relationship between producers and the elite institutions in those regions.

Cylinder seals and their iconography also tell a great deal about the Middle Bronze Age economy (Teissier 1996). For example, a link may be drawn between the craftspeople who produced these seals and the elite consumers who used them in commercial transactions. Seals produced at Hazor and Syrian sites such as Qatna suggest the work of specialists, as their production entailed not only intricate carving skills but knowledge of the contemporary artistic canons as well.

Several of the largest cities in the region functioned as major economic hubs where all sorts of production and commerce took place. Hazor, for example, was a gateway community in which people from the hinterlands could come to exchange their goods with the urban population, serving as a central node in the "international" networks that were emerging (Yadin 1967; Maeir 2000). Megiddo dominated the Jezreel Valley, which was a key point along the inland trade routes, and people living at coastal cities such as Ashqelon benefited from their proximity to both maritime and overland trade routes. These large urban markets served as commercial centers where staple goods produced in the countryside (such as wheat) were converted into labor-intensive goods produced by specialists and where goods from the highlands (such as oil) were exchanged.

International Trade

The Canaanites of the Middle Bronze Age were involved in extensive trade networks extending from Syria and Anatolia to Egypt, a trend that can be documented with both archaeological and textual evidence. Cities of northern Canaan generally looked toward Syria and Anatolia, as demonstrated by affinities in pottery styles. Monochrome Painted Wares appearing throughout Middle Bronze Age Canaan point to ties with Amuq/Cilicia (Gerstenblith 1983; Ilan 1991), and Canaanite pottery of the MB2 has affinities with ceramics from the Khabur region in Syria (Ilan 1996). Evidence for contact can also be seen in other areas of material culture such as cylinder seals, where a style of glyptic art combining Mesopotamian and Egyptian motifs with local motifs, known as the "Syrian Style," emerged during the eighteenth century B.C.E. In addition, metal goods similar to examples from Syria have been found at a number of Canaanite sites, such as Shiloh.

Although the Syrian influence prevailed in the north, southern Canaan was actively engaged in maritime trade with the Egyptians to the south. The metal and ceramic assemblages at Tel el-Dab'a (Avaris) suggest that by the middle of the Middle Bronze Age this city had shifted its focus on trade with Byblos toward cities of the southern littoral (Bietak 1991). Hyksos peoples living at Avaris maintained close ties with Levantine cities such as Ashqelon and Tel el-Ajjul (City 2), where a number of scarabs with royal Hyksos names have been recovered. By this time, large quantities of Egyptian scarabs had made their way north to Hazor (Ben-Tor 1997). The tomb painting from the Egyptian site of Beni Hassan depicting Asiatics with a donkey whose cargo includes a pair of bellows suggests there may have been itinerant metalsmiths along trade routes.

Trade with Cyprus and the Aegean began to develop during this period, and though limited, laid the tracks for what would later become a "Pan-Mediterranean" world system (Stern and Saltz 1978). Cypriote painted jars (for example, Red-on-Black Ware) first appeared at coastal sites such as Tel Mevorakh. At Tel Nami (Kislev, Artzy, and Marcus 1993), there is evidence for contact with Syria, Egypt, Cyprus, and the Aegean in the early part of the Middle Bronze Age, when the city served as a way station between Egypt and Byblos. From Nami, a range of imported goods worked their way to interior sites such as Megiddo, Beth Shean, and the Jordan Valley via overland routes.

Various luxury goods, including copper from Cyprus, arrived at the port cities, then moved east toward the interior. The presence of Cypriote pottery, which was usually handmade and covered with painted decoration, increased during the period, though it did not peak until the Late Bronze Age (Stern and Saltz 1978). Glass, usually small beads, appeared for the first time (Peltenburg 1987; Ilan, Vandiver, and Spaer 1993). Other important items of trade probably included linen and textiles, often "invisible" in the archaeological record, as well as various horticultural goods. The discovery of *Lathyrus clymenum,* a legume of Aegean origin, in storage units, again at Tel Nami, indicates that exchange networks may have reached as far as Greece by the time of the early Middle Bronze Age (Kislev, Artzy, and Marcus 1993).

Textual evidence from this time also helps explain how trade was organized at the interregional level. In the Mari texts, Hazor and Laish (Tel Dan) were specifically named as the recipients of tin in a vast trade network. During the course of the Middle Bronze Age, Hazor emerged as the largest city in all of Canaan, playing a variety of roles and serving as the commercial, royal, and religious center of a broad polity. The relationship between trade activities and the royal court is clearly implied in a letter written by the Assyrian king, Shamshi Adad, to his son Iasmah Adad. In this missive, the ruler of Mari refers to envoys from Hazor who were afforded special status, in one case receiving an escort from Qatna.

The textual evidence also implies that Hazor's prominence stemmed from its central inland location and its role as a point of articulation between the peoples of Egypt and Mesopotamia (Horowitz and Shaffer 1992; Ben-Tor 1992). Syncretisms are apparent in glyptic art of the "Syrian style" involving elements from both states, and examples of these seals have been discovered at Hazor. It is also the only Canaanite city mentioned in both the Egyptian "Execration Texts" and the Mari texts.

LATE BRONZE AGE

The archaeological evidence from the Late Bronze Age is intriguing in that it offers the picture of a society that was at once both prosperous and poor. Wealthy tombs with imported luxury goods, vast administrative centers, and elaborate temples can be observed throughout the region during a time that otherwise gives the impression of being a period of decline (Bienkowski 1986; Knapp 1989). Shlomo Bunimovitz sums up this problem by posing the question, "How can the demographic and settlement crisis . . . as well as the gradual degeneration in certain aspects of the material culture be reconciled with the remains of elaborate palaces and patrician houses, temples and graves?" (2003, 325). However, this apparent paradox itself may explain part of the problem, for it appears the economy was lopsided, with a concentration of resources in the hands of a few and an inefficient overinvestment in conspicuous consumption.

Yet, while the elite members of society lived a life of luxury, the commoners of Canaan faced an even bigger problem: Egyptian domination. Indeed, the impact of the Egyptian presence during the mid- to late second millennium B.C.E. was so pervasive that Canaan is generally construed as an Egyptian colony or vassal state during the Late Bronze Age (Bunimovitz 2003). Though certain parts of the country may have been able to elude Egyptian control at times, the powerful pharaohs of the New Kingdom, by commandeering strategic centers such as Beth Shean, were able to put a stranglehold on the economy of virtually the entire region.

One effect of Egyptian domination was a diversion of resources, felt most acutely by the people living in areas peripheral to the sphere of Egyptian control, for these people were unable to benefit from either agricultural surpluses or profits from trade (Bunimovitz 2003, 325). Similarly, Piotr Bienkowski (1986, 137) has argued that the maintenance of the Egyptian colonial administration contributed to a negative flow of resources out of these areas. Nevertheless, cities of the densely populated coastal plain and northern inland valleys, located in proximity to the major arteries, benefited from the wealth that spilled over into the local community as they gradually came under direct Egyptian control.

The Egyptian influence, in fact, may have resulted in a fundamental restructuring of the Canaanite economy altogether. The independent and competing economic entities of the Middle Bronze Age, once under Egyptian domination, were transformed into vassal city-states of the empire (Knapp 1989, 1992). During this period, there had been true economic power emanating from the Canaanite kingdoms, each functioning as an independent city-state with its own internal system and settlement hierarchy based on economic integration and local political affiliations. During the Late Bronze Age, however, Canaan was generally reduced to a few large urban centers that served as intermediary nodes in a much broader system network. A good portion of the staple wealth that fed the Egyptian empire no doubt derived from Canaan, as the Egyptians controlled agricultural production, thereby appropriating the local material base. Though a few cities (for example, Hazor, Megiddo, and Lachish) enjoyed a reasonable measure of prosperity, others would remain impoverished as Egyptian power surged toward the end of the period (LB2b, c. 1300–1200 B.C.E.).

The large centers that had boomed during the Middle Bronze Age were the same ones that managed to survive, if not thrive, under the Egyptian influence, and probably for the same reason: Their locations gave them access to major trade routes and/or vital resources. Many of the more marginal cities and rural villages may have found that imperial demands exceeded their capacity for production, causing them in some cases to simply fold in the face of adversity (Na'aman 1981; Ahituv 1978; Redford 1992; Bunimovitz 2003). Generally speaking, it was the large urban centers that interested the Egyptians, and it is possible that the combined effect of Egyptian transplants and the cosmopolitanism of local urbanites allowed these cities to prosper in the face of major economic change. There is evidence for palaces, temples, and tombs that exhibit Late Bronze Age wealth, yet, as Shlomo Bunimovitz has advised, these should "not be simplistically interpreted as symbols of localized prosperity, but as evidence for conspicuous consumption aimed to maintain power relations within an economically impoverished . . . country" (2003, 356).

Although a few urban centers flourished during the Late Bronze Age, pastoral life in the hinterlands was also active. Bunimovitz (1994) has proposed the "Shifting Frontier Model" based on the premise, originally discussed by Owen Lattimore (1940) and Robert McC. Adams (1978, 1974) that ecological frontiers often oscillate within broad parameters, depending in large part on the strength of the dominant political power. At times of security and development, the frontier in Canaan shifted southward and eastward while there was general stability and prosperity in the lowlands. In less stable times, these areas quickly reverted to frontier zones, populated primarily by mobile groups. Thus, upon the collapse of the Middle Bronze Age city-states and the incursion of the Egyptians, the frontier shifted from the hilly regions to the coastal plain, Shephelah, and inland valleys.

Some of these pastoral groups, previously nameless nomads with no specific identity forthcoming to archaeologists, begin to come into sharper focus around this time. In the Amarna Letters, the term *'Apiru* was used, often as a pejorative, to describe some of the people who roamed southern Canaan (for example, "The *Apiru* descended from the hills" [Na'aman 1986, 275–276; Marfoe 1979, 9–10]). Initially used to refer to an economic class, only later did the term assume an ethnic connotation.

Specialized Production

Local methods of pottery production changed little from the Middle to the Late Bronze Age, but forms did change gradually over time. Large amphorae used for storage were typical of the period, with the most notable change in local assemblages being the disappearance of Tel el-Yehudiyeh Ware. Evidence for ceramic production during the Late Bronze Age appears at a few sites, and at least two different types of kilns have been observed: kidney-shaped kilns with one central support, and keyhole-shaped kilns (Kletter and Gozalczany 2001; Killebrew 1996). Over time, Late Bronze Age pottery styles became rougher and coarser, and varieties of cheap, local ceramics were mass-produced. Canaanite potters also copied Cypriote and Mycenaean pottery using their own techniques (Mazar 1990).

The production of metal also played an important part in the Late Bronze Age economy. By the thirteenth century B.C.E., extensive mining operations, involving the excavation of vast horizontal galleries and deep (30 m, or about 98 ft.) vertical shafts, were carried out at Timna, the mining region of the Aravah near the modern city of Eilat. These operations were conducted either by Egyptians or under their direct control, as suggested by the presence of New Kingdom pottery, which dominates the assemblage found in the vicinity of the mines. Evidence for the smelting of copper was found at an Egyptian copper-smelting camp with a bowl-shaped furnace dated to the twelfth century B.C.E., as well as a rock-cut furnace with heavily slagged walls, a tuyére in situ, and ring-shaped slag cakes (Rothenberg 1998). Production was well organized, with Egyptian officials and soldiers as well as workmen from the Arabian Peninsula, as suggested by "Midianite" pottery (Rothenberg and Glass 1983; see also Mazar 1990, 286). Yet again, a link between economy and cult may be inferred from the presence of an Egyptian temple to Hathor, the patron deity of the mine.

Trade

One of the primary features of the Late Bronze Age economy was the expansion of trade networks, which increasingly involved peoples from Cyprus and the Aegean. In the north, Tel Nami served as a port for transshipment, which peaked during the mid-thirteenth century B.C.E. Of course, trade between Egypt and its vassal was lively and constant. The Papyrus Anastasi, which mentions a number of coastal cities (for example, Jaffa), refers to trade along the "Way of Horus."

The north Canaanite city-state of Ugarit played a major role in the thirteenth-century-B.C.E. trade networks, serving as a meeting point between land and sea routes. Further south, Tel Abu Hawam may have played a similar role, though on a much smaller scale. The city of Akko, on the other side of the same bay, also provided anchorage around this time (at about the time of the reign of Thutmose III), but it is unclear whether the two sites were contemporary or if Abu Hawan supplanted Akko (Balensi, Herrera, and Artzy 1993).

One of the most important of these port cities was Tel Dor, where small samples of pottery from the Late Bronze Age have yielded examples of almost every type of Minoan, Mycenaean, and Cypriote ware known to have been imported into Canaan (Stern 1995). At Tel el-Ajjul, limited material from renewed excavations has already produced nearly 1,000 ceramic imports dating from the end of the Middle through the Late Bronze Age, most of which come from Cyprus, though Mycenae, Egypt, northern Syria, and southern Lebanon are also presented (Fischer 2002).

Questions remain about which goods were actually being traded. Much of the Mycenaean pottery found in Canaan was highly decorated and somewhat eccentric in form, an outstanding example being the "Charioteer Vase" from Tel Dan. In some cases, the pottery itself was probably the object of exchange and not the vessel contents, and Mazar (1990) has suggested that Mycenaean ceramics were traded as objects of art and valuable tableware used for feasting and drinking rites. Certain closed Mycenaean forms (for example, stirrup jars) may have been used to deliver precious liquids such as perfume and

5.5   In the port city of Tel Dor, small samples of pottery from the Late Bronze Age have yielded examples of almost every type of Minoan, Mycenaean, and Cypriote ware known to have been imported into Canaan. (Photo courtesy of Zev Radovan, Land of the Bible Picture Archive)

unguents, the vessels also serving as marketing tools. It is clear that these imported goods were considered an important component in burial kits of the elite, as some of the best examples are found in the wealthy tombs of the Late Bronze Age. For instance, the "Mycenaean Tomb" (Tomb 387) at Tel Dan contained imports from Cyprus, Mycenae, and the Lebanese coast.

One of the most important items of trade in the Late Bronze Age world was copper, which was widely circulated in the form of ingots, most notably in the "ox-hide" form, named for their shape, which resembles a hide (see Fig. 5.6). Much of the copper is thought to have derived from mines in Cyprus and was subsequently transported to destinations around the Mediterranean world, including Mycenae, Rhodes, Ugarit, and southern Italy, in addition to the southern Levant. Recent studies based on lead-isotope analysis of 100 copper ox-hide ingots from around the Mediterranean, as well as from slag heaps at smelting sites throughout Cyprus, confirm that Cypriote copper was indeed distributed to all of these places, but not until after 1250 B.C.E. (Stos-Gale et al. 1997; Stos-Gale, Maliotis, and Gale 1998). Evidence for the maritime copper trade also comes from the sea itself—in particular, at Cape Gelidonyah and Bodrum off the coast of Turkey, where ox-hide ingots have been found among the submerged remains of shipwrecks (Bass 1967). Copper ox-hide ingots were also imported into Egypt, as they appear several times in Egyptian wall paintings of the period.

5.6   Copper ox-hide ingot (Drawing by J. Golden)

Another vital trade item, the tin ingot, was produced in a variety of forms. Near Kfar Samir, a cache of five irregular, bun-shaped ingots were discovered with one copper ox-hide ingot. These ingots, which date to the fourteenth to twelfth centuries B.C.E., weighed roughly 2–4 kg (about 4–9 lbs.), while rectangular, brick-shaped tin ingots weighed 11–22 kg (24–49 lbs.) each. In some cases, these appear to have been cut from larger blocks of metal, and as George Bass (1967) suggested, the discovery of copper and tin ingots together may indicate that some ships may have had smith's workshops on board. Incised markings chiseled into the ingots are related to the Cypro-Minoan script group (which probably dates to the late second millennium B.C.E.).

Despite the plethora of imported goods found in Canaan during the Late Bronze Age, overall the distribution of Cypriote and Aegean imports suggests that direct trade with the Aegean was less active in southern Canaan. This may be less true, however, of certain coastal cities such as Tel el-Ajjul (Steel 2002). By the end of the thirteenth century B.C.E., the Cypriote and Mycenaean imports virtually disappeared altogether, pointing to an abrupt disruption of the trade networks. Seminomadic groups began to inhabit the hill country, and once again, economic change was afoot.

IRON 1: THE ECONOMY OF THE HIGHLANDS AND "PROTO-ISRAELITES"

In the beginning of the twelfth century, a new process of settlement was under way, and populations began to surge through the highlands. The roots of this population and those responsible for establishing the highland culture of the early Iron Age have been the subject of extensive debate. Much of the discussion centers on the economic background of the Iron 1 peoples, specifically, whether they were farmers or herders (Finkelstein 1988, 1995). Some insight may be gained by considering ethnographic research on various pastoralists of the modern Middle East (for example, Spooner 1972). This research has shown that most groups tend to practice a multiresource strategy as one way of managing risk. In these mixed economies, various combinations of subsistence practices in the ecological continuum between the sedentary and nomadic economies are employed.

Evidence gathered from surveys and excavations suggests that the region was home to pastoral groups in the early Iron 1 and that at least some of the early settlers had nomadic roots, persisting in their reliance on pastoral production even after the process of establishing agricultural communities had begun. For instance, at Tel Dan, the earliest Iron Age occupation seems to reflect this process, where twelfth-century-B.C.E. squatters combined herding with limited farming and hunting. The remainder of the previous Late Bronze Age city (Laish) was pierced by clusters of large storage pits that provide vital information regarding economic life during this phase (Biran 1994; Biran, Ilan, and Greenberg 1996). The pits themselves probably represent the arrival of a nomadic people who lived in semipermanent structures and used them for storage. The faunal remains found within the pits included mainly sheep and goats with some cattle, an assemblage typical of seminomadic herders, and the fact that some pits were lined with stone suggests that they were used for the storage of dry goods (such as grain).

People inhabiting the highlands began to cultivate the valley bottoms adjacent to their hilltop villages, and by the beginning of the first millennium B.C.E., intensive farming with assistance of the plow became the primary means of subsistence for people of the highlands. An important ecological consideration for settlement in the hill country was the availability of farmland, and as the settled population of the highlands continued to expand, large-scale landscaping projects were undertaken. The amount of arable land was greatly increased by the creation of terraces along the hill-slopes, resulting in changes to the Levantine landscape still visible today. Bringing land under the plow in the hill country would have also involved the arduous task of clearing heavily wooded areas. A number of scholars (for example, Stager 1982; Callaway 1985) have proposed that terracing was an innovation of the Iron 1 peoples that allowed them to inhabit the hill country. Israel Finkelstein (1995), however, has argued that the earliest phase of Iron 1 settlement was in areas of the hill country that did not require terracing, that is, the desert fringe, the central range's intermontane valleys, and flat areas (for example, the Bethel Plateau). He also points out that the technique of terrace farming was known during the Middle Bronze Age and possibly even in the Early Bronze Age (Finkelstein 1995; Finkelstein and Gophna 1993). It is unknown whether the Iron 1 settlers of the central hill country came from an agricultural or pastoral background; the terraces themselves do not provide a conclusive answer.

At first, cereal crops, especially wheat, were the primary agricultural product. The highland peoples also began to invest in horticulture, especially olive and grape cultivation, which, despite requiring a longer period of initial development, was ideally suited to the climate of this region. Olive oil presses dating to the Iron Age have been found at sites throughout the central hill country, such as a group of installations in southern Samaria (Finkelstein 1995). Thus, this shift in economic strategy was interrelated with long-term settlement and population growth in the highlands, and ultimately led to an increase in specialization.

Large in-ground storage units, used by the broader community to store grain, have been discovered at a number of settlements. In the broad inland valleys (such as Jezreel and Huleh), Canaan's perennial breadbasket, large silos like those excavated at Megiddo (Storage Pit 1414) and Hazor (Area G Silo) would have held a sizable surplus. This surplus could then have been used for trade with people of the hill country, who found it more difficult to produce and maintain a staple surplus. An open court excavated at 'Izbet Sartah had forty-three stone-lined silos (Str. II) with an estimated total capacity of 53 metric tons of wheat and 21.35 metric tons of barley (Finkelstein 1986). Smaller, decentralized silos such as these may indicate that individuals and extended families, the primary units of production at the time (Hopkins 1985, 1987), engaged in farming on a small scale without a high level of organization (Finkelstein 1988).

Another ecological challenge posed by life in the highlands concerns the availability of water and the management of the water supply. At sites such as Ai and Raddanah, cisterns were cut out of the bedrock and lined with plaster as a way of catching and storing rainwater. At one point, this was thought to be one of the major innovations that allowed Israelite settlement to thrive in the hill country (Albright 1939). This theory, however, can be refuted on several different counts. First, there was extensive settlement in the highlands during both the Early and Middle Bronze Ages, and thus Iron Age settlement in the hill country was not in and of itself unique. It has also become clear that Middle Bronze Age and perhaps even Early Bronze Age peoples made use of cisterns as well. Finally, it is now apparent that many Iron Age settlements did not depend on the use of cisterns for their water supply but rather used large pithoi to shuttle water from springs sometimes located at a distance of several kilometers from the site, as at Giloh.

Though archaeologists often speak in general terms about a highland-lowland dichotomy, it is important to note that within the hill country different cultural processes can be observed between the south and north. Finkelstein (1995) has pointed out that south of Shechem, pastoral groups remained a significant force even after sedentary populations increased. Small-scale herding remained an important activity throughout the period, particularly in marginal regions such as the Negev and on the eastern slopes of the highlands (Finkelstein 1988; Banning and Köhler-Rollefson 1992). A massive cemetery in the Jabal Hamrat Fidan dating to the eleventh and tenth centuries B.C.E. attests to the presence of nomadic tribes in the Faynan District of Jordan (Levy 2002b).

In some areas, hunting was still practiced as a way of supplementing the diet. The slopes of Mount Hermon north of Dan were teeming with gazelle as well as fallow and roe deer, and the remains of dogs, gazelles, and birds found at Dan suggest that its inhabitants were hunting the latter two, probably with the assistance of the former. A closer examination of the faunal assemblage from Dan reveals both lean and fatty cuts of meat, indicating that the entire kill was brought back to the village for consumption (Biran 1994). Fishing, too, was practiced by the Danites, as demonstrated by the presence of freshwater fish-bones and mollusks in the aforementioned pits.

Craft Specialization

The tradition of metalworking continued in the region at the beginning of the Iron Age, and though iron technology itself was not widespread until the tenth century, bronze production thrived at a number of sites. In fact, early in the Iron 1, most weapons and tools were still made of bronze, and many of the Late Bronze Age forms, such as axes, arrowheads, and spearheads, persisted. Bronze workshops dating to the Iron 1 have been excavated at a number of sites, including Tel Deir 'Alla, Tel Qasile, Beth Shemesh, Tel Mor, Tel Masos, Tel Dan, and Tel Harashim in Upper Galilee. At Tel Dan, a metal workshop (Courtyard 7026) dating to the early twelfth century B.C.E. (Str. VI) has been detected based on the recovery of crucibles, bronze slag, basalt tools, and circular installations; just north of the courtyard were a furnace, crucibles, blowpipes, and unused metal. In the following phase (Str. V), several workshop areas, also with crucibles, blowpipes, and circular installation, were located in a large open work area (No. 7061).

Certain cities or regions became known for their prowess in a certain area of production, and it appears the Danites gained renown for their metalworking skills. According to Avraham Biran (1994), a passage in 2 Chronicles (2:13–14) can be interpreted to mean that the King of Tyre was touting an emissary's credentials as a metalworker by making note of his Danite background.

Many of the bronze artifacts from this time represent luxury goods. Bronze wine kits, including a Canaanite-style bowl, jug, and strainer, were highly coveted in the early Iron 1. Examples of these kits have been found at Megiddo, Beth Shean, and Tel es-Sa'idiyeh, but they seem to have gone out of style by the eleventh century B.C.E. The Canaanite figural tradition continued, as exemplified by a seated god from Hazor (Level XI) and a bull from the Samarian Hills, while new types of bronze goods, originating from and/or influenced by Cypriote and Aegean styles, appeared at Tel Qasile, Tel Zeror, Megiddo, and Akhziv. Bronze goods also appear in the Jordan Valley—for example, a bronze bowl with a handle and a tripod reminiscent of the Cypriote style were found at Tel es-Sa'idiyeh (Tubb 2002). Bronze weapons of the period include double axes and long spearheads. Textual evidence, including multiple biblical passages referring to bronze, reflects the continued importance of the bronze tradition throughout the Iron Age.

Economic integration developed gradually during this time, and much of the on-site production activities were probably geared toward immediate consumption. The production of horticultural goods, especially wine, would have required individuals with developed skills, and the discovery of olive press installations in groups (Finkelstein 1995) suggests specialized production, but not on a grand scale. Certain textiles, such as flax and wool, were produced locally, as indicated by the discovery of bronze crochet hooks at a number of sites (such as Samaria; see Crowfoot, Crowfoot, and Kenyon 1957).

Trade Relations

Though the Egyptians had lost their vassal state, their influence persisted in the southern Levant during the early Iron Age. An inscribed pot from Tel Sera (on the Nahal Gerar) dating to the beginning of the twelfth century refers specifically to "Year 22," which can be attributed to the reign of Rameses III. The inscription also makes reference to a record of grain measured in the quadruple *hekat,* an Egyptian unit of measure (a hekat was equal to roughly 4.5 liters, or just over a gallon; the quadruple hekat was commonly used during the New Kingdom). This suggests that the agricultural potential of the southern Levant continued to be an important factor in the regional economy.

Traffic on the old routes saw a limited revival in the beginning of the eleventh century B.C.E., mainly owing to the activity of the Phoenicians. Phoenician Bichrome Ware appears at Megiddo, Tel Masos in the Negev, and the Egyptian Delta. Donkeys were still employed in overland transport, but the camel was probably in use by this time as well.

By the end of the eleventh century B.C.E., maritime trade activities were also revived. At Dor, the Sikil-Phoenician city, the ceramic assemblage indicates that contact with Cyprus and the Aegean had slowed to a trickle at the end of the Late Bronze Age but resumed with vigor in the latter part of the century. At this point, the port city played an important role in the maritime trade networks, as demonstrated by the presence of Cypriote pottery at the site (Stern 1995). Cypriote pottery has been found at inland cities such as Megiddo, while the Cypriote influence is also apparent in the bronze assemblages of the Iron 1; of course, many of the Cypro-Aegean goods were brought to this region by people who would become known as the Philistines.

Tel Masos, strategically located in the northern Negev between the Aravah and routes to the north, emerged as an important node in the copper trade (Kempinski 1978). Evidence for metal production at the site suggests it may have functioned as a processing center, which then shipped the metal on. Ceramics that probably originated from northwestern Arabia, biblical Midian, and the Hejaz, hence "Midianite Ware" (Rothenberg and Glass 1983), were also found at the site, suggesting the far-reaching contacts of the people of Masos. Mining at Timna, however, ceased rather abruptly in the middle of the twelfth century, perhaps as a result of Egyptian withdrawal from the region (Rothenberg 1998). At this point, Cypriote mines became the primary source for copper throughout the Mediterranean world, while Sardinian sources were also exploited (Stos-Gale et al. 1997).

IRON 1: THE ECONOMY OF THE SOUTHERN COASTAL PLAIN

For much of Canaan, the thriving "pan-Mediterranean" trade network of the Late Bronze Age slowed considerably at the beginning of the Iron 1 as trade networks collapsed and/or the Levant was largely circumvented. This does not apply, however, to the region as a whole. By this time, a distinct cultural group, the Sea Peoples, or Proto-Philistines, were becoming a dominant force on the southern coastal plain. All lines of evidence point west toward Cyprus and the Aegean for their origins.

At first, many of the newcomers arriving on the coast may have lived as squatters. At Deir el-Balah, there was evidence for Sea Peoples occupation amid the remains of an Egyptian fortress that was already defunct at the time. Within a matter of decades though, as people continued to filter into the region, they had found a solid economic footing. The Sea Peoples' economic ascendancy in the coastal region is attested to by the decline of Tel el-Sultan, a Canaanite city of modest wealth during the twelfth century B.C.E., which diminished in economic importance as the large Philistine city of Ashdod continued to grow just 10 miles south along the coast (Dothan and Dothan 1992).

Gradually, the Sea Peoples' sphere of influence began to move inland. At first, important cities emerged at points on the coastal plain that provided a conduit to the interior: Ashdod at the mouth of the Wadi Sukreir, which provided a route to the Judean hills; Ashqelon at the mouth of a tidal river, the Wadi Eskale; and Tel Qasile in the Yarkon River Valley. Already in control of the fertile valleys of the coastal plain, where they focused mainly on the cultivation of wheat and barley, they continued to expand inland, setting the stage for territorial disputes in the following period (Iron 2).

The Sea Peoples recognized the great potential for horticulture in the rolling hills of the Shephelah. The primary focus on vineyards and olive groves, that is, wine and oil production, began on a small scale but reached an advanced level later in the Iron Age. As for animal husbandry, the Philistines engaged in the herding of sheep and goats, though their penchant for indulging in pork and beef marked a clear change from the Canaanite cuisine, which emphasized goat and mutton (Hesse 1986; Dothan 1995).

From the beginning of the Sea Peoples' tenure on the Levantine coast, their economy was based largely on their involvement in networks of exchange in the Mediterranean. Revenue from this maritime economy would have come from several directions, as they dealt directly in the import of goods for exchange with local peoples while exacting fees for the delivery or passage of other parties' goods. Initially, they controlled the coastal overland route (the "Way of Horus") and, in time, the maritime routes as well.

Tel Mor on the southern coastal plain may have served as the port for Ashdod. After the destruction of the Egyptian fort at the end of the Late Bronze

Age, a Philistine settlement typical of the Iron 1, as indicated by the pottery, was established at the site.

By the end of the twelfth century B.C.E., Philistine control of trade extended far inland. The relatively sudden appearance of Philistine pottery at Megiddo suggests that the Philistines supplanted the Egyptians in places as far north as the Jezreel Valley. This theory is also supported by a reference in the "Tale of Wen–Amon," the story of an Egyptian temple official from the eleventh century B.C.E. who travels to Phoenicia, which states that Sea Peoples and Phoenicians, not the Egyptians, controlled the major trade routes at the time (Wilson 1969, 25–29; see also Mazar 1986, 65–68).

Excavations at Qasile revealed that its inhabitants were actively engaged not only in maritime trade, as suggested by Cypriote pottery, but in specialized craft production, including ceramics, metals, and textiles (Mazar 1985). This is part of a broader trend. The first waves of Sea Peoples maintained close economic ties with their western counterparts, but in time they became increasingly independent. Not long after settling in the southern Levant, the Sea Peoples set about producing their own pottery, and during the course of the Iron 1 the volume of ceramics that were imported decreased, though local producers emulated the Cypro-Aegean style. The widespread use of kilns throughout the eastern Mediterranean in the Iron Age gave potters more control over their firing techniques (Hocking 2001). At Tel Miqne–Ekron, evidence for pottery production has been discovered in an eleventh-century-B.C.E. context, where square and horseshoe-shaped kilns were used to manufacture Aegean-style pottery (Dothan 1995). At Tel Jemmeh in the northern Negev, a large kiln dating to the twelfth century B.C.E. used mud-brick, with four radial arches to support the floor separating the fire chamber from the chamber where the pottery was placed; it is not entirely clear that this was Philistine, however (Van Beek 1987, 1993).

The same is true of metal goods, which during the earliest phase of Sea Peoples occupation were imported (Stager 1991). By the end of the twelfth century B.C.E., the people of Tel Miqne–Ekron were processing their own metal, using a huge installation with a crucible found in the industrial area. Ironsmiths at Jemmeh may have already employed the technique of quenching in order to strengthen their metal, and at Qasile there is limited evidence for carburization, though in both cases this could have been accidental (Waldbaum 1999). Though it was once thought that the Philistines should be credited with the spread of iron, this now seems doubtful (see Waldbaum 1999). (See sidebar, "The Coming of Iron.")

Homespun production also played a role in the subsistence economy of the Philistines. The eleventh-century-B.C.E. settlement at Tel Qasile offers a unique window on economic organization at the household level. It appears that Sea People, or Proto-Philistine families, relied on the home production of dairy goods and probably kept small numbers of animals in a partially roofed courtyard attached to the house. The open side of the courtyard was used for a range of domestic tasks, as evidenced by the discovery of hearths and grinding stones. It also served as a workspace for "cottage industries" as families produced goods for immediate consumption (for example, olive oil and wine), as indicated by presses. Bronze crochet hooks were found at Jemmeh, and evidence for weaving is indicated by the unbaked clay loom weights found at Tel Miqne–Ekron, Ashqelon, and Ashdod. This type of weight, known from Cyprus and Mycenae, was new in the southern Levant in the eleventh and twelfth centuries B.C.E. (Stager 1991).

As part of their eastward push, the Sea Peoples appear to have been attracted to settlements straddling the area where the coastal plain meets the foothills. Signs of their presence abound at Tel Miqne–Ekron; in addition, excavations at Tel Beit Mirsim have revealed a rural Philistine settlement dating to the Iron 1 (Str. B2). Though it seems to have been sparsely settled, a number of stone-lined silos were discovered. A Sea Peoples presence has also been noted at Tel Halif, and although neither this nor Beit Mirsim can be dubbed Sea Peoples' settlements, the site demonstrates their influence away from the coast. The economic impact of the Sea Peoples was also felt in the Jordan Valley. Jonathan N. Tubb (2002) has argued that their presence at Tel es-Sa'idiyeh was mainly at the behest of Egyptians who hired them as military personnel and/or industrial specialists.

With specific regard to the economy, it is probably inaccurate to conceive of the Sea Peoples as a unified body with singular economic interests as early as the Iron 1. For instance, the port at Tel Dor was established by the Sikils, another component of the collective Sea Peoples, who later "founded" Sicily, according to textual sources.

IRON 2: THE ISRAELITE ECONOMY

During the Iron 2, large city-states served as economic centers for much broader regions. The inland valleys of Huleh, Jezreel and Beth Shean, which flourished as the great breadbaskets, all supported large cities with large populations. Based in part on Steven E. Falconer's (1987) work, William G. Dever (1995) has estimated an "urban threshold"—defined as the point at which population growth is such that a settlement requires qualitative organizational changes in order to continue to support itself—for cities of the Iron 2 of roughly 20 acres and some 2,000 people. According to this standard, the Israelite cities that qualified are Dan, Gezer, Hazor, Jerusalem, and Lachish (only Tel Miqne–Ekron would qualify in Philistia).

For many of these cities, the Iron 2 was an era of great prosperity. Megiddo was a major administrative center during the tenth and ninth centuries B.C.E., even under Neo-Assyrian rule at the end of the eighth century. Elongated structures with square columns and stone troughs, dated to the ninth century B.C.E. (Str. IVA), have been excavated at the site. This discovery touched off a great debate concerning whether they represent the types of stables ascribed to Solomon (Yadin 1972), or if they were royal storehouses (Aharoni 1982; Herzog et al. 1984; for a summary of this debate see Routledge 1995). According to John S. Holladay Jr., the emerging Israelite state required all sorts of specialized producers of goods and services, including select stock of bred horses to

The Coming of Iron

The southern Levant played a prominent role in the history of metal throughout ancient times, and this goes for the coming of iron, one of the great enigmas of Old World archaeology. Though the first iron weapons began to appear in the Levant before the end of the twelfth century B.C.E., iron was still relatively rare through the eleventh century. Bronze production continued on a broad scale and even surged during the early Iron Age, with workshops operating at Tel Masos, Tel Mor, Beth Shemesh, Tel Qasile, Tel Deir 'Alla, Tel Dan, and Tel Harashim in Upper Galilee. It was not until the tenth century B.C.E. that the use of iron became widespread, and iron gradually became the metal of choice for many tasks.

There are a number of reasons why people would have shifted to the use of iron over bronze. Iron actually entered the material record much earlier, but it was generally restricted to some stray decorative items, such as jewelry. Iron is not optimal for this genre because it is less fluid and less lustrous than bronze. Iron, however, even in this early phase of the technology, was harder and more durable than bronze and would ultimately prove far superior to its predecessor for the purposes of making utilitarian goods such as tools, weapons, and building materials.

Where agriculture was concerned, iron was used for axe heads and hoes and would have facilitated the clearing of forests. The more efficient plow tip allowed for deeper plowing, and the iron sickle expedited the process of harvesting. All these innovations may have facilitated the expansion of settlement in the wooded hills of the central highlands. Iron also found widespread application in the world of weaponry and warfare. The Hittites to the north based much of their military prowess on their mastery of iron, using it to build their arsenal, which included helmets, projectile points, and chariot wheels. The Hebrew Bible alludes to the impact of this technology on geopolitics and warfare, stating that the Israelites "could not drive out the inhabitants of the valley because they had chariots of iron" (Judg. 1:19).

The adoption of iron technology was a gradual process, but once it did take hold, it spread rather rapidly throughout the entire Near East, including the southern Levant. As with the advance of any new technology, the dissem-

draw the military chariots and thousands of trained stallions (Holladay 2003). In either event, these and similar structures found at other early Iron 2 cities attest to centralized control of economic activities. Other architectural works, such as an underground water-supply system and a huge city wall and gate system, also attest to the city's wealth.

Hazor (Str. X) was also an important city of the early to mid Iron 2, though considerably smaller than the Canaanite cities at the site. Large storehouses were located near the city gate, and the city's builders showed great ingenuity ination of iron depended largely on the discovery of widespread application and use. Advances within the field accelerated the process as it allowed iron-smiths to more fully exploit the metal's properties. For instance, by the late tenth century B.C.E. and possibly earlier, smiths were aware of more advanced techniques such as carburization, which serves to strengthen the metal, and the use of iron for the production of tools increased significantly (McNutt 1991; Waldbaum 1999). Other techniques, such as quenching, where the hot metal is plunged into cool water, may also have been employed to strengthen the metal.

Of course, one must also consider the spread of iron within its broader social, economic, and political context. For example, it has been suggested that market forces such as tin shortages may have contributed to the shift away from bronze; in other words, stable supplies of copper notwithstanding, a shortage of tin would still drive up the cost of producing bronze. It is also typical for a new technology, especially one with the potential to confer military advantage on those who can monopolize it, to be deliberately withheld from adversaries. It is possible that this was the case in the southern Levant, and some scholars have suggested that the Philistines at one point held a monopoly on metal production. A passage in 1 Samuel (13:19–22) states, "Now there was no smith in the land of Israel; for the Philistines said 'Lest the Hebrews make them swords or spears.'" It should be noted, however, that this line does not refer to any specific metal. The traditional association between the Philistines and their use of iron has led to much speculation about their role as the purveyors of iron technology into the southern Levant, yet this stems mainly from the biblical tradition and there is little archaeological evidence in support of the idea (Waldbaum 1999).

Whether it was the specific properties of the material or monopolies on its production that led to its widespread adoption, the impact of iron technology on society cannot be underestimated. By the end of the second millennium B.C.E., iron would enable progress in subsistence practices and changes in settlement patterns. Iron was also instrumental in the emergence of great empires, playing a pivotal role in the delicate balance of power between the Hittite and Egyptian empires that enveloped the peoples of the southern Levant.

in sinking a deep shaft from the middle of the city in order to have constant access to water, a solution that was as much defensive as economic. In time, Dan would replace Hazor as the primary population center of the Huleh Valley, and the city continued to expand into the early seventh century B.C.E. According to Avraham Biran (1994), great prosperity at Dan was evident in all areas of Stratum 1 that were excavated, especially Areas B and H, which had massive buildings with walls 1.2 m (about 4 ft.) thick and 30 m (about 98 ft.) long.

The open space just inside the great city gates at Dan, Gezer, Hazor, and

Megiddo were places of commerce where people peddled their wares. Goods were shipped from here and received here as well. One interesting find from Tel Dan was a room on the southern slope of the tell containing more than 300 juglets. The juglets were positioned in a way suggesting that they had once sat upon shelves, leading excavator Biran (1994) to infer this was a shop that villagers might pass on their way toward the city gates.

Trade Relations

The Iron 2 was a period of great trade, especially along the vast overland networks. New types of goods from the Arabian trade routes traveled mainly through the Zered–Beer Sheva Depression. As many as 3,000–5,000 camels were used to bring spices and semiprecious stones from East Asia as well as gold, ivory, hides, and blackwood from Africa (Van Beek 1993). In the north, Dan, at the crossroads of the Huleh Valley, played a role as intermediary in trade between the coast and the central Jordan Valley, as suggested by various elements in the ceramic assemblage, including an amphoriskos from Transjordan, a Neo-Assyrian-type vessel, and a Corinthian juglet. Trade with the Phoenician coast was especially active at this time, and Phoenician influence can be seen in much of the region during the Iron 2. The cedars of Lebanon became vital elements of royal architecture for the Israelites as strong links were established between the monarchy and the rulers of Tyre (Holladay 1987, 2003). At Hazor, the rise and fall of the Phoenician influence can be observed in the pottery assemblage. Imported Phoenician wares, or imported-style copies, were rare in the early Iron 1 (3–4 percent in Str. XII-XI). They increased dramatically from 1000 to 885 B.C.E., at the beginning of the Iron 2 (14–18.5 percent in Str. X-IX), and finally dropped off again with the end of the Omride Dynasty (8.5 percent in Str. VIII). Israelite interaction with the Philistines, further down the coast, however, was limited.

Craft Production

The city of Dan upheld its long tradition as a center for bronze production into the early part of the Iron 2. Extensive evidence for metalworking, including a large space (Area B) with circular installations and fragments of crucibles, slag, basalt tools, and blowpipes, has been dated to the late eleventh and early tenth centuries B.C.E. (Str. IVB). Several smaller shops may have also been in operation at other parts of the site (Biran 1994). Furnace design varied during the Iron 1, though the use of bellows and clay tuyeres seemed fairly consistent. At this time, most of the copper came from abroad, primarily Cyprus.

The Jordan Valley played a critical role in the regional economy of the tenth to eighth centuries B.C.E. Recent research at the site of Tel Hammeh (as-Zarqa) in Jordan has revealed the remains of an iron-smelting operation, evidenced by slag, ore, tuyeres, and molten and vitrified clay. Pottery production at the beginning of the Iron 2 became more standardized (Aharoni 1982; Dever 2003b), a trend best exemplified by the ubiquitous pithos jars, long considered a trademark of Israelite material culture. By the eighth century B.C.E., the industry became even more standardized as pottery was mass-produced (Zimhoni 1997).

Economic Organization

Economic organization during the Iron 2 reached a level of complexity not seen before in the southern Levant. The Israelite monarchs may have made use of corvée labor for their large construction projects, perhaps drafting lowland farmers whose primary occupation was seasonal (Holladay 2003). It appears that some form of public works departments or conscripted labor system was implemented to carry out Solomon's alleged building projects, for 1 Kings (5:27–33) reports about 30,000 laborers, 70,000 porters, 80,000 quarriers, and 3,300 administrators and officials involved with the project (Rainey 1996). Holladay (2003) suggests that labor may have been contracted in several ways, following perhaps a system of social debt enacted through practices such as feasting and remuneration of brideprice. It is also possible that landholders could lease property in exchange for labor.

Questions concerning whether the state collected taxes, and if so, how, have also been raised. Large communal storage facilities were generally rather rare at this time (Holladay 1992), but Israel Finkelstein (1988) has argued that the various surplus goods (for example, grain, wine, oil, and dried fruit) kept in exterior storage pits found at sites such as 'Izbet Sartah were subject to taxation. According to Holladay (2003), people would have paid taxes, perhaps via tithing, but the families who produced these goods maintained individual control of their stores, selling them privately in local markets or in bulk to professional buyers, who took them ultimately to international markets.

The nuclear family remained the basic economic unit during the ninth and eighth centuries B.C.E. (Netzer 1992), and families continued to control agricultural production, employing diversified subsistence strategies. However, in time, ownership became increasingly concentrated in fewer hands, leading to a rise in agricultural specialization. It is important to note that the ecological situation in the highlands, though allowing for productive dry-farming and horticulture, did not necessarily lend itself to extensive, government-controlled agricultural production (particularly in comparison to Mesopotamia and Egypt). Even in the time of the Israelite and Judean states, the family-based agricultural system remained the primary mode of production for most people (with the exception of royal wineries).

THE ECONOMY OF PHILISTIA IN THE IRON 2

Craft Production

Economic life in Philistia became increasingly complex over the course of the Iron Age as industries related to the production of horticultural goods developed in tandem with the state. Although many people, particularly in the countryside, continued to produce independently to meet their household needs, centralized production developed in the cities. In a ceramic workshop excavated at Ashdod, every step of the production process was carried out in well-defined areas. In a large courtyard, archaeologists found the remains of storerooms and workshops where potters prepared the raw clay and threw their ceramics on wheels (Dothan and Dothan 1992). Nearby was a row of un-roofed structures with kilns inside. The kilns had lower chambers that were set in the ground and an upper portion that had to be removed by destroying it af-ter each use. Successive layers in the lower chamber suggest the kilns were used over a long period of time. A range of pottery types were produced along with ceramic cult figurines, but it is not clear if the temple controlled the shop or commissioned the work from a privately run shop.

In some cases, there was in-house production for the royal court, as in the winery at Ashqelon during the seventh century B.C.E. (Stager 1991). A large ashlar masonry building housed a series of storage units as well as pressing rooms, with multiple presses that were lined with fine cement and plaster (Stager 1996). This shop functioned as the royal winery for Agá, the last Philis-tine king to rule the independent city-state prior to its destruction by Neb-uchadnezzar in 604 B.C.E. (as known from the Babylonian Chronicle).

Nowhere is the process of integration and centralization of economic activi-ties more evident than at Tel Miqne–Ekron, which emerged as a major regional producer of olive oil under Assyrian rule. Excavations at the site have uncov-ered not fewer than 100 oil presses along the perimeter of the city, just inside the fortifications. The volume of production, estimated through experimental archaeology, was vast. Based on the amount of oil produced in reconstructed press installations multiplied by the number of installations found at Tel Miqne–Ekron, Seymour Gitin (1995) has calculated that some 290,000 U.S. gal-lons of oil, filling 48,000 24-liter jars could have been produced each year. Ulti-mately, the oil would be bottled in jars with inscriptions indicating their con-tents, *smn* (oil), and their volume, *bt*, a standardized measurement of roughly 24 liters, though some bt-containers held up to 32 liters (Gitin 1995).

The most important clues regarding the reach of this industry are, of course, the ones that do not survive: the olive trees and the laborers. It is estimated that an operation of this size would have required roughly 12,500 acres of land and a labor force of some 2,000 people. Based on all of this evidence, Gitin (1993) has argued that Ekron was the biggest supplier in the region, if not the entire Near East at the time.

Oil production, however, was possible only four months out of the year, and thus the overall productivity of the facility was optimized through the manu-facture of textiles during the remainder of the year. Both operations were car-ried out in a series of factory buildings, each of which had three rooms. The middle room of each building contained a four-horned altar, demonstrating the connection between production and cult (Gitin 1995).

Trade Relations

The Philistines and Phoenicians seem to have benefited from a situation of eco-nomic cooperation. Trade between the two groups is evident, though the ques-tion of the interface between them on the coast somewhere south of Dor, a Phoenician city from the end of the eleventh century B.C.E., is one that requires further research. It is also interesting to consider the distinction between for-mal exchange and cultural influence; for instance, the Phoenician style is ap-

5.7 Remains of the olive pressing industry at Miqne-Ekron (Courtesy of E. Cohen, Tel Miqne–Ekron Publications Project)

parent in examples of silver jewelry from Tel Miqne–Ekron, but it is not clear whether this reflects goods obtained via trade or an influence on the local smiths themselves (Golani and Sass 1998).

Based at coastal centers such as Dor, Akko, Sidon, and Tyre, the Phoenicians had extensive contacts with people from the Aegean. The earliest examples of Greek pottery come from tenth-century Tyre (Waldbaum 1994), while Geometric Period pottery from the East Greek Islands, such as Rhodes, Samos, and Lesbos, began in the latter half of the eighth century and increased thereafter. In the mid-seventh century, the earliest Proto-Corinthian material appeared. Phoenician storage jars have been found in seventh-century-B.C.E. contexts at Ashqelon and Ekron.

The Assyrian Impact

The economic impact of the Neo-Assyrian expansion into the southern Levant must not be underestimated. The Neo-Assyrians' interest in the region was most likely motivated by their increasing need for a steady supply of both raw material and finished goods, especially luxury items (Gitin 1995). It is clear from the example of the Tel Miqne–Ekron oil industry that they envisioned the potential for mass production in the eastern end of Philistia and exploited the opportunity fully.

In order to facilitate the economic assimilation of disparate regions and peoples into their rapidly expanding empire, the Neo-Assyrians aspired to establish a universal form of currency, and it appears that silver provided the solution. According to Amir Golani and Benjamin Sass (1998), two separate hoards of silver from Tel Miqne–Ekron, composed of damaged jewelry and cut pieces (*Hacksilber*), represent caches of currency. Assyrian economic expansionism may have been motivated in part by the perpetual demand for new sources of silver.

Economic development in Philistia, and the far-reaching contacts they established, reached its zenith in the early seventh century B.C.E. Toward the end of the century, however, this economic bubble seems to have burst. As the Neo-Assyrians' interests were redirected eastward, their economic influence declined in the region. Egyptians were quick to try to fill the void, but they do not appear to have been very successful. Oil production at Tel Miqne–Ekron declined significantly immediately thereafter. Approximately one century later, the Neo-Babylonians would conquer virtually all of the southern Levant, exiling Judahite and Philistine alike.

SUGGESTED READING

Bar-Yosef, Ofer, and Anatoly Khazanov, eds. 1992. *Pastoralism in the Levant: Archaeological Materials in Anthropological Perspectives.* Madison, WI: Prehistory Press.

Biran, A. 1994. *Biblical Dan.* Jerusalem: Israel Exploration Society.

Dayton, J. 1971. "The Problem of Tin in the Ancient World." *World Archaeology* 3: 49–70.

Epstein, C. 1998. *The Chalcolithic Culture of the Golan.* Jerusalem: Israel Antiquities Authority.

Finkelstein, Israel, and Ram Gophna. 1993. "Settlement, Demographic, and Economic Patterns in the Highlands of Palestine in the Chalcolithic and Early Bronze Periods and the Beginning of Urbanism." *Bulletin of the American Schools of Oriental Research* 289: 1–22.

Gitin, Seymour, ed. 1995. *Recent Excavations in Israel: A View to the West.* Dubuque, IA: Kendall Hunt.

Golden, Jonathan. Forthcoming. *The Dawn of the Metal Age.* London: Continuum.

Gophna, R. 2002. "Elusive Anchorage Points along the Israel Littoral and the Egyptian-Canaanite Maritime Route during the Early Bronze Age I." In *Egyptian and Canaanite Interaction during the Fourth–Third Millennium B.C.E.,* edited by E. van den Brink and T. Levy, 418–421. London: Leicester University Press.

Grigson, Carolyn. 2003. "Plough and Pasture in the Early Economy of the Southern Levant." In *The Archaeology of Society in the Holy Land,* 3d ed., edited by T. E. Levy, 226–244. New York: Facts on File.

Hesse, B. 1986. "Animal Use at Tel Miqne–Ekron in the Bronze Age and Iron Age." *Bulletin of the American Schools of Oriental Research* 264: 17–27.

Maeir, A. 2000. "The Political and Economic Status of MB II Hazor and the MB II Trade: An Inter- and Intra-Regional View." *Palestine Exploration Quarterly* 132: 37–57.

Marcus, E. 2002. "Early Seafaring and Maritime Activity in the Southern Levant from Prehistory through the Third Millennium B.C.E." In *Egyptian and Canaanite Interaction during the Fourth–Third Millennium B.C.E.*, edited by E. van den Brink and T. Levy, 403–417. London: Leicester University Press.

Piggot, Vincent C., ed. 1999. *The Archaeometallurgy of the Asian Old World.* Philadelphia: University Museum, University of Pennsylvania.

Rosenfeld, Amnon, Shimon Ilani, and Michael Dvorachek. 1997. "Bronze Alloys from Canaan during the Middle Bronze Age." *Journal of Archaeological Science* 24: 857–864.

CHAPTER 6

Social Organization

CHALCOLITHIC PERIOD

Settlement Patterns

During the Chalcolithic period, people settled in a variety of environments, with populations concentrated in the northern Negev and Golan as well as in and around the Jordan Valley. Any discussion of settlement patterns during this time must also take into account a sizable transhumant population. On the margins of the desert and zone of settlement, a symbiotic relationship developed between settled peoples and pastoral nomads, a recurrent pattern seen throughout the history of the ancient and modern Near East (Levy 1992; Grigson 2003). As a result of this direct economic interdependence, mobile groups interacted with the villagers on many levels (for example, social and political).

Village Life

Many people lived in small villages made up of single-family homes. Houses were built of mud brick, often with stone foundations, and followed the "broad room" plan, characterized by a rectangular structure with an entrance on the long side. The floors were often coated with a layer of mud plaster and resurfaced on a fairly regular basis. Subterranean structures built at Shiqmim and the Beer Sheva sites may have been used as dwellings, but it is also plausible that they were used for storage, refuse, burial, or perhaps even refuge during times of conflict. In addition to hearths and grinding stones used for domestic food production, the discovery of loom weights and spindle whorls demonstrates that people engaged in various household crafts. People continued to use bone awls and other tools for various tasks, as well as fan-shaped scrapers for tanning hides. Various goods were stored in pits in house floors and in small alleys just outside the home.

Villages such as Ghassul, Gilat, and Shiqmim grew to a substantial size, making limited use of town-planning methods, with houses aligned along narrow streets. At Shiqmim and Abu Matar, it appears that a number of people engaged in small-scale metal production in and around the courtyards of their homes. At Abu Matar, production activities would ultimately become concentrated in several workshop areas.

Social Organization

Several lines of evidence point to disparities in wealth during the Chalcolithic period. To begin, only a limited number of people seemed to have access to luxury goods such as ivory pendants, figurines, and metal scepters. The development of a prestige-oriented metal industry, in particular, seems to reflect the expression of power relations and the emergence of rising elites concerned with ways of legitimizing their authority (Levy et al. 1991; Levy and Shalev 1989). Investment in the development of metal technologies required sponsorship. It is possible that resources became concentrated in increasingly fewer hands as a result of control over large herds and/or agricultural surpluses by landholders, with luxury goods representing converted wealth.

The mortuary evidence from the Chalcolithic period also reflects a certain level of social hierarchy. Small children were still buried in the vicinity of the home, usually in the alleys between houses, often in jars. For the first time, adults were buried in clearly designated cemeteries outside of the village itself. The extensive cemetery at Shiqmim included a number of secondary burials involving small circular structures. It is possible that greater investment was made in some of these grave rings (Levy and Alon 1985), though burial goods were generally modest.

The most compelling evidence for social hierarchy during the Chalcolithic era has just begun to emerge over the past few decades with the discovery of a series of wealthy cave tombs. The Peqi'in burial cave included numerous individuals with a demographic distribution and grave goods that suggest it was used over a long period of time by an extended family or kin group with access to considerable wealth. Another noteworthy tomb has been found at Nahal Qanah, where archaeologists discovered a range of expensive items, including the earliest gold in the region (Gopher and Tsuk 1996).

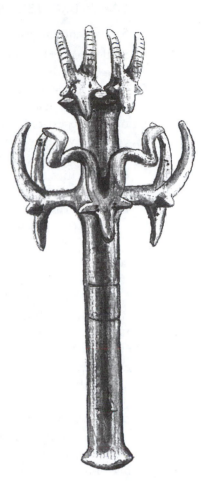

6.1 The "Ibex standard" from the Nahal Mishmar hoard (Drawing by J. Golden; adapted from Bar-Adon 1980)

It is not clear what happened at the end of the Chalcolithic period, but this developed social system appears to have collapsed. David Ussishkin (1980) has invoked a social crisis theory suggesting that the Nahal Mishmar hoard represents the deliberate hiding of booty, belonging perhaps to the nearby temple at Ein Gedi, but others have disputed this interpretation (Moorey 1988). The maceheads of Nahal Mishmar indicate a rise in the manufacture of weapons, which may reflect an increase in conflict toward the end of the period. In any event, by the middle of the fourth millennium B.C.E., roughly two-thirds of the Chalcolithic sites were completely abandoned, with many never to be inhabited again.

EARLY BRONZE AGE

Settlement Patterns

Settlement patterns changed significantly at the beginning of the Early Bronze Age, when the population gravitated toward more fertile areas of the Mediterranean climatic zone on the coastal plain, in the Shephelah, and in the central hill country (Gophna 1974; Broshi 1986; Gophna and Portugali 1988). In the north, most people lived in small hamlets (5–20 dunams) and unfortified agricultural villages (40–70 dunams) as well as in large towns such as Kabri, Kedesh, and Tel el-Far'ah North (80–100+ dunams). There were also a handful of large cities reaching 200 dunams, such as Tel Dan, Beth Yerah, and Shimron. In some cases, the central town was surrounded by a handful of satellite villages and rural farmsteads (thus, a peer-polity system with a three-tier site hierarchy) (Esse 1989; Joffe 1991; Ben-Tor 1992; Finkelstein 1993, 2003).

During the second part of the Early Bronze Age (EB2, 3050–2650 B.C.E.), the southern Levant witnessed a substantial growth in population, with a notable increase in the number of towns and villages (some 260 sites in western Canaan). The most densely settled regions were the coastal plain, the central foothills, the Shephelah, and the Jordan Valley, as well as the highlands and valleys of the northern region (Helms 1987; Greenberg 1990; Portugali and Gophna 1993; Tubb 2002). Assuming a population density of 100 people per acre, there was an estimated population of some 150,000 in the southern Levant, with roughly half the population living in the hill country by this time (Gophna and Portugali 1988; Broshi 1986). As in the Chalcolithic period, a sizable transhumant population would have circulated around the settlements.

In the south, a regional center of roughly 100 dunams emerged at Arad. The EB2 city was enclosed by a vast wall system with circular towers, while a number of monumental buildings were constructed inside (Amiran and Ilan 1996; Amiran et al. 1978). By the third part of the Early Bronze Age (EB3, 2650–2200 B.C.E.), however, Arad was abandoned as power shifted northward toward Tel Halif (Esse 1989). Another great city that flourished during the EB3 was Yarmuth. In the north, large urban centers surrounded by massive fortification systems with rectangular towers developed at Megiddo, Ta'anach, and Tel el-Far'ah North (Miroschedji 1993). Hazor, first settled in the EB2, emerged as one of the most important cities in the north by the EB3, when it served as the center of a large polity, controlling much of the surrounding countryside while maintaining active trade ties with the cities of Syria.

Evidence for social change can be seen once again during the EB2–3 transition. Ruth Amiran (1989) has attributed this to an influx of peoples from the north, while Israel Finkelstein (1995) has argued that it was the result of widespread social upheaval toward the end of the EB2. In either event, by the beginning of the EB3 a revival in urban culture was under way. New cities were established in the Golan, Galilee, and northern valleys, though many of the rural sites were not resettled. By this time, Megiddo had become the primary center in the Jezreel Valley, undergoing major renovations of public architecture that reflect a resurgence of investment in public works (Esse 1989; Kenyon

1958). Renewed urbanism is also in evidence at northern Jordan Valley centers such as Hazor, Beth Shean, Dan, and Beit Yerah (Finkelstein 1995).

Population

The origins of the Early Bronze Age population are unclear. Traditionally, it has been thought that southern Palestine was all but deserted at the end of the Chalcolithic period and that the land was repopulated by groups spilling over from cities of the north. It is more likely that many of the indigenous people remained in the region, resorting to transhumance and land-squatting, while thriving Chalcolithic centers were abandoned. Both continuity and change can be detected in the material culture of the early EB1, suggesting that locals and newcomers comingled, forming the basis for the urban population of the EB2–3.

If people did migrate from the north, they were physically indistinguishable, at least to the archaeologist of today, from the existing southern population. Well-preserved human remains from the Early Bronze Age are rare, but the limited assemblage indicates a generally consistent Mediterranean type for the entire southern Levant, and based on limited genetic studies the southern population is indistinguishable from those to the north and east (Smith 2002). There was little change in physical body type from preceding periods, with males averaging 168 cm (about 5 ft., 6 in.) and females 155 cm (about 5 ft., 1 in.) in height.

City Life, Domestic Life

The larger urban centers of the Early Bronze Age are characterized by features such as town planning and monumental architecture that is not usually present in the smaller communities. To accommodate their growing populations, large cities such as Tel el-Far'ah North, Megiddo, and Khirbet Zeraquon in the Jordan Valley employed the grid system, a key component of urban development that enables more efficient use of space. At Arad, the city was divided into distinct precincts, such as the residential zone and a nearby public area where monumental buildings were located; whether these were used as elite dwellings or temples is unclear. At both Jericho and Megiddo, distinct cultic complexes were demarcated by enclosure, or *tenemos*, walls.

In southern Canaan, a style of domestic architecture known as the "Arad house" was common during the early part of the Early Bronze Age. Arad houses had a "broad-room" plan, usually built with stone foundations and mud-brick upper walls, and with the floor sunken below the street level. Most houses had a single unit, with a central post to support the roof, and sometimes a small additional room for storage. Low benches often lined the interior walls of the main room, sometimes extending into larger platforms. These could have been used for a variety of purposes, including workspace or sleeping. The main room often had a small storage bin, in some cases lined with flat stones. A unique and informative find was a ceramic model of a typical Arad house discovered at Arad itself (Amiran and Ilan 1992).

In the northern region, curvilinear and rectilinear architectural elements were more common. Groups of oval-shaped houses, roughly 50 square meters (540 sq. ft.) in area, have been excavated at En Shadud, Tel Teo, and Jebel Mutawwaq (Braun 1989; Golani 1999). At Yiftahel, the houses usually comprised one small room with a courtyard. There are also examples of houses with multiple rooms that either housed large extended families or belonged to wealthy owners. Apsidal buildings, a style employed at Byblos and thought to derive from the north, appear to have been built at Aphek, Jawa, Megiddo, and Mezer. Buildings with rounded corners may represent a transition between the "sausage-shaped" structures of the early EB1 and the rectilinear angled-corner architecture of the EB2. According to Amir Golani (1999), this "hybrid form" reflects an attempt to maintain the curvilinear style in the face of the growing emphasis on efficient use of space that came with urbanization.

Social Organization

There are some indications that a system of social ranking was in effect during the Early Bronze Age, though whether there was "institutionalized" social stratification according to descent is less clear (Esse 1989). As noted above, disparities in wealth and class are evident in the size and types of people's homes. At Arad, there was considerable variation in house size, and the larger and smaller homes tended to form clusters, suggesting distinct neighborhoods (Amiran et al. 1978). The appearance of luxury residences at a number of sites in the EB2–3 (for example, at Megiddo) could reflect the emergence of a ruling elite, a phenomenon also typical of the shift from a ranked to a stratified society.

Douglas Esse (1989) has pointed out that seminomadic and sedentary peoples would have had different forms of social organization, with pastoral groups operating as segmentary societies. Much of the pastoral population, which had thrived in tandem with the agricultural societies at the beginning of the Early Bronze Age, was absorbed into the urban culture as it took hold at the end of the EB1. Studies of modern pastoral groups suggest that they would have had a rather different social structure, probably some form of kin-based tribal organization, from people in the emerging cities, who would have been more oriented toward a ranked society where kinship was less important. It is unclear, however, how these different forms of social organization were negotiated when the populations generally merged.

An increase in social complexity can be inferred from evidence for the production and exchange of luxury goods. New classes of bureaucrats, administrators, landholders, and merchants arose, adopting the use of "Egyptianized" seals and emulating Egyptian social practices. In at least one instance, there seems to be an attempt to re-create Egyptian burial practices in Canaan. Excavations at Halif Terrace have uncovered a large subterranean structure with a narrow ramp flanked by stone walls that descends into a large chamber (see Fig. 6.2). This chamber was originally a natural cave over which a stone superstructure was built. This style of construction is unique in the region, though it recalls Egyptian-style burials such as the royal tombs at Helwan (Levy et al. 1997).

6.2   The Egyptian-style "tomb" at Halif Terrace, view from the base of the ramp (J. Golden)

Although the Halif example may represent some form of elite tomb, the recognition of linear descent groups is evident in the consistent reuse of family tombs spanning several generations at cemeteries such as Bab edh-Dra and at *nawamis* (circular stone-built burial chambers) in the Sinai. The value of grave goods in the tombs varied, though poor preservation of the human remains precludes the identification of patterns based on age and gender. On the whole, luxury goods and various trappings used to denote wealth and status were somewhat rare during the Early Bronze Age.

INTERMEDIATE BRONZE AGE

Toward the end of the Early Bronze Age, the urban culture of southern Canaan began to decline. One city after another was either abandoned or depopulated. This period was followed by two centuries known as the Intermediate Bronze Age (IBA, 2200–2000 B.C.E.), when many people returned to pastoralism and nomadic alternatives throughout the region (Finkelstein 1991).

Although Talia Shay (1983) has argued that the Intermediate Bronze Age was essentially an egalitarian society with little evidence for pronounced social gaps, a more comprehensive view of the period's burial practices suggests that some form of social hierarchy was in effect (Palumbo 1987; Dever 2003a).

Gaetano Palumbo (1987), performing cluster analysis on the same data as Shay (1983), reported that there was variation in both the types of grave goods and body treatment, concluding that this was not an egalitarian society.

The cemeteries, in many cases isolated from any nearby settlement, were utilized by successive generations of nomadic and seminomadic tribes. It is likely that social groupings were organized according to kinship and tribal relations. Recently, a number of Intermediate Bronze Age shaft tombs were excavated at the site of Shuni, where ceramics and metal goods link the site with cultures of the Syrian Coast (Peilstöcker 2002).

MIDDLE BRONZE AGE

Settlement Patterns

Middle Bronze Age culture began as a semisedentary, tribal society that ultimately underwent a process of reurbanization, emerging as a culture of great city-states. Again, there was a significant shift in settlement patterns, as fewer than one-third of the Early Bronze Age sites were resettled (Tel Poran and Megiddo are notable exceptions). However, the rapidly rising population required fertile land, and during the second part of the Middle Bronze Age (MB2, c. 1800–1650 B.C.E.), more than 300 new sites were established throughout the region. This was the first significant population of the Mediterranean coastal plain, as communities were founded along coastal drainage systems.

There was also a population surge in parts of the Jordan Valley such as at the site of Hawran. According to regional surveys conducted in the central highlands, this area was steadily repopulated over the course of the Middle Bronze Age, with the creation of roughly 250 settlements and 30 cemeteries. A string of important settlements, including Tel el-Ajjul, Tel el-Far'ah South, Tel Malhata, and Tel Masos, was also established in the northern Negev along the Wadi Beersheva–Wadi Gaza later in the period. Although there were a total of some 500–600 settled communities during the Middle Bronze Age, seasonal encampments and cemeteries not related to any settlements also suggest a sizable transhumant population, especially in the steppelike southern foothills.

The population in the southern Levant was roughly 100,000 for the first part of the Middle Bronze Age (MB1, 2000–1800 B.C.E.) and 140,000 for the MB2 (Broshi 1986). Although the overall size of the population was not much different from that of the Early Bronze Age at its height (EB2–3), there were significant shifts in the pattern of settlement. The lowland regions, particularly the northern valleys, were the most densely populated, accommodating more than one-third of the population. A sizable population also lived in the foothills, though, as during the Iron Age, most of the highland population (roughly 75 percent) was concentrated in the north, while semisedentary groups of pastoral nomads dominated the foothills south of Shechem.

Population

The relatively sudden appearance of new cultural elements in Canaan at the beginning of the Middle Bronze Age suggests an influx of peoples into the region. In some instances, the parallels between the material culture of Canaan and areas to the north (especially Syria) are quite striking. Although this trend is certainly attributable in part to the exchange of various goods, several lines of evidence, including osteological evidence, suggest human migration (Smith 2002).

New architectural styles and techniques that appeared in Canaan also suggest the arrival of new peoples. One interesting example was the mud-brick arch. This feature, first used earlier in the drier regions of Syria, was untenable when attempted in the more humid southern Levantine environment (Ilan 1995). This and other Syrian architectural traditions with a history dating back to the Early Bronze Age appeared rather suddenly in the Middle Bronze Age, another indication that these ideas originally evolved outside of Canaan. In addition, new burial practices appeared in Canaan side by side with older ones, suggesting that new arrivals had settled in the region, maintaining their own customs (Ilan 1995; Tubb 1983).

Linguistic evidence also reflects the influence of new peoples in Canaan. Specifically, Hurrian names more at home in Syria first appeared in seventeenth-century-B.C.E. inscriptions from Gezer, Hebron, Shechem, and probably Hazor as well (Shaffer 1988, 1970). By the fifteenth century, the number of Hurrians had increased significantly, with names appearing frequently at sites such as Ta'anach and Shechem. The Egyptian pharaoh Thutmose III and his successors actually referred to the southern Levant as "Hurru" at this time. In most cases, the various peoples appear to have lived side by side.

Based on the osteological evidence, researchers estimate a death rate of about 4.5 percent per annum for cities of the Middle Bronze Age. Group tombs excavated at Jericho that may represent singular incidents of mass burials have given rise to theories that an epidemic may have afflicted this small city's inhabitants.

City Life, Domestic Life

By the early MB2, urbanism was once again fully under way, and a growing number of people flocked to large cities. At the same time, the number of smaller villages and hamlets was much greater in the MB2, suggesting that people generally lived in either large cities or rural settings, with relatively few options in between. The cities can generally be divided into a few regional centers and large gateway communities, subregional centers, small provincial villages, and farmsteads of the hinterlands.

Hazor was the largest city, with a population of more than 15,000. Other large cities included Gezer, with roughly 10,000 citizens, and Ajjul, Aphek, and Lachish, with populations in excess of 5,000 each. Often these sites served as the centers for large city-states; for instance, Ashqelon, with up to 15,000 people living within its ramparts, had influence over an area of roughly 500 square kilometers (190 sq. mi.) as well as over a number of smaller sites (Stager 1991; Finkelstein 1992). Tel Dor, further north on the coastal plain, commanded an area of more than 700 square kilometers (270 sq. mi.), with close to 30 smaller sites and some 7,000 people. Two factors, however, must be considered when calculating these population estimates. For one, figures based on gross site size may overrepresent the actual number of city dwellers because the earthen ramparts themselves, which account for much of the actual site size, were not occupied (Broshi 1986; Finkelstein 1992a). Furthermore, population estimates should also take into account the large numbers of semisedentary people, who, though less visible in the archaeological record, no doubt played a major role in the social organization of the Canaanite city-states.

The new form of enclosed "rampart settlement" began to appear throughout the countryside during the Middle Bronze Age. Sloping earthen ramparts, square in plan, surrounded cities both large and small, giving these mound sites their unique form today. In some cities, such as Dan, Gezer, and Yavne-Yam, impressive gate structures were built into the rampart systems. At Hazor and Shechem, the gate area would have been bustling with activity and a focal point of city life, as indicated by the size of this space and the large roads worthy of chariot traffic that radiated from it. At Shechem, a large central marketplace was excavated in one section of the town.

Archaeologists' knowledge of city layout is hampered by the fact that many Middle Bronze Age sites have seen centuries of subsequent occupation, rendering the excavation of broad, horizontal areas difficult. Nonetheless, limited exposures have revealed evidence for urban design with well-planned grid systems and distinct districts, a model that probably originated in Syrian cities such as Ebla. Large-scale public buildings were often aligned at right angles, creating streets and walkways while defining open piazzas. The long streets of Tel el-Ajjul ("City II") divided parts of the city into distinct districts, including religious and administrative precincts as well as an industrial quarter.

There were, of course, residential neighborhoods as well. At Megiddo, parallel streets on the eastern portion of the mound demarcated blocks of residential units, providing one of the best examples of a residential neighborhood. At Tel Dan, new homes were constructed up against the site's upper slope as the growing population required additional housing. In some cases, houses lined cobbled streets 2 meters (about 6.5 ft.) wide. Middle Bronze Age houses were generally designed with several small rooms surrounding a central courtyard. At least some of the buildings had a second story that served as the domicile, while the first floor could have been used for a variety of purposes (for example, as a storefront or pen). At Jericho, several homes contained loom weights and saddle querns, suggesting that families engaged in production for immediate consumption right inside the home; in some cases, families ran small "cottage industries."

Social Organization

Archaeological evidence from the Middle Bronze Age suggests increasing disparities in wealth and status during the period. In some cases, this can be inferred from residential/domestic contexts. A number of mud-brick houses were excavated at Jericho, and though the majority were small and irregular in design, others were considerably larger and more elaborate. In some cities, whole neighborhoods reflect varying wealth and/or status. For example, several of the larger settlements had lower and upper cities, with the latter, often called "citadels," reserved for the homes of the rich and famous, and in some

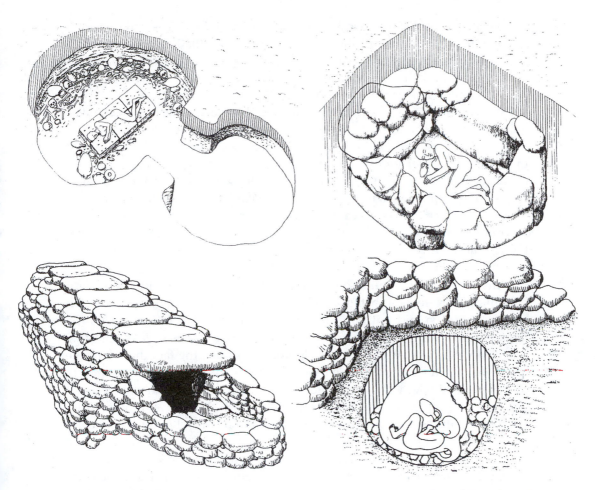

6.3   Four different styles of MBA tombs and burials (Drawing courtesy of David Ilan; adapted from "The Dawn of Internationalism: The Middle Bronze Age." 2003a. In *The Archaeology of Society in the Holy Land*, 3d ed., edited by T. E. Levy, 297–319. New York: Facts on File.)

cases, administrative and/or religious activities. Cylinder seals were used by a limited number of people, most likely the elite (Ilan 2003).

Middle Bronze Age social organization is best understood through the mortuary evidence: human remains and grave goods. Both intramural and extramural burials have been observed. In some cases, people buried their dead within urban areas beneath house floors and in courtyards. There were two major types of tombs: (1) multiple burials, with individuals buried roughly one at a time over an extended period of time; and (2) mass burials, representing a single event. Examples of continuous burials have been excavated at Tel Dan, Gibeon, and Jericho. These tombs, each with an average of twenty individuals, were probably used by nuclear families over the course of several generations, suggesting the importance of descent groups. At Hazor, one large tomb appears to have been used for a period of at least fifty years. The composition of the tomb's population in terms of age and sex suggests that two or three generations of one nuclear family were buried there. The group burials were more common toward the latter part of the Middle Bronze Age, which may reflect the increasing importance of group affiliation and social hierarchy. Contemporary texts from Syria indicate that descent groups and lineages there played a critical role in power structures.

Differences in status and wealth can also be observed, as there was considerable variation in the methods of burial afforded different people. The primary tomb types of the Middle Bronze Age were jar burials (for infants), simple pit or cist burials, shaft tombs, rock-cut chamber tombs, and masonry cist and chamber tombs (see Fig. 6.3). To some extent, these various tomb types correspond to differences in age. At Tel Dan, for instance, the cist tombs were used for children three to twelve years old, while the masonry chamber tombs were reserved for adolescents and adults. The masonry chamber tombs were probably the most costly to construct and would have been reserved for elites and wealthy individuals.

Differences in status can also be inferred from some of these tombs. At Jericho, there were several instances where the body of a male, perhaps a clan leader, had been laid out on a mud-brick platform and, in one case, on a wooden bed. The number of grave goods, however, varies little, suggesting that differences in wealth were not significant. Rather, the fact that all of the tombs contained a significant number of offerings implies that the community in general had attained a certain level of affluence. The inclusion of grave goods (for example, small juglets and jewelry) with children and infants suggests that status was ascribed through birth. At Tel el-Ajjul (Group 6), a child buried with gold ornaments under the corner of Palace 2 may have been a member of a noble or royal family. At Ashqelon, a tomb dated to approximately 1500 B.C.E. contained the remains of an adolescent girl. The tomb comprised a mud-brick-lined vault covered with wooden boughs and plaster, and it had grave goods including two toggle pins, three Egyptian scarabs, and an ivory roundel found on her midsection. There were also base-ring juglets from Cyprus and two bowls, one of which may have contained a cut of lamb or goat and a small bird (dove or partridge).

A rare burial custom of the period was the so-called "warrior burial." These burials, reserved for adult males, often included a variety of bronze weapons, such as ribbed daggers and axes of the fenestrated and duckbill varieties; in rare cases, horses were included. The warrior burials may in fact reflect the existence of a distinct class of individuals who had attained status for achievements such as bravery in battle; alternatively, the military motif may have been a way of representing the higher status ascribed to members of certain lineages. Although women were included in the wealthy group tombs, evidence for individual women of distinction does not appear. Ora Negbi (1966) has argued that gender distinctions can be detected in the varying burial kits (for example, at the Temple at Byblos). Among the pastoral tribes, evidence for high-status males can be inferred from the "Tale of Sinuhe," where an Egyptian sojourner in Canaan relates, "Much also came to me because of the love of me; for he had made me chief of a tribe in the best part of his land" (Lichtheim

1973, 227). Thus, pastoral tribes may have had a sociopolitical structure independent of the city-state based on the power of tribal chiefs.

The "Tale of Sinuhe" also describes some of the luxuries bestowed upon the "chief of a tribe," providing an interesting window on the practice of feasting among Canaanite elites. One passage reports, "Loaves were made for me daily, and wine as daily fare, cooked meat, roast fowl, as well as desert game. For they snared for me and laid it before me, in addition to the catch of my hounds. Many sweets were made for me, and milk dishes of all kinds" (Lichtheim 1973, 227).

Social complexity peaked at the end of the Middle Bronze Age (MB2b, c. 1650–1550 B.C.E.), but this system may have led to its own undoing thereafter. A number of scholars have argued that the diversion of resources in response to demand by both the temple and bureaucracy for luxury goods (for example, tin used to make bronze) and the construction of monumental public works may have put an excessive strain on resources. By about 1450 B.C.E., virtually every urban center, especially those in the central highlands, was either substantially depopulated or abandoned altogether, in some cases apparently destroyed in conflagration. This process of urban decay, which affected all of Canaan, may have taken as long as a century or more to play out. Egyptian interference as described in contemporary texts may have hastened this process, but the stability of Canaanite cities was already threatened by internal factors.

LATE BRONZE AGE

Settlement Patterns

Rapid change at the end of the Middle Bronze Age had a profound impact on social life in Canaan during the centuries that followed (Bunimovitz 2003). There was a sharp decline in urbanism coupled with broad-scale demographic changes, an important trend being the rise, yet again, of transhumance. Major urban centers such as Gezer, Lachish, and Megiddo were still occupied at this time but were much smaller in scale than during the Middle Bronze Age and exerted less control over surrounding rural populations. However, any sort of "social crises" at the end of the Middle Bronze Age would have been experienced differently in various regions.

Population

The core of the Canaanite population, though smaller than in the Middle Bronze Age, remained largely intact, as suggested by continuity in material culture (for example, the ceramic assemblage). At the same time, there were incursions of new peoples from several directions, and the population was more diverse than ever. The flow of Hittites from the north increased; people from Cyprus and the Aegean began to arrive in significant numbers; and the Egyptians, who held political control over most of Canaan, became a dominant force in the region.

It appears that the Canaanite identity itself was threatened in the aftermath of Middle Bronze Age collapse and repeated Egyptian incursions. Tel el-

Yehudiyeh, a strong cultural marker of the Hyksos, disappeared entirely from Canaanite pottery assemblages at the beginning of the Late Bronze Age, a development that may reflect animosity that the ascendant Egyptians had toward the "wretched Asiatics" associated with negative memories of Hyksos rule. Certainly there was a sizable population of Egyptians living in Canaan during the Late Bronze Age, many being government officials and important commercial players. Yet, it is often difficult to distinguish between this foreign, Egyptian contingent and the many local elites of Canaanite society who adopted their cultural trappings and aspired to emulate their social habits. The Aegean influence began as an adoption of style, perhaps a cosmopolitan fad of the day. At Tel el-Ajjul, Aegean pottery was coveted as exotica for grave offerings but was rare in domestic contexts, that is, not used for daily activities. Overall, much of Aegean material may have come to Canaan as a result of the Egyptian taste for these goods (Steel 2002).

In the north, the Hittite influence can also be observed at this time. After the collapse of the Hittite Empire at the end of the thirteenth century B.C.E., refugees entered Palestine via the northern coast. This is evident in the frequency of Hittite names as well as in the mortuary data. Double-pithos burials, a style ubiquitous in the contemporary Hittite Anatolia, have been found at a few thirteenth- and twelfth-century-B.C.E. sites such as Nami and Zeror, where some sixty were excavated. Hittites also made their way into the Jordan Valley, with their influence observable at Dan and Sa'idiyeh (Biran 1994; Tubb 2002).

City Life, Domestic Life

City life was not abandoned altogether, and despite depopulation, many Late Bronze Age settlements retained their urban character. At Tel el-Far'ah South, a massive building of roughly 550 square meters (5,920 sq. ft.) was located in the northern section of the city. Some degree of urbanism can also be observed at Ta'anach, for instance, with its large "West Building."

The structures called "patrician houses"—the Late Bronze Age equivalent of luxury homes—have been excavated at sites throughout Canaan, including Aphek, Megiddo, Ta'anach, and Tel Batash (Timna). Several examples from Batash (Str. IX-VII) each had a large pillared hall, storage rooms, and a staircase leading to the second floor (Kelm and Mazar 1982). One of these buildings had in its final Late Bronze Age phase (Str. VII) two rows of stone bases on which stood wooden columns, a style that would become popular in the succeeding Iron Age. These houses generally included an open courtyard or atrium.

Again, the region saw a return to seminomadism and the pastoral lifestyle by many people, though "ruralization" was not nearly as dramatic as during the Intermediate Bronze Age. Nomadic groups dominated the no-man's-lands between city-states. Several specific groups are named in the Egyptian literary sources, including the 'Apiru of the Amarna Letters and the Shasu, and it is clear from references to them, particularly to the latter, that they were not held in high regard. (See sidebar, "Who's Who.")

Who's Who: Ethnicity in Ancient Canaan and Israel

Anthropologists use various aspects of a culture, such as language, geographical area, or type of environment, cuisine, clothing, and religion, to study ethnicity. Of course, one of the key ways that people create and maintain identity is by drawing distinctions between themselves and others. For instance, an important factor in the creation of the Israelite identity was a definition of Israelite as *not Philistine*.

The Bronze Age

Much of what archaeologists know about the different ethnic groups populating the eastern Mediterranean prior to the fully historical periods comes from analysis of pottery styles, which can be quite precarious, and examination of Egyptian art. Beginning as early as the late fourth millennium B.C.E., certain conventions, such as headgear, hairstyles, and facial hair, were used to represent what were conceived of as different peoples. The Narmer Palette (Early Bronze Age) and the Beni Hassan tomb (Late Bronze Age) are two well-known examples of Egyptian depictions of people from Canaan.

The reconstruction of ethnicity from the Middle Bronze Age is based on textual evidence mostly from Syro-Cilicia and Lebanon as well as from a few local Canaanite texts. Most textual evidence indicates that the population of Syria and Palestine was mainly West Semitic or "Amorite." The Amorites (Amurru in cuneiform sources) originated as a semisedentary people in the semiarid, northern fringe of the Syrian Desert, gradually expanding as a people. By the end of the Middle Bronze Age, a growing Hurrian presence existed in the southern Levant that increased over time. Personal name forms in the Mari Archive (c. eighteenth century B.C.E.), as well as a few rare inscriptions from the southern Levant (for example, Gezer, Shechem, and Hazor), reflect a cognizance of different ethnicities and/or nationalities. The later Amarna Letters from Egypt offer a similar picture. In many of these texts, clear distinctions can be drawn between West Semitic (Canaanite) names and Hurrian names. The linguistic evidence can also be used to approximate a rough ethnoregional map. For instance, while there is a mix of Canaanite and Hurrian names for rulers of the interior cities, the coast south of Lebanon is almost exclusively West Semitic.

The Iron Age

One of the most intriguing problems of Iron Age archaeology concerns the emergence of new peoples such as the Philistines, Phoenicians, and Israelites, as well as the Canaanites, who hung around well into the Iron Age. Although these various peoples are fixtures in the Hebrew Bible, identifying them as tangible historical entities has proven difficult. Features that can be used to

(continues)

Who's Who: Ethnicity in Ancient Canaan and Israel *(continued)*

address this question include linguistics (particularly names), evidence for diet, and geography (that is, culture areas). For instance, during the Iron Age, Canaanites lived primarily in the lowlands as opposed to the hill country or Negev, areas that are associated with Israelite settlement.

Even as the written record increases, definitive evidence regarding ethnicity is not forthcoming. This has prompted Victor Matthews to refer to this period as "the cauldron out of which the tenth- to eighth-century cultures emerged. One of these will ultimately be defined as the kingdom of Israel, but the ethnic origins of this people are most likely as mixed as the evidence associated with their culture" (2001, 32).

The earliest extra-biblical reference to the Israelites as a people comes from Egypt and the "Merenptah Stele" (c. 1200 B.C.E.), a 7-ft.-high stele carved from black granite that was discovered among the remains of this pharaoh's funerary temple in western Thebes. Most of the stele is devoted to recounting conflict with Lybians and Sea Peoples, but the last three lines of the inscription describe how Merenptah led a military campaign into Canaan: "Canaan has been plundered in every sort of woe. Ashqelon has been overcome. Gezer has been captured. Yano'am was made non-existent. Israel is laid waste and his seed is not" (Rainey 1991).

The text refers to both cities and peoples conquered by Merenptah, and though the spellings of Ashqelon, Yano'am, and Gezer include the determinative for a city (that is, a hieroglyph meaning "city"), the word for "Israel" has a glyph that denotes a people without a place. Although the Merenptah inscription reflects the existence of the people of Israel in Canaan as early as the thirteenth century, it provides little insight into who these people were.

An outstanding example of the artistic representation of ethnicity comes from the wall of the Cour de la Cachette at Karnak, where a scene carved in relief accompanied by an inscription describes an Egyptian military campaign into Canaan. Frank Yurco (1990) attributed the inscription and the deeds described therein to Merenptah. The relief, in fact, recounts what is almost certainly the same campaign into Canaan that is described in the Merenptah Stele, though it is possible that the latter refers to Rameses II (Redford 1992). More problematic still is the identity of the vanquished, for the linking of the text, which names several peoples, with the corresponding image (several different groups are depicted) is challenging. Not surprisingly, there has been considerable debate as to who's who. If Yurco is to be believed, it is the men with the ankle-length clothes and shaved heads with headbands, who are riding chariots, that are the Israelites. However, Anson Rainey (1991) disagrees with Yurco, pointing out that the dress is more typical of Canaanite soldiers and that their chariots, too, are Canaanite. Instead, he points to a representation of men in knee-high garments with turbanlike headdresses, arguing that these were the Israelites.

They may be one and the same with the Shasu, who are also mentioned several times in the Karnak wall reliefs as well in the Papyrus Anastasi, where they are represented as captives of Egypt. In the relief, short kilts and turbans distinguish them from the Canaanites. Others, however, have argued that the Egyptian texts seem to maintain a distinction between Israel and the Shasu in the records of military campaigns into the region and that the latter were minor players in these conflicts, harriers at most (Yurco 1990).

The Hebrew Bible, of course, makes multiple references to the Canaanites. Two of the more memorable instances include the story of the Israelite conquest, when Canaanite cities, armies, and kings were defeated, and the exhortations of prophets who criticized the Canaanites' ways and chided those Israelites who followed them. Though there is some level of historical fact preserved in the Book of Joshua, the conquest of Canaan could not have happened precisely as it was described in the narrative.

Traditionally, archaeologists have pointed to a suite of cultural traits thought to be exclusive to the Israelites, including agricultural terraces, cisterns, large collared-rim storage jars, and the so-called four-room houses, all of which may represent a unique cultural-ecological adaptation to the highland environment.

Although it has often been assumed that these were Israelite innovations, this model has recently come under scrutiny. Some scholars, for example, have argued that the early Israelites borrowed a number of these ideas from their Canaanite neighbors (Dever 2003b). Structures similar to the pillared four-room houses have been observed at Tel Batash (Timna) and Lachish, which at the time were likely home to Canaanites. This style of architecture has also been observed at the coastal cities Ashdod and Qasile in Philistia and at Tel Keisan in Phoenicia. Several other elements, such as ashlar masonry and the dromos bench type, thought to be diagnostic of Israelite culture may have actually derived from Sea Peoples/Philistine culture (Dever 1995c; Esse 1992).

Do these apparent "suites of traits" simply reaffirm with circular logic what the Hebrew Bible says? One may begin to answer this question by examining whether they were truly exclusive to the Israelites. Some of these features and practices may have evolved not as a way of expressing cultural identity, but as parallel solutions to similar problems—for instance, water management in the highland zone. The pillared courtyard house, which evolved into the four-room house, represents a standardized form of housing that might be expected with the rise of urbanism. In fact, a number of researchers have argued that the people who ultimately emerged as Israelites were ethnically, for the most part, indigenous inhabitants of Canaan (Finkelstein and Silberman 2001; Dever 1995c, 1998). Pottery assemblages, particularly domestic wares, display little change from Late Bronze Age Canaanite cities to the early Iron Age and what is commonly held to represent Israelite material culture.

(continues)

Who's Who: Ethnicity in Ancient Canaan and Israel (continued)

Identifying the people known as the Philistines has also proven difficult. Although their Cypro-Aegean roots cannot be denied, there are questions about how the so-called Sea Peoples came to be one people, the Philistines. Within a few generations of landing on the coast, they began to intermingle with local Canaanites, establishing a new cultural tradition altogether. The diversity of the Sea Peoples conveyed in the Egyptian wall carvings at Medinat Habu raises questions about which group(s) became the Philistines.

Like any ethnic group, the Israelites are defined as much by who they are as by who they are not. On a very broad level, it is possible to draw some basic distinctions between the cultures of the Israelites and Philistines. They ate different foods, as seen in the abundance of pig remains in the Philistine faunal assemblages (roughly 20 percent at several sites and exceeding sheep and goat), a phenomenon only partly explained by ecological factors; it is important to note that Philistine forebears, such as the Mycenaeans, had an appetite for pig meat as well (Hesse and Wapnish 1998). The limited number of artistic representations that exist reflect two peoples with a dissimilar sense of fashion and style; for instance, the Philistines are associated with several different forms of headgear. The Philistines' flare for the eccentric can also be observed in the style of pottery decoration—for example, the Bichrome Wares, with colorful bands and bird motifs. According to Lawrence Stager, who has excavated at the Philistine site of Ashqelon for two decades, "in contrast to the Israelites, especially the rustic ridge-dwellers of the central hill country, the Philistines of the plain appear to have been far more urbane and sophisticated" (1991, 31).

As for the Hebrew Bible, it is unequivocal in its delineation of distinct cultural groups, and if there was any group its authors preferred not to be associated with, it was the Philistines. The numerous references to this people range from neutral to derogatory—none can be characterized as flattering. The Hebrew Bible, however, being an Israelite document, may, in order to strengthen the Israelites' own identity, at times overemphasize the differences between these peoples.

Any discussion of culture and ethnicity, of course, must also raise the question of language. It is problematic that no mention is ever made in the Hebrew Bible of a distinct language spoken by the Philistines. This in itself, however, does not prove much, for it is possible that the Philistines did speak a distinct language but that the authors of the Bible simply did not report this—as in later epics, such as The Iliad (and even in most Hollywood movies today), where everyone speaks the same language as the authors (or producers). Though texts ascribed to the Philistines are rare, the few that do remain seem to indicate that their original language was not Semitic, but perhaps Indo-European. For instance, certain terms, such as seren (lord/ruler) and k/gova (helmet), and personal names (achish and Golyat) recall elements from the Anatolian branch (Machinist 2000). An inscription discovered in the Temple Complex (650) at Ekron suggests an affinity with Phoenician, a connection that may relate to contact between Ekron and the cities of Sidon and Tyre (Gitin, Dothan, and Naveh 1997), and it is possible that this reflects a shared ancestry, that is, both derive from the same or similar Aegean dialect(s).

Culture area is certainly one of the best ways to define the Philistines, who began on the coast but quickly pushed their way inland. Again, biblical references are useful if read critically, making clear that the land of the Philistines was on the coastal plain. Most of these references relate to the time when the highland states were just beginning to coalesce and having well-defined boundaries was important to them. Border conflicts between Judah and Philistia are suggested in 1 Kings (15:27, 16:15–17) and 2 Chronicles (17:10–11, 28:18). By defining the Philistine area in this specifically delimited fashion, the Bible's authors also undermined and delegitimized Philistine expansionism.

Yet, despite all of the animosity reflected in the biblical text, archaeological discoveries of the past few decades offer glimpses of a less hostile relationship. During the seventh century B.C.E. at Tel Miqne–Ekron, for instance, there is evidence for economic interaction between the two peoples in the way of Judean ceramic forms, which constitute some 7 percent of the entire assemblage, and Judean shekel weights. Though the four-horned altars, widely used by Israelites from the tenth century B.C.E. on, had fallen out of use by the seventh century B.C.E., they made a surprisingly strong comeback at this time at Tel Miqne–Ekron (Gitin 1995). The two peoples also have in common the inclusion of music in their religious rites with similar instrumentation (Dothan and Dothan 1992); however, music may have been common to all of the ancient Near Eastern religions.

Much has been made of the distinction between Israelites and Canaanites, and clearly, this tradition stems from the Hebrew Bible, with its memorable accounts of Joshua's conquest of Canaan and the stormy relationship between Samson and Delilah. Yet, outside of the biblical narrative, in the archaeological record, the distinction is difficult to discern. Thus, the question remains: How much of the tale of these two peoples is fiction, and how much is fact? Perhaps further archaeological discovery will provide more definitive answers.

Social Organization

Wealth and Status.   Several lines of evidence point to the existence of a wealthy, elite social class. There was, for one, the penchant for "patrician houses," and the Canaanite thirst for Aegean wines is evident in the pictorial *kraters,* deep bowls that were fairly common in the northern Levant and in

6.4 Depiction of a Canannite noble in Egyptian-style clothing from a Tel Hazor plaque (Drawing by J. Golden; adapted from Yadin 1972)

Cyprus, though rare in the south and in Egypt. At Megiddo, Aegean pottery was evenly distributed among the tombs of the tell's southern slopes, while their distribution within the city itself was restricted to three areas: near the palace (Palace 204), near the city gate, and within a residential neighborhood in the city's south end (Leonard and Cline 1998). Although these burials may form part of an elite cemetery, it appears that in living contexts only certain wealthy and important individuals had access to imported goods.

Overall, the sumptuary goods of the Canaanite elite reflect an unprecedented emphasis on conspicuous consumption by certain individuals. Canaanite nobles adopted Egyptian styles, and since the known names of rulers are generally male, it is likely this was the case for nobility as well.

Burials. Members of this elite class of the Late Bronze Age also expressed their status through extravagant burials. At both Megiddo and Ta'anach, there were extraordinarily wealthy tombs that appeared not long after destruction levels at both cities (Bunimovitz 1989). Jewelry and wares found with elaborate burials could represent the presence of new nobility from the north (Na'aman 1994). In fact, most elite burials contained a large number of foreign goods, though it is not always clear whether those interred were actually of foreign origin or simply included exotic grave offerings. The Egyptian influence can again be seen in the adoption of certain Egyptian burial practices. In particular, "Egyptianized" anthropoid coffins have been excavated at Deir el-Balah (Fig. 6.5), the last station on the "Way of Horus," as well as at Beth Shean, Tel el-Far'ah South, and Lachish; one example from Lachish bears a hieratic inscription. Yet, the extent of Egyptian influence differed in various regions. Some fifty such coffins of the Egyptian naturalistic style have been found at Beth Shean, which is not surprising since it was the site of an Egyptian outpost. Five examples of the "grotesque style," showing an Aegean influence, also made their way to Beth Shean; each depicts a person wearing a headdress, one with a feathered helmet that recalls those worn by Sea Peoples at Medinat Habu. Amihai Mazar (1990) infers that these may have been Sea People who came to Beth Shean while it was under Egyptian rule.

One of the most outstanding examples of an Aegean-style burial is Tomb 387 from Tel Dan (Biran 1994), which is commonly referred to as the "Mycenaean Tomb" because of the wealth of Mycenaean material found in it. The tomb was built of rough stones in a style similar to that of contemporary tombs in Ugarit and Enkomi in Cyprus. The grave goods included more than 100 ceramic vessels, many of which were imports from Mycenae (roughly one-fourth), Cyprus, and Phoenicia. Some of the styles represented include the piriform amphoriskos, stirrup jar, pyxides, flasks and bowls, alabastron, and the unique "Charioteer Vase," with its elaborate painted design. Chemical analysis (NAA) of the Charioteer Vase and some of the other vessels indicates that they came from near Argolid in Greece. This particular style helps date the tomb to the late fourteenth to thirteenth centuries B.C.E. (Mycenaean 3A2 to early 3B). As noted above, the direct influence from Cyprus and the Aegean was stronger in the north. The domed tomb entrances at Tel el-Far'ah and Beth Shean were reminiscent of Mycenaean *dromos* tombs (Waldbaum 1997); other forms of burials that indicate foreign influence include the *Larnax* (a chest-shaped coffin or sarcophagus, usually ceramic) tombs at Gezer and Acre and the cist graves at Tel Abu Hawam. Wealthy burials, including structural tombs, have also been found at both Megiddo and Dan.

Most burials in the highlands were in caves used as multiperson tombs. In the coastal region, however, individual pit burials were more common. In addition to foreign influence, this practice may also reflect social differences between pastoral tribes of the sparsely populated highlands, where kinship structures were emphasized, and the more cosmopolitan, consumer-oriented societies on the coastal cities.

By the end of the Late Bronze Age, at a time when the general level of prosperity was at something of a low, it appears that this elite class may have become a burden on the rest of society. As the Canaanite urban elite struggled to maintain their power, they created a vicious cycle by overtaxing this already depressed underclass (Bunimovitz 2003). Equally if not more important in terms of social change were developments elsewhere in the eastern Mediterranean. One after another, the kingdoms of the broader region fell apart, and great movements of peoples ensued. Thus was the end of the Bronze Age.

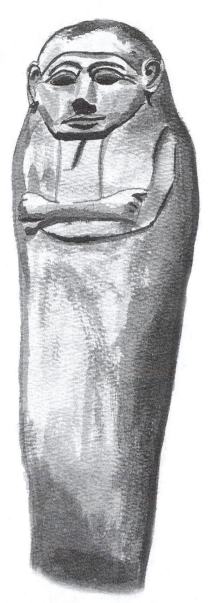

6.5 Anthropoid coffin showing Egyptian influence from Deir el-Balah (Drawing by J. Golden; adapted from Trude Dothan and Moshe Dothan. 1992. *People of the Sea: In Search for the Philistines*. New York: Macmillan.)

IRON AGE I

Settlement Patterns

There was social upheaval throughout much of the ancient world at the end of the second millennium B.C.E., and this turmoil is clearly reflected in the settlement patterns of the time. Pastoral groups dominated marginal ecological zones such as the Negev and the eastern slopes of the highlands (Finkelstein 1988; Banning and Köhler-Rollefson 1992). However, both archaeological and survey data suggest that in some parts of the region nomadic groups began to settle down. Israel Finkelstein (1996; Finkelstein and Silberman 2001) has suggested that the layout of houses at Tel Esdar and 'Izbet Sartah seems to mimic the plan of a pastoral tent camp, though the latter site was only partially excavated and this reconstruction is largely conjectural.

A similar pattern where seminomadic squatters begin to lay down the roots of settled life has also been observed at Dan (Str. VI) (Biran 1994, 128). A biblical passage (Judg. 18:12) referring to the site as Mahaneh Dan (the camp of Dan) may also reflect the city's nomadic heritage. The most significant change of the Iron 1, however, was the establishment of new settlements throughout the highlands at locations where there had been no previous Late Bronze Age settlement. For instance, some 25 sites were observed in the Meron range of the Upper Galilee as well as some settlements in the western Galilee; most of these sites were small villages of no more than 5 dunams (Aharoni 1957). More recent surveys of the northern hill country have led to the discovery of some 100 sites ranging in size from very small (a few dunams) to medium-sized (10–20 dunams) to relatively large (more than 20 dunams) (Zertal 1988).

Although many new settlements may reflect the settling of transhumant peoples, a sizable pastoral population also remained on the move. At Giloh, in the central hill country overlooking the Rephaim Valley, the foundation of a square, stone-built structure, perhaps the tower of some highland stronghold, dating to the eleventh century B.C.E. has been excavated. It is possible that this was used as a place of refuge for a newly settled or semisedentary population. Based on all of the available survey data, Finkelstein (1997) has calculated a total highlands population of some 20,000 for the earlier portion of the Iron 1 and 60,000 by the end of the period.

Population

The character of the Iron 1 population is one of the most fascinating and hotly debated issues in southern Levantine archaeology. Although the Hebrew Bible relates the tale of the Israelites, led by Joshua, conquering and then displacing the Canaanites, this is not reflected in the archaeological record. In fact, it is rather difficult to distinguish the two at the beginning of the Iron Age, and many aspects of Canaanite material culture remained intact. Archaeologists have traditionally pointed to new features in the Iron 1 assemblage that are considered to be diagnostic of highland Israelite culture (for example, collared-rim store jars and four-room pillared houses), but the exclusively Israelite nature of these has recently been challenged by a number of scholars. In addition to the prolonged Canaanite presence, it is also important to note that at the very beginning of the period (Iron 1a), Egyptians still retained a hold on parts of the region. Thus, we see a diverse population as well as one that was not fixed. There was generally uniformity in the basic pot forms of the Iron 1, yet regional differences are apparent at sites such as Tel Keisan.

City Life, Domestic Life

Urbanism returned to the Negev during the Iron 1 with the establishment of large settlements such as Arad, Beer Sheva, Tel Esdar, and Tel Masos. Undoubtedly a major population center for this region, the cultural identity of the latter is unclear. The large, spacious structures appearing in the Negev highlands (for example, 'Ain Qudeis) around this time were originally thought to have been fortresses representing either penetration of the Israelite population into the Negev or some deliberate royal initiative. More recently, it has been argued that they were used as pastoral enclosures (Finkelstein 1988).

The nuclear family, in some cases along with domestic servants, formed the basic social unit in the Iron 1 (Stager 1985; Meyers 1997; Bloch-Smith and Alpert-Nakhai 1999). Most people lived in pillared, or "four-room," houses; some of these courtyard houses actually had three rooms, and there were a number of variations on the general plan. The house was designed to meet specific needs such as food storage and animal enclosure (Holladay 1992, 2003). Based on ethnographic research from Iranian villages, John S. Holladay Jr. (2003) estimated the annual grain consumption for a family and its animals at around 1,800 kg (3,970 lbs.) of wheat and 1,080 kg (2,380 lbs.) of barley, an amount too large to store in jars and bins, and thus grain pits were used. In some cases, houses would have had a second story used for sleeping quarters, while the first floor was used for basic household activities (Netzer 1992). The open court doubled as an animal pen by night and a work area during the day. Interior pillars were used to support the roof: On the coastal plain, wooden posts rested on stone bases; in the northern Negev, stone drums were stacked; and in the central highlands, singular stone pillars were used. Pillars were also used to delineate roofed and unroofed space within the domestic unit.

Social Organization

The populations of small Iron 1 settlements were composed primarily of large extended families or small lineages (Stager 1985; Holladay 1992). It is possible that all inhabitants were members of a single clan (Holladay 2003). Beyond the village, a segmentary society comprised of clans and tribes may be inferred from the settlement patterns of small, unfortified villages and hamlets broadly spaced about the highlands and Upper Galilee (Aharoni 1957; Finkelstein 1988).

Over the course of the period, society became increasingly complex and urban in nature, culminating in the state structures of the Iron 2. Gender hierarchy during the Iron 1 has been the subject of debate. Although some scholars hold that men had greater status at the time (Simkins 1999; Stager 1985), others have suggested that prior to the Iron 2 state, there was some degree of gender equality (Meyers 1988, 1997). By the time of the Iron 2, however, it is clear that women had lower status. Changes in burial customs in the early Iron 1 also indicate the development of a class structure.

IRON 1: SOCIAL ORGANIZATION AMONG THE COASTAL PEOPLES

A period of profound social change began during the Iron 1 with the arrival of new peoples, en masse, on the coastal plain. In fact, the evidence for this intrusive element beginning early in the twelfth century B.C.E. is one of the criteria that have allowed archaeologists to distinguish the Iron 1 from the Late Bronze Age. The first wave of settlement, with as many as 25,000 people, concentrated mainly in five major cities, known as the Pentapolis. According to Lawrence Stager, in order to achieve such large numbers so rapidly, "boatload after boatload of Philistines, along with their families, livestock and belongings, must have arrived in southern Canaan during stage 1" (2003, 344).

By 1100 B.C.E., this new people began a period of expansion. The original coastal sites of Philistia were strategically located in order take advantage of access to the interior. For example, Ashdod, at the mouth of the Wadi Sukreir, had direct access to the Judean hills. Moving north, examples of Philistine pottery appeared rather suddenly at Megiddo, gradually reaching the farming village of Afula; in the south, they moved inland, appearing at Tel Eitun. Much of this pottery, however, may have been locally produced in the Philistine style. Overall, inland settlements were smaller, with fewer cities, exempting Tel Miqne–Ekron (Machinist 2000; Schniedewind 1998).

Population

The new people arriving on the Levantine coast are known collectively as the "Sea Peoples," but the question of diversity within this broad category remains the subject of great debate. What is certain is that much of Sea Peoples culture, though alien to the southern Levant, had strong parallels among contemporary peoples of Cyprus and the Aegean. Their cuisine, for instance, specifically the consumption of pork and other pig products, suggests Mycenaean origins, as does the style of pottery from which they ate. However, upon settling on the coastal plain and no doubt mingling with local Canaanites, these people developed a new culture of their own. Archaeologists have traditionally referred to the people of the southern coast as Philistines, based, of course, on the biblical tales of this people and their cities. The early Iron 1 was certainly a formative stage, when foreign elements were most strong, and even once this culture crystallized, perhaps at the end of the Iron 1, the Philistines continued to absorb cultural elements from their neighbors—and subjugators—for centuries to follow.

City Life, Domestic Life

One of the most fascinating aspects of Iron 1 settlement on the coastal plain is that this immigrant population must have arrived with some form of urban system intact. This migration may relate in part to social crises among the Aegean cities (Stager 2003). As large units of people arrived at once, it is not surprising that most of this population was concentrated in towns and cities such as Ashdod, Ashqelon, and Tel Qasile on the coast and Tel Miqne–Ekron further inland. Urban design is well attested at the site of Ashdod, where opportunistic outlanders, on the vestiges of the Egyptian-Canaanite settlement of the Late Bronze Age, founded a new city of some 8 hectares early in the Iron 1 (Str. XIII). In the western part of the settlement (Area H), an upper city was established comprising two main blocks of public buildings, aligned along a north-south axis and separated by a wide street running west. The street sloped toward the west in order to allow for water runoff. The north end of the city hosted an industrial quarter, including a ceramic workshop (Rm. 4106), where potters did their best to emulate the Mycenaean (3c) bowls and cooking jars that they were accustomed to (Dothan and Porat 1993). Excavations in the residential quarter of Tel Qasile have also provided evidence for town planning, with streets 3 meters (about 10 ft.) wide laid out according to a grid system. The houses of the early Philistines (eleventh century B.C.E.) were rectilinear, with wooden pillars set on stone bases used to support the roof. A central courtyard, half of which was covered, was used to house livestock, to conduct household chores, and for recreation.

Social Organization

Evidence from domestic contexts suggests that some members of this early Philistine society were wealthier than others. The upper city at Tel Qasile (Area H, noted above), located near the highest point of the site, served as both the city's administrative center and as a neighborhood for some of the city's wealthiest citizens (Dothan and Dothan 1992). The range of elaborately decorated kraters used for wine, in addition to jewelry such as a gold ring found in the courtyard of a house, suggest that the individuals living there could afford to indulge in luxury goods.

The mortuary evidence also suggests disparities in wealth and status. At Tel el-Far'ah South, there was a large cemetery consisting primarily of simple pit burials, and it is presumed that this form of burial served commoners throughout the region. However, there were also elite burials at the Tel el-Far'ah South cemetery—five caves transformed into dromos tombs. These tombs were designed with steps leading down into a rock-cut burial chamber, where the bodies of the deceased were laid out on broad benches. Grave goods, also placed on the benches, included Canaanite Wares, local "Proto-Philistine" pottery, and Aegean imports, but no imports from Cyprus. Anthropomorphic coffins similar to those at Deir el-Balah (Late Bronze Age) were found in two of the tombs, attesting to the eclectic character of this culture. By the later phase of Cemetery 500, however, burials were characterized primarily by Philistine pottery.

The spread of Philistine burial customs can also be observed in the distribution of small female figurines rendered in the "mourning gesture." These figurines have been found at Tel Jemmeh and Azor as well as Tel Eitun, where five of these figures were attached to a krater. Again betraying their Cypro-Aegean roots, these figures have affinities with examples known from Mycenaean 3c cemeteries (such as Perati) on the Greek mainland, at Rhodes (Ialysos), and at Naxos. Another trend worth noting is the shift away from group graves. Whereas most Canaanite graves of the Late Bronze Age were communal burials, at some twelfth- and eleventh-century sites in the Aegean and in Philistia individual burials began to appear; at Azor, for example, twenty-five individual graves were excavated.

IRON 2: HIGHLAND CULTURE

Settlement Patterns

Early in the Iron 2 (approximately mid-eleventh to tenth centuries B.C.E.), settlement in the Judean hill country was nearly double that of the preceding period (Ofer 1994, 102), and the survey data seem to indicate a significant jump in settlement during the time of the Iron 1–2 transition. Finkelstein (1999) has argued that there was a settlement hierarchy, with a few primary sites, such as Tel Rumeida and Ras et-Tawil, and smaller, second-order sites such as Khirbet ez-Zawiyye and Khirbet Attir (Ofer 1994), but suggested this was not the case until later in the period.

Population
City Life, Domestic Life

People of the Iron 2 lived in small farming villages as well as in large cities. The largest urban centers were at sites that had been occupied on and off for centuries—Dan, Gezer, Hazor, and Lachish. Jerusalem, still a relatively small site in the preceding period, began to emerge as a political, commercial, and religious center. At Dan, evidence for city planning has been uncovered, including a distinct residential quarter and a religious area (Biran 1994). At the city of Lachish (eighth century B.C.E.), houses were built along the perimeter of the site. Large public districts with administrative, commercial, religious, and/or royal buildings were found at all four of these major cities.

Town planning is also evident in the standardization of domestic architecture. The four-room pillared house, a style that has been seen at Tel Beit Mirsim, Tel Masos, Beer Sheva, Tel en-Nasbeh, and Hazor, crystallized as a fixed plan during the Iron 2. At Tel es-Sa'idiyeh (Pritchard 1985), houses dating to the ninth to seventh centuries B.C.E. (Str. V) were almost identical in plan and size (for example, Houses 3–12). Generally, houses were built of stone and/or mud brick, with a single doorway opening from the street into a large front room. In some cases, half of the room, which was partitioned by a row of columns, was paved with stones. The artifacts found inside the houses represent a range of activities. Clay ovens, mills for grinding, and bins for storage were used to process food for daily consumption. Concentrations of loom weights (in, for example, houses 3, 5, and 6) indicate limited domestic production, and gaming pieces were also found in some houses.

In a number of instances, houses shared back and side walls, forming a block. Overall, the standardization of houses and town planning may have been part of a broader trend toward a more specialized use of space concomitant with the rise of the state (Faust 2002a). House design also seems to reflect an increasing division between public and private space.

Social Organization

During the Iron 2, Israelite society became increasingly complex in terms of both political and social organization. The nuclear family continued to be the basic economic unit, and agricultural and pastoral goods were still gathered by individual households. However, each family belonged to a larger 'bet 'ab' (literally, "house of the father," referring to the extended family), and much of the produce a household collected may have been considered to be at the disposal of the 'bet 'ab' (Holladay 2003, 393).

Socioeconomic inequality in the Iron 2 can be inferred from several lines of evidence. To begin with, wealthy people lived in large luxury homes, many of which were furnished with fancy trappings, such as furniture decorated with carved ivory inlays. Fragments of these intricately sculpted inlays dating to the ninth and eighth centuries B.C.E. have been found at a number of sites. Most remarkable are the hundreds of examples found in excavations of the Assyrian destruction level at Samaria, though these may be heirlooms that go back to the ninth century B.C.E. (Crowfoot and Crowfoot 1938; Barnett 1982). Biblical references support the notion that these were perceived as luxury goods in their day, for in the Book of Amos (6:4 and 3:15), the prophet by that name admonishes the rich Israelites for their greed and arrogance, pointing specifically to ivory furniture as an example of their excesses. Examples of outstanding elite dwellings, or "palaces," have been found at sites such as Megiddo and Arad.

Disparities in wealth can be observed not only in the ownership of luxury goods but in access to basic staple resources as well. At the Iron 2 (tenth to ninth centuries B.C.E.) settlement of 'Izbet Sartah (Str. II), the distribution of grain pits suggests that some had more to store than others. Spatial analyses of some forty-three stone-lined silos, surrounded by five houses, indicate that most of these pits actually belonged to the largest household (Holladay 2003; Rosen 1986–1987; Finkelstein 1986). Social ranking was also apparent in thousands of engraved seals and seal impressions dating to the ninth to sixth centuries B.C.E. William Dever (1995) showed that many of these were rather mundane, made of nonprecious stones, undecorated, and often bearing personal names only. However, a few examples were made from semiprecious stones with ornate designs, and sometimes bound with gold rings (Avigad 1986; Hestrin and Dyagi-Mendels 1979). The owners of these fancier seals made frequent use of various high-status titles, such as steward, prince, and priest as well as "servant of [the king]," "who is over the house," and "who is over the tax."

In recent decades, there has been a windfall in evidence for writing, leading to theories about widespread literacy in Israelite society (Millard 1972; Mazar 1990), though Nadav Na'aman pointed out that in both the eighth and seventh centuries B.C.E. the archaeological contexts for the inscriptions are mainly public, administrative, and military in nature and not private. In addition to inscribed ostraca, such as a group of sixty-three written in Hebrew that were found at Samaria, inscriptions appear on vessels, weights, and the seals mentioned above; there are also a number of important inscriptions from Arad. Dever (2003b) conceded that the masses may have been functionally literate, meaning they could use graffiti to execute transactions, as indicated by the nonbiblical inscriptions written in what seems to be some form of vernacular Hebrew. Yet, true literary works, in fact most of the Hebrew Bible, circulated among a small, well-educated elite class, out of the reach of the masses.

Of course, with the increase in literacy comes an increase in the amount and depth of information about society available to the archaeologist. Dever has extracted information about the different social classes that are either alluded to or implied in the Hebrew Bible. These include: administrative functionaries; military personnel; aristocrats, nobles, and wealthy landholding families; professionals and people of the law; merchants; artisans and craftspeople; people forming the general labor force; farmers, ranging from estate-holders to peasants; and finally, the lowest class, which included the poor and landless, aliens, and various nonfreemen (for example, indentured servants).

Social ranking is also apparent in the mortuary evidence. A lack of evidence for burials indicates that, on one hand, many people were buried individually in small pits, most of which were not preserved. On the other hand, some of the wealthier members of society were interred in large, multichamber rock-cut tombs, such as those dating to the eighth and seventh centuries B.C.E. found at Khirbet el-Qom and in and around Jerusalem, especially Silwan (see Chapter 9 sidebar, "The Silwan Necropolis"). A few aboveground tombs with ornate facades are also known. Many of the tomb chambers were lined with benches and had niches carved out for the body. Repositories for previous burials indicate that families used the tombs over successive generations in order to ensure the preservation of wealth and status through the male lineages (Bloch-Smith 1992). In addition, the architecture of the Judean tombs seems to mirror the four-room buildings in which the deceased had dwelt in life. The tombs generally contained a range of precious goods, such as jewelry, model furniture, and imported ceramics from Cyprus and Egypt as well as scarabs and seals; some of the tombs had early Hebrew inscriptions with blessings and warnings to enemies that reflect a Phoenician influence. References to rock-hewn tombs appear in the Hebrew Bible (for example, Isa. 22:15–16). Royal tombs, some of which can be directly related to specific kings, have been excavated at Jerusalem and Samaria.

Owing to the wealth of both archaeological and textual evidence, it is possible to make inferences with regard to gender-based social differences. With the increased social complexity concomitant with political changes of the Iron 2, the status of women became patently subordinate to that of men (Meyers 1988, 1997; McNutt 1999; Yee 1999; Faust 2003). Reading into the ceramic assemblage, Avraham Faust (2002b) has argued that varying status afforded to each gender was evident in the types of pottery used for masculine and feminine activities: Women's pottery was plain earthenware, but vessels used by men were elaborately decorated. This can be interpreted as a male-female/nature-culture dichotomy. Moreover, gender-based activities were divided in terms of space, with the work of women conducted in private areas of the house while men entertained in the public, communal space (Bloch-Smith and Alpert-Nakhai 1999). A review of references to domestic life in the Hebrew Bible also reflects differences in economic, social, and political life based on gender. For example, passages that concern eating and entertaining reveal that tasks related to food preparation generally fell to female members of society, while communal feasting was reserved for men (Meyers 1997, 1988; Bloch-Smith and Alpert-Nakhai 1999; Faust 2002b).

Conflict between groups was fairly common during the Iron 2, and society became more warlike at this time. This shift is suggested in part by the location of settlements in relation to one another (Faust 1999a, 2002a). Additionally, there are multiple references in Judges and 1–2 Samuel that describe conflict within and between various social groups. At the same time, there is also evidence, as in the Beersheba Valley sites, for coexistence and interaction between different ethnic groups, such as the Judeans and the Edomite-oriented groups, in addition to seminomadic peoples.

IRON 2: COASTAL CULTURE

After the initial Iron 1 population explosion on the coastal plain, it appears the influence of Philistine culture continued to expand inland. Although the biblical narrative tells of perennial conflict between coastal peoples (that is, Philistines) and inland peoples (that is, Israelites), it is not clear to what extent this represents historical reality. Some of the differences between these peoples, for instance, may have been somewhat exaggerated—both by the ancient authors of the time and slightly later, and by biblical scholars in modern times.

Population

The first few generations of Sea Peoples that settled on the coast in the Iron 1 maintained close relations with their counterparts in Cyprus and the Aegean. In time, though, the affinities between these early Philistines and the peoples of their homeland(s) would diminish, and a new, unique Philistine culture would emerge. Moreover, the Sea Peoples began to assimilate practices from the inland Canaanite and Israelite traditions as well as from the Phoenicians, who were themselves a relatively new hybrid culture. As the Aegean influence in cultic practice faded, religious elements from the local cultures were absorbed. At Ashdod (Str. X), the distinctive, decorated Bichrome Wares were out of use, and the red burnished "Ashdod Ware" that replaced it had stylistic affinities with pottery of both the inland Israelites and Phoenicians. One scholar has even suggested referring to this culture as "Southern Phoenician," emphasizing the connection with peoples at Dor and other northern cities (Dever 1995b). By the seventh century, what may have been a Phoenician-inspired script, attested at both Tel Miqne–Ekron and Ashqelon, provides further evidence that this was a time of rapid culture change. It is also important to note that during the eighth century B.C.E. Neo-Assyrians launched a series of devastating attacks on cities throughout the southern Levant, and in the seventh to early sixth centuries B.C.E. Neo-Babylonians would conquer Philistia.

City Life, Domestic Life

During the Iron 2, most of the people still lived in cities. On the coast, Ashqelon developed into a large city, while Tel Miqne–Ekron, further inland, emerged as the primary center of Philistia during the tenth and ninth centuries and into the time of Assyrian domination. The archaeology of the Philistines has generally focused on the larger urban centers, and few rural settlements have been excavated. Tel Zippur, a rural town first settled in the Late Bronze Age, may have played host to Philistines in the Iron 1. The biblical figure David is said to have been living in the "field of the Philistines" (*bisdeh Pelishtim*) (1 Sam. 27:7), which may refer to the lands surrounding the large cities. Biblical references also indicate that Philistines lived in unwalled villages (*kofer happ Erizi*) as well as fortified cities (*ir mivtsar*) (1 Sam. 6:18).

There is evidence for town planning, with cities usually split into distinct quarters. Several of the Philistine cities had upper-class neighborhoods, which were often located in a high spot (acropolis), as at Tel Miqne–Ekron's Northwest Acropolis and Ashdod Area H, where an acropolis was situated near the cult center. When Ashdod expanded in the late eighth century B.C.E. (Str. VIII), a potters' quarter was marked off by walls. Distinct industrial and residential quarters have also been excavated at Tel Miqne–Ekron and its satellite, Batash-Timna. At Tel Qasile, excavations in a residential neighborhood revealed that during the late tenth and early ninth centuries B.C.E. (Str. IX-VIII) people lived

6.6   Inscription discovered in the Temple Complex (650) at Ekron (Photo courtesy of Zev Radovan, Tel Miqne–Ekron Publications Project)

in four-room houses no different from those used by contemporary peoples of the hill country.

Social Organization

Cities such as Ashqelon and Tel Miqne–Ekron achieved great prosperity during the course of the Iron Age. At the latter, the booming olive oil industry and the city's attraction as a vibrant cult center drew people and wealth from the surrounding region. An upper class emerged, as demonstrated by the discovery of expensive luxury items, particularly in the way of jewelry and personal adornments. Six hoards of silver were found in seventh-century-B.C.E. contexts at Tel Miqne–Ekron, several of which may have been private caches belonging to wealthy individuals. One such cache contained some thirty-one items of jewelry, mostly silver (Gitin 1995, 69). The most outstanding piece from this hoard was a silver medallion inspired by Assyrian cultic iconography, suggesting that the city's elites were either Assyrians, perhaps local officials and dignitaries, or locals attempting to adopt Assyrian status symbols (Gitin and Golani 2001).

Burials also give an indication of disparities in social status and wealth. In a courtyard of the acropolis (Area H) at Ashdod, archaeologists found what is probably a "warrior's burial": an adult male interred with a horse and a dagger with an iron blade similar in form to objects from Greece dating to about 1000 B.C.E. (Dothan and Dothan 1992). A wealthy cemetery near the Philistine city of Qatif-Rukeish, just south of Gaza, showed influence from Assyria and Phoenicia, suggesting a cosmopolitan population.

PHILISTINE HIGH CULTURE

The Philistines are often imagined as barbarians; indeed, the term is invoked in modern English to describe a person lacking in culture and indifferent to aesthetic values (and the term is defined as such in English dictionaries). However, archaeological research on this group has suggested that this is an unfair representation (Stager 1991). Research at Ashqelon and Tel Miqne–Ekron, in fact, tells the story not of a brutish people but of a rich culture that celebrated life with art, wine, and song. The artistic abilities of Philistine craftspeople can be observed in their elegant and colorfully painted wares of the Iron 1, as well as in ceramic cult stands of the Iron 2. The royal winery at Ashqelon dating to the seventh century B.C.E. supports this view, and there is also evidence for music. The lyre appears a number of times in various decorative motifs; for example, an eighth-century-B.C.E. clay figure of a man playing a lyre was found at Ashdod, and a cult stand from the same city depicts a four-piece ensemble.

SUGGESTED READING

Banning, Edward B., and Ilse Köhler-Rollefson. 1992. "Ethnographic Lessons for the Pastoral Past: Camp Locations and Material Remains near Beidha, Southern Jordan." In *Pastoralism in the Levant: Archaeological Materials in Anthropological Perspectives,* edited by O. Bar-Yosef and A. Khazanov, 181–204. Madison, WI: Prehistory Press.

Bloch-Smith, E.1992. *Judahite Burial Practices and Beliefs about the Dead.* Sheffield, England: Sheffield Academic Press.

Dever, William G. 1987. "The Middle Bronze Age: The Zenith of the Urban Canaanite Era." *Biblical Archaeology* 50: 148–177.

Faust, Avraham. 2000. "Ethnic Complexity in Northern Israel during Iron Age II." *Palestine Exploration Quarterly* 132: 2–27.

———. 2003. "Residential Patterns in the Ancient Israelite City." *Levant* 35: 123–138.

Finkelstein, I., Z. Lederman, and Shlomo Bunimovitz, eds. 1997. *Highlands of Many Cultures: The Southern Samaria Survey—The Sites.* Tel Aviv: Institute of Archaeology of Tel Aviv University.

Golden, Jonathan. Forthcoming. *Dawn of the Metal Age.* London: Continuum.

King, Philip J., and Lawrence E. Stager. 2001. *Life in Biblical Israel.* Louisville, KY: Westminster/John Knox Press.

Levy, Thomas E. 1992. "Transhumance, Subsistence, and Social Evolution." In *Pastoralism in the Levant,* edited by O. Bar-Yosef and A. Khazanov, 65–82. Madison, WI: Prehistory Press.

Lichtheim, Miriam, trans. 1973. "Story of Sinuhe." In *Ancient Egyptian Literature.* Vol. 1, *The Old and Middle Kingdoms,* 223–233. Berkeley: University of California Press.

Shiloh, Y. 1978. "Elements in the Development of Town Planning in the Israelite City." *Israel Exploration Journal* 28: 36–51.

Steel, Louise. 2002. "Consuming Passions: A Contextual Study of the Local Consumption of Mycenaean Pottery at Tell el-'Ajjul." *Journal of Mediterranean Archaeology* 15: 25–51.

Tubb, Jonathan N. 2002. *The Canaanites.* London: British Museum.

CHAPTER 7

Politics

Along with increased economic and social complexity in the southern Levant came the development of power structures and political establishments. Like the social and economic systems that developed in the region, there was great variation in the level of organization over time, and it was by no means a direct progression from simple to more complex. Rather, the forms of political bodies that emerged in the southern Levant were related to demographics, internal historical developments, and foreign influences that changed frequently and dramatically over the course of some four millennia. The amount of information regarding political organization that is available to archaeologists also varies with each period, particularly where historical evidence is concerned. With prehistoric societies, of course, there is no historical record, and during the protohistorical period virtually all of the relevant texts derive from the annals of adjacent regions (Egypt and Syro-Mesopotamia). For the later periods, especially from the Iron 2 on, traditional scholarship has turned to the Hebrew Bible for historical data; this approach, however, has come under increasing scrutiny in recent years. Beyond historical information relating to specific individuals (such as kings), archaeologists must work with indirect evidence such as royal architecture and iconography; ideally the historical and archaeological evidence is used in conjunction whenever possible.

CHALCOLITHIC PERIOD

Though historians know nothing about individual leaders or specific polities in the southern Levant during the Chalcolithic period, evidence points to site hierarchies and territoriality as well as warfare among various peoples. As yet, no elite residences dating to the period have been found, but evidence for the rise of powerful elites can be seen in the production and trade of valuable prestige goods and the establishment of rich tombs replete with these potent luxury goods. One such cave tomb is Givat Ha'oranim in the foothills overlooking the coastal plain, northeast of Jerusalem, which contained luxury and/or ritual goods including metal artifacts, fenestrated incense burners, basalt bowls, and impressive ivory carvings (Scheftelowitz and Oren 1997). Evidence for rich and powerful individuals was also discovered in the Nahal Qanah cave in the western Samaria hills. There, archaeologists found a set of eight gold and electrum rings—the earliest gold artifacts in the southern Levant—in a small niche, along with a metal scepter and a "crown fragment." These finds have correlates in the Nahal Mishmar hoard (Gopher and Tsuk 1991, 1996). Peqi'in,

7.1 Map showing Chalcolithic sites, including recently discovered cave tombs (J. Golden)

a cave tomb in the Upper Galilee, contained a similar range of burial goods in addition to more than 250 ossuaries ranging in size and shape. The great number of individuals represented in the cave suggests that it may have been used over a long period of time, serving as the burial site for an extended population, perhaps from a number of villages (Gal, Smithline, and Shalem 1997).

There can be no doubt that those interred in these tombs had attained great wealth and honor, and the fact that these were corporate burials is testament to the status of certain groups as a whole, that is, a certain kin group or lineage. These elites probably came to power via control over farming and grazing lands, accruing surplus food stores and large herds. Ultimately, they were able to convert this wealth into power, using symbolic displays such as tombs and prestige goods to promote themselves.

Settlement patterns also reflect some form of territorial organization. In the northern Negev, where Chalcolithic culture blossomed, arable land was limited, and competition for such terrain may have led to greater political integration and to territorial conflict (Levy 1986; see also Carniero 1970, 1981). The larger villages, such as Shiqmim, were surrounded by smaller satellite sites, suggesting small regional polities. The location of the tombs, spread across the countryside and never in proximity to settlements, may reflect an effort by these powerful lineages to assert control over broad areas. Evidence for violent conflict can be seen in the maceheads made of hard stones (for example, limestone) as well as copper alloys found at sites throughout the Chalcolithic countryside. Owing to the exotic nature of the materials used and the investment required for their production, maceheads are often regarded as prestige goods, but when hafted onto elastic wooden shafts, they would have also made highly effective weapons. In Egypt, with which there was already limited contact, the macehead had already begun its long career as a symbol of power.

It is unclear what happened at the end of the Chalcolithic period. Some scholars, such as David Ussishkin (1980), have argued that there was a break-

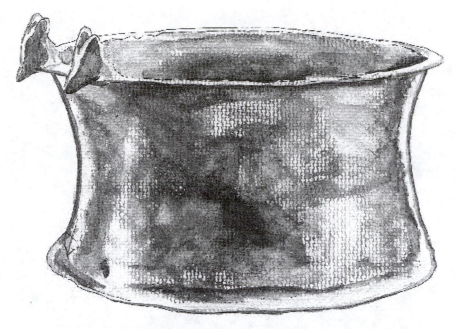

7.2   The "crown" from the Nahal Mishmar hoard (Drawing by J. Golden; adapted from Bar-Adon 1980)

down in the Chalcolithic sociopolitical system altogether. As evidence for this theory, Ussishkin pointed to the proximity of the Nahal Mishmar hoard to the Ein Gedi temple and suggested that the treasure found at Ein Gedi represents goods rescued from the temple that were hidden at a moment of crisis—an intriguing theory indeed, but one that is difficult to confirm.

EARLY BRONZE AGE: THE FIRST URBAN REVOLUTION

At the beginning of the Early Bronze Age, most people lived in small farming villages organized as a series of small-scale, autonomous chiefdoms, but later in the period (EB1–2) the first wave of Levantine urbanism was under way (Esse 1989; Joffe 1991). The Jordan Valley was dominated by three primary centers—Dan, Beit Yerah, and Khirbet et-Makhruuq, while the northern Jezreel Valley was dominated by the cities of Kabri and Shimron. Continuing into the EB3, population density increased as much of the population converged into a few large polities (for example, the Huleh Valley) dominated by cities with as many as 20,000 people (Greenberg 1990).

Seeking to explain the emergence of urbanism in the southern Levant, an early generation of archaeologists, including William Foxwell Albright, Kathleen Kenyon, and G. Ernest Wright, attributed this phenomenon to the incursion of peoples from beyond the region. It is true that from this point on, the movement of peoples in and out of the southern Levant played a vital role in the political history of the region. More recently, however, researchers have attempted to frame the problem within a local, social context (Esse 1989;

7.3   The walled Early Bronze Age city of Arad (Photo courtesy of Zev Radovan, Land of the Bible Picture Archive)

Kempinski 1992). Douglas Esse (1989) has applied the concept of "secondary state formation," explaining that while many of the features typically associated with primary states—institutionalized power structures, centralization, and socioeconomic stratification—are observable in the Early Bronze Age, the influence of the original Egyptian and Syro-Mesopotamian states cannot be ignored. Esse thus argued that while these "pristine states" achieved an advanced level of integration through internal processes, secondary states such as that seen in Canaan emerged as the result of the interaction and competition between expansive primary states.

The presence of some form of municipal body is evident in public architectural works of the period, most conspicuously the construction of massive city walls. Though only a few settlements of the EB1 were protected by fortifications (for example, Tel Erani and Tel Shalem), by the EB2–3 formidable city walls with bastions began to appear at a number of sites, including Megiddo, Ta'anach, Yarmuth, Jericho, and Arad (Fig. 7.3).

The rapid appearance of wall systems during the EB2–3 and their subsequent expansion and renovation suggests an increase in tension and competition between rival cities, even if their primary purpose was political posturing. Investment in public works, for instance, may reflect competitive emulation between rival polities trying to outdo one another with displays of power and wealth through investment in highly visible public works. At the same time, archaeological evidence for the use of metal weapons and artistic representations of armed individuals suggest that there was indeed violent conflict dur-

7.4 Serekh of Narmer inscribed on a wine jar from Halif Terrace
(Photo courtesy of T. Levy and E. C. M. Van den Brink 2003)

ing the period, though it is uncertain whether conflict was between local feuding cities or if there was some external threat.

Egypt is a usual suspect, yet opinions concerning the nature of the Egyptian presence in the southern Levant vary. The famous Narmer Palette from the Egyptian site of Heirakonpolis has traditionally been cited as evidence for Egyptian conquest. The slate palette bears an expertly carved relief that depicts the Egyptian ruler "smiting the enemy," and prisoners are also shown. These victims of Egyptian aggression are thought to be Asiatics because of their hair and beards as well as the presence of symbols that bear a resemblance to the walled cities of southern Canaan (Yadin 1955; Yeivin 1960). Yet, beyond the interpretation of this artifact, there is little archaeological evidence to support such conquest theories. Much of the Egyptian textual evidence cited in support of military theories has been questioned by William Ward (1991); indeed, the whole matter of the feasibility of an Egyptian invasion at this time is questionable.

Whether there was conflict or not, economic relations between the two regions were often implemented on behalf of political leaders. Clay bullae with Egyptian (or "Egyptianized") seal impressions found at several southern sites reflect the involvement of a bureaucracy, and the discovery of wine jars bearing incised serekhs (for example, at Arad, Erani, and Halif Terrace) suggests that at least some trade was carried out on behalf of Egyptian kings. No doubt, interaction with Egypt would have influenced EB1 political structures as the demand for goods enhanced the wealth and status of those with contacts in the Egyptian administration. Relations with Egypt, however, slowed to a trickle during EB2, having a negative impact on much of southern Canaan and beyond.

During the latter part of the Early Bronze Age (EB2–3), a majority of the Levantine population was integrated into a system of city-states, or peer polities. Each unit would have been administered from the city with a political economy that reached into the agrarian hinterland, as suggested by the three-tier settlement hierarchy. Each polity probably had its own leader who ruled from a large center such as Hazor, Beth Shean, Dan, or Beit Yerah; there is, however, no direct evidence for specific rulers in Canaan during this time. That there was some form of municipal governing body may be inferred from archaeological finds, such as the huge granary at Beit Yerah, which implies economic integration at the level of the city-state and some political figure or group to oversee the (re)distribution of a sizable staple surplus. At Arad, a complex of houses demarcated with a surrounding wall was identified by the excavator as a palace (Amiran et al. 1978), though it could represent a housing compound used by a wealthy extended family (Mazar 1990).

THE END OF THE EARLY BRONZE AGE AND THE INTERMEDIATE BRONZE AGE

By the last quarter of the third millennium B.C.E., the Early Bronze Age political systems had all but collapsed entirely. Many people abandoned the cities, returning to a more rural lifestyle. The power of the urban elite was in decline, and political alliances of the urban system would have fallen apart as people reverted to segmentary societies based on kin group affiliations. During this period, known as the Intermediate Bronze Age, political allegiance shifted away from city-based rulers or chiefs toward the heads of large clans or tribes.

Several different factors contributed to the disruption of the economy and political systems of Early Bronze Age societies. Climatic deterioration toward the end of the third millennium B.C.E. played a large role as people struggled to adapt to a drier climate and as the flow of staple goods on which political power was premised dried up (Rosen 1995). There were also external factors, for it is clear that by the end of the Early Bronze Age, relations with Egypt had turned hostile. Evidence for Egyptian aggression can be seen in a Fifth Dynasty tomb relief from Dashasheh that depicts an Egyptian army's siege of an Asiatic city, and textual accounts from the early Sixth Dynasty describe a series of devastating military raids against the cities of Canaan conducted by Pepi I. Rock carvings discovered in the mining region of southern Sinai suggest that competition for access to these mineral resources was one source of conflict.

CANAANITE KINGDOMS: MIDDLE BRONZE AGE

Political Organization

Early in the second millennium B.C.E., urbanism once again took hold throughout much of the southern Levant. A hierarchical relationship in the size of settlements indicates that large urban centers served as the seat of political power for what may be loosely described as city-states, though there is disagreement with regard to the degree of political complexity reached during the Middle Bronze Age. What would ultimately evolve into one of the great urban cultures of the second millennium B.C.E. had its roots in the tribal societies of the preceding Intermediate Bronze Age and early Middle Bronze Age. For instance, many of the large earthworks that surrounded the later Canaanite cities were actually established prior to urban development, serving, perhaps initially, as enclosures for the tents and semipermanent structures used by seminomadic tribal groups.

Information about political organization in the early Middle Bronze Age is also offered by Egyptian texts. The "Tale of Sinuhe" refers to pastoral groups with an internal sociopolitical structure, sometimes including several tribal leaders. The most important source of textual information for this period comes from the Twelfth Dynasty Egyptian inscriptions known collectively as the "Execration Texts." This series of curses on foreign places and peoples considered enemies of Egypt in effect creates the equivalent of a rough geopolitical map for Middle Bronze Age Canaan. More important, the texts all date from the mid-twentieth and mid-nineteenth centuries B.C.E. (that is, c. 1950 B.C.E. and 1850 B.C.E., following Kitchen 1989), thereby providing a before-and-after picture for the process of urbanization. The earlier texts, on one hand, tell of tribes, sometimes with multiple leaders, and a landscape dotted with but a few cities (for example, Ashqelon and Jerusalem). The later group, on the other hand, lists the names of numerous cities, including Acre, Hazor, Jerusalem, Laish, Qadesh, and Shechem, conveying a sense of widespread urbanization.

By the later Middle Bronze Age, the Canaanite countryside was divided up into a series of territorial units, probably distinct city-states or kingdoms resembling "early state modules," as described by Colin Renfrew (1971; also Finkelstein 1992a). Evidence from archaeological surveys reflects an eight-tier settlement hierarchy system by the later MB2 (MB2b–MB2c). Hazor and Avaris (Tel el-Dab'a) alone may be classified as first-order gateway cities, and both are entirely unique cases. Hazor, which reached some 80 hectares, was more akin to Syrian cities of northern Canaan, while Avaris was a Canaanite city established in northern Egypt. Ashqelon (60 ha), Yavne-Yam (65 ha), and Kabri (35–40 ha), all located in coastal areas or along central routes, are considered second-order gateway cities. Third-order gateway settlements, such as Tel Dan (16 ha) and Tel Dor (10 ha), also situated along land and sea routes, were smaller, though perhaps equally wealthy. The inland valleys were dominated by regional centers such as Megiddo (more than 20 ha, including the upper and lower cities), Acco, Beth Shean, Kabri, Shimron, and Shechem. Primary centers of the coastal plain and Shephelah also included Tel el-Ajjul, Aphek, Gezer, Lachish, and Tel es-Safi. Survey data from this period also indicate a rise in the number of rural settlements, suggesting that there were a few relatively large centers surrounded by numerous small villages and farmsteads.

The Second Urban Revolution

By the middle of the Middle Bronze Age, Canaan was divided into distinct political units subsuming urban, rural, and nonsedentary populations. These polities ranged from large chiefdoms to some of the region's first true city-states. Jericho, for example, was a small, autonomous community organized according to family and kinship structures, led, perhaps, by a council of clan heads. Shechem had broad influence in the hill country, which also played host to several autonomous polities of moderate size. Several vast city-states with large urban centers emerged. Hazor, all but abandoned during the Intermediate Bronze Age, saw rapid growth, developing into a bustling urban center that was the core of the consummate Canaanite city-state.

In Syrian texts from this time, Hazor is often mentioned as a contemporary of other kingdoms such as Carchemish, Ugarit, Babylon, Eshnuna, Qatna, Yamhad, and Kaptara (Cyprus or Crete). Reference is also made to emissaries from Babylon who took up long-term residence at Hazor, suggesting that there may have been formal standing political ties between the various city-states. Owing to its status and location, Hazor occupied a unique position as mediator between the Canaanite kingdoms and those of Syro-Cilicia. In many ways, Hazor was more similar to city-states of the Syro-Mesopotamian world system than to the rest of the southern Levant, and it was exceptional with regard to political organization. Avaris (Tel el-Dab'a) may have played a similar role as Hazor's southern counterpart, mediating between Canaanite city-states and Egypt. In both cases, political development in Middle Bronze Age Canaan must be understood in the context of a land situated between two developed states.

The Canaanite city-states no doubt had kings, but it is not until the end of the Middle Bronze Age, when local Canaanite/Amorite texts first appear, that it becomes possible for historians and archaeologists to speak of specific rulers. Textual sources show that kingship in Syria was passed down along descent lines, and mortuary evidence from the southern Levant suggests that descent groups were recognized and that status was hereditary; it is unclear, though, how this figured into the structure of political power. A number of cylinder seals and at least one scarab with the name of Hyksos rulers (for example, Aa-user-re) discovered at Tel el-Ajjul point to political ties between Egypt and southern Canaan. "Warrior burials" may represent the graves of individuals who served some royal court or guard.

Monumental Architecture

In the absence of direct evidence for specific kings and political institutions, archaeologists may infer from the wealth of evidence for monumental architecture that some political body was able to command the contacts and resources necessary for sponsoring extensive public projects. Such projects are seen throughout Canaan. Palaces and "governors' residences" have been excavated at sites such as Tel el-Ajjul, Kabri, Hazor, Lachish, Megiddo, and Aphek. At the latter site, two governors, Takuhlinu and Haya, are mentioned by name in cuneiform tablets dated to about 1230 B.C.E. (Singer 1983; Beck and Kochavi 1985). These massive buildings, some larger than 1,000 square meters (nearly 11,000 sq. ft.), were elaborate in design, with broad, pillared halls, multiple storage rooms, and large courtyards. At both Megiddo and Shechem, the palace was located in the vicinity of the temple, though it is not clear that there was a direct connection. A northern influence is observable in a number of Canaanite palaces, particularly at Tel el-Ajjul and Lachish, which incorporated massive sandstone slabs, or orthostats, reminiscent of those in Syrian palaces. It would appear, therefore, that Canaanite kingship was modeled at least in part on the political structures of Syrian city-states.

The massive earthworks that surrounded many Middle Bronze Age cities also point toward the existence of centralized power structures. They represent a significant investment of resources, above all, labor. The construction of the ramparts at Shiloh required an estimated 250,000 workdays—that is, it would have taken some 3,000 laborers roughly five years to complete the project— and the earthworks at Tel Dan would have taken an estimated 1,000 workers some three years. In a number of cases, such as Dan and Yavne-Yam, small populations relative to the size of the ramparts suggest that much of the labor force responsible for their construction was drawn from beyond the city itself. Those overseeing these projects would also have had access to the expertise of specialists (for example, designers and architects) as well as various other resources, including draft animals and building materials. The function of these massive rampart systems, however, is not always clear. Traditionally, it has been held that the earthen ramparts served as fortification systems, yet recent scholarship has challenged this view. For instance, what armies and types of attack were these structures built to defend against (for example, battering rams)? And would they have been successful against a siege? Numerous other questions have been raised. At Ashqelon, the earthen ramparts were capped by walls, yet it is not clear whether this system was intended to defend against surface attacks or against tunneling meant to penetrate the city surreptitiously (Stager 1991). Some of these ramparts were actually built prior to urban development within them.

Other explanations tend to emphasize the symbolic aspects of these structures. In the central hill country, ramparts formed small citadels, or "highland strongholds," that served primarily as political centers, hosting large public buildings, temples, and storage facilities. In some cases, such as Ashqelon and Dan, elaborate gates were built into the ramparts, serving, on the one hand, as prestige architecture, and, on the other, as an effective way to monitor the movement of goods and people in and out of the city.

Regardless of their specific function, these massive constructions would have stood as highly visible symbols of power. Surely, there were rivalries between neighboring city-states as they vied for grazing and farmland as well as for access to trade networks. Monumental architecture served to enhance the status of local leaders and the cities in general while fostering a strong sense of identity based on location (for example, hailing from a certain city). The ruling political bodies of the city-states thereby engaged in "competitive emulation" or "one-upmanship." Visible from afar, these imposing fortresses and lofty citadels could have facilitated the extension of political power from the cities out into the surrounding regions. In the words of one researcher, the massive rampart systems represented "dynastic propaganda typical of early states striving for legitimacy" (Finkelstein 1992a).

7.5 A model of the reconstructed mud-brick gate and towers of the city of Laish, later captured by the Tribe of Dan (Photo courtesy of Zev Radovan, Land of the Bible Picture Archive)

Warfare and Conflict

Evidence for conflict during the Middle Bronze Age comes from both archaeological remains and text. As for archaeological evidence, weapons such as daggers and spearheads made from the state-of-the-art metal, bronze, have been
found at virtually all of the major cities. Horses were sometimes included in
the warrior burials and were probably used to drive chariots. If the earthen
ramparts were built in response to a need for defensive systems, it is still unclear whether the threat was internal, that is, from conflict between rival
Canaanite cities, or external. Clearly, the infiltration of Asiatics into the Delta
did not please the Egyptians, and texts dating to this time reflect growing animosity toward these intruders. The term "Hyksos," which comes from the
Egyptian *hekau khasut*, literally, "foreign rulers," refers to the Asiatics who
founded the Fifteenth Dynasty in Lower Egypt (c. 1750 B.C.E., MB2b). That
these Asiatics were Canaanites in origin is indicated by the Semitic form of
Hyksos names as well as from the evidence of material culture at sites such as
Tel el-Yehudiyeh and Tel el-Dab'a (Avaris) in the Delta. At the latter site,
Canaanite material of the MB1 appears in the early phases (Str. F-G), suggesting a gradual and peaceful migration into the Delta (Dever 1991). By the middle of the period (MB2), the city's population grew, and Avaris (Tel el-Dab'a,
Str. E) came to be dominated by Asiatic rulers who usurped political control
over the Delta and established the Fifteenth Dynasty (c. 1650 B.C.E.). Archaeo-

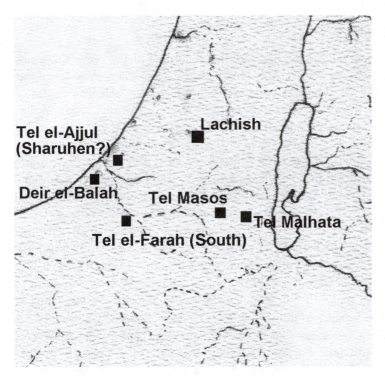

7.6   Map showing key sites in the southern Levant relating to the "Expulsion of the Hyksos" (J. Golden)

logical evidence for this phenomenon can be observed in the burial of royal and/or noble family members in underground vaults.

According to the literary tradition, the Hyksos were defeated at Avaris in about 1550 B.C.E. Following their expulsion from the Delta, a vindictive Egyptian army, led by the pharaoh Ahmose, pursued them into southern Canaan, destroying the city of Sharuhen, which is usually identified as Tel el-Ajjul. The destruction of such an important city would have had a major impact on southern Canaan and beyond. The demise of several southern cities, including Tel el-Far'ah South, Tel Masos, and Tel Malhata, has also been attributed to the Egyptians, though it is likely that the Canaanite cities were already in a state of decline well before the time of the presumed Egyptian invasion.

By the late Middle Bronze Age (MB3, c. 1650–1550 B.C.E.), sociopolitical complexity in the southern Levant had peaked, and with this rapid expansion in population and exploitation of arable land, the Canaanite societies may have reached a critical point where agricultural production failed to keep pace with demand. The very wealth and power of these Canaanite city-states may have contributed, in the end, to their own undoing. Investment in monumental public works continued while the hunt for tin was on. It is conceivable that the demands of both religious and political institutions resulted in an irreversible diversion of resources, ultimately putting a strain on the agricultural base that was too difficult to sustain.

LATE BRONZE AGE

Much of Canaan was under the direct political control of the New Kingdom pharaohs during the Late Bronze Age. Owing to the great interest that the land of Canaan held for the kings of Egypt and Syria, there is a relatively large body of texts from both regions, in addition to some local inscriptions, that complement the archaeological evidence. The thirteenth century B.C.E., in particular (LB2a), is illuminated by the extensive correspondence between rulers from Syro-Palestine and the Egyptian King Amenhotep IV, c. 1350 B.C.E.

Some of the key Egyptian texts yielding information about political organization during Late Bronze Age Canaan are the "Poetical Stela" of Thutmose III, the "Papyrus Anastasi I," the "Onomasticon of Amenemope," and a series of long topographical lists drawn up by the scribes of Thutmose III. Though some scholars have argued that references to Canaan are not explicit and are thus unreliable (Lemche 1991), others have countered that Canaan was clearly recognized as both a land and a people, which is precisely why this term is taken for granted in these ancient texts (Na'aman 1994; Rainey 1996). Canaan was divided into independent political entities of various sizes, as indicated by both textual and archaeological evidence (Na'aman 1996; see also Alt 1925). Regional surveys indicate that there was less integration in the Late Bronze Age than during the Middle Bronze Age in most parts of Canaan (for example, Jezreel), with perhaps the exception of the central hill country (Bunimovitz 1994).

Political History

Following Ahmose's efforts to force the Asiatics out from their seat of power in the Delta, several subsequent pharaohs expanded the scope of the offensive, pursuing the Hyksos deep into southern Canaan in repeated campaigns. This is especially true of Thutmose III, who in year twenty-two of his reign (mid-fifteenth century B.C.E.) launched the first of several attacks on Canaanite cities, including Gezer, Megiddo, and Ta'anach, as recorded in inscriptions from Karnak (Dever 1992b). The Canaanite kingdoms of the Middle Bronze Age had always operated independently of one another, but when confronted with the threat of Thutmose III's armies, the Canaanite and southern Syrian kingdoms formed a coalition under the leadership of the king of Kadesh, with the support of Mitanni. Megiddo apparently served as the headquarters for this "league of Canaanite rulers." Defeat came nonetheless, and Thutmose III established rule over the region, extending the Egyptian sphere of control to as far north as the Orontes.

Much of this information comes from Egyptian sources, and the historical reality of these accounts has been legitimately questioned. Examination of these texts suggests that Egyptian stories about their struggle against a hated foreign power could contain some element of hyperbole. As for the archaeological evidence, destruction levels at southern and inland sites dating to the late seventeenth and early sixteenth centuries B.C.E. seem to support the general historicity of certain events (Weinstein 1981), though the pattern of destruction cannot be so neatly defined. The political upheaval experienced toward the end of the Middle Bronze Age was probably a long, drawn-out process, and some of the problems leading to the Middle Bronze Age collapse were well under way irrespective of Egyptian aggression, a factor that only hastened the process (Bunimovitz 2003; Ilan 2003). Convalescence for the Canaanite cities following these events came slowly or not at all (Gonen 1984). There was a notable decrease in the number and size of Late Bronze Age settlements. Though a number of cities retained their urban character, they seem to have had less control of the hinterlands, where nomadic peoples were once again on the rise.

At the end of Eighteenth Dynasty, Egyptian hegemony over Canaan appeared to be slipping, but with the transition to the Nineteenth Dynasty, further devastation was visited upon the region. Rameses I and his co-regent, Seti I, set out to reestablish dominance and even to outdo their predecessors, launching a series of campaigns into the region in the early thirteenth century that reached into Syria to the very margins of Hittite territory. Rameses II, whose influence in Canaan is demonstrated by the discovery at Tel Dan (Area Y) of a scarab bearing his name, further extended control over Canaan, seeking also to contain the rapidly growing Hittite city-states to the north. Peace between Egypt and Hatti was not yet meant to be, and a great battle was fought between the two near Qadesh on the Orontes early in the thirteenth century B.C.E.

7.7   Map of the Eastern Mediterranean indicating the extent of the Hittite and Egyptian Empires, with Qadesh, the site of the great battle between their armies (J. Golden)

Kings, Regents, and Vassals

Certain titles used in both Egyptian and Babylonian texts suggest that Egyptians bore ranks and designations in administrations associated with Canaan (Rainey 1996). A letter from Alashiya, probably Cyprus, indicates Canaan as a "province" of greater Egypt (Rainey 1996), though some scholars have objected to the specific use of this term (Moran 1992; Na'aman 1975). Several sources, including later biblical texts (for example, Num. 34:7–11), allude to specific borders delimiting Canaan and its cities. There are also references to Canaanite city kings, suggesting that the region comprised city-states with local rulers under the governance of the Egyptian New Kingdom empire. The Amarna Letters coming from Byblos, Beirut, and Tyre also allude to monarchs. For instance, passages concerning Rib Haddi of Byblos refer to the "kings of Canaan" (El Amarna [EA] 109:44–46), while passages from Tyre refer to the "king of Sidon" and the "king of Hazor" as well as to the "king's territory" and the "king's land" (EA 148:39–47; see Moran 1992; Rainey 1996). The Amarna Letters also confirm that many of the local rulers had Hurrian and other foreign names—for example, "Milkilu" from Gezer and "Zimredda" from Lachish (Na'aman 1994)—and by the time of Thutmose III, Canaan was considered part of Hurru. Based on the distribution of names, it generally appears that the city-states of southern Palestine had kings of West Semitic (Amorite) origin, whereas the northern region, including Lebanon and much of southern Syria, usually had Hurrian kings (Na'aman 1994), and the two overlapped in the central hill country. It is important to note, however, that the names that survive heavily favor royalty as opposed to members of the general population.

The pervasive Egyptian presence makes it difficult to distinguish between local, Canaanite political structures and those imposed by Egypt. For much of the Late Bronze Age, Egypt maintained a network of centers and garrisons in order to facilitate its domination in parts of Canaan that were under Egyptian control. It is also unclear whether the Egyptian presence was limited to government and administrative entities, or Egyptian civilians actually settled in Canaan. Political power was played out on an increasingly international stage. A mud-brick fortress dating to the Late Bronze Age has been found at Tel Sera (Str. X), where the material culture included Canaanite and Egyptian as well as Mycenaean and Cypriote goods. This trend is also reflected in the artistic styles of the day. A new form of hybrid iconography known as the "International Style," which combined elements from multiple cultural traditions, emerged during this period. Luxury goods of the hybrid style circulated within a broad supraregional system of interaction, becoming part of a royal vocabulary to which the kings of the day subscribed (Feldman 2002).

The existence of Late Bronze Age kings and regents is evident in the royal architecture from the period. Egyptian-style residencies, or "governors' residences," have been unearthed at several sites, including Beth Shean (Fig. 7.8), which functioned as an important administrative center and garrison in the Egyptian colony. Elaborate buildings interpreted as palaces have also been found at a number of sites apparently not under Egyptian control, indicating

7.8　The Egyptian residence at Beth Shean (J. Golden)

that local rulers enjoyed a certain degree of wealth and power. Whereas during the Middle Bronze Age the temple and palace at Shechem were built as part of one large complex, by the Late Bronze Age the two were distinct and the palace was relocated closer to the city gate. It is possible that this represents a split, perhaps even a rivalry, between the religious and political institutions.

The same trend can be seen at Megiddo of the fourteenth century B.C.E. (Str. VIII), which has some of the most impressive examples of monumental architecture from the Late Bronze Age. In area AA, two palaces flank the city gate, one of which included a large room that was used as either a reception hall or perhaps a large bathhouse. Room 31, hidden in the back of the building, may have served as a treasury. Leading up to the palace area was a gatehouse with six piers constructed of ashlars. It is likely that the gate was more ceremonial in function than defensive, as it lacked side towers. In fact, there was a shift away from the construction of defensive works during the Late Bronze Age, prompting Amihai Mazar (1990) to suggest that the Egyptians may have banned the construction of fortification systems. A cache of carved ivory inlays found in a twelfth-century-B.C.E. palace addition represents the remains of elaborate furnishings. Similarities between the overall plan of the thirteenth- and twelfth-century-B.C.E. palace at Megiddo and a contemporary palace at Ugarit have been observed, and as a general rule, kings of southern Canaan continued to look northward for inspiration in royal architecture and iconography.

The End of The Late Bronze Age

Egyptian domination of Canaan continued into the mid-thirteenth century B.C.E. Appearing at Aphek in a "Governor's Building" dating to this time was a letter from the governor of Ugarit, named Takuhlina, to Haya, the Egyptian high official in Canaan. The clay tablet is inscribed in Akkadian, the lingua franca of international political correspondence at the time. However, by the end of the thirteenth century B.C.E., the 'Apiru and other groups in Canaan were beginning to challenge Egyptian imperialism. At Beth Shean, two basalt victory stelae were erected to commemorate Seti I's suppression of a rebellion headed by two nearby cities in the Jordan Valley, Tel el-Hama-Hamat and Tabaqat Fahil-Pella.

The end of the Late Bronze Age is often characterized as somewhat chaotic, and a number of sites dating to this time, including Debir, Tel Halif, and Tel Beit Mirsim, display evidence for destruction and great burning. The thirteenth-century-B.C.E. city at Tel Sera also saw a violent destruction but was rebuilt not long thereafter. The fall of Hazor (Level XIII) in the thirteenth century B.C.E., destroyed by conflagration, is perhaps the most nefarious event of this era. Hazor was prominent for the duration of the Bronze Age, and surely the conquest of this great Canaanite city was catastrophic for the entire region. In fact, an entire chapter of Joshua (11) is devoted to the story of this city's demise. Hailed as the "head of all those kingdoms," Hazor led a northern coalition in the battle at the Waters of Merom but was defeated. The Book of Joshua (11:13) goes on to explain that although the cities overtaken by Israel were generally spared complete annihilation, Hazor, as the archetype of Canaanite wealth and power, had to be obliterated.

This trend continued into the twelfth century B.C.E., when a number of sites, such as Gezer and Lachish (Str. VI), were destroyed. It is not clear who was responsible for the downfall of these cities, but several, such as Lachish, fell after the reign of Rameses III. One suspect is Seti I, who is known to have campaigned as far north as Qadesh on the Orontes in an effort to reassert Egyptian domination of Syria (Amurru). An Egyptian wall relief from the Temple of Karnak known as the "Cour de la Cachette" refers to a campaign into Canaan where the pharaoh captures Gaza and Megiddo, but there has been debate as to whether these attacks should be attributed to Rameses II (see Singer 1988; Dever 1992a) or to his successor, Merenptah (Merneptah) (Yurco 1990; Stager 1991). There is also the widely discussed "Victory Stele of Merenptah," which consists of a list of places and peoples destroyed by the king on a military campaign into Canaan. That the same campaign is described here as on the wall reliefs from Karnak is all but certain (Yurco 1990). In addition, a fragment from a stele found at Megiddo, one of the victimized cities, refers to Merenptah, though the precise dating of this artifact is uncertain. The Egyptian presence continued for the duration of the Late Bronze Age, but by the end of Rameses II's reign, there was a new threat: the Sea Peoples.

IRON AGE 1: THE HIGHLANDS AND INLAND VALLEYS

The period known as the Iron Age 1 spanned but 200 years (1200–1000 B.C.E.), yet it was a time of considerable political change. Although Egypt did not have the grasp on Canaan that it did for most of the Late Bronze Age, there was still a strong presence at the end of the thirteenth century and into the twelfth century B.C.E. under Rameses III, and perhaps as late as Rameses IV (Weinstein 1981, 1992). The Egyptian influence was still felt in a number of places, continuing as late as the reign of Rameses III and in some cases Rameses IV (Weinstein 1992, 1981). At Beth Shean, several of the Egyptian buildings from Stratum VI were rebuilt, including Building 1500, which was probably either an Egyptian governor's residence or an administrative center. Large anthropoid coffins similar to those from Deir el-Balah appear in cave tombs of Beth Shean's northern cemetery, suggesting that important Egyptian officials or soldiers lived at the site.

A number of finds represent the Egyptian presence at Lachish (Str. VI), including a Twentieth Dynasty cartouche and several votive bowls with hieratic inscriptions, as well as a tomb with an anthropoid coffin bearing a hieratic inscription. In Area P, a temple designed with Egyptian elements similar to that at Beth Shean was excavated. In the Jordan Valley, the authority of Egypt was also felt as late as Dynasty 20 (c. 1196 B.C.E.). Egyptian-style buildings and a cemetery at Tel es-Sa'idiyeh (Str. XII) indicate Egyptian influence into the twelfth century B.C.E. (Pritchard 1985; Tubb 2002).

The Late Bronze Age fortress at Tel Sera (Str. X) was rebuilt in the twelfth century B.C.E. (Str. IX), and although Egyptian material (including an Egyptian bowl with a hieratic inscription referring to "Year 22" of what is most likely the reign of Rameses III), continued at the site, the Aegean and Cypriote imports ceased. The fortress was destroyed again during the twelfth century B.C.E. at around the same time that the Egyptian presence declined. Tel Mor, located at the mouth of the Nahal Rubin, shared a similar fate. The small fortress (11 x 11 m) was burned near the close of the thirteenth century and rebuilt in the Iron 1a (Str. VI-V). Egyptians also maintained their hold on domination in the Timna copper mines, as demonstrated by multiple occurrences of Rameses III's cartouche at the site.

Much of what archaeologists know about the Iron 1 period comes from biblical and historical sources, with the result being a tendency to underestimate the level of cultural continuity that existed (Dever 1992b). Vestiges of the Canaanite culture appear throughout the southern Levant, and in fact, not only did many cities persevere, but in areas such as the Jezreel and Beth Shean Valleys, there seems to have been localized florescence. The city of Megiddo rebounded shortly after its thirteenth-century-B.C.E. destruction (Str. VIIb), retaining a distinctively Canaanite character thereafter (for example, with red and black painted wares). The palace near the city gate was rebuilt with an annex that contained a hoard of ivory, serving, perhaps, as a palace treasury (Mazar 1994). In the eleventh century B.C.E., Megiddo (Str. VIA) boasted a large palace located near the city gate.

The Canaanite city of Gezer seems to have remained autonomous, and biblical references relate that neither Joshua nor David were able to bring the site under Israelite control (Dever 1992a). In the mid-tenth century B.C.E., Gezer was among the lands that were conquered by Egypt, but an agreement was brokered whereby the city was turned over to Solomon as part of the dowry of the pharaoh's daughter. In the Jordan Valley, Tel es-Sa'idiyeh, identified as either biblical Zarethan or Zafon, also retained a Canaanite character. It is difficult to determine how political organization among the Canaanites may have changed as a result of broader regional trends, but the Hebrew Bible gives the impression that the Canaanites still had kings.

The perseverance of the Egyptians and Canaanites notwithstanding, clearly there was considerable change during the Iron 1. Hundreds of new villages appeared in the highlands in the twelfth century B.C.E., but where these people came from has been the subject of debate. Current scholarship has them as Canaanites, some displaced in the wake of the Sea Peoples' arrival on the coast (Dever 1995c; 2003b), others pastoralists who fled to the hills during the turbulent thirteenth century B.C.E. (Finkelstein 2003; 1996b). According to Israel Finkelstein and Neil Asher Silberman, "The emergence of early Israel was an outcome of the collapse of the Canaanite culture, not its cause"(2001, 118).

Of course, the Hebrew Bible tells of conquering Israelites, but this explanation has found little support in the archaeological evidence. Several Canaanite cities do appear to have been destroyed at the end of the twelfth century as well as in the eleventh century B.C.E. (for example, Deir 'Alla in the Jordan Valley), but it seems more reasonable to assume that Egyptians and Sea Peoples, well documented at the time, played the part of conquerors. For want of a better term, William Dever (1992a) has suggested using the term "Proto-Israelite" to describe the new highlanders, yet this term must be applied with caution. The Victory Stele of Merenptah (c. 1207 B.C.E) constitutes the first known reference to "Israel," but this example remains unique. Archaeological evidence for political organization during the Iron 1 is rare. One notable exception is Har Adir in the Upper Galilee, where a fortress protected by a casemate wall dating to the eleventh century B.C.E. has been excavated. It is possible that the fortress was constructed as a response to a growing threat from Tyre, Sidon, or some Phoenician power (Mazar 1990).

IRON AGE I: SOUTHERN COASTAL PLAIN/PHILISTIA

The political history of the Philistines, a people who settled and ultimately took control of the southern coastal plain at the beginning of the twelfth century B.C.E., is vague. As the term "Sea Peoples" is somewhat ambiguous, referring to a number of different groups, it is difficult to determine at what point archaeologists should begin speaking of them as "Philistines." To begin with, there are questions about their arrival. In some cases, the incursion of Sea Peoples was violent. At Dor, the Sikils appear to have taken the city by storm in the beginning of the twelfth century B.C.E. (Stern 1995). A letter sent to the king of Alashiya (Cyprus) by Ammurapi, the last king of Ugarit, was found in the

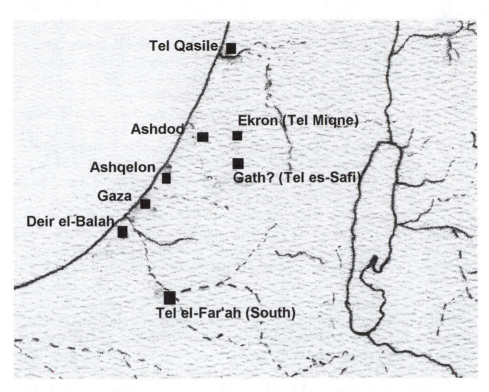

7.9 Map showing major cities of Philistia, based on archaeological research and descriptions in the Hebrew Bible (J. Golden)

ruins of that city (c. 1185 B.C.E.) and describes a desperate situation: "enemy boats have arrived, the enemy has set fire to the cities and wrought havoc. . . ." In the region that would become Philistia, the southern coastal plain and Shephelah, the destruction of several Late Bronze Age cities coincided with the arrival of Sea Peoples. They landed on the coast in droves, and as their numbers increased, they began pushing inland. There can be no doubt that this migration had an immediate and profound impact on the balance of power in the southern Levant.

The chronological framework for this cultural phase is provided in large part by securely dated finds relating to Egyptian royalty. In the eighth year of his reign (c. 1174 B.C.E.),[1] Rameses III recognized the threat posed by these new peoples and engaged them in a great battle recorded in vivid color at Medinat Habu. In addition, two cartouches found at southern Levantine sites (Acco and Deir 'Alla) bear the name of Queen Tausert (c. 1187–1185 B.C.E.), and a cartouche of Seti II (1199–1193 B.C.E.) was found in the "governor's residence" at Tel el-Far'ah South. In several instances, these artifacts were found in association with Philistine Bichrome Wares. A scarab with Seti II's *prenomen*, the king's throne name, also appears at Tel Masos (Fritz and Kempinski 1983).[2]

The Hebrew Bible provides some insight into political organization during the Iron 1 in Philistia. In 1 Samuel 31:9, there is a reference to the "Land of the Philistines" (*'eretz Pelishtim*), and the Book of Joshua (13:2) mentions the "Regions of the Philistines," which may imply that there were political subdivisions within the broader Philistine polity (Machinist 2000). Philistine cities are also mentioned in biblical passages, particularly Judges 14–16, which describes the so-called Pentapolis, the five primary cities of Philistia: Ashqelon, Ashdod, Ekron, Gaza, and Gath. (See sidebar, "The Philistine Pentapolis.")

Archaeological research has also revealed other important Philistine centers. Tel Qasile was not only an economic center but also the seat of political power for the Yarkon basin. Iron 1 levels at Tel Aphek have yielded Philistine pottery, and a Philistine cemetery has been excavated at Azor. A Philistine town has also been discovered at Beth Shemesh (Str. III), where the coastal region meets the foothills. As the biblical sources (1 Samuel and Judges) had it, Beth Shemesh was an Israelite city—but this is not borne out by the archaeological evidence. The city is mentioned in 1 Samuel in conjunction with the "Battle of Even Ha'ezer," and thus, it seems that Beth Shemesh was a site of contention between various groups, perhaps at the border between the distinct polities.

The archaeological and textual evidence relating to the early Philistines conveys a climate of perpetual conflict during the Iron 1. The construction of fortification systems at cities such as Ashqelon gives some indication that Philistine cities were not at ease. The famous wall paintings from Medinat Habu clearly document at least one major battle between a coalition of Sea Peoples and the Egyptians. The Hebrew Bible also describes conflict, particularly along the border between Philistia and Israel-Judea, which is described in both Judges 13–14 and 1 Samuel 6 as running north-south along the western flank of the hill country. The story of Samson (Judg. 13–16) also refers to distinct boundary lines, and the overall relationship between the two peoples is generally described as adversarial.

The cities of Philistia served as the political centers for broader city-states, and both the textual and archaeological evidence suggest that each was ruled by its own local king. The twelfth-century-B.C.E. city at Tel Miqne–Ekron (Str. VII-V) boasted a number of large monumental structures, several of which featured rectangular and circular hearths. These types of hearths are best known from the royal architecture of the Aegean, where palaces incorporating the design have been excavated at Pylos, Mycenae, and Tyrins. Though the Aegean examples are larger, they are remarkably similar in terms of overall design (Dothan 1995). The wide scope of research at Tel Miqne–Ekron has carried archaeologists beyond the site proper, revealing that the city at one point commanded authority over a much broader area and was at the helm of a large city-state, implied by the borders of Ekron as described in the Bible.

Tel el-Far'ah South was another important city of Philistia. The large mudbrick fortress already extant at the site appears to have been appropriated by Philistines who inhabited Tel el-Far'ah toward the end of the Iron 1. In the impressive "governor's residence" excavated at the site, one room had some forty-five vessels and stoppers with Egyptian stamp seals. Other buildings at Tel el-Far'ah South were similar to private houses from Egypt, indicating that Egyptians may have lived at the site. Thus, it is not entirely clear who actually controlled the city at this time. According to the biblical tradition, each city of

The Philistine Pentapolis

The archaeological search for this Pentapolis has generally been successful: Though the identity of two cities, Gaza and Gath, remains unresolved, the other three have been excavated and identified with relative certainty. Archaeological research at Ashdod has confirmed the existence of the Philistine city by this name. Ashqelon was a great port city known from cuneiform texts as well as from the Bible. By 1150 B.C.E., a massive fortification system with a glacis and mud-brick tower was built, and the city grew to some 60 hectares (Stager 1991). The Philistine city that is best known through archaeology is the site of Tel Miqne–Ekron (Gitin and Dothan 1987), which was by far the Philistines' most important inland stronghold. Tel Miqne–Ekron was probably founded sometime in the beginning of the twelfth century and grew relatively quickly into a major fortified city of roughly 20 hectares (50 acres), including an upper and lower city (Gitin and Dothan 1987; Gitin 1995). It was long believed that the massive archaeological site, located precisely where the Bible places ancient Ekron, was indeed the Philistine city by that name, and with the discovery of an inscription at the site referring to Ekron by name, this identification is all but certain.

Identifying Gaza and Gath has proven more complicated. The large tell site at modern-day Gaza City is generally believed to be the ancient city by that name, but owing to the location of the modern city directly atop the mound, as well as conflict in the area today, systematic investigation of the site has been limited. Gath, in contrast, remains "at large" in the sense that there has, as of yet, been no positive identification of the ancient site, though there are several candidates.[3] For some time, it was believed that Tel Erani was the fifth Philistine city and that both the local modern town of Qiryat Gath and nearby Kibbutz Gath had taken their names from the ancient city. However, multiple seasons of excavation at Erani have produced but scant remains of Philistine material culture, raising doubts about its identification as a major Philistine center. Rather, archaeologists have turned their attention toward Tel es-Safi (Zafit) in the southern Shephelah, just south of Ekron (Maeir and Ehrlich 2001). The location of the site, situated in a fertile alluvial basin along local conduits that make it accessible from the coastal plain to the hill country as well as to international trade routes, is consistent with that described in the Bible. More important, recent excavations at Tel es-Safi have revealed the remains of a city that was clearly Philistine in character, and it has thus emerged as the best candidate for the city of Gath (Maeir 2002).

Philistia had some type of local king, referred to as *seren*, a term that is probably related to the Greek word *tyranos*. An interesting exception was Achish, the ruler of Gath, who is referred to by a Semitic term for king (*melek*) several times in 1 Samuel, thus raising questions about Philistine hegemony over the city (Kassis 1965).

After this initial age of fluorescence, by the end of the Iron 1 and the beginning of the Iron 2 Philistia seems to have experienced a period of political disorganization. By the tenth century B.C.E., Ekron, partly destroyed, and its size severely reduced, began a period of some two and a half centuries of decline. Evidence for sitewide destruction dating to the ninth century has been detected at Tel es-Safi.

The Phoenicians at this time held several important cities, including Tyre and Sidon on the northern coast. Phoenician kings are mentioned in both biblical and extra-biblical texts, often in terms of having friendly relations with the Israelites and not-so-friendly relations with the Egyptians. At the port city of Tel Dor, there was an important harbor and a glacis fortification system.

IRON AGE 2–3: THE ISRAELITES

The Rise of Israelite Culture and "the United Monarchy"

The Iron 2 is one of the most fascinating periods politically in the history of the region, and there is a relative wealth of archaeological and historical material concerning this era. City-states had flourished throughout Canaan during the Bronze Age, but it was not until the tenth century B.C.E. that anything akin to a centralized political unit emerged in the southern Levant. The process of state formation had begun somewhat earlier, probably during the Iron 1–2 transition, when the highland population began to expand. As noted previously, there is evidence for widespread settlement in the central hill country and Galilee during the Iron 1, but this was generally restricted to small farming communities with little political integration. In time, this population grew to a point where sites were located fewer than 3–4 km apart, creating a situation where a subsistence mode of herding and farming could no longer sustain the society. According to Frank S. Frick (1985), the processes of state formation were set in motion as an adaptive response to a changing sociopolitical landscape that involved agricultural intensification and demographic expansion. Seeking to expand their resource base, the highlanders came into direct competition with their neighbors—the Canaanites and Philistines—a situation that can often lead to qualitative changes in society.

Irrespective of where the people came from—either as immigrants, indigenous Canaanites, or both—the region saw a population increase that began to put pressure on the land and its resources. Adam Zertal (1998, 242; 2001, 38) has proposed that Israelites, unable simply to seize land, may have gained access to resources through diplomacy and exchange; however, there is no evidence with which to test this model. As competition increased, society became more politically integrated, organizing under the leadership of chiefs (Finkelstein 1989), who would have negotiated, in turn, with tribal elders willing to cede some of their power in the interest of group protection (Gottwald 1979,

1983). State formation thus began during the tenth century B.C.E. when previously autonomous tribes merged into larger political units. According to Victor Matthews, "The competitive nature of neighboring chiefs, circumscription, aggressive incursions by the city-states, and the tenuous system of choosing tribal leaders all contributed to the dissolution of tribal autonomy" (2002, 40). In support of this reconstruction, he pointed to the story of Saul's rise to power and his constant struggle to maintain it in 1 Samuel. At the time when Saul is supposed to have lived, there was as yet neither a centralized bureaucracy nor any state religious institutions, but within a century there would be a bureaucracy and centralized control over production and distribution as well as efforts to establish a state religion. The account of Saul was surely written in later times and might reflect certain memories about an ancient reality.

As the Hebrew Bible would have it, the United Monarchy, beginning in the tenth century B.C.E., was a relatively short period lasting roughly seventy-five years. Upon the death of Solomon in approximately 930 B.C.E., the United Monarchy fell apart. The tribes of the north revolted against Jerusalem, establishing the Kingdom of Israel with Jeroboam as its king. The southern tribes remained loyal to Rehoboam, the son of Solomon, who took the throne of the southern Kingdom of Judah. Although traditional scholarship has treated this as the start of the era when kings and dates can be treated as reliable historical fact, this view has recently been challenged by those who argue that the biblical account was little more than myth. The archaeological evidence, settlement data, and extra-biblical sources, in many cases, do not concur with the Hebrew Bible.

Monumental Architecture

A distinctive vocabulary of royal architecture can be observed in the archaeological record of the Iron 2. Typical features include casemate walls, six-chambered gates, and Proto-Aeolic capitals; ashlar masonry using dressed stones represents an appropriation of the Phoenician royal style. Many of these elements have been observed at Megiddo, the seat of an administrative center during the tenth century B.C.E. (Str. IVB-VA). Two large public buildings (1723 and 6000) at the site were probably palaces. Palace 1723 was part of a larger complex enclosed by a fieldstone wall and piers of ashlars. It also had a four-chambered gate with stone Proto-Aeolic capitals, a feature considered a standard in royal Israelite architecture by many scholars. Other buildings display northern Syrian and southern Anatolian influences. The city also had a massive six-chambered gate (18 x 20 m) built of ashlars, though the dating of the gate is uncertain. Near the gate, a wall built in the elaborate "offset-and-inset" style was found. Another structure at Megiddo, consisting of small, individual units, has been the centerpiece of one of the great debates of southern Levantine archaeology (see Routledge 1995). There are questions concerning the dating of this feature, that is, whether it belongs to the tenth or ninth century B.C.E. Even more controversial is the interpretation of its function: It was initially said that the units represented royal stables, such as those ascribed to Solomon in the Bible, but others have argued that they were storage units.

Six-chambered gates have been discovered at a number of sites, including

Hazor, Megiddo, Tel Ira, Lachish, and Gezer. Recently, some scholars have downplayed the importance of these gates as evidence for state architecture (Niemann 1997; Finkelstein 1996a), arguing that at the very least there are no grounds for attributing them to Solomon, or to any specific king, for that matter. The gates clearly had a practical purpose as part of the city's defensive works. The Gezer gate system included a platform atop the tower from which to defend the city against would-be intruders while providing a way to monitor movement in and out of the city. Furthermore, gates of the same style have been found at Canaanite and Philistine sites (for example, Ashdod), raising questions about whether they should be regarded as unique to Israelite architecture.

Regardless of who was responsible for the construction of these monumental works, they suggest a number of things about Iron Age societies. Clearly, all of these monumental structures point to a developed urbanism (Master 2001), which is indicative of both population growth and agglomeration. They also reflect the command of extensive resources, including materials and, above all, labor. Politically, they contributed to the identities of these cities. Huge residential buildings served as palaces for local rulers, while other structures were the focal point of political and administrative activity. The massive walls and gate systems represent defensive measures as well as prestige architecture designed to project an image of prominence. The key question with regard to these projects concerns to what extent they represent political integration at a broader level. That is, were they independent undertakings, or was the centralized state involved? David Ussishkin (1977, 1985), excavating at Lachish (Level IV), ascribed the construction of the massive brick fortification wall and triple-chambered gate to a Judahite king, either Rehoboam or Jehoshaphat. Cities of the Negev, such as Arad, Beer Sheva, and Malhata, also had great walls and other monumental works in the late tenth and ninth centuries B.C.E., and it is likely that their construction was financed, at least in part, with state funds from Jerusalem (Rainey 2001).

It is, of course, during the Iron Age 2 that Jerusalem came to prominence as a great political center, and there are several reasons for this. Jerusalem was situated on a defensible highland perch. Geographically speaking, it occupied a centralized location in the highlands, the heart of Israelite culture, with access to routes of communication via the Jordan Valley. According to the Hebrew Bible, it was not among the cities taken during the initial conquest, which gave it an air of neutrality and thus prevented internal squabbling between rival tribal leaders (Na'aman 1996; Ben-Tor and Ben-Ami 1998; Matthews 2002); that is, Jerusalem was a "disembedded capitol" (see Blanton et al. 1993). In addition, as the story goes, David conquers the Jebusite city, making it the capital of the great expansionist kingdom (2 Sam.), and his successor, Solomon, builds Jerusalem into a great city. (See sidebar, "The Archaeology of Jerusalem.")

Yet, questions concerning the historicity of the biblical account relating to Jerusalem and the monarchy remain. The text itself is not always consistent, but more important, substantial excavations in Jerusalem have turned up virtually no evidence for any of Solomon's great buildings, and the dating of buildings attributed to him elsewhere (for example, Megiddo and Hazor) are

The Archaeology of Jerusalem

The Canaanite city of Jebus was first established sometime during the Middle Bronze Age, perhaps around 1800 B.C.E., on a low hill surrounded by the mountains of Judea. Located near the Gihon Spring in the Kidron Valley, Jebus was one of the first sites in a wave of settlement in the central hill country. It probably served as a commercial center where people from nearby villages would congregate, and as a central point in the long-distance trade networks emerging at the time.

The Middle Bronze Age occupation is attested by archaeological evidence, including a long stretch of wall dating to the eighteenth century B.C.E., and the city enters the historical record with its mention in the Execration Texts (c. 1900–1800 B.C.E.). There are several references to Jerusalem (Urushalim) in the Amarna Letters indicating that it was a city-state with its own king during the Late Bronze Age, yet there is scant archaeological evidence representing this phase. One explanation for this apparent gap is that the Temple Mount was built (mainly during the Islamic period) on top of Late Bronze and early Iron Age cities, thus obliterating most traces of the mid–second millennium occupation (Knauf 2000).

One of the most intriguing and controversial topics in all of the archaeology of the southern Levant concerns the occupation of Jerusalem during the Iron 2. The beginning of the Iron 2 is generally understood to be the time when the biblical kings David and Solomon ruled from Jerusalem. Yet the archaeological evidence dating to this period is slim: Stratum 14 in Areas D1 and E and the eastern slope have yielded some remains dating to the tenth century B.C.E., but there is little more. Some scholars have cited the general lack of archaeological remains from this period as evidence against the existence of a Jerusalem-based monarchy at that time, and the historicity of the biblical account has been called into question (Finkelstein 1999; Finkelstein and Silberman 2001). Others have countered that this "negative evidence" proves little, as Herod (first century B.C.E.) is supposed to have razed the entire area during his extensive building projects, wiping out the traces of earlier structures. It is worth noting that a similar situation exists with the city of Byblos, where no archaeological remains from Late Bronze or Iron Age times have been discovered, despite the fact that it is documented in texts from the period.

The density of modern occupation in this critical area of ancient Jerusalem, as well as the current political situation, has limited the amount of archaeological research on the Iron Age occupation. Nonetheless, a few outstanding archaeological features dating to this period have been excavated. On the eastern slope of the Iron Age city, archaeologists have uncovered a large stepped structure preserved to a height of 16.5 m (about 54 ft.) that can ten-

(continues)

The Archaeology of Jerusalem *(continued)*

tatively be dated to the tenth century B.C.E. (Shiloh 1993). Though some have been tempted to associate this structure with David's "fortress of Zion" (Metsudat Zion) as described in 1 Chronicles 11:5, it is more likely that it served as a retaining wall employed in the construction of the citadel. But where the early part of the Iron 2 is concerned, opinions about the history of the city vary widely (for a recent summary of these arguments see Rainey 2001; Finkelstein 1999; Abu el-Haj 1998).

Jerusalem expanded rapidly during the eighth and seventh centuries B.C.E., reflecting a broad shift in the demography of Judah as a whole. Sprawling over an area of more than 150 acres, with a population as high as 20,000, the city dwarfed many of the major towns in the Judean countryside. Lachish, the second largest city in Judah, occupied only 20 acres, while other Judean towns averaged only 5 to 8 acres in area. Excavations in the Jewish Quarter of the Old City reflect the city's growth around this time, and many of the archaeological discoveries suggest this was a time of conflict and stress for the city.

Nahman Avigad's famous excavations in the Old City revealed the remains of new homes built on the Western Hill, reflecting the settlement's northward expansion. At the summit of the Western Hill, a section of a massive stone wall, commonly known as the Broad Wall, was discovered. More than 7 m (23 ft.) wide, the wall would have stood an estimated 9 m (29.5 ft.) high. While serving to widen the city limits, it appears that some of this wall's construction entailed the destruction of some of the aforementioned new homes, suggesting to the excavator that this may have been a time of crisis. In fact, the sheer size of the wall, designed perhaps to withstand the might of Assyrian battering rams, has led to theories that it was built by Hezekiah in preparation for the coming of Sennacherib (Avigad 1983; see also Mazar and Hanan 1988).

Jerusalem of the eighth century B.C.E. is also represented by the large corpus of stamped la-melekh jar handles dated to this time. Fragments of a Proto-Aeolic capital and the rubble of ashlar masonry, though not found in situ, provide additional evidence for the Iron 2 occupation, and perhaps, more specifically, the presence of an administrative building or palace. This may roughly correlate with the fall of Israel in 722 B.C.E. and the subjugation of much of Judah at the end of the century at the hands of Neo-Assyrians.

The Iron 2 occupation is also represented by residential structures such as the "lower terrace housing" (Area E1) and the "Ashlar House," which dates to the seventh century B.C.E. The "House of the Bullae," which probably dates to the end of the century, was in all likelihood an archive or administrative building, since some fifty bullae with seal impressions were among the remains of the burnt structure (Avigad 1983). Also dating to the seventh century was the four-room style "House of Ahiel" (Shiloh 1993).

There is evidence for the planning and construction of massive public works in late Iron Age Jerusalem, especially the extensive municipal water systems that brought water from the Gihon Spring to a point inside the city walls. One system, known as "Warren's Shaft," involved a sloping tunnel with rock-cut stairs leading down to a vertical shaft some 14 m (46 ft.) deep, the base of which met another tunnel that led to the spring. Although the precise date of this system is unknown, most scholars agree that it falls somewhere between the late tenth century B.C.E. and the time of Hezekiah, late in the eighth century B.C.E.

The other major water system is known as "Hezekiah's Tunnel," though its construction cannot be linked to this particular king with certainty. The winding tunnel cuts through more than 500 m (1,640 ft.) of bedrock beneath the city, making partial reuse of the earlier Warren's Shaft system. Like the latter, Hezekiah's Tunnel cannot be directly dated, yet some scholars have interpreted it as part of the precautionary measures taken in anticipation of Sennacherib's impending offensive in the eighth century B.C.E., as described in the Hebrew Bible (2 Kings 20:20; 2 Chron. 32:1–4, 30). An inscription carved on the cavern wall near its southern end, marking the meeting point of two work crews tunneling toward each other, thereby commemorated the completion of the project.

The fortification system of this period also included a large tower located just north of the massive wall. The tower, perhaps part of a gatehouse system, was preserved to a height of about 8 m (26 ft.) with walls 4 m (13 ft.) thick built of large, rough-hewn stones and ashlar corners. The tower displays evidence for burning along with arrowheads and other material dating to the sixth century B.C.E. (late Iron Age), suggesting a violent end at this time. Indeed, a number of structures dating to the early sixth century B.C.E. (for example, the Burnt House, the House of Ahiel, and the Ashlar House) appear to have experienced violent destruction by fire. Scholars have attempted to tie this archaeological evidence with biblical references to the destruction of the First Temple by the Babylonians in 586 B.C.E. (Shiloh 1993). And while it is difficult to determine the precise date of the destruction levels in Jerusalem, such an association could also explain why excavations have revealed few remains of royal buildings near the Temple Mount.

problematic; there are no extra-biblical sources (for example, inscriptions) associated with Solomon.

There is evidence for massive public architecture in Jerusalem during the later Iron Age (eighth century B.C.E.). One of the best examples is a city wall no less than 7 meters (about 23 ft.) wide that was probably built at the end of the eighth century B.C.E., perhaps in anticipation of an impending attack by Sennacherib (c. 701 B.C.E.). This wall also served to expand the city limits, which may also reflect the population growth seen throughout Judah around this time.

7.10   The eighth-century "Broad Wall" in Jerusalem (J. Golden)

Early in the ninth century B.C.E., Samaria emerged as the capital of the northern Kingdom of Israel, which now extended into Transjordan in the area north of
the Arnon River, as it is described in the Meshe Stele. It would remain the capital
for some 150 years until its destruction by the Assyrians in about 720 B.C.E. This
was a prime location owing to its proximity to Shechem as well as to the roads
leading to the coast and to Phoenicia, an important political ally for the Om-
rides. Massive ashlar walls, built using the "header and stretcher" design, enclosed the royal acropolis at Samaria, which covered an area of some 4 acres.

Writing and Bureaucracy

By the eighth century and perhaps earlier, a great scribal tradition had developed in Israel. The use of Egyptian hieratic signs and numerals indicates extensive borrowing of the script, if not of the Egyptian bureaucratic model altogether (Mathews 2002; James 1988). Most of the scribes' work was concerned
with maintaining records of transactions and public works. Scribes and administrators also made extensive use of bullae, as indicated by the multiple examples discovered in Jerusalem and elsewhere.

In some cases, portions of the Hebrew Bible may represent authentic lists of
actual individuals grafted directly into the body of the narrative. For example,
the detailed lists of officials and advisers in David's court (2 Sam. 23:8–39),
written in prosaic style and contrasting sharply with the meter of the rest of

7.11   The "Tomb of the Pharaoh's Daughter" at Siloam in Jerusalem (J. Golden)

the text, are more consistent with the format of geographical and personnel lists observed elsewhere in the Near East (Hess 1997). Similarly, in 1 Kings, there are lists of Solomon's high officials, the twelve districts of his administration, and a resumé of building activities. The term *lsr r*, a designation for the governor or mayor of the city, is known from extra-biblical texts, including one of the Kuntillet 'Ajrud jar inscriptions, and 1 Kings 22:26 and 2 Kings 23:8 refer to the mayors of Jerusalem and Samaria. These titles contrast with those from the time of Saul, which are mostly kin-based (Edelman 1985), and may represent the development of a meritocracy or a new emphasis on alliance building. This trend may also be reflected in 2 Samuel 20:23, when David, organizing his armies, hired mercenaries as well as loyalists and made high-profile appointments that included non-Israelites (Matthews 2002). These measures, too, may have been taken to promote an ideology of the state.

Foreign Relations

As for foreign affairs, political relations between the Israelites and their neighbors varied over time. Archaeologically, there is a clear influence from Phoenicia in the royal architecture of Israel in the ninth century B.C.E. According to the biblical tradition, at this time there was considerable internal political struggle in addition to concerns over the Aramean threat. King Ahab of Israel is said to have married Jezebel, the daughter of the Phoenician king of Sidon, in order to forge an alliance and strengthen ties with the Phoenicians. Similarly, Solomon married an Egyptian princess at a time when Canaan served as a buffer between Egyptian and Phoenician rivals. Solomon, in fact, may have been playing both sides, for he also concluded a treaty with King Hiram of Tyre (Matthews 2002).

One of the most significant developments in foreign relations in the late Iron Age is the emergence of trade with South Arabia. Limestone altars and South Arabian inscriptions found at sites in Judah, such as Jerusalem, Beersheba, and 'Aroer, attest to the existence of a trade route that led from South Arabia through Edom and the Negev to the coast. The famous biblical story about Queen Sheba may relate to this development, reflecting a later process rather than an actual event during the Solomonic days (see Finkelstein and Silberman 2001).

Economic Control

The rise of the state in the Iron 2 also entailed centralized control over economic resources. Archaeologists have uncovered the remains of large granaries at Beth Shemesh, Megiddo, and Hazor, in each case situated in the vicinity of other buildings that served either as royal storage facilities or stables. A large palace granary was also discovered at Samaria, the capital of the Northern Kingdom. There is textual evidence for centralized economic power. The kings probably held or controlled vast tracts of land, as suggested by the royal stamped jar handles referring to royal vineyards (Mazar 1990; Avigad 1986; Hestrin and Dyagi 1979). Some of the more ornate seals made use of titles such as "servant of [the king]," "who is over the house," "who is over the tax," and "prince." The title Sar 'ir, found in several instances, including on inscribed jars from Kuntillet 'Ajrud, refers to a city governor or mayor. According to the Hebrew Bible (1 Kings), King Solomon was able to accumulate great wealth through an advanced system of taxation and investment in extensive trading expeditions, at one point in partnership with Hiram, the king of Tyre. He also had access to a huge labor force through conscription; again, there is no archaeological evidence to support this account.

Israelite Kingship

The Hebrew Bible, particularly the prophetic works, is replete with references to specific kings and often provides information about the political state of affairs. For instance, the reign of Jehu is said to have been characterized by conflict between the Omride and Davidic Dynasties (2 Kings 8–9), and peace was not restored until the time of Jeroboam II. One of the most controversial topics concerning the Iron Age is whether David was an actual historical figure. The life and deeds of David are recounted throughout 1 and 2 Samuel, but, as always, it is difficult to tease apart fact from myth through the archaeological record. More convincing are the several instances in the Bible (2 Sam. 7:26 and 1 Kings 2:24) and at least one extra-biblical text (Dan inscription), and quite possibly two (Meshe Stele), where the term "House of David" is used in reference to the King of Judah. This term appears as a counterpart to "King of Israel," which denotes the ruler of the Northern Kingdom. As for later kings, di-

7.12   Stamped "lamelekh" jar handle from Lachish (Drawing by J. Golden; adapted from Amnon Ben-Tor. 1992. *The Archaeology of Ancient Israel.* New Haven, CT: Yale University Press.)

rect textual evidence often refers to the individuals mentioned in the Hebrew Bible (for example, the dedication of Hezekiah's Tunnel in Jerusalem), including texts from other regions (for example, Sargon II's "Khorsabad Annals"). At Samaria, archaeologists discovered tomb chambers belonging to the kings of Israel hewn into the rock beneath the royal palace (Franklin 2002).

Superpowers from the East

Indigenous state structures, however, would not last long, and during the last few decades of the eighth century B.C.E. most of the southern Levant was under constant threat of a new imperial power, the Neo-Assyrians. In 734 B.C.E., Tiglath Pileser III launched campaigns into both Phoenicia and Philistia, turning his attention next to the Galilee, conquering that region and exiling its people. The citizens of Samaria stood fast for another decade but soon succumbed to a similar fate—conquest and exile in about 720 B.C.E.—only to be subjected to forays conducted by Sargon II and Sennacherib in the final decades of the eighth century and by Esarhaddon and Ashurbanipal in the seventh century. Maintaining a consistent presence in the region and occasionally using force, the Neo-Assyrian kings forged the "global" empire of its day and for a period of some seventy years dominated what was called *pax Assyriaca,* an economic policy explained in ideological terms. For a brief time, the Judean King Hezekiah gained political control over a number of cities, including the Philistine center of Ekron, but Sennacherib reasserted Neo-Assyrian ascendancy in all of Philistia and beyond (for example, Lachish III) at the end of the eighth century B.C.E.

Much of what archaeologists know about this period derives from the annals of two later Neo-Assyrian kings, Esarhaddon and Ashurbanipal. The accuracy of both the historical and biblical accounts of the Assyrian onslaught is corroborated by archaeological evidence. At Tel Dor, one of the earliest examples of a Greek bowl in the southern Levant, dating to the late eighth century B.C.E., was found on the floor near the city gate, and the city is said to have been destroyed in 733 B.C.E. (Stern 1995). Neo-Assyrian power in the region began to fade, however, as the Assyrians were forced to shift attention to a growing threat on their eastern border, and the Egyptians made immediate attempts to seize control. Soon another superpower from the east, the Neo-Babylonians, would fill the vacuum left by the Assyrians.

Nebuchadnezzar was attempting to complete the destruction of the already weakened Israelite cities by launching a major military campaign through the countryside. This operation culminated, according to the Hebrew Bible, in the destruction of Solomon's Temple in Jerusalem at the hands of Nebuchadnezzar in 586 B.C.E.[4] Here is one case in which events described in the Hebrew Bible can be documented archaeologically, as excavations at a number of sites in Judea have produced evidence for destruction that generally coincides with this date. At Lachish (Str. II), there is evidence for destruction by heavy fire, and among the burnt debris of the Stratum II city gate, archaeologists recovered an ostracon bearing a distress letter written by a certain Hoshayahu to his commander, Yaush. At the southern fortress of Arad, several ostraca containing references to the mobilization of forces and supplies were found in a destruction level. Indeed, there is evidence for the destruction of Jerusalem itself, with extensive traces of burning and arrowheads in the houses located near the city's northern fortifications. With the fall of Jerusalem, some four centuries of Israelite kingship came to an end.

IRON AGE 2–3: THE PHILISTINES

During the tenth through the eighth centuries B.C.E., the coastal plain and certain inland areas remained in Philistine hands, but they were not nearly as powerful as they had been during the Iron 1. Toward the end of the eighth century B.C.E., the growing Neo-Assyrian superpower from the northeast began to loom. Several prominent Philistine cities would fall to the armies of Sargon II, but ironically, in several cases this actually led to a cultural renaissance.

A wall relief from the Assyrian city of Khorsabad documents the destruction of Ashdod by Sargon II in 712 B.C.E. Ekron, too, denoted as *?mqar(r)úna* in the Neo-Assyrian sources, fell to Sargon II, but the Assyrians were not inclined to stay. After a brief interlude under the rule of the Judean King Hezekiah, all of Philistia was conquered in 701 B.C.E. by Sennacherib, who had grand designs for colonization. Ekron occupied a prime site in relation to trade routes and access to resources, and its potential contribution to the empire's economy was immediately recognized, as reflected in Neo-Assyrian texts claiming it as a vassal state (see Gitin 1997). As a result of the revolt and Sennacherib's campaign, control over the territories in the Shephelah transferred from Judah to the Philistines.

In the seventh century B.C.E. (Str. IC-IB), the upper city of Ekron was revived, the lower city was reoccupied, and there was expansion to the north. The city, which hosted a large administrative center of the Neo-Assyrian Empire, grew to roughly 35 hectares (85 acres). An inscription discovered in the Temple Complex (650) specifically names a succession of five kings, two of whom were already known from the Neo-Assyrian annals: Ikausu, to whom the dedication is made, and who was probably the same as the aforementioned Achish; and Padi, his father (see Gitin, Dothan, and Naveh 1997). Aside from Ikausu, all the names of eighth- to seventh-century Philistine kings mentioned in Neo-Assyrian records were Semitic. This detail has important implications (see Gitin, Dothan, and Naveh 1997; A. Mazar 1985; B. Mazar 1992). In the Neo-Assyrian texts, the title used for both of these individuals was "king," yet in the Ekron inscription the title flips to "ruler," a subtle difference that may reflect a sign of deference to the ultimate Assyrian monarch; alternatively, this was the local Philistine-Canaanite term. Finally, the reference to the construction of a temple at Ekron more or less confirms that Tel Miqne is Ekron of the Bible.

The reach of the Neo-Assyrian Empire can also be observed at the Negev site of Tel Jemmeh, where a building dating to about 675 B.C.E. was built in the Neo-Assyrian style using a variety of techniques to create mud-brick vaults (Van Beek 1987). Two ostraca from Jemmeh bear names with the ending s˘in, which may also represent a common Philistine title of the seventh century B.C.E. (Naveh 1985). Neo-Assyrian influence can also be seen in the existence of the Palace Ware Vessels, which imitate Assyrian metal vessels and were found in the Negev and other Judean sites.

The Philistines, of course, also play a large part in sections of the Hebrew Bible relating to this period. As in the Iron 1, they are presented as a distinct regional entity often at odds with their Israelite neighbors. For example, border conflicts between Judah and Philistia are mentioned in 1 Kings and 2 Chronicles. There are also multiple uses of the collective terms for "Philistine" and "Philistia," as well as an allusion to a single city (Ashdod in Isa. 20:1). Yet there is no indication of a true polity, as in the united Pentapolis represented in the earlier references, and in truth it is only the Hebrew Bible that describes this Pentapolis as existing during any period.

In 604 B.C.E., Ashqelon and Ekron were both destroyed by the Neo-Babylonian king Nebuchadnezzar. The king of Ekron, Adon, appears to have written a letter earnestly conveying his impending sense of doom at the advance of Babylonian armies. The "Adon Letter" was written to the Egyptian pharaoh, patron to the Philistine ruler, beseeching him to come to his aid as the Babylonian armies moved within a single day's march. Nevertheless, all efforts to avert disaster were unsuccessful. Ashqelon may have been the last of the Philistine cities to fall, and the last Philistine king, Aga', along with his sons, his staff, and a number of nobles, was banished from the city and sent into Babylonian exile.

NOTES

1. Date based on Egyptian Low Chronology.

2. The provenience for the Masos scarab is less secure (Fritz and Kempinski 1983).

3. Two sites, Tel Jemmeh and Tel Erani, have been published under the name Gath, but neither is currently accepted. William Flinders Petrie was the first to excavate the site of Tel Jemmeh, which he believed was the Philistine city of Gath, but further review of the site has raised doubts about whether it was truly a Philistine city during the Iron 1.

4. A date of 587 B.C.E. has also been proposed for this event, though most scholars tend to support the later date.

SUGGESTED READING

Ash, Paul S. 1999. *David, Solomon and Egypt: A Reassessment.* Sheffield, England: Sheffield Academic Press.

Finkelstein, Israel. 1999. "State Formation in Israel and Judah: A Contrast in Context, a Contrast in Trajectory." *Near Eastern Archaeology* 62: 35–52.

Finkelstein, I., and Na'aman, N., eds. 1994. *From Nomadism to Monarchy: Archaeological and Historical Aspects of Early Israel.* Jerusalem: Israel Exploration Society.

Galil, Gershon. 1996. *The Chronology of the Kings of Israel and Judah.* Leiden and New York: E. J. Brill.

Garbini, G. 1988. *History and Ideology in Ancient Israel.* New York: Crossroad.

Grayson, A. K. 1996. *Assyrian Rulers of the First Millennium BC, II (858–745 BC).* Toronto: University of Toronto Press.

Hess, R. S. 1997. "The Form and Structure of the Solomonic District List in 1 Kings 4:7–19." In *Crossing Borders and Linking Horizons, Studies in Honor of Michael C. Astour on His 80th Birthday,* edited by G. Young, M. Chavalas, and R. Averbeck, 279–292. Bethesda, MD: CDL Press.

Knauf, E. A. 2000. "Jerusalem in the Late Bronze and Early Iron Ages: A Proposal." *Tel Aviv* 27: 75–90.

Lemche, N. P. 1998. *The Israelites in History and Tradition.* Louisville, KY: Westminster/ John Knox Press.

Master, D. M. 2001. "State Formation and the Kingdom of Ancient Israel." *Journal of Near Eastern Studies* 60: 117–131.

Moran, W. 1992. *The Amarna Letters.* Baltimore: Johns Hopkins University Press.

Na'aman, N. 1996. "The Contribution of the Amarna Letters to the Debate on Jerusalem's Political Position in the Tenth Century B.C.E." *Bulletin of the American Schools of Oriental Research* 304: 17–27.

Rainey, A. 2000. "Mesha and Syntax." In *The Land That I Will Show You,* edited by M. Graham and J. Dearman, 291–311. Sheffield, England: Sheffield Academic.

Schniedewind, William M. 1998. "The Geopolitical History of Philistine Gath." *Bulletin of the American Schools of Oriental Research* 309: 69–77.

Stern, E. 2001. *Archaeology of the Land of the Bible.* Vol. 2. New York: Doubleday.

Thompson, T. L. 1992. *Early History of the Israelite People.* Leiden: E. J. Brill.

Ussishkin, D. 1977. "The Destruction of Lachish by Sennacherib and the Dating of the Royal Judean Storage Jars." *Tel Aviv* 4: 28–60.

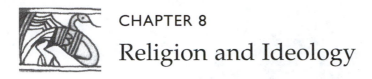

CHAPTER 8

Religion and Ideology

CHALCOLITHIC PERIOD

Places of Worship and Ritual

The site of Gilat, located along the Wadi Patish northwest of modern-day Beer Sheva, provides some of the earliest evidence for cultic architecture and public worship. The cult center includes a large complex comprising several buildings that appear to have served as some form of cultic center (Alon and Levy 1989; Levy et al., in press). The cultic area incorporates open courtyard space and several buildings, including Room A, which had a high concentration of symbolic items, including more than sixty "violin-shaped" figurines. The site of Teleilat Ghassul also featured a cultic center (Area E) with several temples (Hennessy 1982). Vivid murals were painted directly onto plastered walls using a variety of materials for pigment, including red ochre. In one scene, at least six individuals and one central figure were depicted in a procession scene (Cameron 1981); it is possible that the central figure was a deity (Stager 1992). Other motifs seen in the murals include a schematized star, several human figures with pronounced eyes, and a horned animal. At Both Gilat and Ghassul, the temples were in use over a considerable length of time.

Another cultic complex, at Ein Gedi, included four separate structures and a large open-air courtyard (Ussishkin 1980). This site is located on a high cliff overlooking the Dead Sea, far from any settlement. Open-air sanctuaries made up of large, walled, circular enclosures and *massebot,* or stele-like standing stones, have been found throughout the Sinai and Negev (Avner 1984). Based on their form and location, it is thought that these served the pastoral transhumant population.

Ritual Paraphernalia

The Chalcolithic people used a variety of figurines for ritual purposes. The "violin-shaped" figurines are schematic representations of humans, sometimes females. The numerous examples found at Gilat were made from a variety of stones imported into the site from outside the region (Levy 2003a; Goren 1995). Violin-shaped figurines also occur at Ghassul, along with "eye figurines," which appear to have Syro-Mesopotamian connections. Later in the Chalcolithic period, anthropomorphic statuettes made of ivory began to appear at sites in the northern Negev. These figurines are more naturalistic and display considerable detail, with gender clearly indicated. Their pronounced noses have inspired theories about the ritual "breath of life." One bone figurine from

8.1   The anthropomorphic image from the sanctuary at Ghassul (Drawing by J. Golden; adapted from Dorothy O. Cameron. 1981. *The Ghassulian Wall Paintings*. London: Kenyon-Deane Ltd.)

Shiqmim combines elements of the two traditions (Levy and Golden 1996). At the cemetery of Quleh on the coastal plain, a male ceramic figurine (20 cm, or almost 8 in.) with damage to the genital area was discovered inside an ossuary (Milevski 2002).

Two of the most outstanding objects of art from the period—the "Gilat Lady" (Fig. 8.2) and "Ram with Cornets"—come from the sanctuary (Alon 1977). The first is a ceramic representation of a female figure sitting on what may be a birthing stool, with a churn on her head and either another birthing

In Fuller's Notes

stool or a drum under her other arm. The churn and birthing stool suggest that this statue, along with the "Ram with Cornets," may have been related to ritual beliefs concerning fertility (Amiran 1989). Also found in the sanctuary at Gilat were eccentric vessel types such as miniature churns and "torpedo" vessels, which may have been used in some forms of ritual.

Ceramic ossuaries used for burials may have also had some ritual function. Between 250 and 300 ossuaries ranging in size and shape were discovered in the cave tomb at Peqi'in, along with several figurines (Gal, Smithline, and Shalem 1997). In some cases, the ossuaries incorporate anthropomorphic elements, especially human faces. The discovery of ossuaries similar in style throughout the countryside of the time suggests widespread beliefs concerning death.

EARLY BRONZE AGE

Places of Worship and Ritual

There is little evidence for cultic architecture during the EB1, with the major exception of Megiddo. By the EB2–3, however, places of worship appear at a number of large centers. The basic plan for Early Bronze Age cultic architecture is traditionally known as the "broad room": a rectilinear structure with an entrance near the center of the long side. Over the course of the period, temples generally increased in size and scale, and there were elaborations on this basic temple plan. The cultic center at Megiddo is one

8.2   Cult vessel in the form of a woman with a churn on her head. Found in Gilat (northern Negev), Chalcolithic period, ca. 4000 B.C.E. (Photo courtesy of Zev Radovan, Land of the Bible Picture Archive)

of the best examples of cultic architecture during the Early Bronze Age. This site had a distinct religious precinct (300 square meters, or approximately 3,230 sq. ft.) featuring a double temple with annex rooms and a third structure, each with walls nearly 2 meters (about 6.5 ft.) thick. Adjacent to the temples was a circular platform, nearly 8 meters (about 26 ft.) in diameter, that most likely was used for rituals (Dunayevsky and Kempinski 1973; Loud 1948, see Fig. 8.3). The addition of a wall enclosing the entire precinct sometime around the EB3 indicates that the cultic center remained in use for most of the period. The location of what is probably a palace in proximity to the cultic complex suggests a connection between religion and political structures (Kempinski 1989).

A similar double temple plan with flanking annex rooms was also observed at Arad, where excavators found several platforms and installations (Amiran et al. 1978). The adjacent courtyard allowed for viewing of the installations

8.3   Megiddo, remains of the Canaanite temple with the large round altar dating from c. 2500–1850 B.C.E. (Photo courtesy of Zev Radovan, Land of the Bible Picture Archive)

and could have accommodated public worshippers.[1] An example of this style of architecture has also been discovered at Ai, atop the site's highest point, and is thus known as the Acropolis Temple. The large broad-room building here (roughly 100 square meters, or 1100 sq. ft.), which remained in use during the EB2–3, featured a main chamber with a row of stone pillar bases, and its walls were coated with plaster. The interior of this elaborately designed temple yielded a number of cultic objects. A large structure at Erani, with nine pillars lined in three rows, has also been interpreted as a temple (Kempinski and Gilead 1991). Plaster-coated walls were also found at a temple at Yarmuth, hence the name, the "White Building." A raised platform opposite the entrance may have been used for rituals and/or to support a cultic figure (Miroschedji 1993). Cultic installations and features included raised platforms and large, flat massebot, which often appeared in groups, as seen at Hartuv (Mazar 1996). It is not clear what their function was, though they may have represented deities.

One recurrent motif from the seal impressions depicts a group of figures with arms interlocked, perhaps engaged in a dance. In at least one example from an EB3 jar, the dancers appear above a row of rectangles that recalls the "palace facade" motif, known from many seals, suggesting public ceremonies involving dance. Dancing may have played a vital role in rituals associated with the harvest, and it is possible that in this instance the dancers performed in or near some monumental structure, such as a temple. At Bab edh-Dra, one

8.4   The "Dumuzi Stele" from EBA Arad. (Drawing by J. Golden; adapted from Ruth Amiran. 1972. "A Cult Stele from Arad." *Israel Exploration Journal* 22: 86–88.)

scene shows four figures with upraised hands, bracketing what may be a palm branch.

Glyptic Evidence

Insight into Early Bronze Age religion can also be inferred from the iconography known from cylinder seal impressions and incised potsherds and stones. The most common motifs involve animals, particularly horned animals, along with lions and humans (for example, at Hazor and Dan). During the EB2–3, there are affinities between these seals and examples from Syria (Ben-Tor 1978; Kempinksi 1989).

At Megiddo, a large corpus of seal impressions depicts horned animals and lions. The open plaza of the cultic complex was paved with stones incised with the figures of horned animals and humans that appear armed, representing, perhaps, hunters or warriors (Kempinski 1989). A group of ivory and stone bulls' heads dating to the EB3 (for example, at Ai, Jericho, and Beit Yerah) may also have some link to cult. The bull motif represents a long-standing tradition in the Near East, and it was ubiquitous in Mesopotamia, where the bull is often associated with supernatural beings.

At Arad, the excavators discovered one unique artifact, an incised stone slab, or stele, that may reflect religious beliefs (Fig. 8.4). The stone, 24 cm (about 9.5 in.) tall, depicts two superimposed "stick" figures—one that stands with arms upright and a second below lying horizontally inside a rectangular box. It has been suggested that the boxed figure represents a burial, while the upright figure rises, thus the scene as a whole may relate to a death-rebirth motif (Amiran 1972). The heads of both figures also resemble plants, suggesting a connection to the agricultural deity from Mesopotamia, Dumuzi.

MIDDLE BRONZE AGE

Places of Worship and Ritual

The archaeological evidence for religious and ritual activity during the Middle Bronze Age, including burial offerings, sacred deposits, artistic representations, and cultic architecture, is vast. By the later Middle Bronze Age (MB2–3), large temples stood at a number of Canaanite sites, including Tel el-Hayyat, Hazor, Tel Kitan, and Shechem. These imposing structures were built with massive stone foundations that generally followed a plan incorporating one long main hall, though these varied from the broad-room design. One form, the "Migdal temple," had a symmetrical, direct-axis plan, and there was often a small niche at the back of the broad hall that may have been used for ritual practice or display.

One of the best examples of this tradition was the massive Migdal temple at Shechem. The temple had walls reaching up to 5 meters (6.4 ft.) thick and was erected atop a large earthen platform similar in construction to the ramparts, creating an "acropolis" effect. Those visiting the temple at Hazor would have ascended a set of stairs lined with trimmed basalt stones, anticipating the use of orthostats. There was also the "Langhaus" design (late MB2), which had long, massive walls. Examples have been discovered at Tel Haror, Tel Kitan, Megiddo, and Shechem, and in several cases, they were built on the sites of earlier temples. At some of the smaller centers, such as Tel el-Hayyat, "Megaron-style" chapels, featuring a columned porch, were found (Fig. 8.5).

Several of the basic design elements in the Canaanite temples display a distinct northern influence. The general floor plan of temples in Canaan has parallels with structures found in the great Syrian cities of Alalakh, Ebla (Tel Mardikh), and Ugarit (Ras Shamra), but it is not clear whether this represents the spread of a widely held belief system or the emulation of architectural style. A similar plan, in fact, was also employed in a temple from Avaris (Tel el-Dab'a), the center of Hyksos-Asiatic life in the Egyptian Delta. Temples and chapels have also been identified at a number of Middle Bronze Age sites on the coastal plain, including Ashqelon, Tel Mevorakh, and Tel Michal (Dothan 1981).

Buildings and open courts designated for religious practice were often grouped together within a city, forming cultic precincts. At Megiddo (Str. XII), a small platform mound (0.1 ha) may have been reserved for cultic activities, while the religious precinct from the Early Bronze Age was transformed into an open plaza with massebot. The cultic area at Nahariyah had a similar open plaza, and the open-air site at Jebel el-Rukba in southern Samaria had an oval platform, roughly 16 x 9 meters (52 x 30 ft.), built of stone, which may have functioned as a gathering place for rituals (Finkelstein 1995). Massebot have been found at a number of sites, the most outstanding example being Gezer,

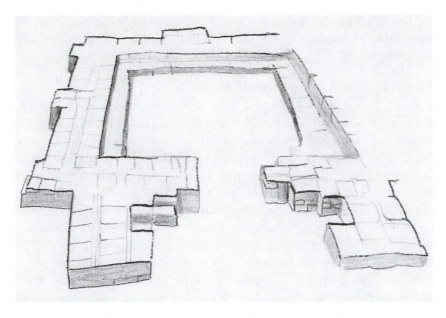

8.5   "Megaron-style" chapel at Tel el-Hayyat (Drawing by J. Golden; adapted from David J. Kilne Ilan. 2003. "The Dawn of Internationalism: The Middle Bronze Age." In *The Archaeology of Society in the Holy Land,* 3d ed., edited by T. E. Levy, 297–319. New York: Facts on File.)

8.6   The "High Place" with megalithic massebot at Tel Gezer (Photo courtesy of BiblePlaces.com)   *In Fuller's Notes*

where the "high place" featured a group of eleven massive massebot, which still straddle the mound's crest today. Byblos, too, featured a cluster of large standing stones.

Public Worship and Common Belief Systems

Overall, the evidence for religious activity during the Middle Bronze Age indicates a trend toward increased public worship. Impressive temples with massive walls were sometimes built atop small "citadels" where they could be observed from afar. Perhaps this is echoed in a passage from the Hebrew Bible that refers to "the high places at which Baal worship occurred within Israel" (Num. 22:41). The megalithic massebot erected in open spaces also suggest that worshippers sometimes gathered in large groups. Parallels in the iconography of the glyptic art, pendants and figurines, in addition to affinities in architectural style, reflect the widespread exchange of religious ideas and beliefs within the broader region. Indeed, many of the artistic conventions suggest a shared Canaanite system of practices spanning much of the eastern Mediterranean, from parts of southern Anatolia (such as Kultepe) to Hyksos Egypt in the Delta.

Cultic Imagery and Iconography

The art and iconography of the Middle Bronze Age, including cylinder seals, jewelry, and bronze statuary, provide glimpses into the world of Canaanite mythology. It is immediately apparent that there was an association between rare and precious metals and religious icons, as attested by the large corpus of figurines and pendants made of bronze, gold, and silver. Anthropomorphic figurines generally took two forms: small pendants made of gold, silver, and bronze sheet metal, with engraved schematic designs, and cast bronze statuettes that are somewhat more naturalistic. The pendants, usually 10–20 cm (about 4–8 in.) in height, often bear the image of a female face and stylized body with a triangle used to emphasize the pubis. Based on this, as well as the use of vegetal motifs for decoration, it is thought that they represent a Canaanite goddess. Examples of these pendants have been found at Tel el-Ajjul and Gezer as well as in the Hyksos cemetery at Avaris (Tel el-Dab'a).

Bronze statuettes have also been found at a number of Middle Bronze Age sites in the southern Levant (for example, Nahariyah), and at Byblos similar statuettes often appear as grave goods. These, too, were primarily female, though males are also represented (Negbi 1976). The females are frequently depicted nude with hands on hips, sometimes with horns or a conical headdress, and may represent the goddess Astarte. The function of these statuettes is unclear, but they may have been used as objects of worship (that is, idols) or as offerings to the gods. Some figurines are in the form of daggers shaped like women, reflecting the association between Canaanite female deities and both love and warfare. This particular motif, which can be found throughout the ancient Near East, is thought to derive from the "Syrian-Hittite" tradition.

The production of ritual goods sometimes took place in the immediate vicinity of the temple, where the religious establishment directly sponsored "at-

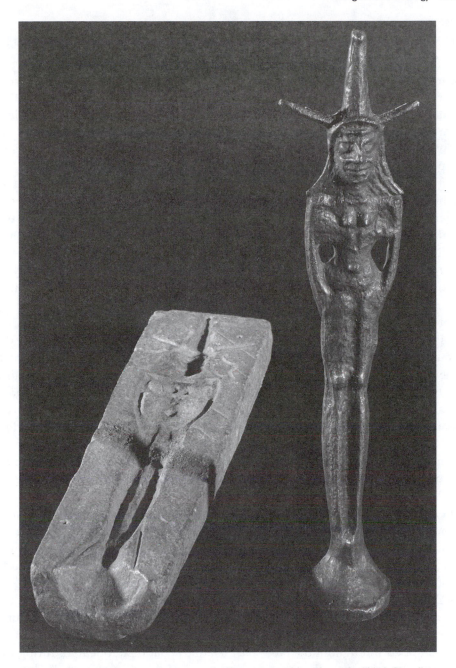

8.7   Ancient mold and modern cast of a Canaanite goddess from the "High Place" in Nahariyah. Late Bronze Age, Canaanite. (Erich Lessing/Art Resource, NY)

tached specialists." For example, at both Tel el-Hayyat in Transjordan and Nahariyah on the coast, evidence for ceramic production was found in the cultic area. At the latter site, a ceramic mold used to cast bronze statuettes in the form of a goddess was found in the vicinity of a temple, linking the cult with metal production as well.

The Canaanite "Pantheon"

In addition to the glyptic art and statuary, archaeologists' understanding of Canaanite divinity is also based upon literary evidence, including texts from Syria. These various sources, however, rarely corroborate, and the resulting patchwork "pantheon" is often difficult to sort out. Although there are close parallels between the Syrian and Canaanite mythology, for instance, it is not always clear whether artifacts represent regional variants of similar deities or separate individuals altogether.

This is particularly true of the goddesses worshipped in ancient Canaan, which include Anat, Asherah, Astarte, Ištar, and Kudhsu. Anat was more popular in northern Canaan and Phoenicia, but it is sometimes difficult to distinguish between Astarte, Anat, and Asherah. Each goddess probably had some role associated with love and/or war, as indicated by their representations in glyptic art, especially cylinder seals. Another female figure, known simply as the "Naked Goddess," was often depicted on Syrian seals of the late nineteenth and eighteenth centuries B.C.E., but again, there is ambiguity with regard to her identity in relation to other deities.

Perhaps the most intriguing of these female deities is Asherah, who over the course of many centuries fulfilled a variety of roles. She was a mother figure in the divine family, associated with fertility and warfare. Bronze statuary dating to the fourteenth to thirteenth centuries B.C.E. from Syrian sites such as Ugarit (Ras Shamra) features a goddess widely thought to be Asherah. In many instances, she appears in a full-length dress, sometimes exposing the shoulders and breasts. Commonly conceived as a fertility goddess, in some myths she assumes a more maternal character, complementing her consort, the patriarch El, while the more sexual aspects of fertility are left to her daughter, Anat (Korpel 2001). Asherah, too, had a creator role, hence her association with the tree of life, and she sometimes bears the Semitic epithet, qds˘, "holy." She was also sometimes referred to as Ilat, or Elat, a feminine variation on El. In some instances, Asherah assumed elements of the Egyptian goddess Hathor (for example, wearing cattle horns), and she was also associated with the sea ("Lady Asherah of the sea").

On the male side of the pantheon were the supreme god, El, and his son, the storm king and warrior Hadad/Baal, brother of Anat.[2] We know from a number of sources, including the archives from Mari and Ugarit, that Hadad was worshipped throughout the Near East. Hadad/Baal first appeared during the eighteenth century B.C.E. with the emergence of the "Syrian style." The god was often represented in association with a pair of symbols: the "quadripartite" disc and the crescent moon, which was sometimes incorporated into his headgear. Epithets for Hadad/Baal include the "Rider of the Clouds" and the "Storm Bringer." Several passages in the Hebrew Bible referring to Israel's propensity to lapse into Baal worship (cf. Judg. 2:11; 3:7; 8:33; 10:6, 10; Hosea 2:13) imply that Baal enjoyed a rather long-lived tenure as a Canaanite divinity. There was also the "solar deity," but little is known about this god.

The senior god of the Canaanites was El. El is best known from the Ugarit texts, where he often bears the title *bâniyu binwâti,* "creator of the created

8.8   The "silver calf" from Ashqelon, ca.1600 B.C.E. The calf is standing next to a miniature clay shrine, in which it was found. (Photo courtesy of Zev Radovan, Land of the Bible Picture Archive)

things" (in Corpus des tablettes en cunéiformes alphabétiques (CTA) 4.II.11; 4.III.32; 6.III.5; 11; 17.I.25; Herdner 1963). He is also called the "father of the gods" in several instances, while other deities are referred to as his family or his sons. One rare text from the southern Levant (Hazor) refers directly to El. The bull and calf, which had a central place in Canaanite iconography, were often associated with either El or Baal. For example, El often bears the epithet "Bull," referring to his virility, while the bull was also linked with the storm god, who is depicted riding the bull, demonstrating the association between fertility and rainfall. One of the most outstanding examples of this motif is the exquisite "silver calf" from late Middle Bronze Age Ashqelon (c. 1600 B.C.E.) (Stager 1991; see Fig. 8.8). The statuette was made of bronze and originally plated with silver. The calf was found housed in a ceramic model of a beehive-shaped shrine. This motif recalls a scene from a Middle Bronze Age Anatolian cylinder seal depicting a bull poking its head out of a shrine much like the one from Ashqelon. The statuette was discovered in the storeroom of a sanctuary situated on the slopes of the rampart facing the sea, which may have served as a point of worship for travelers reaching the city by sea (Stager 1991).

Burials and Ritual Deposits

Mortuary practices from the Middle Bronze Age also reflect spiritual beliefs. Virtually all burials from this period had some sort of grave goods, even if modest. The inclusion of food items or burnt offerings (animal bones) and furniture in some tombs suggests a belief in the afterlife; a burial at Tel el-Ajjul contained the remains of a feast.

Another Middle Bronze Age practice was the burial of small caches without human remains, perhaps some form of offering deposit. At Tel Dan, one such deposit contained a number of bronze tools and weapons as well as decorative items such as amulets and silver female figurines. Offering deposits have also been observed at Megiddo (Str. XIII), Kfar Shmariyahu, and Tel el-Hayyat; at Nahariyah and Byblos, similar deposits included miniature ceramic goblets found with animal bones. It is noteworthy that each of these sites served as cultic centers. This practice, which was abandoned by the MB2–3 (Ilan 1995), may represent the ritual interment of valuable prestige goods, or the artifacts may have been part of poorly preserved shrines.

Religious Eclecticism in Egypt

The Hyksos infiltration of the Delta brought Canaanite religious practices to Egypt. The unique culture that emerged in the Delta at this time was eclectic, displaying both Egyptian and Asiatic influences, and Cypro-Aegean material began to appear. The Baal-Seth cult, for instance, represents some form of hybrid religion involving both local Egyptian and Asiatic cultic practices. One temple at Avaris (Tel el-Dab'a) was clearly Asiatic in style, incorporating architectural elements seen in the temples of Ebla, Alalakh, and Ugarit. During the MB2a/b transition at Avaris (Tel el-Dab'a, Str. F), a temple complex was established in Area A/II at the site (Forstner-Müller 2002).

LATE BRONZE AGE

Despite the fact that Egyptians dominated Canaan for much of the Late Bronze Age, much of the Canaanite religious tradition remained intact, which is not surprising considering that religion is often one place where cultural identities find refuge when threatened. Temples dating to the period have been discovered at several sites, including Beth Shean, Lachish, and Tel Mevorakh. At Megiddo and Hazor (Area H), temples originally built at the end of the Middle Bronze Age were used right though to the Late Bronze Age. At this point, both were renovated, but with limited changes to the basic broad-room design, where the main hall was entered via a front porch. Some of these temples contained a small room where access was limited, which probably served a specific cultic function, that is, as "holy of holies" (Mazar 1990). As during the Middle Bronze Age, these temples had affinities with the temples of Syria. The temples at Ugarit, Alalakh, and Hazor had similar building plans and main halls of similar dimensions, and at Alalakh the temple had lion orthostats and a basalt altar similar to that from Hazor.

Hazor was a preeminent religious center during the Late Bronze Age and provides some of the best evidence for cultic practice at this time. In Area H, a new gateway and altar were added in the beginning of the period (Str. XV), but by the fourteenth century B.C.E. (Str. XIV) the Hazor temple was destroyed.

8.9 The reconstructed "stele shrine" from LBA Hazor, with a group of eleven massebot (J. Golden)

When rebuilt shortly thereafter, it still conformed to the general parameters of the previous temple, but the entire building was lengthened, with the addition of a new entrance hall and finely cut orthostats made of basalt lining the hall's inner walls. Large orthostats in the form of seated lions were found out of their original context, but presumably two such lions would have been built into the door jam so as to guard the entrance to the new hall. This temple was probably dedicated to Hadad/Baal, as suggested by the basalt altar bearing his symbol, the spoked wheel, as well as a basalt statue of a figure standing on a bull.

In addition to the main temple at Hazor (Area H), the site also featured a small cult shrine built on the interior slope of the Middle Bronze Age rampart (Area C). This structure consisted of a single broad room, which contained an offering table and statues of a seated lion and a seated man, perhaps a deity. The shrine also contained a row of eleven massebot or stelae, the central one having a carved relief of a moon and crescent symbol above two hands raised as in prayer (Yadin 1970; Beck 1990, 1983; see Fig. 8.9). A ceramic mask and silver scepter found in this shrine probably served as cultic paraphernalia. The location of the shrine is itself interesting, as it demonstrates that in addition to central, public worship, people also made use of smaller local shrines. Religious activities at Hazor (fourteenth to thirteenth centuries B.C.E.) were also conducted in an open cult space found in Area F, where archaeologists found a large stone altar built with a channel for drainage.

Other notable temples include the Megiddo temple, which featured two ashlar towers in the front, and a new temple (Temple 2) at Shechem, erected on the ruins of the Middle Bronze Age temple. It, too, followed Hazor and the Syrian temples in the broad-room plan and had an altar and massebah, which stood in the front courtyard. The unmistakable Syrian influence on many of these temples suggests that common belief systems continued on a broad scale.

Despite the continuation of Canaanite customs, in certain places the Egyptian impact can be clearly seen in religious practice. A temple at Beth Shean departs from what is typical of Canaanite cultic architecture, being squarer in plan (200 square meters, or about 2,150 sq. ft.) and entered via a bent axis. It also featured benches along part of the wall, and two columns in the center of the hall supported the roof. A "holy of holies" was approached via a seven-stepped staircase, and a small adjacent chamber may have served as a treasury. One of the more unique features at the Beth Shean temple is the use of Egyptian-style papyrus-shaped capitals. This temple was destroyed at the end of the thirteenth century B.C.E., but it was subsequently rebuilt during the time of Rameses III (Str. VI), this time with an Egyptian frieze. The Egyptian influence at Beth Shean is also reflected in a stele that depicts an Egyptian official performing some sort of ritual or act of supplication before the Canaanite god Mekal (see Mazar 1990, 289), which suggests the integration or fusion of practices.

At Lachish, a temple similar in plan to that of Beth Shean, also featuring a "holy of holies" with a staircase, was established in the center of the city (Area P). The Egyptian influence is evident in the two main columns with papyrus stalk capitals and in the decorative columns with Egyptian-style fluted shafts. The plastered interior walls were adorned with painted designs in red, yellow, blue, white, and black; only fragments have been preserved, but it is likely that other buildings of this period originally had similar "frescos." Reverence for Egyptian gods is also attested in the mining region of Timna, where the people working in this industry prayed in a temple to Hathor.

Lachish also hosted the "Fosse Temple," a unique example of religious architecture standing just outside the city wall in the Middle Bronze Age moat. This temple had a small entrance corridor leading to a main hall with rows of wooden columns, and though it was rebuilt several times during the fifteenth to thirteenth centuries B.C.E., the plan remained largely the same. The floor of the thirteenth-century temple, which saw violent destruction, was permeated by *favissae*, small caches of valuable goods (for example, an ivory statue). A building similar to the Fosse Temple has also been found at Tel Mevorakh, and it is possible that these unique temples represent a separate current of ritual practice distinct from the main Canaanite cult of the Late Bronze Age (Mazar 1990).

Another structure thought to be a temple was found near the present-day airport of Amman. It contained, in addition to Aegean ceramics, a large amount of Egyptian material, including pottery, seals, scarabs, and jewelry. The burnt remains of humans, both adults and children, were found, but there is no consensus regarding the significance of this building.[3]

8.10   The Egyptian Hathor temple in the mining region of Timna (J. Golden)

IRON AGE

Places of Worship and Ritual

There is little evidence regarding religious practices among the highland peoples of the Iron 1. There were virtually no urban centers at this time and no established temples remain, though open-air and temporary sites of worship may have been used. One intriguing and controversial feature of highland religion was the *bamah* (pl. *bamot*). Commonly translated as "high place," the term appears in more than 100 references in the Hebrew Bible, yet scholars disagree about what the bamot actually were and how they were used (Nakhai 1994). The most common theory is that they were ritual platforms used at open-air cult sites.

Two isolated sites in the central hill country, Mt. Ebal and the "Bull Site," have been interpreted as bamot. Both sites were located on high, remote perches in the hills near Shechem. The Mt. Ebal site features a rectangular stone platform, roughly 9 feet high, that was approached by a ramp; two enclosures flanked the platform on its southwest side. More than 100 installations containing a variety of goods have been found (Str. IB). The site is generally devoid of domestic architecture, and the large assemblage of animal bones, many of which were burned, differs in composition from those typically found in domestic contexts. In addition to the ceramic assemblage, Mt.

Ebal can be dated by a seal and two Egyptian scarabs to the late thirteenth century B.C.E. (Brandl 1986–1987). In addition to these finds, the site's impressive location and the structure's unique design have led the excavator (Zertal 1988) to interpret the site as an open-air shrine. There are parallels between this structure and one said to have been built by Joshua on Mt. Ebal (Josh. 8:30–35; Deut. 27:1–10); however, some scholars have rejected this interpretation (for example, Dever 1992), arguing instead that the Mt. Ebal site represents a farmstead or an isolated fortress.

The Bull Site, named for a bronze bull figurine discovered there, has also been dated to the early Iron Age and is believed to have been an early Israelite cult site, or "high place" (Mazar 1982; Zertal 1994). The site is located on a prominent hilltop near Mt. Gilboa in the northern central hill country in the vicinity of at least four small Iron 1 settlements, but otherwise isolated. The figurine itself is a small (5 x 7 in.) bronze representation of a humped bull, perhaps a Zebu bull (*Bos indicus*). Originally, the eyes would have been inset with stone and/or glass. Excavations at the site revealed the remains of a ring of large stones some 20 m (66 ft.) in diameter. At the eastern side of the ring, a large stone, probably a massebah, was found lying on its side in a small paved area, along with a small ceramic cult stand or incense burner. This site, insofar as the bull motif recurs, demonstrates some level of continuity with earlier Canaanite traditions (Bloch-Smith and Nakhai 1999), such as the worship of the storm god, Baal/Hadad. Continuity with the Canaanite Bronze Age is so strong, in fact, that Israel Finkelstein (1998) has suggested that this site was first established in the Middle Bronze Age and subsequently revived in the twelfth century B.C.E. with the construction of the enclosure and massebah.[4]

The lack of monumental architecture at open-air sites does not mean that large numbers of people did not congregate for worship. The central hill country probably hosted a large seminomadic population at this time, and the large open space surrounding the small shrines such as the Bull Site could have accommodated mass gatherings. At the same time, the construction of monumental structures at places of centralized worship later in the Iron Age does not preclude the possibility that people continued to engage in outdoor worship, and there are other indications that this practice never ceased entirely.

Shiloh and Shechem may have also hosted religious activity during the Iron 1. Shiloh was the site of a Late Bronze Age temple, and it may have continued to serve as a regional cult center for seminomadic peoples in the Iron 1. Much of the evidence dating to this period was disturbed by later activity at the site, but a range of artifacts, including pottery with cultic motifs, animal bones, and storage units associated with the temple, points to cultic activity during the twelfth and eleventh centuries B.C.E. (Finkelstein 1985, 1986). In addition, in the Hebrew Bible, a tabernacle or shrine is said to have stood at Shiloh (Judg. 21:12; 1 Sam. 1:3). At Shechem, the long-standing tradition of the site as a center for worship was upheld as people continued to use the temple (Field V), established during the Late Bronze Age, well into the twelfth century B.C.E.[5] Canaanite gods were probably still worshipped at the small eleventh-century-B.C.E. temple at Hazor.

8.11   Mount Gilboa, near the "Bull Site" (J. Golden)

Four-Horned Altars

During the Iron 1 and carrying on into the Iron 2, one of the most important cult items was the four-horned altar, a rectangular limestone altar with a rim creating a depression on top and a horn at each corner. Horned altars are described in the Hebrew Bible (Lev. 4:7, 18, 25) and appear to have served at least two different purposes: animal sacrifices and the burning of incense. The horn, like the longtime Canaanite bull motif, was a symbol of strength and security. According to the biblical tradition, horned altars were prepared for the Tent of Congregation in the desert, and later for Solomon's Temple in Jerusalem. According to 1 Kings 1:50, the altars were used by individuals who sought protection by fleeing to the temple and grasping the horns.

IRON 2–3

Religion and Politics

Throughout the Iron 2 period, politics played an influential role in religion. Whereas during the Iron 1, religious practice was decentralized, there was a shift toward increased centralization and standardization in practice during the Iron 2. This trend is reflected in the archaeological record, especially in the location and design of temples, as well as by religious paraphernalia. Accord-

8.12 Four-horned altar from Tel Dan (Photo courtesy of Zev Radovan, Land of the Bible Picture Archive)

ing to Beth Nakhai, the shifting political climate of the day required "the strengthening of national solidarity and the promotion of loyalty to the king through the promulgation of the official religion in outlying areas" (1993, 21). Nevertheless, the actual degree of uniformity in religious practice at this time has been questioned.

The biblical narrative provides numerous examples of kings and prophets inserting themselves into each other's affairs and engaging in political jockeying as played out through the religious establishment. For instance, we read in Amos 7:13 that upon the division of the kingdom into Judah and Israel (c. 930 B.C.E.). Jeroboam, the first ruler of the latter, built royal sanctuaries at Bethel and Dan, cities on opposite ends of his kingdom. This move was designed in part to stake out territory, but these temples, replete with golden calves, also represented a direct challenge to the primacy of Jerusalem in the southern Kingdom of Judah. Thus Jeroboam was making a statement of defiance toward his rivals.

The whole notion of a centralized religious establishment, of course, is premised on the existence of the Solomonic Temple in Jerusalem. The Hebrew Bible describes in rich detail a temple that King Solomon, the master builder, established for the "God of Israel on Mount Moriah in the City of David (2 Chron. 3:7). There are detailed accounts of this structure and its elaborate furnishings—massive gates gilded with gold and silver and beams made from the cedars of Lebanon—as well as references in 1 and 2 Kings to temples that Solomon constructed at Gezer, Hazor, and Megiddo. Although temples dating to the Iron 2 have been excavated at the latter three sites, virtually no evidence relating to the First Temple in Jerusalem remains today. Thus, questions about the reality of the Solomonic temple have become the centerpiece of ongoing debates involving archaeologists, biblical scholars, and a highly interested segment of the general public.

In the archaeological record, places of worship dating to the Iron 2 have been identified at a number of sites, including Et-Tell, Bethsaida, Beth Shean, Hazor, Tel Kedesh, Lachish, Tel el-Mazar, Tel Michal, Tel Qiri, Tel Rehov, and Ta'anach in the eleventh through ninth centuries B.C.E. and Tel Beit Mirsim, Tel el-Far'ah North, Jerusalem, and Samaria in the eighth century B.C.E. Sanctuaries located at Dan and Arad enjoyed long-term use from the tenth through seventh centuries B.C.E. In the tenth century B.C.E., two new temples (Building 338 and Shrine 2081) were established at Megiddo. Both of these temples were furnished with similar assemblages of ritual paraphernalia, including four-horned altars, round limestone offering tables, and three-legged mortars and pestles made of basalt (Ussishkin 1989). In Building 338, there were also ceramic models of shrines and a male figurine. The latest discoveries concerning religious practice during this time come from the excavations at Tel Rehov (Mazar et al. 1999). In levels dating to the ninth and tenth centuries B.C.E., Area E features a cultic complex with a bamah and massebot standing on a platform adjacent to a large courtyard with various ovens and installations that may have been used to prepare ritual feasts. Excavation of this area also yielded several ceramic female figurines and a cult stand.

At Lachish, archaeologists have found what may be a single-room shrine. The structure (Room 49), which dates to the mid-tenth century B.C.E., was lined with benches on which probably sat a set of chalices, cult stands, and a limestone altar. It also had a small massebah and a raised platform in the southwest corner. A similar feature observed at Ai contained fragments of an elaborate cult stand found next to the benches and a platform on which they probably stood.

One of the more enigmatic examples of religious architecture from the Iron 2 is the sanctuary at the northern Negev fortress, Arad. The date of the Arad temple is uncertain, but the most recent reevaluation of the site's stratigraphy suggests a ninth-century-B.C.E. date for its initial construction (Herzog 2001).[6] Inside the temple's main broad-room hall, near the center of the western long wall, a set of steps lead up to a small (4 x 4 ft.) niche, or "holy of holies," that had a stele with red paint and two massebot. Limestone incense burners flanked the steps. In addition to auxiliary rooms on the northern and southern sides, there was a large open courtyard adjacent to the main hall, in the center of which was an altar built of unhewn stones. One outstanding artifact from the temple was a small bronze lion figurine. Some of the older presumptions

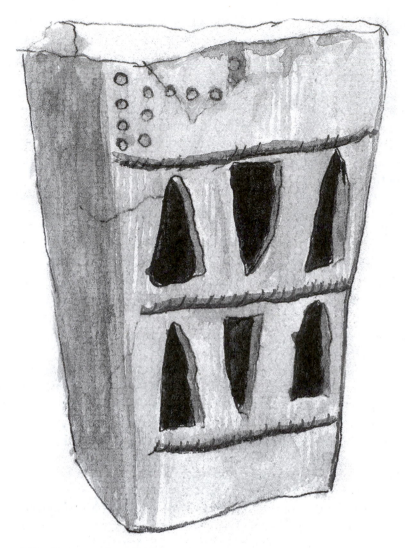

8.13   Cult stand from Tel Rehov; the stand may have been a "hybrid form" that originally had four horns as suggested here. (Drawing by J. Golden; adapted from Mazar et al. 1999)

about the Arad temple—that it was identical in plan to the one in Jerusalem and that it was destroyed in two phases—are not supported by the archaeological evidence (Herzog 2001). The temple was abandoned by the late eighth century B.C.E., which would generally conform with the date (c. 715 B.C.E.) given for Hezekiah's reformist campaign against secondary places of worship outside of Jerusalem (Rainey 1994; Herzog 2001). It must be assumed, however, that as Arad was an official fortress, the royal establishment at some point sanctioned worship at its sanctuary (Ahlström 1991).

As previously noted, it is difficult to discern just how centralized religion actually was at various times during the first half of the first millennium B.C.E. The Hebrew Bible's description of the struggle to limit worship outside of

8.14   The "High Place" at Tel Dan, Area T. (Photo courtesy of Nelson Glueck School of Biblical Archaeology, Hebrew Union College)

Jerusalem implies that this was a recurring phenomenon. One trend reflected in the archaeological record is the performance of private rituals outside of formal places of worship. In addition to public worship at temples, private shrines are indicated by cultic paraphernalia, especially ceramic stands, found in houses at sites such as Ai, Beth Shean, Hazor, Lachish, and Megiddo (Negbi 1993). There is also evidence for the use of local, that is, neighborhood, shrines at cultic installations dating to the tenth and ninth centuries B.C.E., which were excavated at Tel el-Far'ah North, Lachish, Megiddo, Tel el-Mazar, Tel Qiri, and Ta'anach.

The tradition of outdoor worship continued into the Iron 2, as bamot and open-air sanctuaries are found at several sites. One of the best examples of an open-air sanctuary complex from this time is the "High Place" at Tel Dan, which features a large open platform, or bamah, and an adjoining (*lis˘ka*) temple. The temple was probably used for burnt offerings, as it included an altar with iron shovels used to clear the ash. Cultic paraphernalia included a pedestaled oil lamp with seven spouts, horned altars of various sizes, and figurines.

The construction of bamot during the Iron 2 may also reflect the mixing of politics and religion, for during the United Monarchy there was a deliberate effort to integrate the use of bamot into the state religion as a way of consolidating control over and unifying the disparate elements of the population, including newly conquered peoples (Nakhai 1994). According to the biblical accounts (for example, 2 Kings 12:31), there was a proliferation of bamot during the Divided Kingdom, facilitated by kings of both the north and the south. It is interesting to note that in the ninth century B.C.E., the platform at Dan was renovated and enlarged, and in the following century a staircase roughly 10 m (33 ft.) wide leading up to the platform was added, suggesting, perhaps, an increase in traffic. Yet, even at Dan, with its elaborate centralized "High Place," there is evidence for the use of other, smaller cult installations in the plaza near the city gate (Dever 1991; Biran 1994).

Cultic Paraphernalia

Change in ritual practice is indicated by the introduction of a new form of paraphernalia: the cult stand. Cult stands have been found at a number of Iron 2 sites throughout the countryside. Though made from a variety of materials (for example, bronze, stone, and ceramic; see Devries 1987), they were most often ceramic with a high cylindrical or square foot and an open bowl on top. Each stand is unique, and the designs on some of the more elaborate examples offer a glimpse of the religious iconography of the day. Cult stands found in the southern temple of Beth Shean (tenth century B.C.E.) incorporate a range of snake and bird motifs, and one is in the form of a two-story house. One remarkable cult stand comes from Ta'anach, where it was found in a multiroomed temple. The base of the Ta'anach cult stand is square in shape and divided into four superimposed registers. In the top register, there is a winged sun disk, and in the two central registers there are a pair of winged sphinxes with female heads, wearing the Hathor headdress, and goats eating from a stylized tree, flanked by two lions. In the lowest register, two lions are shown flanking a nude female, who grasps their ears. The top register also has a Proto-Aeolic capital, which recalls the capitals that flanked the entrance to the Solomonic Temple.

It has long been thought that the cult stands were used for burning incense (May 1935), but it has been pointed out that they rarely show traces of burning (Fowler 1985). The Hebrew Bible is replete with images of animal sacrifice, and there is some archaeological evidence for this practice. For instance, one of the Ta'anach cult stands was found with iron knives and astragali, the knuckles of sheep and goats. Astragali were also found at Megiddo in association with cult objects from Shrine 2081.

There is also evidence that some of the Iron 1 practices were continued. Four-horned altars dating to the early part of the Iron 2 have been found at Megiddo, Arad, and Tel Beer Sheva. The Beer Sheva altar, which probably dates to the ninth century B.C.E., was nearly 2 meters (6.5 ft.) tall and constructed of well-cut ashlars. Figurines are found throughout the countryside in a variety of contexts and perhaps served as protective household idols. There are various types of figurines, including birds with pillar bases, a horse and rider motif, all sorts of zoomorphic figures, and, in rare cases, male figures, but the overwhelming majority are female figures thought to represent Asherah.

Deities Worshipped

Though it was during the Iron 2 that the concept of monotheism first began to take hold, the archaeological record clearly reflects the recognition of multiple deities throughout the period. Some of the most important discoveries concerning early Israelite religion come from the site of Kuntillet 'Ajrud, an eighth- to seventh-century-B.C.E. station, or caravanserai, in the Sinai, about 50 km (30 mi.) south of Kadesh Barnea (Meshel and Meyers 1976; Meshel 1978). The site featured a sanctuary comprising two buildings where inscriptions were discovered. Several of these inscriptions, including a rare poem, were clearly religious in nature. The poem, perhaps a psalm, reads, in part, as follows:

> and when El appears on the summits of the mountains . . .
> . . . then the mountains melt and the hills are pounded.
> . . . and my god uprooted [. . .]
> . . . in order to bless Baal on the day of the bat[tle . . .]
> . . . for the namesake of El on the day of the bat[tle]

This passage is significant for several reasons. For one, it documents the recognition of the Canaanite gods El and Baal in addition to YHWH perhaps as late as the seventh century B.C.E. (Dever 1980, 1982). It also implies that El, who in the poem appears in his solar aspect and then blesses Baal, was the more powerful of the two deities (Dijkstra 2002a). In addition to these texts, inscribed store jars found in the plastered "bench-room" of the Kuntillet 'Ajrud shrine refer to Asherah (Pithoi A and B), and illustrations on the vessels portray what may be the Egyptian god Bes as well as a lion woman who may represent Asherah.

Asherah's place within Canaanite and Israelite religion represents one of the most intriguing topics in the study of the Iron Age. The goddess is best known from the ubiquitous Asherah figurines, also called pillar figurines, which make rare appearances as early as the tenth century B.C.E. but do not become common until the eighth century B.C.E. The style of the Asherah figurines varies in terms of overall form[7] and in the level of detail, though all can be described as schematic, with no attempt to individualize. There are also differences in manufacture, for instance, handmade and mold-made.[8] At Ta'anach, the discovery of a mold used to make Asherah figurines in a tenth-century installation indicates that they were manufactured on-site.

Mentions of Asherah also appear in extra-biblical texts, such as the inscription from Khirbet el-Qom (Dever 1969–1970), and numerous times in the Hebrew Bible itself. Yet her role in Canaanite religion is ambiguous. Although there are some indications that she was worshipped alongside YHWH, perhaps as his consort, there were also attempts to eradicate her from the "official" religion, particularly by the eighth and seventh centuries B.C.E. (Dever 1996; Binger 1997). The ubiquity of the Asherah figurines, especially in household contexts, suggests that if this was part of some forbidden cult, it was fairly widespread.

In several instances, such as cult stands from Ta'anach and Kuntillet 'Ajrud and an ewer from Lachish (Beck 1982; Hestrin 1987), Asherah is associated with the "Sacred Tree," a symbol common in religions of the Near East. A variation on the Sacred Tree theme appears in the form of petal-shaped chalices with thick, trunklike stems and lotus branches that may have been used in some ritual. Other female deities appeared during the Iron Age, including the "Naked Goddess" (Watzinger 1933–1935; Tuffnel 1953) and the "Syrian goddess" (Winter 1983; Briend 1993). Later, during the time of Assyrian rule, the goddess Ištar is depicted on seals from Beth Shean and Tel Dor, where she appears with a circle of stars. Tallay Ornan (2001) has argued that along with Ashtarte, Ištar was associated with the cult of the "Queen of Heaven" mentioned in the Hebrew Bible.

 BROAD TRENDS IN THE EVOLUTION OF ISRAELITE RELIGION

For the earlier part of the Iron Age, the term "Israelite religion" should be used loosely. A number of features, such as the use of massebot, altars, and "holy of holies" cult niches, remained a part of ritual practice, betraying the Canaanite roots of the later religion that would evolve among the highland peoples. This is also evident in the fact that the cults of Canaanite gods such as Asherah and Baal continued to retain adherents. However, as culture changed and new identities were formulated in this region, religious practice began to change. By late in the eighth and seventh centuries B.C.E., there was an increasing emphasis on centralized worship. According to the biblical tradition, rulers such as Hezekiah and later Josiah attempted to assert the primacy of Jerusalem, campaigning against worship at regionally based sanctuaries such as the one at Arad. Just how successful this campaign actually was remains unclear.

The concerns of the central religious institution were compounded when, upon the destruction of the Northern Kingdom, Assyrian colonists settled in the region, bringing with them Mesopotamian deities (Becking 2002). With pervasive political upheaval during the first half of the first millennium, religion became an increasingly important part of identity, and the god that people worshipped was one way of distinguishing themselves from others. This appears to have been the case with peoples of the highlands (that is, the Israelites) and peoples of the coastal plain (that is, the Philistines), although, in some rare instances, overlap can be observed.

IRON 1: EARLY PHILISTINE RELIGION

The first few generations of Sea Peoples that arrived on the southern Levantine coast brought religious beliefs from their native lands with them. This is reflected in the many archaeological finds from this phase that display a strong

Cypro-Aegean influence. This trend can be seen at Tel Miqne–Ekron, where terra-cotta figurines, libation vessels, and *kernoi,* hollow, ring-shaped vessels that were probably used for libations, all with clear foreign parallels, demonstrate the transfer not only of Cypro-Aegean style but of ritual practices as well. Similarly, artifacts from Tel Qasile, such as a lion rhyton and an incense stand with a bird-shaped bowl, both associated with an Iron 1 temple, also reflect Aegean religious influences.

Ritual Paraphernalia

It would appear that these immigrants continued to worship some form of mother goddess, as suggested by the ceramic Ashdoda figurines found throughout Philistia at this time. These figurines, which portray a seated goddess who merges with a four-legged offering table, are often decorated with the characteristic Philistine black and red paint. The general motif is similar to the slightly earlier Mycenaean tradition of seated clay goddess figurines (sometimes with child) that are known from Cyprus, Rhodes, and the Greek mainland. In an example from Ashdod (Str. XII), the seated woman had a lotus flower pendant painted on the torso to appear as though hanging from her neck between her breasts. Zoomorphic vessels and figurines were also common during the Iron 1. Generally, these were used in the home, though zoomorphic vessels are sometimes found in burials.

There is also evidence for the use of cult stands. Near the bamah of the temple at Ekron, the remains of a wheeled cult stand—three bronze wheels and part of a frame with a loop for inserting an axle—were found. Parallels from Cyprus (for example, Larnaka) have also been found. A similar item (called a "mechanot/laver stand") is described in 1 Kings 7:27–33 as having been made by the Phoenician King Hiram of Tyre for Solomon's Temple in Jerusalem (Dothan 1995).

A range of artifacts were used for ceremonial purposes, including libation vessels and rhytons as well as figurines. At Tel Miqne–Ekron, elaborate knives, made with an iron blade secured with bronze rivets to an ivory handle and incorporating a ring-shaped pommel, were found in the temple, suggesting that they were used in some form of ritual sacrifice.[9] Though having foreign parallels, these knives were quite rare in the southern Levant. Another item that may have had a ritual function was the incised cow scapulae found at Tel Miqne–Ekron and Tel Dor, another city with Sea Peoples roots. These bones were inscribed with parallel lines and are similar to examples found on the benches of temples at Enkomi and Kition in Cyprus (Webb 1985). It is possible that they were used for divination (that is, scapulamancy), and the Hebrew Bible (Samuel, Isaiah, and 1 and 2 Kings) refers to this as a Philistine practice. Some scholars have pointed to the incised lines, arguing that they were musical instruments (Dothan and Gitin 1990; Stern 1995).

Places of Worship and Ritual

Information about formal worship in Philistia comes from the Iron 1 temples built at Tel Miqne–Ekron and Tel Qasile. The founders of Tel Miqne–Ekron es-

8.15 Ceramic Ashdoda figurine (Photo courtesy of Zev Radovan, Land of the Bible Picture Archive)

tablished a temple in the center of the lower city sometime during the twelfth century B.C.E. The first phase (Str. VIB) of the temple (Building 351) had a thick coating of plaster and floors with plaster and pebble pavement. In the following phase (Str. V, Building 350), as the entire city expanded, an enlarged temple was built in its place. The main hall had pillars along the north-south axis, much like the temple at Tel Qasile. Adjacent to the columns, in the center of the hall, was a hearth. The eastern side of the building was divided into three separate rooms, the center room (Room B) having a raised platform (bamah) preserved to a height of roughly 1 meter (Dothan 2002, 1995). Precedents for this feature are found in both Canaan and the Aegean.

At Tel Qasile, there was a temple complex that underwent three successive phases of reconstruction spanning the twelfth and eleventh centuries B.C.E. (Str. XII-X). The temple began as a relatively small (6.6 x 6.4 m, or 21.65 x 21 ft.) brick structure with one main room furnished with benches and a small platform. Around the beginning of the eleventh century B.C.E. (Str. XI), the temple was rebuilt with stone and slightly enlarged. In the southwest corner of the building there was a storage room containing a number of cultic items. A separate, ancillary chapel with benches and a small platform was built adjacent to the larger structure, a tradition that was probably Aegean or Cypriote in origin. In its final phase, the temple (Str. X) was significantly enlarged and the general plan modified. A small entrance chamber was built, restricting access to the sanctuary by creating a bent axis approach, and the courtyard adjacent to the temple, featuring a square altar, was enclosed. Both of these modifications may reflect a greater emphasis on control over religious practice. The centerpiece of the Tel Qasile temple was a raised, keyhole-shaped hearth, most likely part of the original design. The hearth had a circular depression in the center, and the platform, with the broken sherds of storage jars impressed into it, was similar to examples known from Enkomi, Cyprus (Dikaios 1969).

The continual remodeling of these temples suggests that the newly arrived peoples were still in the process of developing their own style of religious architecture (Mazar 1990). Though there are similarities to local Late Bronze Age Canaanite temples such as the Tel Mevorakh shrine and the Fosse Temples of Lachish, many elements of the Tel Qasile temple design draw on earlier traditions from Cyprus (for example, Kition) and the Aegean (for example, Mycenae).

In addition to large temples, smaller shrines were also used. At Tel Miqne–Ekron, in a residential area near the margins of the industrial zone, there was a series of superimposed shrines, the latest of which had a white plastered floor, benches, and a raised platform. A deposit containing figurines and bichrome pottery, including a portion of a lion-headed rhyton, was found adjacent to the shrine. Cultic items, such as cult stands and decorated chalices, were also found in a residential part of the eleventh- to tenth-century city at Tel Qasile (Str. VIA). The diversity of form seen in these stands and their residential context suggest private worship in households or at neighborhood shrines.

Deities of the Early Philistines

In these formative years of the Philistine culture, people still worshipped the goddess that hailed from their native homeland. As this culture evolved into something altogether new, the Aegean influence faded. A new entry into the Philistine "pantheon" was the god Dagon, who had been worshipped by

Canaanites long before the arrival of the Sea Peoples. The Hebrew Bible mentions the existence of Dagon temples at Gaza (Judg. 16:23) and Ashdod (1 Sam. 5), though these have not been identified archaeologically. In the story of Samson, which itself may have Aegean roots (see Dothan and Dothan 1992; Stager 1991), the temple at Gaza is described as having two large columns. In several instances, Baal is also referred to as *bn dgn,* meaning Son of Dagon, and it appears this was meant to be taken literally.

IRON 2: PHILISTINE RELIGION

As the Philistine culture evolved, Canaanite traditions continued to make their way into the Philistine ideology. One clear trend was the shift toward male-oriented deities. By the eleventh century B.C.E., male figurines increased in frequency relative to females as the use of Ashdoda figurines declined sharply. This general pattern seems to reflect the ascendance of Dagon, and in time, this god displaced the Cypro-Aegean goddess. During the ninth and eighth centuries B.C.E., another Canaanite god, Baal Zebub, gained popularity among the Philistines.[10] This god is known from Ugaritic texts as well as from the Hebrew Bible (2 Kings 1:2–3, 6, 16), which connects him to the city of Ekron.

After auspicious beginnings in the Iron 1, the Philistine culture seems to have gone into a period of decline early in the Iron 2. Religious practice, of course, did not cease (anthropological studies imply that ritual practice usually increases during tough times), and various cultic items are still found, but it would appear that the social and economic resources needed to erect monumental temples were not available. A small shrine with a mud-brick platform was built at Ashdod during the ninth or eighth century B.C.E. (Str. IX). Throughout the sanctuary, and in pits surrounding it, various cultic vessels (for example, kernoi) were found, along with anthropomorphic figurines much like the earlier Ashdoda figurines, though primarily male. The grand Iron 1 temple at Tel Qasile (Str. XII-X) was destroyed sometime during the early tenth century, along with much of the city, but was rebuilt by the end of the tenth or beginning of the ninth century B.C.E. (Str. IX-VIII). At Ashdod, a cult center was located near the upper city, or acropolis.

With the coming of the Neo-Assyrians and outside investment, a certain level of prosperity returned to the region. Nowhere is this more evident than at Ekron, which had become a key vassal city-state in the Assyrian Empire. The massive (57 x 38 m, or about 187 x 125 ft.) Temple Complex 650 at Tel Miqne–Ekron was situated in the elite part of the city and was perhaps founded by noble patrons. Its overall plan was a hybrid based on local design concepts as well as on those drawn from Neo-Assyrian royal and religious architecture. The complex comprised a courtyard surrounded by a number of rooms. The entrance had a threshold flanked by socket stones, indicating heavy double doors. The main reception hall included a small room at one end with a raised platform approached by a staircase. The complex also included a long sanctuary hall with two rows of four columns, which was entered via the great hall. Inside the hall were two large vats that may have been used for ablutions (Gitin, Dothan, and Naveh 1997). Inside the sanctuary, an inscription was found on a large building block that may have formed part of the western wall. Overall, the style of this sanctuary is reminiscent of Phoenician temples such as the one at Kition. Complex 650 also had multiple storerooms, and throughout the complex, a range of valuable goods made of gold, silver, ivory, bronze, and iron were found.

Open-air shrines were also used during the late Iron Age (seventh to sixth centuries B.C.E.). One example comes from Horvat Qitmit in the Beer Sheva basin, which may have been an Edomite site. The complex included open-air enclosures with stone altars, a plaster basin, and a smaller annex with massebot; adjacent to the court was a tripartite building. The largest of the rectangular enclosures contained a number of ritual items, including various vessels and cylindrical cult stands decorated with applied figures of animals and humans, who in some cases held either weapons or birds. Among the figurines was a bull's head with a black triangle painted on its forehead, and there are both ceramic and bronze examples of the "three-horned mitra." These figurines and other items have strong parallels with material from Ashdod.

Cultic Paraphernalia

Evidence for cultic practices can be inferred from several different kinds of artifacts. Two varieties of chalices—painted and petal-decorated—were likely used in some form of libations or ablutions ceremony. The first group is characterized by painted designs, often using triangles, reminiscent of the fenestrated forms with triangular windows. This type was exclusive to Timna (Tel Batash) and Tel Miqne–Ekron, where they were found in association with limestone altars (Gitin 1993). The second type of chalice, the petal form, had usage that was more widespread. The vessel form, with its thick stand and petals, may be related to the Sacred Tree motif and therefore may represent a sign of Asherah's comeback.

Pillar figurines similar to those found in Israel and Judah were also found in Philistia, though the Philistine versions often have mold-made heads with large ears, rosette pendant necklaces, and long hair worn down to the shoulders. The two styles could represent two different conceptions of a similar goddess, or perhaps no more than different fads among the women of the two cultures. There were also handmade pillar figurines, which differ from the Israelite figures in terms of their greater detail. The hollow base pillars were usually made on the wheel (Kletter 2001).

The use of zoomorphic libation vessels increased late in the period (Iron 2c), and they gradually became more uniform in appearance. At Tel Miqne–Ekron, bovine vessels were found in the temple as well as at the shrines of the oil factory. One of the most outstanding artifacts from the period is the gold cobra, or *uraeus* (a Greek term for the raised cobra, a typical pose), from Ekron.

Limestone altars similar to those used a century or so earlier in Judea and Israel appeared a number of times at seventh-century-B.C.E. Tel Miqne–Ekron. It is intriguing that these four-horned altars were no longer current in Israelite religious practice, nor were they found elsewhere in Philistia (except for one at

Ashqelon), representing, perhaps, the emergence of a unique cult at Ekron. Nineteen altars in total have been found, at least one in every part of the site. The altars come in a variety of shapes—block, round, and shaft—and range from small (0.13 m, or about 5 in.) to quite large and immovable (1.66 m, or about 65 in.); the horns were either round or triangular. (See sidebar, "The Inscriptions from Tel Miqne–Ekron.")

Local and Household Practice

As during the Iron 1, religion was practiced on two levels during the Iron 2: People worshipped at both large temples as a group activity and individually or in small groups at local shrines. At Tel Miqne–Ekron, altars were found in all quarters of the city except the fortifications and in most cases appear in contexts that would otherwise not be interpreted as cultic (Gitin 1993). Variation in the types of altars as well as in the contexts in which they have been found indicates that mode of practice was flexible in the sense that a variety of forms were considered acceptable. The location of the altars suggests that worship could be performed outside of the central temple, and the fact that they were found in elite and nonelite residential areas alike suggests pluralism in worship (Gitin 2002).

Outside Influences

The system of Philistine religion at this time was eclectic and reflects the adoption of practices from several of the neighboring peoples. As noted above, the use of four-horned altars at Tel Miqne–Ekron was unique, and it is possible that this tradition was actually brought there by Israelite refugees after the fall of Israel (Gitin 1995). Regardless of its origin, this convention clearly played an important role in the cultic practices of Ekron and reflects a familiarity with and acceptance of an Israelite tradition.

In addition to this Israelite element, the silver medallion from Ekron reflects a Neo-Assyrian influence. The design on the medallion represents a crude example of a common motif of a worshipper before a goddess, who stands on the back of a lion, arms raised. Shown in the sky above the two figures are a winged solar disc, the moon, and seven circles that represent the stars of the Pleiades (Gitin 1995). Both the lion and the celestial symbols identify the figure as the Assyrian goddess Ištar. This image also reflects a shift in stance toward female deities, as not only Ištar but also other "foreign" goddesses were invited into the Philistine pantheon at this time.

It is possible that Ashtoret, the Phoenician-Canaanite goddess, came to Philistia sometime during the Iron 2. One of the jar inscriptions from Tel Miqne–Ekron read *qds l'asrt*, where the *t* ending for the name Asherah may indicate a Phoenician derivation. According to Seymour Gitin (1995), this version of the goddess's name, the three lines used to denote the quantity (noted above), and the general paleography all point to a Phoenician influence. William Dever (1995), however, has argued that this actually refers to the local goddess Asherah and pointed to the parallel use of the *asˇrt* spelling in the Khirbet el-Qom and Kuntillet 'Ajrud inscriptions of the eighth century B.C.E.,

The Inscriptions from Tel Miqne–Ekron

In the ancient world, as today, it was important for people to denote information about the contents of a vessel—for instance, what was in it and for whom it was intended. It was not uncommon, therefore, for various inscriptions to be written directly onto the vessel body. In Iron 2 Philistia, these inscriptions were often placed below the shoulder of the jar, above the handle. Many of these jars, however, are poorly preserved, and the inscriptions are often elusive. Employing a process of washing the sherds with acetic acid, however, it is sometimes possible to detect inscriptions otherwise unseen.

At Ekron, six examples of a common jar type (ovoid Corpus 1) bearing inscriptions have been recovered from a seventh-century-B.C.E. destruction layer (Str. IB). This corpus of inscriptions, which were generally dedicatory, reveals a great deal about the religious beliefs and customs of Ekron's late Iron Age citizens. One store jar had an inscription with the words *mqm...t* and three horizontal lines, which has been translated as "for the shrine, thirty units of produce set aside for the tithing" (Gitin 1995, 72), indicating that the temple collected tithes from worshippers. The use of the word *maqom* in several of the inscriptions may imply that when the term *Asherat* was used it referred to the goddess or perhaps her cult, but not to the shrine itself. The use of the term *qodesh* at Ekron as a benediction or dedication in conjunction with *Asherat* supports this conclusion. Finally, archaeologists have learned about a west Semitic influence from an inscription that reads *bn nt,* meaning "son of the goddess Anat" (Gitin 1995).

The surviving portion of another, partly damaged inscription reads *qd_ l(h)q(n)d_*.[11] The beginning, *qodesh l'*, means "dedicated to"; thus the missing word is most likely the name of a person or deity. Furthermore, the name was probably Aegean/Philistine in origin, as indicated by the *shin* ending (Naveh 1985). So far, all of the Ekron inscriptions come from one building in the elite zone (Gitin 1993).[12]

Recent excavations at a newly discovered site near Tel Aviv have yielded hundreds of vessels, many of which were cultic in nature, including ceramic cult stands or incense burners (Kletter 2002). Painted in red, black, and white, a number of these vessels, which date to the tenth and ninth centuries B.C.E., also bear inscriptions that now await translation.

which almost certainly referred to Asherah. The link between Ashtoret of the Philistines, Ashtarot of the Israelites, and Asherah remains unclear. In 1 Samuel 31:10, there is a reference to an Ashtoret temple located somewhere in the Jezreel Valley near Beth Shean, but once again, there is no archaeological evidence for this. One of the Ekron inscriptions also refers to *Ptgyh,* a figure whose identification remains uncertain. It is possible that this is the name of a goddess of non-Semitic origin, perhaps some unknown Philistine or Indo-European goddess.

Religious eclecticism in Philistia may stem in part from the fact that over the course of several centuries the people of this region had been exposed to a variety of cultural influences. The original Sea Peoples, who arrived on the coast displaying a heavy Cypro-Aegean flavor, subsequently blended with local Canaanite traditions in order to produce the Philistine culture. Israelites (briefly), Neo-Assyrians, and then Egyptians, all prior to the city's final destruction at the hands of the Neo-Babylonians, subsequently ruled parts of this region (for example, Ekron). Moreover, while an isolated find such as the Assyrian motif mentioned above can be attributed to the presence of an individual expatriate practicing his own religion in a new land, the frequency with which the four-horned altars appeared cannot be explained this easily.

The Social and Economic Context of Religion

There are some indications that there was a priestly class supported by the public. For instance, textual evidence demonstrates that tithes of oil and fig-cakes were collected by the temple (Gitin 1993, 253). Evidence from both Ashdod and Ekron suggests that musicians were also associated with the cult and that music may have been performed as part of certain ceremonies.

There is also evidence for a link between cult and production, whether it was production for the cult, or the infusion of ritual beliefs into the production process. In the potter's precinct at Ashdod (Area D), where male figurines were manufactured, cultic vessels were also found. At Ekron, fancy chalices and limestone altars have been found together in association with olive installations. The four-horned altars may have been employed in some form of production ritual.

NOTES

1. The religious nature of these features has been questioned by Mazar (1990).

2. In some rare cases, Dagan is described as the father of Hadad (Baal).

3. For a summary of the various theories surrounding this topic, see Mazar (1990, 255–257).

4. Finkelstein (1998) takes into account Zertal's (1994) more recent analysis of pottery from the area that is up to 90 percent Middle Bronze Age and the Middle Bronze Age style of the bull figurine.

5. Though the temple was Canaanite in style, several scholars argue that by the Iron 1 the Shechem temple was used for early Israelite worship.

6. According to others, the temple may have been built as late as the seventh century B.C.E.

7. Examples from Judah often depict the goddess from the waist up only.

8. Handmade examples are usually slightly smaller than molded ones.

9. Three ivory knife handles of the same type were also found at Miqne, with the metal blade most likely recycled. One of the Ekron knives (from Field 1) was found near a puppy burial, though it is not clear that they were related (Dothan 2002).

10. The name Baal Zebub may be a dysphemism for Baal Zebul.

11. The inscription was carved into a vessel, and some sherds bearing portions of letters have not been recovered.

12. The excavators acknowledge that this apparent distribution could be an accident of sampling (Gitin 1993).

SUGGESTED READING

Alon, D. and T. Levy, eds. 1998. *Archaeology, Anthropology, and Cult: Excavations at Gilat (Israel): Archaeological and Geological Records.* London: Leicester University Press.

Becking, Bob, Meindert Dijkstra, Marjo C. A. Korpel, and Karel J. H. Vriezen, eds. 2002. *Only One God? Monotheism in Ancient Israel and the Veneration of the Goddess Asherah.* London: Sheffield Academic Press.

Bloch-Smith, Elizabeth. 1992. *Judahite Burial Practices and Beliefs about the Dead.* Sheffield, England: Sheffield Academic Press.

Dever, William G. 1995. "'Will the Real Israel Please Stand Up?': Archaeology and the Religions of Ancient Israel—Part II." *Bulletin of the American Schools of Oriental Research* 298: 37–58.

Devries, L. 1987. "Cult Stands: A Bewildering Variety of Shapes and Sizes." *Biblical Archaeology Review* 13: 26–37.

Dothan, Trude. 2002. "Bronze and Iron Objects with Cultic Connotations from Philistine Temple Building 350 at Ekron." *Israel Exploration Journal* 52: 1–25.

Gitin, Seymour. 1993. "Seventh Century B.C.E. Cultic Elements at Ekron." In *Biblical Archaeology Today, 1990, Pre-congress Symposium: Population, Production and Power (Proceedings of the Second International Congress on Biblical Archaeology)*, edited by A. Biran and J. Aviram, 248–258. Jerusalem: Israel Exploration Society.

Herzog, Zeev. 2001. "The Date of the Temple at Arad: Reassessment of the Stratigraphy and the Implications for the History of Religion in Judah." In *Studies in the Archaeology of the Iron Age in Israel and Jordan*, edited by A. Mazar, 156–178. Sheffield, England: Sheffield Academic Press.

Hestrin, Ruth. 1987. "The Lachish Ewer and the 'Asherah." *Israel Exploration Journal* 37: 222–223.

Mazar, Amihai, ed. 2001. *Studies in the Archaeology of the Iron Age in Israel and Jordan.* Sheffield, England: Sheffield Academic Press.

Meshel, Zeev. 1978. *Kuntillet 'Ajrud: A Religious Centre from the Time of the Judean Monarchy on the Border of Sinai.* Jerusalem: Israel Museum.

Negbi, Ora. 1993. "Israelite Cult Elements in Secular Contexts of the Tenth Century B.C.E." In *Biblical Archaeology Today, 1990*, edited by A. Biran and J. Aviram, 221–230. Jerusalem: Israel Exploration Society.

Ottosson, Magnus. 1980. *Temples and Cult Places in Palestine.* Stockholm: Almqvist and Wiksell International.

Rainey, Anson. 1994. "Hezekiah's Reform and the Altars at Beer-Sheba and Arad." In *Scripture and Other Artifacts: Essays on the Bible and Archaeology in Honor of Philip J. King*, edited by M. Coogan, C. Exum, and L. Stager, 344–354. Louisville, KY: Westminster/John Knox Press.

Smith, Mark S. 2002. *The Early History of God: Yahweh and the Other Deities in Ancient Israel*, 2d ed. Grand Rapids, MI: William B. Eerdmans.

CHAPTER 9

Material Culture

CHALCOLITHIC PERIOD

Ceramics

Early pottery assemblages of the Chalcolithic period represent a transitional phase, known as the "Wadi Rabah horizon," which includes red-slipped and burnished pottery, sometimes with painted decoration similar to examples from Syro-Cilician traditions (that is, the Halaf). This assemblage also includes pottery decorated with bands of fingernail impressions. Pottery related to the Wadi Rabah horizon has been found in the earliest levels at Ghassul and Gilat. There is also the "Qatifian assemblage," a type of poorly fired pottery, usually with thick bases showing rounded reed impressions. This pottery, identified at Qatif (Y-3) and Teluliot Batashi, may represent a regional variant of the Wadi Rabah assemblage. Basins decorated with vertical thumb impressions also belong to this phase.

During the course of the early Chalcolithic period, new forms of pottery entered the assemblage, including cornets, jars and pithoi, and churns used for the processing of dairy goods. There are also some eccentric types, such as the so-called "torpedo vessels" and miniature churns, which are rather rare.[1] Later assemblages of the Chalcolithic period are characterized by the Cream Wares, thin-walled ceramics made with a fine grit–tempered fabric, typically light buff in color. In some cases, such as the finer "V-shaped" bowls, a red band was painted on the rim. Hemispherical vessels are common in domestic assemblages, which also include ceramic spoons.

Lithics and Groundstone

Blades, most often sickle blades, as well as bifacial axes and adzes, dominate the lithic assemblage of the Chalcolithic period. Microlithic tools, bladelets, and "micro-end scrapers," made from an extremely fine flint, are generally more typical of the earlier phase. Fan-shaped scrapers made from a fine, chocolate brown flint are also diagnostic of the Chalcolithic assemblage. These are made in the tabular flint tradition, where the cortex has been carefully ground to a smooth finish, and some rare blade tools made in this tradition seem to presage the later Canaanean blades (Rowan and Levy 1994).

There are a range of groundstone artifacts, including maceheads, palettes, and bowls, made from various stones including basalt, limestone, and granite. One outstanding example is the fenestrated incense burner (Fig. 9.2). Usually made from basalt and thought to be used for burning incense, these stands

9.1 Painted pottery from Shikmim, Chalcolithic period, 3d millennium B.C.E. (Photo courtesy of Zev Radovan, Land of the Bible Picture Archive)

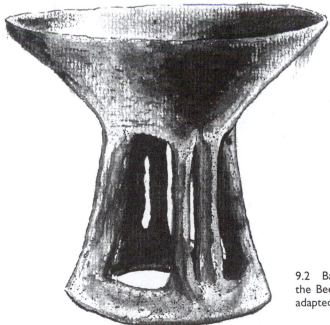

9.2 Basalt "fenestrated" incense burner from the Beer Sheva culture (Drawing by J. Golden; adapted from Perrot 1984)

were initially rather squat in design but became increasingly "high-footed" later in the period.

Architecture

Houses of the Chalcolithic period, made with mud bricks set on stone foundations, were typically designed for nuclear families. A unique style of architecture that appeared during this time was the system of subterranean structures involving bell-shaped chambers connected by tunnels. Possible functions for these features include housing, refuge, storage, and burial, though this is not clear. Examples of cultic architecture have been found at Gilat, Ghassul, and Ein Gedi. Temple complexes at these sites include large structures, sometimes with walls covered by painted murals (for example, Ghassul), large open courtyards, altars, and massebot.

Ritual Paraphernalia and Works of Art

Several forms of small statuary and figurines were used during the Chalcolithic period. These include anthropomorphic and animal figurines made of ceramic and stone. Violin-shaped figurines have been found at a number of Levantine sites, especially Gilat, which had more than sixty examples made from a variety of materials. Some are clearly female, as certain examples have breasts. A corpus of small ivory figurines from sites in the Beer Sheva area probably dates to later in the period. These figurines include representations of both sexes and are indicated by detailed genitalia. There are also stone-carved heads, sometimes referred to as "Pinocchio figurines," the schematic style of which, particularly their pronounced noses, link them to the ivory tradition. One unique bone figurine from Shiqmim shares elements of both the earlier violin-shaped tradition and the Beer Sheva ivories (Levy and Golden 1996; Fig. 9.3).

Two outstanding ceramic sculptures from this period both come from Gilat, including the "Lady of Gilat" and the "Ram with Cornets." The former is a representation of a female figure sitting on what may be a birthing stool and holding a churn on her head, while the latter is a ram with three cornets protruding from its back. As both were found in a cultic context, and both concern aspects of pastoral production, they have been interpreted as relating to ritual beliefs concerning fertility (Amiran 1989). A ceramic figure of a bull similar in style to these has been found at Ein Gedi.

Metal

During the earliest part of the Chalcolithic period, metal technology had not yet come to the southern Levant (Golden, Levy, and Hauptmann 2001). Some of the earliest metal artifacts, made from relatively "pure" copper, may have been imports, though this is not clear. Typical forms include chisels, awls, and axes. Soon these types would be produced locally, and they are found at settlements as well as in elite burials. Around the same time, a distinct industry focused on the production of elaborate items (for example, standards), and various forms of maceheads developed, several drawing on the various animal motifs recurrent in much of the art from this period. The latter were made us-

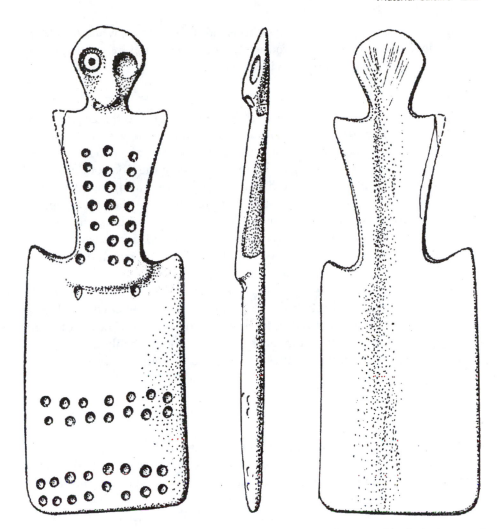

9.3   Bone anthropomorphic figurine from Shiqmin combining elements of both the ivory and the violin-shaped figures (Drawing by Daniel Ladiray; adapted from Thomas E. Levy and Jonathan Golden. 1996. "Syncrestic and Mnemonic Dimensions of Chalcolithic Art: A New Human Figurine from Shiqmim." *Biblical Archaeologist* 59: 150–159.)

ing a variety of "natural alloys," that is, copper with significant amounts of arsenic and antimony, and employing the lost wax-casting technique.[2] The location of the workshops that made these items remains unknown. At Nahal Qanah, the earliest gold in the southern Levant appears at a cave tomb in the form of large, ring-shaped items, the function of which is not clear (Gopher and Tsuk 1996).

Industrial Remains

Micro-end scrapers made of an extremely fine flint are found at Gilat, as is evidence for their production in the way of blade blanks and a rare bladelet core. By the end of the fifth millennium B.C.E., an advanced metals industry was emerging. Centered in the Beer Sheva region, some sites (for example,

Shiqmim) had small neighborhood or household workshops, while Abu Matar has evidence for several large production zones indicated by crucibles, slag, ore, "raw" copper, and simple bowl furnaces.

Burials

The Neolithic practice of infant jar burials carried over into the early Chalcolithic period. It is most likely out of this tradition that the use of ceramic ossuaries, also called "bone boxes" or "charnel houses," evolved. The first large extramural cemeteries in the region were used during the Chalcolithic period. At the cemeteries at Adeimeh and Bab edh-Dra, several different types of graves have been observed. Cist burials, rectangular stone-lined pits roughly 1 meter long, were used for both primary and secondary inhumations. Tumuli consisting of a mound of stone cover finely constructed cairns. Cairn burials without the superstructure have been noted at Shiqmim (Levy and Alon 1985) and Fidan Site 009 (Adams 1991).

Midway through the period, there developed a new tradition of wealthy tombs, usually created through the landscaping of natural caves, such as at Nahal Qanah, where a few individuals were buried with a range of exotic grave goods. Peqi'in, with hundreds of ossuaries, was probably used over the course of several generations (Gal, Smithline, and Shalem 1997).

EARLY BRONZE AGE

Ceramics

Whereas during Chalcolithic times there were several regional pottery styles, ceramic production became increasingly standardized during the Early Bronze Age, resulting in a more prosaic assemblage. Potters had better control of firing conditions, producing in some cases superior quality ceramics, and used the wheel on a more consistent basis. By the EB2–3 it appears that certain wares were mass-produced.

Early Bronze Age ceramics can be divided into groups by function: cooking and storage wares, table wares, and a separate line of funerary wares, including a corpus of miniature vessels. The assemblages of pottery associated with burials differ markedly from the "living" assemblages, most notably in that cooking and larger storage vessels are essentially absent. Kathleen Kenyon's (1979) Proto-Urban A and B findings, which include amphoriskoi, saucers, and "teapots" (spouted juglets), are generally considered to be too small to have had utility and probably represent a class of ceramics made exclusively for burials. Some of these (group A) have a red slip but are otherwise undecorated; others (group B) are painted with the "line group" designs. Kenyon's group C includes bowls, some of which are high-footed or have a stem, and are thus called chalices. These are often covered with a gray slip and highly burnished. In the past, foreign origins have been sought for some of these types, but more recently their uniqueness to the region has been noted and hence local origin has been emphasized instead (Ben-Tor 1992).

One of the more common forms of cooking pots was the "holemouth" jar, a neckless vessel with a flat or rounded base, the latter appearing mainly in the south. These are often furnished with handles, such as the wavy-ledge handles, and are commonly decorated with painted line group designs. Serving vessels include bowls, cups, and platters. There were a few forms of specialized vessels, such as the large kraters with spouts beneath the rim that were probably used to make beer. Small juglets, usually with flaring rims, may have stored precious liquids (for example, oil), while flat vessels with clear signs of burning were used as lamps.

Early Bronze Age ceramics often had a red or purple-brown slip and were highly burnished. Pottery with painted decoration is also common. For instance, the Line Group Painted Wares featured vertical bands of reddish brown painted onto a white slip background. One of the key diagnostic features for Early Bronze Age pottery, found on a number of different pottery types, was the ledge handle. These pot handles often had a series of impressions, giving them a "pie-crust" or wavy-ledge form.

Overall, the quality of pottery increased over time, as more pots were wheel made, superior fabric with finer temper was used, and improved firing techniques were employed. In general, production became more standardized, as seen in a greater regularity of forms. There is also less variety in decoration, as the use of red slip and burnish became increasingly common, although the slip and burnish are sometimes applied in an elegant lattice pattern. One of the key pot types from later in the period is the so-called Abydos Ware, which comprises jugs, juglets, and jars (Fig. 9.4). Wheel made, well fired, and of fine fabric, Abydos Wares represent some of the finest ceramics produced during the Early Bronze Age. These vessels are replete with elegant red painted bands filled with geometric shapes, especially triangles, that adorn the vessel shoulders Although this type of pottery is found throughout the region, its appearance is rather limited in time, thus providing a useful chronological hinge.[3] Holemouth jars and ledge-handles known from the EB1 continue to appear into the EB2–3.

Although the pottery was locally made, differences in the material culture of the north and the south exist, largely owing to stylistic influences from northeastern Anatolia and Syria. The key diagnostic ceramic type from the north was the Gray or Dark-Faced Burnished Ware. These wares were mainly open vessels with a thick, dark gray, and highly burnished slip, and sometimes a "grain wash" or "band slip." Bowls were usually carinated, often decorated with a rope design and knobs of varying shapes. Holemouth jars of the north usually have flat bases. Bowls with high-footed or fenestrated bases continue from the Chalcolithic period.

A new form of high-fired ceramics, known as Metallic Ware, appeared during the EB2. Produced perhaps in shops of the northern Jordan Valley, Metallic Wares peaked in popularity during this period but declined by the EB3. Other features typical of the northern ceramics include combed surface decoration and large, flat platters with a sharp, inverted rim and red slip, sometimes highly burnished. By the EB3, the main "fossil type" for the north was Khirbet Kerak Ware (also known as Beit-Yerah Ware). This type of pottery is known for

10 cm

9.4 "Abydos Ware" of the EBA (Drawing by J. Golden; adapted from R. Amiran, U. Puran, Y. Shiloh, R. Brown, Y. Tsafir, and A. Ben-Tor. 1978. *Early Arad: Chalcolithic Settlement and the Early Bronze Age City I. First–Fifth Seasons of Excavations, 1962–1966.* Jerusalem: Israel Exploration Society.)

its distinctive, highly burnished black slip on the outside and its red interior, often decorated with geometric designs. The handmade Khirbet Kerak Ware comprises a range of forms. Large platters and bowls with a highly burnished red slip were also common. The Metallic and Khirbet Kerak Wares were mainly found in the north and were quite rare in the south.

During the EB1, Egyptian imports are found at a number of sites in southern Canaan. By the latter part of this phase, locally produced Egyptian-style wares, ubiquitous at sites such as Halif Terrace and En Besor, generally replaced the imported vessels. The types of wares commonly include bread molds, bag-shaped vessels, and wine jars.

Lithics and Groundstone

The lithic assemblage comprised a range of blade tools, the most memorable type being the Canaanean blade. This somewhat eccentric form was up to 15 cm (6 in.) long and 3 cm (a little over 1 in.) wide, sometimes trapezoidal in cross section and usually retouched in order to smooth the blade surface.[4] The Canaanean blades were made with a high-quality, fine-grained flint found in the western Negev and Sinai, which hints at continuity with the Chalcolithic "tabular scraper" tradition.

The Egyptian presence in the southern Levant can also be seen in the lithic assemblages, particularly in a form known as the Hammemiah knives (razors). Though many were probably local imitations, some were Egyptian imports.[5] The groundstone assemblage includes maceheads, often of limestone, and some bowls, although many of the stone bowl types, including fenestrated stands known from the Chalcolithic period, were replaced with ceramic copies during the Early Bronze Age (Ben-Tor 1992).

Glyptic Art

The various types of glyptic art that appear in the Early Bronze Age, especially seal impressions, form an important part of the material culture of the period. The stamps and cylinder seals themselves that were used to make these impressions have not been found, however, as many may have been made from wood. Seal impressions from Egypt or Egyptian-style stamp seals have been found throughout southern Canaan at sites such as Halif Terrace, Arad, and En Besor.

Seal impressions from cylinder seals are known from a number of northern sites, including Beit Yerah, Dan, Hazor, Megiddo, and Tel Qashish. Typical geometric designs include spiral, herringbone, and lattice patterns, which suggest a connection with Asia Minor or perhaps the Aegean (Ben-Tor 1992). Seals from Jawa, in the semiarid region east of the Jordan Valley, show a Syrian influence (Helms 1987), while a Byblite and Mesopotamian (Jemdet Nasr) influence is evident in many seals. Figurative designs involving lions and horned animals were also used, many forming schematic motifs, as seen in seals from Megiddo and Jericho.

Pictographic art also appears in the form of engraved images found in stone and on pottery. At Megiddo, horned animals were incised on the stones used to pave the cultic area, and at Arad the Dumuzi Stele depicts human stick figures. Serekhs, essentially the insignias of Egyptian kings that ruled at the end of the fourth millennium B.C.E., were incised on the bodies of vessels, often wine jars. The symbols of several different rulers (for example, Narmer and Hor-Aha) were also found on sherds from a number Levantine sites, including Ai, Arad, Azor, Halif Terrace, and Tel Malhata.

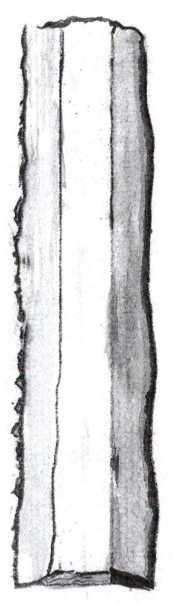

9.5   Canaanean blade typical of the Early Bronze Age (Drawing by J. Golden)

Metals

A quick comparison of Chalcolithic and Early Bronze Age metallurgy might invite speculation that the art of metalworking was in decline during the latter period. No doubt, the collapse of Chalcolithic society had an impact on the

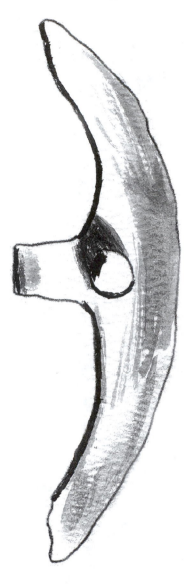

9.6a   Crescentic axehead of the EB3 (Drawing by J. Golden; adapted from Roland de Vaux. 1971. "Palestine during the Neolithic and Chalcolithic Periods." In *The Cambridge Ancient History*, Vol. 1, Pt. 2. 1: 499–538. Cambridge: Cambridge University Press.)

metal industry, with a shift in the nature of demand and patterns of consumption, and a concomitant shift in the organization of production (Golden 2002c). A certain level of continuity can be observed in metal production from Chalcolithic times to the Early Bronze Age. For one thing, copper continued to be the primary material used, as the use of bronze did not begin until later in the Early Bronze Age. There is also continuity in terms of the "utilitarian" forms that were produced—for instance, awls, axes, and adzes from the two periods are generally similar. It was once thought that awls for each period could be distinguished by their shape—Chalcolithic examples were round in section while those from the EB1 were square—but recent discoveries have shown this not to be the case.[6] At the beginning of the Early Bronze Age, there was a shift in the types of weapons produced, with a complete cessation of metal macehead production and a switch to spearheads and daggers. It also appears as though copper use may have declined between the final phase of the EB1 and the EB2 (Tadmor 2002).

Metal weaponry of the later Early Bronze Age includes spearheads, a number of which were quite long and with a central rib, and several types of daggers, some rhomboid in section with no tang, and others with a sizable tang and a central rib. There was also a range of tools, including axes, adzes, chisels, knives, pegs, and a saw. Axes and adzes come in a variety of sizes and forms, one distinctive type being the "crescentic axehead," examples of which have

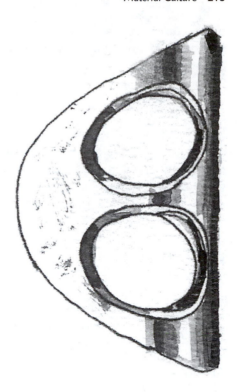

9.6b "Fenestrated axehead" of the IBA (Drawing by J. Golden; adapted from Ram Gophna. 1992. "Early Bronze Age Fortification Wall and Middle Bronze Age Rampart at Tel Po-ran." *Tel Aviv* 19: 267–273.)

been found at Jericho and at Bab edh-Dra in EB3 contexts (Fig. 9.6a). Many of these items are represented in the Kfar Monash Hoard, an isolated assemblage of copper weapons and tools discovered on the Sharon Plain believed to date to the late EB1b (Tadmor 2002; Hestrin and Tadmor 1963). This hoard also included a saw (Tadmor 2002, 245) and disc-shaped objects, which, along with some of the other items, have Egyptian (for example, Minshat Abu Omar) and Nubian (Qustul) parallels.

Precious Metals and Miscellaneous Prestige Goods

Gold continued to be quite rare during the Early Bronze Age. There are beads made of gold, and a gold disk, possibly from Asia Minor, found in a burial cave near Beit Yerah. Silver, even more rare and valued than gold at the time, was also used to make beads, and one of the most outstanding singular artifacts from this period is the silver bowl from Tel el-Far'ah North. Ivory was used to make various items, notably bulls' heads, which have been found at Beit Yerah, Jericho, and Ai in EB3 contexts, all of which display a remarkable similarity in style. Carved bone handles with geometric designs (for example, spirals and herringbone patterns) similar to those appearing on seals have also been found at these sites, bolstering the possible connection with Asia Minor.

Industrial Apparatus

Sites in the mining regions of Sinai and Faynan, as well as settlement sites such as Arad, Tel es-Shuna North, Halif Terrace, and Ashqelon-Afridar, have artifact assemblages that represent the tools of copper production, including crucibles, smelting furnaces, and molds as well as ore, slag, and "raw" metal. Ceramic workshops have also been found at sites such as Tel el-Far'ah North, which had two kilns and other industrial debris.

INTERMEDIATE BRONZE AGE

Ceramics

Most of the material representing the Intermediate Bronze Age comes from shaft-tomb assemblages. Pottery forms typical of the period include amphoriskoi, four-spouted lamps, flat bowls, and tall, wheel-made jars with flaring necks. Holemouth jars and spouted jugs similar to those of the Early Bronze Age continue, while forms such as the mug, goblet, and jug with short spout represent new forms that first appear during the period. Large bowls and basins were also used, and chalices decorated with incised wavy lines appear, though these are rare. Fine, wheel-made wares, often with painted decorations, were imported from Syria.

Incised decorative motifs in the form of dots or combed lines appear on some pots. Applied elements reminiscent of the Early Bronze Age, such as ledge and loop handles, sometimes appear on Intermediate Bronze Age pottery, but in a degenerate form.

Architecture

Much of the Levantine population during this time practiced a seminomadic lifestyle, though scattered settlements such as Beer Resisim have been excavated. Circular, semisubterranean houses have been excavated at villages in Transjordan (Palumbo 1987). Scant evidence for human occupation has been found in recent excavations at Beth Shean (Area R), but no significant architectural remains (Mazar 1997a).

Metals

One of the most significant developments to occur during the Intermediate Bronze Age was the first appearance of true tin bronze. To date, the earliest examples of tin bronze appear sometime around 2200–2000 B.C.E. (Merkel and Dever 1989). At the Enan burial cave just north of Hazor, a number of bronze artifacts have been discovered, including daggers with a midrib, tang, and rivet holes with strong Cypriote parallels (Eisenberg 1985). Fenestrated axes (Fig. 9.6b) with shaft holes derived from the crescentic axes of the Early Bronze Age, first appeared during the Intermediate Bronze Age, while another form, the broad axe, also is generally restricted to this time. Several different forms of ribbed javelin heads, some longer and broader, others shorter and narrower, are known from the Intermediate Bronze Age. Another form, long and square in section, may represent javelin or spear butts. Copper was transported throughout the region in the form of long, thin ingots; examples of these have been found at Beer Resisim, Jericho, and Lachish. Though evidence for foreign contacts during the period is relatively limited, connections can be seen in the metals, both in terms of technology and materials, as well as in forms, such as the daggers from Enan that have Cypriote parallels (Eisenberg 1985).

The Coming of Bronze

Bronze, an alloy of copper and tin, did not appear in the southern Levant before the end of the Early Bronze Age, and possibly only later. The new alloy did not see widespread use in the region until the ensuing Middle Bronze Age. The addition of tin to copper—a true technological breakthrough—resulted in a metal that was more fluid and stronger than copper that could be used to make superior castings, weapons, and tools. The optimal proportion of tin to copper is roughly 1:10, though through the Middle Bronze Age these proportions varied considerably at times, and the use of copper without any tin persisted in the production of some metal weapons (for example, spearheads from Shiloh). Variation in the use of these materials suggests that much of the metal circulating during the Middle Bronze Age was recycled and/or that metalsmiths of the time were still experimenting with this relatively new medium.

The evolution of metal use in the southern Levant generally followed a particular sequence, moving from copper to copper-based "natural" alloys and finally to tin bronze, but this transition was gradual. At first, there was little change either in the shape of the tools produced or in the method of manufacture, and upon the introduction of tin bronze, copper with arsenic, antimony, and other "alloying" materials continued to be used. According to Northover (1998), a linear, evolutionary approach to understanding this problem, with each successive "improvement" in technology supplanting the other, is inaccurate; rather, each development served to widen the choices available to the metalsmith. Arsenical copper and bronze were used interchangeably to manufacture many of the same types of goods, a trend observed at Ashdod, Jericho, and Samieh in Jordan.

Over time, percentages of arsenic in metal began to steadily decline and the use of tin became more common, though the recipe for this alloy was quite variable at first. In order to strike an optimal balance between strength, toughness, and wear resistance, a range of 6 to 12 percent tin could be used (Northover 1998). The properties of bronze, such as a lower liquidus temperature and viscosity, allowed for an expansion in casting techniques, and more intricate forms could be manufactured using the "lost wax" process. Bronze also gave the metalworker a harder, stronger, and more tensile material that would become less brittle during hammering. But despite the practical advantages of this new metal, much of it saw only limited or no use, as many of the bronzes were at first created specifically for burial.

By the Middle Bronze Age, however, the widespread adoption of bronze was apparent in the duckbill and shafthole axes from Levantine sites such as Ashqelon, and a dagger blade (Type C) from a Jericho tomb, G83a, had roughly 12 percent tin (Moorey and Schweizer 1972). Ingots with low per-

(continues)

The Coming of Bronze *(continued)*

centages of tin were found at Har Yeruham in the Negev, and ingots and rough castings have also been discovered at Tel ed-Duweir and Jericho. At first, bronze was probably something of a novelty or luxury item and used to make "prestige weapons," and the technology involved in producing alloys may have been restricted to certain prosperous cities and to specific goods available only to the wealthy.

The question of where bronze was first invented and how it made its way into the southern Levant has not been resolved. Several scholars have suggested northwestern Iran, which was also an area that made considerable use of arsenical copper. Bronze appeared in Mesopotamia and Syria prior to the middle of the third millennium B.C.E.—for instance, appearing in the Royal Tombs of Ur around 2500 B.C.E —and probably traveled from Syria sometime thereafter. Many of the Canaanite bronzes (such as spearheads) are quite similar to examples from Syria and Lebanon. At the same time, bronze artifacts from the Enan burial cave near Hazor seem to reflect a Cypriote origin (Stech, Muhly, and Maddin 1985; Philip 1991), and James Muhly (1999) has suggested Cyprus as one place where this technology may have been discovered early on.

There is also considerable debate regarding the sources and availability of tin, key limiting factors in the bronze industry. The mining area at Kestel in Turkey has been identified as one potential source of tin during the Early Bronze Age (Yener and Vandiver 1993), and contemporary evidence for the processing of metal, such as crucibles from nearby Göltepe, has been offered in support of this theory. This entire reconstruction has been challenged by Muhly (1993), who has questioned whether the areas at Kestel thought to have been exploited during the third millennium B.C.E. for their tin deposits contained sufficient quantities of the metal to make extraction worthwhile. Textual evidence seems to point toward sources further east, perhaps Afghanistan (Stech and Pigott 1986), and Muhly (1999) has suggested that tin came to Cyprus and Anatolia overland and/or via the Black Sea.

Much more is known about the sources of copper. During the Early and Intermediate Bronze Ages, the Wadi Aravah mines, Timna and Faynan, were exploited on a large scale. An estimated 100 tons of metal were produced in the Faynan district during the Early Bronze Age (Hauptmann 1989), and a vast metal manufactory dating to the period has recently been excavated there (Levy et al. 2002). But as the focus of the metal industry shifted toward bronze, alternative sources of copper were sought. This is reflected in the lack of evidence for Middle Bronze Age activity at these mines as well as in the increase in copper mining on Cyprus and the evidence for Cypriote copper smelting at Enkomi and Kition. But miners would again return to exploit the Aravah deposits. By the Late Bronze Age, when Timna had come under

Egyptian control, there was an extensive mining operation at these deposits, and by the Iron 2b–2c, there was extensive activity at two Faynan district sites: Faynan (Site) and Khirbet en-Nahas ("ruins of copper").

Perhaps the most informative artifact type representing the great bronze trade of the Late Bronze Age is the "ox-hide"–shaped copper ingot. Ox-hide ingots, which were designed for long-distance transport, generally had a standardized weight of 29 kg. Pieces of the ingot would be broken off by the end user (that is, the smith) as needed. This type of ingot has been found at sites throughout the eastern Mediterranean, particularly at early Late Bronze Age sites on the island of Crete, and at Sardinia and Cyprus later. These ingots are depicted in wall paintings at the Egyptian tombs of Rekhmire and Penhet at Thebes. Underwater archaeology at a pair of shipwreck sites near the coast of Turkey has also yielded vital information on the topic. The ship found at Cape Gelidonyah in the Bay of Antalya had thirty-nine copper ox-hide ingots, and the shipwreck of Ulu Burun near Kas in southwestern Turkey had some 200 (Bass 1967; Maddin 1989). The Ulu Burun shipwreck, which occurred sometime during the fourteenth century B.C.E., also had as many as twenty ox-hide–shaped ingots made of tin. Given that this metal was destined to be used to make bronze, the ratio of copper to tin ingots (10:1) is not surprising. The evidence from these sites suggests that Greek ships sailed east via Rhodes and Cyprus and stopped, among other places, along the Levantine coast, in some cases picking up a Canaanite crew.

As bronze technology continued to spread, production became increasingly standardized. The use of open molds became more common, and some degree of uniformity with the cast figurines can be observed. Variation in the materials used, however, suggests the work of multiple workshops. It appears that certain cities served as centers for metal production, as the evidence for metal falls off sharply in peripheral areas. Regardless of its route of diffusion, ultimately tin bronze was adopted on a more general level, and by the Late Bronze Age, bronze was produced on a regular basis. Bronze production, of course, carried on well into the period known as the Iron Age, with recent evidence coming out of excavations at Khirbet en-Nahas in the Jabal Hamrat Fidan, Jordan (Levy et al., forthcoming).

Precious Metals and Various Prestige Goods

Expensive luxury goods are actually quite rare during the Intermediate Bronze Age. One rare exception is the silver vessel from 'Ain Samiya. This piece displays expert craftsmanship with the use of the repoussé technique and was decorated with various mythical beings, pointing to a Syrian origin. Items of personal adornment were sometimes made of copper during the Intermediate Bronze Age. Toggle pins of various types appear, including short, simple types as well as longer examples that sometimes have eyelets or knobbed heads. The latter are similar to contemporary pins from northern cities such as Byblos and Ugarit. Earrings, bracelets, and rings made of copper also appear, usually as burial goods, during the Intermediate Bronze Age.

Burials

The form of burial for which the Intermediate Bronze Age is best known is the rock-cut shaft tomb. Hundreds of these tombs have been discovered at sites such as Shuni, Jericho, and Jebel Qa'aqir (Dever 1987; Peilstöcker 2002). Some 900 shaft tombs were recorded at Khirbet Kirmil and 1,100 at Dhahr Mirzbaneh (Dever 2003a; Finkelstein 1991). Ceramics and metal goods from Intermediate Bronze Age shaft tombs (for example, Shuni) show a Syrian influence (Peilstöcker 2002). In the Golan, Galilee, and Transjordan, thousands of dolmen tombs have been found. In these areas, as well as in the Jordan Valley and northern Negev, tumuli—cist tombs covered with mounds of earth and stone—were also used. The "Northern Cemetery" at Beth Shean featured a number of Intermediate Bronze Age burial caves.

MIDDLE BRONZE AGE

Ceramics

By the time of the Middle Bronze Age, most ceramics were made on the wheel. Typical ceramic forms of the period include goblets, pithoi, "ring-based" bowls, jugs, and juglets. There were several variations on the juglet form, including the dipper juglet, with precedents in the preceding Intermediate Bronze Age, as well as new forms such as cylindrical juglets and the piriform juglet with button base. Storage jars include two-handled jars with modeled rims, but one- and four-handled versions also appear.

Other well-known types from this period include open carinated bowls with a low foot. Over time, this foot became taller, which, along with a sharper carination, gives the vessel a more goblet-like appearance. Kraters, deep bowls with handles sometimes extending from the pot rim to the shoulder, are typical of the Middle Bronze Age. Ceramic pot-stands and oil lamps were also used during the Middle Bronze Age.

Various forms of decoration were employed during the period. One distinctive style of the Middle Bronze Age pottery assemblage was the "Levantine Painted Ware," which comprises both bichrome and monochrome painted pottery. Monochrome Painted Cream Ware was found primarily in the north and though manufactured locally, employed a style, technique, and technology linked to the Amuq (Syria) and to southeastern Anatolia. The distribution of this pottery type is highly localized in the Huleh Valley region around Tel Dan, with only a few pieces found further south in the Jordan Valley.

Ceramics imported into the southern Levant include "Chocolate-on-White Wares" as well as Cypriote Pendant Line pottery, which first appears in the MB1. Cypriote jars—for example, "Red-on-Black Ware"—were adorned with painted decorations. The volume of Cypriote imports, which were usually handmade, increased over the course of the period, mostly on the coastal plain at various sites. A Syrian connection is also evident in the ceramic assemblages, with MB2 pottery similar to ceramics from the Khabur region (Ilan 1996). The Monochrome Painted Wares reflect ties with people of the Amuq/Cilicia region (Gerstenblith 1983; Ilan 1991).

Architecture

Palaces and the "governors' residences" appear at Tel el-Ajjul, Aphek, Hazor, Kabri, Lachish, Megiddo, and Shechem. Often more than 1,000 square meters (over 10,700 sq. ft.), these massive structures were designed with pillared broad halls, multiple storage rooms, and large courtyards. The palaces (for example, at Tel el-Ajjul and Lachish) often show a northern influence, since their use of massive sandstone slabs, or orthostats, is known from the palaces of Syria.

Massive earthworks such as ramparts and glacis made of mud brick are also hallmarks of the Middle Bronze Age. A variety of methods were used to construct these. The sloping ramparts were sometimes built using alternating layers of crushed stone and pottery, as at Gezer. These were often built against a stone core that was actually a reused wall, as was the case at Megiddo and Shiloh as well as at Gezer. Some cities encased their earthen ramparts with a stone glacis, as at Jericho, or with some form of external stone revetment, as at Shechem. The rampart at Hazor, which employed a number of different techniques, reached 15 m (about 50 ft.) high and 60 m (about 197 ft.) wide in spots and was surrounded by a ditch 15 m (about 50 ft.) deep.

Monumental gateways were found, including three-tiered gatehouses that were up to 20 m (about 66 ft.) long and 10 m (about 33 ft.) wide, often with staircases inside the towers. There are strong parallels between gatehouses found at sites such as Gezer, Hazor, and Yavne-Yam and those from Syrian cities such as Alalakh. Arched gateways, again with Syrian parallels, have been found at Laish (Tel Dan) and Ashqelon.

Metal

One key feature of the Middle Bronze Age material culture was the proliferation, after its initial introduction in the preceding period, of the use of true tin bronze. Bronze was utilized to make an array of distinctive weapons, tools, and ornaments. Typical forms of weapons and tools include daggers of the flat-bladed and veined variety, spearheads with socketed shafts, and hafted flat axes and adzes. The duckbill axe head (Fig. 9.6c) was common early in the period but was replaced by the shafthole type later on (early MB2). Many of the metal goods found at Canaanite sites, such as Shiloh, are rather similar to ex-

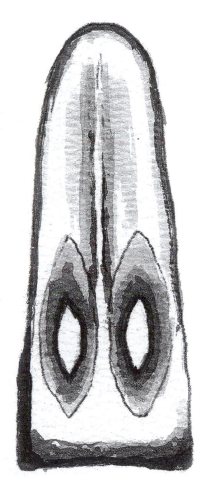

3 cm

9.6c "Duck bill axehead" of the IBA (Drawing by J. Golden; adapted from Ram Gophna. 1992. "Early Bronze Age Fortification Wall and Middle Bronze Age Rampart at Tel Poran." *Tel Aviv* 19: 267–73.)

amples known from Syria, while much of the copper used to make these items probably came from Cyprus.

Ornamental items include stick or toggle pins with "mushroom" or "club-shaped" heads, fibulae or garment fasteners, and statuettes. Silver and gold were also used to make ornamental goods and jewelry, such as ring amulets and "penannular" rings, as well as small figurines. At Tel el-Ajjul, an impressive number of gold objects, including solid-gold toggle pins, as well as silver, electrum, and, in rare cases, lead point to a mastery of metalworking techniques (Khalil 1984); evidence for the local casting of gold has not, however, been discovered in the region.

Glyptic Art

Imported goods from Egypt and Syria are also typical of Middle Bronze Age assemblages, attesting to the networks of international trade that began to emerge during the period. Scarabs bearing royal Hyksos names written in Egyptian hieroglyphics have been recovered at Tel el-Ajjul (City 2). In some cases, the scarabs appear to use the Egyptian symbols in a somewhat random fashion, and at times the glyphs are replaced altogether with geometric shapes. Syrian cylinder seals have also been found at Canaanite cities, mostly in the north.

A particular style of glyptic art called the "Syrian Style," which combines Mesopotamian, Egyptian, and local motifs, emerged during the eighteenth century B.C.E. This syncretistic genre ultimately spawned a number of motifs that are now regarded as uniquely Canaanite, in particular those portraying the deities Hadad-Baal and Astarte. Mythical beasts such as the griffin and sphinx, native to neighboring lands, were spun into local Canaanite versions, while random symbols such as the ankh were used to fill space. Human (or divine) figures are also depicted in many seals. These figures sport the styles of the Canaanite noble class, such as the long robe and beard for men.

One other medium where Canaanite artistic and iconographic styles can be observed is in the small plaques made of bone used as insets to decorate wooden items such as jewelry boxes or furniture. These inlays employ a range of motifs, including naturalistic figures such as birds, lions, cattle, and various other animals, in addition to humans; the men depicted often have an Egyptian "attitude," as do some of the birds, and a symbol that closely resembles the Egyptian Djed column was also used. There are also inlay pieces in the form of strips that may have been used as border trim. These feature a range of geometric designs, including rows of concentric circles, zigzag triangles, and other symbols.

Miscellaneous Imported Goods

Glass, usually small beads, appeared for the first time during the Middle Bronze Age (Peltenburg 1987; Ilan, Vandiver, and Spaer 1993). Other important items of trade probably included linen and textiles, often "invisible" in the archaeological record, as well as various horticultural goods. Egyptian scarabs and other items of either Egyptian origin or influence are much more common at the coastal sites than elsewhere, and this is true to some extent of Aegean/Cypriote goods.

The "Hyksos" Cultural Variant

During the Middle Bronze Age, a distinct subregional style linked to a people commonly known as the Hyksos emerged in the Egyptian Delta. The diagnostic form of pottery for the Hyksos is the so-called Tel el-Yehudiyeh Ware, named for the Delta site where it was first discovered. This assemblage includes small juglets with painted, incised, or punctate decoration. Most outstanding are the ceramics made in the form of humans (usually human heads), fish, and various other zoomorphic forms. Fish and various animals are also found as painted decorations on pots, though abstract geometric designs are more common. Recovered from sites in the Egyptian Delta as well as southern Canaan (for example, Ashqelon), Tel el-Yehudiyeh Ware points to contact between these two regions. Both the metal and ceramic assemblages from Avaris suggest that by the middle of the Middle Bronze Age, the focus of trade relations shifted toward cities on the northern coast such as Byblos (Bietak 1991).

LATE BRONZE AGE

Ceramics

As far as local Canaanite wares are concerned, there was very little change in the Late Bronze Age from the previous Middle Bronze Age. Overall, the pottery seems to have declined somewhat in quality, becoming coarser and rougher. The most notable change was the complete disappearance of Tel el-Yehudiyeh Ware, a ceramic style associated with the Hyksos, who came under attack at the beginning of the Late Bronze Age.

Typical Late Bronze Age storage vessels include "commercial" storage amphorae and dipper juglets, found in houses as well as in tombs. Open vessels were used for serving and eating, and a variety of cooking jars were used. A distinctive ceramic type appearing in the period is the pilgrim flask, a rounded, flattened, small-necked vessel with handles on each side. Oil lamps from this time were often designed for hanging.

Bichrome Wares. Bichrome Wares, kraters and biconical jugs decorated with red or red and black paint applied directly to a buff surface, were imported from Cyprus. The painted designs are typically in the form of a frieze involving triglyphs, which divided the space into metopes (rectangular registers) and various geometric patterns. Animal motifs with deer or gazelle were often used to fill the registers. One notable motif is the Sacred Tree flanked by antelopes, which may derive from a design known in Mitanni glyptic art. In some cases, amphorae were also decorated with metopes. Open bowls were sometimes painted as well.

Imported Wares

Though many of the local wares, especially from the beginning of the period, show continuity with assemblages of the previous period, one of the hallmarks of the Late Bronze Age is the first appearance in significant numbers of ceramic types from Cyprus and the Aegean. The Chocolate-on-White Ware, already known in the Middle Bronze Age, continued through the sixteenth century B.C.E., and though Cypriote forms inspired this style, the wares probably were locally made. It was during the fourteenth and thirteenth centuries B.C.E., however, that Cypriote and Mycenaean imports were most common, and there was a proliferation of forms.

Cypriote Wares.   Cypriote wares began to appear with greater frequency over the course of the Late Bronze Age, peaking in the later fifteenth and fourteenth centuries B.C.E. This pottery was usually handmade and occurred in a variety of forms with an assortment of decorative designs. Typical Cypriote forms include ring-based ware (*bilibil* jugs), white slipped milkware, and the *buchero* (ribbed) vessel. One unique form is the base-ring juglet that resembles the head of a poppy plant, thus giving rise to speculation that such pieces at some point contained opium.

Another style of ceramic, known as Bichrome Ware, began late in the Middle Bronze Age and appeared with increasing frequency in the fifteenth century B.C.E. This pottery is named for its painted decorations in two colors, red and black, with motifs involving birds, fish, and bulls, similar to Cypriote examples (also known as Late Cypriote I style). Bichrome Wares are known from Megiddo (X-IX), Gezer (XVIII), and Tel el-Ajjul (City II). This style was often used to decorate local forms, such as kraters, which is not surprising considering that kraters were probably related to the wine market. It is not clear, though, how much of this pottery was actually made in Cyprus and how much of it represents local production imitating the foreign style. Other diagnostic ceramic forms at the beginning of the Late Bronze Age include Monochrome, White Slip I, and Base Ring I Wares and Syrian-style gray lustrous pottery. Later in the period, Cypriote imports also included the bilbil jug and the Base-Ring II style.

Mycenaean Wares.   Mycenaean Wares, as well as their local imitations, represent an important dimension of Late Bronze Age material culture. Found more frequently on the coast (for example, Tel Abu Hawam), Mycenaean Wares ultimately made their way as far inland as Transjordan. The Mycenaean II first appears in the Levant during the LB1b, or approximately the fifteenth century B.C.E., at sites such as Lachish Fosse Temple and Amman airport.[7] By the fourteenth to thirteenth centuries B.C.E., Mycenaean Wares (IIIA-B) began to flow throughout the eastern Mediterranean. As with the Cypriote-style wares, however, it is not always apparent which examples are true imports and which are local imitations.[8]

The Mycenaean imports are generally of superior quality. They often had a cream slip with a lustrous finish that was then painted, usually dark brown. The painted decorations include a range of motifs, including spirals and concentric circles, horizontal bands, and stylized figures. Various Mycenaean forms are found in the southern Levant, including pyxides (small boxes), Kylix drinking cups, stirrup jars, flasks, piriform amphoriskoi, flat bowls, and kraters.

Other Imports

In the north, ceramics frequently display a Phoenician influence. This is particularly true of pottery forms such as jugs, flasks, bowls, and oil lamps. Egyptian scarabs, especially useful since they sometimes provide absolute dating, are also common during this period.

Architecture

A distinctive architectural form from the Late Bronze Age was the "patrician house," a design that typically included an open courtyard or atrium, storage rooms, and a staircase leading to the second floor. Examples of the patrician house have been found at sites throughout Canaan, including Aphek, Megiddo, Ta'anach, and Batash-Timna. In some cases, the house included a pillared hall made with rows of stone bases supporting wooden columns. One of the most outstanding examples of monumental architecture comes from the site of Hazor, where there was a palace and a temple featuring sculpted orthostats. In terms of overall design, the monumental architecture at Hazor and other sites is similar to examples from northern cities such as Ebla and Alalakh. Examples of Egyptian-style architecture have been found at several sites (for example, Beth Shean).

Metals

Bronze was used to make tools (for example, sickles) and weapons (daggers and arrowheads), which in some cases were decorated. Some of the weapons display a foreign influence, for example, the leaf-shaped arrowheads from Mycenae. Other bronze goods representing the Late Bronze Age include oil lamps, censers, and bowls with animal-shaped handles. The Canaanite tradition of bronze statuary continued in the Late Bronze Age with the appearance of figures such as an armed and striding Baal and the naked Ashtarte. Images of mortals are rare, and these are generally restricted to the few examples of Canaanite nobles, who are depicted in a blessing gesture.

Precious Metals and Miscellaneous Luxury Goods

Jewelry was commonly made of gold and silver during the Late Bronze Age. One diagnostic type from the period was an elongated toggle pin with eyelets. Two such toggle pins, along with an ivory roundel, were found with a female burial at Ashqelon. During the Late Bronze Age, the wealthy sometimes owned fancy vessels made of faience and glass. Other expensive luxury goods include alabaster vases, ivory cosmetic boxes, and various items enhanced with bone and ivory inlay.

Industrial Remains

Among the most easily recognizable artifacts from the Late Bronze Age are the "ox-hide ingots," copper ingots named for their hide-shaped form. These ingots were widely traded throughout the eastern Mediterranean at this time. Notable are the ox-hide ingots found amid the remains of two shipwrecks near the coast of Cape Gelidonyah and Bodrum in Turkey; they are also depicted in ancient Egyptian tomb paintings. Kilns and furnaces that probably date to the Late Bronze Age have been found in association with the temples at Hazor.[9] In Area C, there were two stone-built firing installations, one used for smelting, as indicated by the presence of copper slag. The Area H temple also had a kiln that was most likely used for the production of small votive vessels.

Art

The glyptic art of the Late Bronze Age reflects various foreign influences, including seals in the Mitanni style depicting lions, winged beasts, griffins, and horned animals. Other seals show a Cypriote-Aegean influence, while Assyrian motifs begin to creep in. It is also during this time that Proto-Canaanite and Proto-Sinaitic inscriptions begin to appear. In some instances, such as the celebrated "Charioteer Vase" from Tel Dan, elaborate images were painted onto fancy vessels.

Artistic styles can also be seen in the sculptures that were sometimes incorporated into the architecture of temples and palaces. Lions depicted in sculptural work at Hazor and Beth Shean have parallels with Syro-Cilicia, especially the city of Alalakh. Several unique examples of Canaanite sculptural art of the Late Bronze Age come from the Hazor shrine (Area C), including a group of

9.7 The "Charioteer Vase" from the "Mycenean Tomb" at Tel Dan (Drawing by J. Golden; adapted from David Ilan. 2003. "The Dawn of Internationalism: The Middle Bronze Age." In *The Archaeology of Society in the Holy Land*, 3d ed., edited by T. E. Levy, 297–319. New York: Facts on File.)

small stelae, a statue of a seated male figure, and a small, sculpted lion. Artifacts made of carved ivory were also used, with several outstanding examples from Megiddo, including a long piece of inlay that may be from a knife handle, a pyxis with lions and winged beasts, and a plaque crowded by figures both mythical and naturalistic. Although the latter shows a Syro-Cilician influence, other ivory pieces are more Aegean in style.

Burials

Burial traditions varied from region to region during the Late Bronze Age. For instance, in the highland zones, caves were often used for multiple burials, whereas in the coastal area individuals were more likely to be buried in pits. A burial from Ashqelon dating to early in the period (1500 B.C.E.) consisted of a mud-brick–lined vault covered with wooden boughs and plaster.

Later in the period (thirteenth to twelfth centuries B.C.E.), foreign funerary conventions become increasingly evident. For example, a Hittite influence can be seen in the double-pithos burials at Nami and Sa'idiyeh, Zeror (Tubb 2002), and an Egyptian influence can also be observed, especially in the "Egyptianized" anthropoid coffins from Beth Shean, Deir el-Balah, Tel el-Far'ah South, and Lachish. There were two main styles of coffins: the Egyptian naturalistic style and the grotesque style—the latter displaying an Aegean, that is, Sea Peoples influence; both have been observed at Beth Shean. A Cypriote-Aegean influence is also apparent throughout much of the region, especially on the coast and in the north, where dromos burials reminiscent of Mycenaean tombs appear, and Larnax-style tombs appear at Gezer and Acre. Other forms of wealthy tombs seen in this period were cist graves (for example, at Tel Abu Hawam) and stone-built structures (at Megiddo and Dan).

MATERIAL CULTURE OF THE INTERIOR DURING THE EARLY IRON AGE (IRON 1)

Ceramics

Pottery typical of the Iron 1 assemblage is somewhat pedestrian, with fairly conventional forms and little decoration. Large pithoi, especially the collared-rim variety, have traditionally been regarded as the key diagnostic component for Israelite material culture, but they have also been found outside the hill country (for example, at Tel Qasile and Tel Keisan). One specific version of the pithos jar, known as the "Galilean" type, has a carinated body with handles just below a wide mouth. This type, which appears in the Galilee and Huleh regions, may have had Canaanite precursors. Another form of pithos jar, found in the Galilee and in the northern Jordan Valley, was more at home in Phoenicia (for example, Tyre). Large amphorae were also common in local assemblages. Various jugs and juglets, flasks, and pyxides from Iron 1 contexts (such as Tel Dan, Level VI) remained similar in style to those of the Late Bronze Age, and some Bichrome Wares still appear (Biran 1994). "Midianite Wares," a class of ceramics originating from northwestern Arabia and the Hejaz, were found at the northern Negev site of Tel Masos (Rothenberg and Glass 1983).

Incised and impressed decorations were sometimes used, but painted decoration is rare. Nevertheless, subtle differences in ceramic styles have allowed archaeologists to observe regional variation. Although the Israelite styles dominate sites of the hill country, settlements closer to Philistia and Phoenicia tend to have more mixed pottery assemblages. The Mycenaean and Cypriote imports, on the one hand, virtually disappear at this time. The Egyptian influence, on the other hand, persists into the Iron 1. At Tel es-Sa'idiyeh, for example, scarabs and Egyptian-style carved ivory boxes were found.

Architecture

Monumental architecture from this time is rare, and many sites consist of little more than pits and small houses. The configuration of some highland villages is thought to resemble nomadic tent camps. Large, in-ground storage units have been discovered at some of the larger Iron 1 sites, such as Megiddo (Storage Pit 1414) and Hazor (Area G Silo), although other sites (for example, 'Izbet Sartah) have smaller, stone-lined silos. Plaster-lined cisterns carved out of the bedrock were used for water catchment at sites such as Ai and Raddanah. Another key feature of the Iron 1 highland occupation is the extensive agricultural terraces cut into the hill-slopes.

Metals

Bronze continued to be the primary metal used in the production of both luxury goods and weapons and tools well into the Iron Age 1. Bronze wine kits consisting of a Canaanite-style bowl, jug, and strainer were included in burials early in the period (for example, at Megiddo, Beth Shean, and Tel es-Sa'idiyeh), but these went out of style by the eleventh century B.C.E. Bronze figurines appear during the Iron 1 period, two outstanding examples being the bull from the Samarian Hills ("Bull Site") and a seated god from Hazor (Level XI). New types of bronze goods (for example, bowls with handles and tripods) originating from and/or influenced by Cypriote and Aegean styles have been observed at Akhziv, Megiddo, Tel Qasile, Tel es-Sa'idiyeh, and Tel Zeror.

In the early part of the Iron 1, most weapons and tools were also made of bronze, and a number of forms known from the Late Bronze Age, such as hammer axes, double axes, arrowheads, and long, socketed spear and javelin heads, remained in use. By the eleventh century B.C.E., the earliest iron tools in the region appear, notably a pick from Har Adir in the Galilee. Iron, however, was still relatively rare, its use largely restricted to the manufacture of decorative items.

Industrial Remains

Evidence for bronze production, including crucibles, slag, blowpipes, "raw" metal, various tools made of basalt, and various forms of installations and furnaces, appears at Iron 1 sites throughout the southern Levant. Olive oil presses from the Iron Age have been found at sites in the central hill country, including a group of installations in southern Samaria; however, their dating is less precise (Finkelstein 1995).

ISRAELITE MATERIAL CULTURE OF THE IRON 2

Ceramics

During the Iron 2, ceramics became more standardized in both form and method of production. This trend included a reduction in regional variation observed at the beginning of the period (Aharoni 1982; Dever 1997). By Iron 2b, however, the assemblages of Judea and Israel were more distinct.

Imported Phoenician wares, or imported-style copies, quite rare in the early Iron 1, increased dramatically during the early Iron 2. The Phoenician influence permeates the material culture of the Iron 2 only to drop off again with the end of the Omride Dynasty. Imported ceramics from Cyprus and Egypt, as well as scarabs and seals, continue, and Neo-Assyrian-type vessels appear for the first time.

During the late eleventh and early tenth centuries B.C.E., slipped and burnished wares began to appear in greater quantity (Holladay 1990; Zimhoni 1997; Dever 1997). The presence of these wares peaked during the tenth century, when slips and burnishes were used on up to one-half of the pottery at some sites; for example, at Tel Batash, 48 percent of the ceramics were slipped and burnished, at Gezer (Str. VIII) 37 percent, and at Beer Sheva (Str. VIII) 37 percent.

By the ninth century B.C.E., much of the pottery was mass-produced, with the industry becoming even more standardized by the eighth century B.C.E. (Zimhoni 1997). Typical forms from this time include storage jars, jugs, cooking pots, and large bowls with carinated rims. Amphorae also continued, though they were made with shorter necks and more rounded shoulders. By the seventh century B.C.E., a new form of amphora with carinated shoulders, elongated bodies, and pointed bases was common. Several new forms, such as the decanter, appeared during the Iron 2–3. Vessels used for serving, such as bowls, jugs, and juglets, were treated with a surface slip and burnishing, whereas cooking and storage vessels typically had no surface treatment (Faust 2002a).

The most notable change in the ceramic assemblages of the seventh century B.C.E. was the appearance of imports such as Assyrian-type vessels (for example, bottles and carinated bowls) and the Corinthian juglet. The Phoenician-style "Akhziv Wares" also appear. The elongated amphorae with pointed bases and carinated shoulders continued, and a notable new form, a class of large, heavy bowls, appeared.

One of the most important features of this late Iron Age assemblage is the use of stamps on jar handles. These so-called *La-melekh* jar handles are found at a number of sites, including a large group from Jerusalem. Clay bullae also appear in late Iron Age contexts, again in Jerusalem, where one house contained a cache of fifty, many of which were inscribed (Shiloh and Tarler 1986). (See sidebar, "Bullae.")

Architecture

Although the early Iron Age has little evidence for monumental architecture, there are numerous examples of grand temples and palaces that date to the

Bullae

Seals were used throughout the ancient Near East in order to record and document transactions and legally recognized agreements. Important documents written on papyrus or parchment were rolled, tied with string, and then sealed with a lump of clay, or bulla, which was then stamped with a seal. Seal impressions are also frequently found on jar handles. The seal itself was often made of some semiprecious stone or, in the case of the less affluent users, ceramic. Typically the owner's name or title was carved into it, so as to mark possession or handling of the goods by the stamp's owner.

Excavations at Iron Age sites in the southern Levant have brought to light hundreds of seals and seal impressions written in early Hebrew, mostly dating to the eighth and seventh centuries B.C.E. Among the ruins of what was a residential quarter of Jerusalem at the time, some fifty inscribed bullae and seal impressions were found. Many of these examples were well preserved as a result of burning, which had the effect of hardening the clay, and it has been suggested that this may have been the city that was torched by the Babylonians in 586 B.C.E. (see Avigad 1986). Each of these seals and bulla bore the name of its owner, and it seems that several may now be identified as belonging to specific individuals named in the Hebrew Bible.

One impressed bulla bears a three-line inscription that reads, "Belonging to *Berekhyahu* son of *Neriyahu* the scribe." The suffix *yahu* translates to "of God," as in "blessed of Yahweh," and was common in Hebrew names, especially in Judea. A direct parallel for this person is found in a scribe named Barukh, son of Neriah, mentioned four different times in the Bible (Jeremiah 32:12; 43:1–7; 36; and 45), and he is known as the comrade and confidant of the prophet Jeremiah (Avigad 1978, 1986; Shanks 1987). Based on the genealogy, the style of script used, and the fact that both Baruchs were scribes, Nahman Avigad (1986) has argued that this bulla represents a direct reference to the biblical figure (for further discussion of this and other examples, see also Schneider 1991). Irrespective of whether the bullae can be used to identify specific biblical figures, such finds are particularly important for the study of social and political organization because they represent a vital source of information about personal names, official titles, the administrative system, and the iconography in use at the time.

Suggested Reading

Avigad, Nachman. 1978. "Baruch the Scribe and Yerahme'el the King's Son." *Israel Exploration Journal* 28: 52–56.

———. 1986. *Hebrew Bullae from the Time of Jeremiah: Remnants of a Burnt Archive.* Jerusalem: Israel Exploration Society.

Schneider, T. 1991. "Six Biblical Signatures: Seals and Seal Impressions of the Six Biblical Personages Recovered." *Biblical Archaeology Review* 17: 26–33.

Shanks, Hershel. 1987. "Jeremiah's Scribe and Confidant Speaks from a Hoard of Clay Bullae." *Biblical Archaeology Review* 13: 58–65.

Shiloh, Yigal. 1993. *The New Encyclopedia of Archaeological Excavations in the Holy Land,* edited by Ephraim Stern, 2: 198–172. New York: Simon and Schuster.

Iron 2. These structures often employ a common vocabulary of royal architecture, with ashlar masonry and palmette capitals on columns. Cedar may have been used extensively in the construction of monumental architecture, though it does not survive in the archaeological record. There are, however, multiple references in the Hebrew Bible, as well as in extra-biblical sources, to the cedars of Lebanon, most famously, the description of their use in the construction of Solomon's Temple.

Houses of the Iron 2 varied considerably in size and plan, with some more elaborate than others (for example, pillars sometimes lined the courtyards). Some of the fancier houses were built in the "four-room" style, though after the tenth century they became less common in the southern kingdom. These houses were roughly 100 square meters (1076 sq. ft.), and some examples include a second floor, as indicated by a stone staircase (for example, at Hazor). Excavations in and around the Old City of Jerusalem revealed a neighborhood built sometime in the seventh century B.C.E. and quite possibly destroyed in the city's devastation in 586 B.C.E. Along the eastern slope of what were the Middle Bronze Age ramparts in Jerusalem there developed a residential area, with four-room houses dated to the Iron 2–3, in which the structures conform to the contours of the slope.

City Walls and Gate Systems. Some of the outstanding architectural features from this period include elaborate gate systems found at Beer Sheva, Dan, Megiddo, Timna (Tel Batash), Tel en-Nasbeh, and Hazor; city walls with both a solid and casemate design were also used. Excavations in Jerusalem's Old City have revealed a section of a massive wall, roughly 7 m (23 ft.) thick, built

9.8   The Iron Age water system at the Hazor (J. Golden)

9.9   Proto-Aeolic column of the Iron 2 (Drawing by J. Golden; adapted from Yigal Shiloh. 1977. "The Proto-Aeolic Capita—the Israelite 'Timorah' (Palmette) Capital." *Palestine Exploration Quarterly* 109: 39–52.)

mainly with large, rough-hewn stones, faced with ashlars on its corners (Shiloh 1979; Mazar and Hanan 1988).

Water-Supply Systems.   Two major underground water systems were used in Jerusalem during the later Iron Age. The one called "Warren's Shaft" (late tenth through late eighth centuries B.C.E.) employed a sloping tunnel with rock-cut stairs leading down to a vertical shaft some 14 m (46 ft.) deep, the base of which met the Gihon spring. The other major water system in Jerusalem, known as "Hezekiah's Tunnel," runs underneath much of the city. It must postdate Warren's Shaft because it incorporated a portion of the earlier system.

The complex water system at Hazor, dated to the ninth century B.C.E., consisted of an entrance room with retaining walls and descending ramps as well as a wide, square, vertical shaft linked to a sloping tunnel that reached to the level of the groundwater at a depth of some 40 m (131 ft.). Similar though often less complex systems have been excavated at other sites, including Gezer, Gibeon, and Megiddo.

Metal

By the tenth century B.C.E., the use of iron had become fairly widespread throughout the southern Levant. Farming implements and other tools such as plows, picks, shovels, and knives were typically made of iron. Arrowheads, spearheads, and other weapons were also made of iron, as were various types of equipment used in horsemanship and the manufacture of chariots (for example, spoked wheels).

With the clear advantages of iron for such utilitarian purposes, the role of bronze became limited to the production of luxury goods and works of art. Fancy bronze bowls, decorated with a range of techniques (such as repoussé)

9.10a (*above*) Iron 2 city gate at Hazor.
9.10b (*below*) Iron 2 city gate at Megiddo
(Photos courtesy of Zev Radovan, Land of the Bible Picture Archive)

are found at sites throughout the region. Silver was also used to make fancy wares (for example, bowls) as well as jewelry, and it was used as the standard for monetary payment, with small ingots cast in the weight known as the shekel. Gold was used to make small items of jewelry, such as earrings.

Industrial Apparatus

Despite the rapid spread of iron technology, the great tradition of bronze-work in the southern Levant never ceased. A late-eleventh- to early-tenth-century bronze workshop at Dan includes crucibles, slag, basalt tools, and blowpipes as well as circular installations and furnaces fixed with bellows and clay tuyeres. Some of the earliest evidence for iron production comes from the tenth- to eighth-century-B.C.E. site of Tel Hammeh (as-Zarqa) in the Jordan Valley, where the remains of an iron-smelting operation include slag, ore, tuyeres, and molten and vitrified clay. Evidence for iron processing has also been discovered at Tel Jemmeh.

Gold and silver came into the region in the form of ingots, which were then used by local smiths. At Eshtemoa, a silver hoard including small amorphous lumps of silver was discovered. The Hebrew Bible mentions Tarshish—a location not positively identified but thought to be either in Anatolia or Spain—as one source of this metal. A source of both silver and gold also mentioned in the Hebrew Bible is Ophir (1 Kings 9:28), which is also noted in an ostracon inscription.

Burials

Most common people were probably buried individually in small pits that do not survive in the archaeological record. There are also more elaborate tombs, such as the large, multichambered rock-cut tombs dating to the eighth and seventh centuries B.C.E.; some of the best examples are in Silwan, Jerusalem. Many of the tomb chambers were lined with benches and had niches carved out for the body. In some cases, aboveground tombs with ornate facades were used. Grave goods from some of these wealthier burials included imported ceramics, jewelry, and model furniture. Carved into some of the tombs are early Hebrew inscriptions, some of which reflect the Phoenician influence. (See sidebar, "The Silwan Necropolis.")

PHILISTINE MATERIAL CULTURE OF THE IRON I

Philistine Ceramics and the Mycenaean Influence

During the Iron 1, a completely new material culture complex appeared rather abruptly on the southern coast of Canaan. The arrival of a new people—Sea Peoples, who would later become the Philistines—is evident in many aspects of material culture, above all, in their pottery: at first Monochrome Wares with designs painted in red or black. This ceramic style was observed in the earliest Philistine levels at Tel Miqne–Ekron, and at Ashdod a form of dark, painted Monochrome Ware was found directly above the Late Bronze Age destruction level. This style is directly related to the Mycenaean IIIC:1b ceramics, though

The Silwan Necropolis

The Silwan necropolis comprises some fifty tombs carved into the limestone cliffs of the Kidron Valley's eastern ridge. The multichambered tombs often feature sarcophagi, niches, and benches lining the walls. The entrances to many tombs have a lintel, and in the case of several of the aboveground tombs, the lintels bear inscriptions. The inscriptions provide a rare clue as to their date, for the script used in the inscriptions suggests the eighth to seventh century B.C.E. (Ussishkin 1993).

Positioned in two rows across the face of the cliff, the tombs would have been visible reminders for the living of the wealth and power of the city's elite. One outstanding example is Tomb 3 (also known as the Tomb of the Pharaoh's Daughter). Although the precise identification of the tomb's owner is uncertain, this freestanding structure appears to have an Egyptian connection, as it originally featured a small pyramid on top and an Egyptian-style cornice.

much of it was locally made. Within a few generations, it would evolve into a new style known as Philistine Bichrome Ware, named for its use of both black and red paint to decorate the pot. This genre drew from a variety of influences, elaborating on the Aegean designs with Canaanite- and Egyptian-inspired elements (for example, the stylized lotus). Common motifs on Bichrome Ware included spirals, birds, and occasionally fish, which were painted within registers formed by horizontal bands, tryglyphs, and metopes. The use of slipping and burnishing was also common, peaking at sites such as Ashdod (Str. X) and Tel Qasile (Str. IX), where it was evidenced on a third of the ceramic assemblages.

Despite these changes in the style of decoration, many of the Mycenaean forms remain in the repertoire. Typical forms of this period include bell-shaped bowls with handles, strainer jars, and juglets along with stirrup jars and pyxides; kraters were also common, reflecting the great tradition of wine appreciation in this culture. Libation vessels and rhytons were probably used for rituals and/or ceremonial purposes.

The Mycenaean influence is also evident in the use of ceramic Ashdoda figurines, where a female torso is incorporated into the form of a chair or table. Smaller female figurines, often found in Philistine burials, depict women with their hands on their heads in the "mourning gesture." These also have Cypro-Aegean parallels. The Philistines used ceramic cult stands, often designed with windows featuring human figures, that have been found at sites such as Ashdod and Tel Qasile. Stone seals from this phase usually have schematic representations of human and animal figures, and in some rare cases have inscriptions that, although undecipherable at present, bear a resemblance to a Cypro-Minoan script.

Architecture

Philistine cities often featured massive fortification systems. A glacis and mud-brick tower protected the great port city of Ashqelon; Ekron had a fortification system that enclosed an upper and a lower city; and Tel el-Far'ah South had a large, mud-brick fortress. The latter also featured a "governor's residence" that was built toward the end of the Iron 1, and this, as well as several private houses at Tel el-Far'ah South, displays an Egyptian influence (for example, vessels and stoppers with Egyptian stamp seals). Large granaries, sometimes with a subterranean silo, have also been found at Philistine cities (Tel Qasile, for example).

Philistine temples such as those from Ekron and Tel Qasile typically featured a main hall with pillars along the north-south axis and hearths near the center. The Ekron temple had walls with a thick coating of plaster and floors with a plaster and pebble pavement. Raised platforms similar to the bamah were also part of Philistine religious architecture. The temple complex at Tel Qasile included a separate ancillary chapel adjacent to the main structure, furnished with benches and small platforms. The complex also included a courtyard that featured a square altar. In addition to these large temples, smaller shrines were used as well. One such shrine located in a residential area of Tel Miqne–Ekron had a white plastered floor, benches, and a raised platform.

Metal

Bronze and iron were both used during the Iron 1. Metal weapons and tools from this time include knives, adzes, axes, and various farming implements. There are some rare examples of daggers that employ a polymetallic technique, that is, iron and bronze. In fact, the reconfiguration of the metals industry is reflected in these artifacts as iron, used to make the blades, displaced bronze, which would become relegated to rivets and decorative knife handles. Examples of polymetallic knives have been found at Tel Qasile as well as Tel Miqne–Ekron, where there were several examples of iron blades secured to ivory handles with bronze rivets. The temple at Ekron also contained three bronze wheels and part of a frame representing the remains of a wheeled cult stand. Many of the metal artifacts from this time have parallels from Cyprus and the Aegean.

Industrial Remains

After settling on the coast, the earliest Sea Peoples continued to import metal from abroad, probably from their homelands (Stager 1991), but by the end of the twelfth century B.C.E., local workshops were in operation. Furnaces with crucibles, sometimes bearing the remains of copper and bronze slag, have been found in the industrial area at Tel Qasile and Ekron. Whereas it has traditionally been thought that the Philistines were responsible for the spread of iron, this theory now seems doubtful (see Waldbaum 1999). In any case, evidence from Tel Jemmeh and Tel Qasile suggest that by this time, iron may have been produced using the techniques of quenching and carburization, though this is not certain (Waldbaum 1999).

The potters at twelfth-century-B.C.E. Tel Jemmeh used a large, mud-brick kiln that had four radial arches separating the fire chamber from the section where the pottery was placed (Van Beek 1987, 1993). Horseshoe-shaped and square kilns were used to manufacture Aegean-style pottery during the eleventh century. Artifacts related to textile production have also been found. One building at Tel Qasile, part of a larger complex, contained loom weights and grooved "spinning bowls" (Dothan and Dothan 1992). "Spoolweights," with parallels in Cyprus and the Aegean, have been found at cities such as Ashqelon and Ekron (Stager 2003).

Burials

Simple pit burials, such as those seen in the cemetery at Tel el-Far'ah South, probably belonged to commoners, and it is presumed that this form of burial served throughout the region. Other forms of burial, seen at sites such as Azor and Tel Zeror, include long cist graves and makeshift coffins using large broken vessels.

The eclectic nature of this culture is especially evident in some of the more elaborate burials—for example, the natural caves that were transformed into elite dromos tombs reflecting the Aegean influence. These typically had steps leading down into the rock-cut chambers that were lined with broad benches. There are also examples of anthropomorphic coffins dating to this period, such as those from Tel el-Far'ah South and Deir el-Balah, which display an Egyptian and Sea Peoples influence. Some graves include Canaanite wares, early forms of Philistine pottery, and Aegean imports. During the twelfth and eleventh centuries B.C.E., individual burials became more common.

MATERIAL CULTURE OF THE PHILISTINES IN THE IRON 2

Ceramics

By the Iron 2, the distinctive Bichrome Wares of the previous period were gone from most sites. In a number of cases (for example, Ashdod, Str. X), red-burnished "Ashdod Ware" appears to have replaced this type. This style of ceramics has affinities with pottery of the Phoenicians and inland Israelites. The Philistine pottery of the Iron 2 also reflects the influence of foreign elements, most notably that of the Neo-Assyrians and Egyptians, and in some cases, the Israelites.

Architecture

The style of temple architecture changed during the Iron 2–3. One of the best examples of cultic architecture from this time is Temple Complex 650 at Tel Miqne–Ekron. The general layout of the complex incorporates both local design concepts and those from the Neo-Assyrian tradition of royal and religious architecture. The complex consisted of a central courtyard surrounded by rooms and a main reception hall with a small room at one end that had a raised platform with a staircase. There was also a long sanctuary hall with two rows of four columns each, and two large vats that may have been used for ablutions (Gitin, Dothan, and Naveh 1997).

The Neo-Assyrian influence can also be observed at Tel Jemmeh, where one building dating to approximately 675 B.C.E. employed a variety of techniques in order to create mud-brick vaults (Van Beek 1987). Several Philistine cities, such as Ashdod, featured massive gate systems.

Metal

Metal production continued at Tel Miqne–Ekron and Tel Qasile, where the industrial complex from the Iron 1 remained operational, with revamped blast furnaces for smelting and a large vat attached to two basins installed in the adjacent textiles shop. Silver continued to be used for jewelry and as a form of currency. Gold artifacts are also found, most notably the gold cobra (uraeus) from Ekron. An inscribed ostracon from Tel Qasile mentions Ophir as a source of both silver and gold.

Industrial Remains

Under Assyrian rule, Ekron emerged as a major regional producer of olive oil, and excavations at the site have uncovered no less than 100 oil presses. Kilns, consisting of lower chambers set in the ground and disposable upper components, were found in an open-air ceramics workshop at Ashdod. A winery with plaster-lined presses was discovered in the royal court at Ashqelon in a large ashlar masonry building dating to the late seventh century B.C.E. (Stager 1991).

Burials

Philistine burials during the Iron 2–3, especially those of the wealthy, often show Assyrian and Phoenician influences. Burials also give an indication of disparities in social status and wealth. In some rare cases, adult males were buried with a horse and iron dagger in what are known as "warrior burials." One such burial was found in a courtyard of the acropolis (Area H) at Ashdod.

PHOENICIAN MATERIAL CULTURE

On the northern part of the coastal plain, a separate culture influenced by both local Canaanite traditions and Sea Peoples traditions arose. There was also a constant flow of cultural exchange between the Phoenicians and the Israelites. Phoenician Bichrome Wares with red and black painted decorations have been found at a number of sites including Acco, Akhziv, Atlit, Tel Dor, Tel Keisan, Megadim, and Tel Mevorakh. A distinctive style of red-slipped and burnished vessels known as Akhziv Ware first appeared in the eighth century B.C.E. Typical forms in this assemblage include jugs, often with elongated necks that are sometimes conical. There are also shallow bowls that were often used as lids for burial urns. A form of Cypriote pottery characterized by black stripes and concentric circles painted onto red jugs, juglets, and flasks, known as Cypro-Phoenician Ware, began to appear in the southern Levant sometime around the beginning of the tenth century B.C.E. and continued for the duration of the Iron Age.

9.11   Three Astarte figurines, supporting their breasts with hands. From Judah. Terracotta, pillar-type (1000–700 B.C.E.). Iron Age. (Erich Lessing/Art Resource, NY)

Phoenician architectural conventions had a huge influence on the royal architecture of the Israelites. The Proto-Aeolic capitals and ashlar masonry so characteristic of Israelite royal architecture probably derived from Phoenician traditions. The connections between these two cultures are also suggested by the narratives of David and Solomon in the Hebrew Bible, which refer to relations with Phoenician kings, particularly Hiram of Tyre.

Phoenicians in this region cremated their dead and placed the ashes in an urn, which was then buried. This practice was peculiar to this group at the time. The Phoenicians sometimes buried their dead in rock-cut tombs roofed with large stone slabs, as at the cemetery of Akhziv. Some of these burials had tombstones bearing the inscribed name of the deceased. Overlapping religious traditions between Phoenicians and their southern counterparts, particularly with regard to goddess worship, may be inferred through the use of Astarte figurines (Fig. 9.11).

NOTES

1. Both the torpedo vessels and the miniature churns appear only at Gilat (Levy 2003a).

2. In rare instances, nickel and silver have also been detected in these complex metals.

3. Abydos Ware is known from Egypt, but only during the reign of Djer, the third king of the First Dynasty. At Arad, it is restricted to the EB2 level (Str. III), thus providing evidence for a correlation between the EB2 and Djer's reign.

4. Both the bulb of percussion and striking platform were usually removed.

5. Some examples of Hammemiah knives are made from a pink-colored flint that probably came from Egypt.

6. A. Golani, personal communication.

7. The pottery sequence for Mycenae is divided into three distinct phases, termed Mycenaean I-III, which are then further subdivided by letter (for example, a–d).

8. Neutron Activation Analysis conducted on the "Charioteer Krater" and other ceramics indicates the Mycenaean 3A2 to early 3B (fourteenth- to thirteenth-century B.C.E.) site of Argolid in Greece as a point of origin, suggesting that at least some of these wares were true imports (Biran 1994, 111).

9. It is possible that the Area C kilns date to the Middle Bronze Age, though potsherds found in association with it seem to favor a Late Bronze Age date (Yadin 1975).

SUGGESTED READING

Bunimovitz, Shlomo. 1990. "Problems in the 'Ethnic' Identification of the Philistine Material Culture." *Tel Aviv* 17: 210–222.

Dever, William G. 1987. "The Middle Bronze Age: The Zenith of the Urban Canaanite Era." *Biblical Archaeology* 50: 148–177.

Finkelstein, Israel. 1999. "Hazor and the North in the Iron Age: A Low Chronology Perspective." *Bulletin of the Schools of Oriental Research* 314: 55–70.

Golden, Jonathan. 2002a. "The Early Bronze Age." In *Encyclopedia of Prehistory.* Vol. 8, *South and Southwest Asia,* edited by P. Peregrine and M. Ember, 86–111. New York: Kluwer/Plenum.

———. 2002b. "The Middle Bronze Age." In *Encyclopedia of Prehistory.* Vol. 8, *South and Southwest Asia,* edited by P. Peregrine and M. Ember, 293–304. New York: Kluwer/Plenum.

Gonen, Rivka. 1992. "The Late Bronze Age." In *The Archaeology of Ancient Israel,* edited by A. Ben-Tor, 211–257. New Haven, CT: Yale University Press.

Mazar, Amihai. 1985. "Emergence of the Philistine Material Culture." *Israel Exploration Journal* 35: 95–107.

———. 1990. *Archaeology of the Land of the Bible, 10,000–586 B.C.E.* New York: Doubleday.

Oren, Eliezer D., and Donald W. Jones, eds. 2000. *The Sea Peoples and Their World: A Reassessment.* University Museum Monograph, 108. Philadelphia: Museum of Archaeology and Anthropology, University of Pennsylvania.

Tubb, Jonathan N. 2002. *The Canaanites.* London: British Museum.

CHAPTER 10
Intellectual Accomplishments

The peoples of the southern Levant, in perpetual contact with their neighbors from Syro-Mesopotamia and Egypt, kept up with the scientific knowledge and intellectual accomplishments of the time. When peoples from Cyprus and the Aegean began to appear in Canaan, many new ideas were quickly adopted. At the same time, the Canaanites and Israelites had many great ideas of their own. Two such achievements, in particular, profoundly influenced world history: the alphabetic system of writing and monotheistic religion.

THE ALPHABET (ALEPHBET)

One of the great intellectual accomplishments of the Canaanite societies, and indeed one of their most important contributions to Western cultures, was the alphabet. Written language first evolved in Egypt and Mesopotamia late in the fourth millennium B.C.E. Languages continued to develop and evolve in both regions, with Semitic languages, Akkadian in particular, sweeping through much of the Near East during the second half of the third millennium B.C.E.

The Roots of the Canaanite Script

The alphabet first emerged in Canaan sometime around the beginning of the second millennium B.C.E. Clearly, the roots of the alphabetic system of writing are entwined with the syllabic system of Egyptian hieroglyphics. The difference between a syllabic system and an alphabet is that in the former, each letter represents a syllable (consonant plus various vowels), whereas in the latter each letter represents a singular sound or phoneme. Egyptian hieroglyphics are, for the most part, syllabic, but the potential for an alphabet was present in the evolution of the hieroglyphic script. The Egyptian language employed a combination of glyphs that were trilitteral (three sounds), bilitteral, and unilitteral ideograms; the latter, however, representing a singular sound, were in essence alphabetical signs. In a process that is known as the "acrophonic principle," the picture in some instances came to represent the first consonant of the word for that symbol and not just the item itself. In other words, some of the Egyptian ideographs actually functioned as phonemes.

In fact, the Egyptians did sometimes use their phonemic symbols to spell out the sound of a word in much the same way the letters of the alphabet are used. Known as "group writing" or "Egyptian syllabic orthography" (Gardiner 1957), this manner of spelling was used almost exclusively for loanwords, especially place-names and personal names where there was no Egyptian equivalent. In such cases, words that sounded similar were used (Allen 2000). For example, the city name "Yarmut" (Yarmuth) was written Y3-mt, by spelling Y + a + m(w)t (the latter portion was an Egyptian word for death); thus we see the combination of two unilitteral glyphs and one trilitteral glyph. Canaanite personal names were spelled out in a similar fashion. It is intriguing that loanwords from the Semitic languages, many Canaanite no less, triggered what appears to have been one of the first steps toward a quasi-alphabet. It is also noteworthy that the use of group writing for Semitic proper names first became common during the Middle Kingdom (c. 2040–1780 B.C.E.); that is, around roughly the same time of the first Proto-Sinaitic and Proto-Canaanite inscriptions.

During the Bronze Age, a variety of languages was spoken in the southern Levant. Akkadian continued to be the lingua franca for most of the Near East, with kings and administrative officials corresponding in one common language. Each region, therefore, including Canaan, had scribes trained in Akkadian. Canaanites, or people related to them (for example, the Hyksos), lived in Egypt toward the end of the Middle Bronze Age, and Canaan was essentially an Egyptian vassal state for much of the Late Bronze Age. Canaanite scribes, therefore, also learned to write in this script.

Amihai Mazar (1990) has pointed out that, as neither of these languages was indigenous to Canaan, nor were Canaanites bound by the religious canons associated with them, they may have enjoyed a certain freedom to depart from the conventions of these scripts.[1] With this greater license, the scribes of Canaan were free to experiment and explore. Although archaeologists can only speculate about the how and why of such a process, it is with relative certainty that Egyptian hieroglyphics may be cited as the original source of inspiration for the Proto-Sinaitic and Proto-Canaanite characters.

The Canaanite scribes first made linear drawings of a few hieroglyphs, and in this way, employing the acrophonic principle, they began to produce an alphabet whereby the symbol used was actually the first consonant of the Semitic word. Thus, for instance, the glyph showing a house and representing "H" in Egyptian was given the value "B" because the Semitic word for "house" (beit/bayit) began with a "B." The sign for water was the wavy line, ~ and the word nu, which had the phonetic value for the letter n. The Canaanite scribes took their word for water (maym) and applied the same principle, borrowing the Egyptian water sign and assigning it the value m. Ultimately, the outcome of this experiment was an entirely new concept: the alphabet, or rather, alephbet.

The Evolution of the Script

One form of the Canaanite alphabet emerged in Ugarit, where scribes at the time were writing mainly in Akkadian. One of the most spectacular archaeological discoveries of the twentieth century was the now famous archive at Ugarit, which included some 120 inscribed tablets bearing administrative lists, royal correspondence, and the like. Most of these texts were written in Akkadian. Cuneiform documents, in fact, have also been found at Hazor, Gezer, Hebron, and Shechem. Sometime early in the second millennium B.C.E., a new graphic syllabic script with several hundred characters evolved in Byblos (Mendenhall 1985). It is not clear what happens thereafter, for Biblite Syllabic inscriptions are quite rare after 1800 B.C.E., but this script may have been used up until the thirteenth century B.C.E.,[2] when its replacement by the alphabet was all but complete.

By the beginning of the second millennium B.C.E. (the late Middle Bronze Age in Canaan), the scribes of Ugarit began to use a new script based on twenty-seven cuneiform characters. The southern Canaanites also developed new scripts of their own, two variations in fact—Proto-Sinaitic and Proto-Canaanite—both of which were also based upon the use of acronyms (Albright 1966; Cross 1967; Naveh 1982). Unfortunately, only a few examples of each have been recovered to date, and the ones that do exist are mostly incomplete and therefore difficult to decipher. As a result, some fundamental questions regarding the time of the first Proto-Canaanite scripts and the origins of the alphabet remain unanswered.

Proto-Sinaitic

The Proto-Sinaitic script was first identified at the site of Serabit el-Khadim by none other than Sir William Flinders Petrie. Exploring the region of the ancient turquoise mines, Petrie (1906) discovered, near a desert temple, a statue of a sphinx now believed to date to approximately 1700 B.C.E.[3] In addition to a small dedication to Hathor written in Egyptian, the statue also bears inscriptions in a different set of characters that, while clearly related to the Egyptian, represented a significant departure; this was, in fact, a new script not seen before by modern scholars. Some ten years later, Sir Allen Gardiner (1916) was able to draw on his knowledge of both the Egyptian and Semitic languages to decipher some of the characters, recognizing the word *Baalat* (interpolating the vowels) as the Semitic equivalent for the goddess Hathor.

Today archaeologists know of some thirty to forty Proto-Sinaitic inscriptions that have been found on statuettes and stelae and carved into the rock faces around Serabit el-Khadim. Many of these seem to be dedications related to religious practices. One, for example, which reads, "for [or belonging to] the lady," perhaps refers to Asherah or to some other goddess.

Traditionally, the Sinai inscriptions have been dated to the New Kingdom (Albright 1966), though others prefer a Middle Kingdom date (Gardiner 1962; Sass 1988). Benjamin Sass (1988), for instance, has argued that the style of the sphinx and block statuette on which inscriptions appear is more typical of the Middle Kingdom, perhaps the late Twelfth Dynasty. Although Proto-Sinaitic generally fits into the framework of Northwest Semitic, partly by virtue of its relation to Proto-Canaanite, precisely where it belongs in the linguistic tree remains uncertain.

Proto-Canaanite

Further north, another version of this new script began to emerge. Current knowledge of this script, Proto-Canaanite, is based on some twenty-five inscriptions, the earliest dating to the late Middle Bronze Age and the latest ap-

10.1 Iron arrowhead bearing the inscription "King of Amurru" (Drawing by J. Golden; adapted from Starcky 1982)

pearing at the beginning of the Late Bronze Age. These inscriptions, most of which were found in a relatively small area in the southern Shephelah, span much of the second millennium B.C.E., though there is a notorious fourteenth-century-B.C.E. gap from which no texts have been found.[4] It is doubtful, however, that this absence of evidence reflects a true break in the evolution of the script, since the textual evidence picks right up again in the thirteenth century B.C.E. Furthermore, to the north the record of Ugartic texts continues unbroken.

The earliest known example of a Proto-Canaanite inscription is one word incised on a bronze dagger discovered at Lachish of the MB2 (eighteenth to seventeenth century B.C.E.)(Starkey 1934). At first these inscriptions appeared in rather pedestrian contexts—for example, potsherds from Gezer and Nagila—and may have been used to identify the potter. It is possible that this new script was used more informally at first, while Akkadian remained the official language, which is certainly plausible considering that the new script was more accessible and required less rigorous training.[5]

In the thirteenth and twelfth (and possibly eleventh) centuries B.C.E., Proto-Canaanite inscriptions appear more frequently in the archaeological record, and their distribution is more widespread, though still largely in the south. These include examples from Lachish, Beth Shemesh, and 'Izbet Sartah. The inscription from the 'Izbet Sartah ostracon seems to represent the exercise of a scribe-in-training. On one line appear the letters of the alphabet, but there are several omissions and departures from the order typical of the time, and several odd combinations of signs make portions of the inscription unintelligible (Mazar 1990). By this time, Proto-Canaanite was also used for religious purposes, as indicated by an inscribed ewer found in the Fosse Temple at Lachish (c. 1220 B.C.E.), which bears a blessing to a goddess. Using a unique format, the text is punctuated by representations of gazelles.

Though certain pictographic elements were still used, a more linear and shorter alphabet with some twenty-two letters was clearly in the works, if not yet formalized by this time. It appears that a cuneiform script was still preferred in the north at this time, with the linguistic division somewhere in the Jezreel Valley (Sass 1988). As time went on, several modifications were made to the script. The number of letters was reduced, and the most naturalistic pictographic forms, such as the ox and human heads, were replaced with more schematic symbols (Garbini 1988). It was perhaps around this time (c. 1200 B.C.E.) that the Pre-Islamic Arabic alphabets separated from the Canaanite system (Cross 1979a; Naveh 1982).

The latest Proto-Canaanite inscriptions date to the eleventh century B.C.E. Examples from this time have been found at Rapa and Gerba'al, and a group of five inscribed arrowheads was found near el-Khadr, south of Bethlehem. One reads *'Abd lb't* . . . ; the obverse says *'ben 'anat*, a common Canaanite name known in both Ugarit and Egypt (Cross 1954). In some cases, short texts also appear on jar handles. Aside from the el-Khadr examples and one from Manahat, most of these inscriptions actually come from the area that by this time was considered Phoenicia, and the cuneiform script was all but extinct. At this stage, the script was also quite similar to that used in early Phoenician-language texts.

Unresolved Issues

As noted previously, the evidence for the evolution of these scripts is highly incomplete, and thus certain questions about the origins of the alphabet remain unresolved. To begin with, one must explain the lack of evidence itself. It can be assumed that many early inscriptions were written on some form of perishable material, perhaps papyrus or parchment. The inscriptions that survive were usually written on broken potsherds or rocks or incised into metal and rocks, but most of the Ugaritic inscriptions of the Late Bronze Age were written on clay tablets. If even a small fraction of the daily transactions and political acts that took place were recorded, it is obvious that many inscriptions were simply not preserved in the archaeological record.

Another factor that makes reconstructing the evolution of the early alphabet more complicated is the fact that for some time, a number of different Canaanite scripts were probably used in tandem. In fact, no standard alphabet existed until the tenth century B.C.E. (Cross 1979a; Mendenhall 1993).

Of course, one essential problem is how to define the term "alphabet" itself, and hence how to identify the time and place of its origin. Ignace J. Gelb (1952) wanted to deny the status of early Phoenician as a true alphabet, arguing it to be technically still syllabic in that it lacked independent vowels, which were instead attached to consonants. The Phoenicians did, however, write vowels on occasion: Certain symbols, known as *matres lectionis*, "mothers of reading," were often written to indicate the vowel sounds, a convention seen already in Ugaritic cuneiform texts. In any case, the Phoenician script probably began just before 1000 B.C.E., though some have suggested an earlier date. It is also possible that the Ugaritic alphabet derives from Proto-Canaanite as well. In Ugaritic, a similar principle of creating phonemes out of cuneiform signs was followed, but, as there is no evidence for a formative process in Ugarit, it has been argued that the letter names and order for their cuneiform symbols were borrowed directly from Proto-Canaanite (Millard 1979).

On the southern coast, a distinct writing system—a syllabic linear script similar to Cypriote scripts of the Late Bronze Age, which have not yet been deciphered—was used by the Philistines. The Semitic languages, however, remained important in this region, and Proto-Canaanite script was used in Philistia as well. One of the earliest alphabetic inscriptions from "Semitized" Philistia (Sass 1988, 160) was an ostracon found at the twelfth- to eleventh-century-B.C.E. site of Qubur el-Walaydah, which includes two Canaanite names. Another inscription, which translates as "Belonging to Aba," was discovered in the vicinity of Ekron. Carved in the style typical of Philistia, both this inscription and the one from Qubur el-Walaydah make use of the Proto-Canaanite characters and are generally similar to other Canaanite inscriptions. At the same time, both the form and position of a few of the signs bear a resemblance to early Greek inscriptions, and it is not impossible that Philistines, perhaps with knowledge of Phoenician, played some role in the diffusion of the alphabet.

But is was the Phoenician script—including both the names of the letters and their order—that would be adopted by the Greeks sometime in the eleventh to tenth century B.C.E. (Naveh 1973; Sass 1988). The Greeks built upon this script by assigning distinct letters to the main vowel sounds, creating the alphabet as we know it today. Proto-Canaanite would ultimately evolve into alphabetic Hebrew, becoming the official script in most of the southern Levant, widely used even in Philistia in the eighth century B.C.E.

Implications of the Alphabet

According to Frank M. Cross (1979a), one of the leading experts on ancient Semitic languages, the alphabet was an independent invention that was not repeated. Indeed, after the second millennium B.C.E., virtually all new scripts can be said to descend from Proto-Canaanite. Such widespread adoption underscores the impact of this innovation on society. Certainly, the use of the alphabet simplified writing and may have done something to wrest its mastery from the hands of scribes alone. Changes in the economic, social, and political environment, however, would have made even more of a difference in the spread of literacy than a simplification of writing systems. Benjamin Sass (1988) pointed out, for example, that the use of 2,000 characters in Eastern languages such as Chinese is mastered by most by the age of ten, and widespread literacy on a global level is a fairly recent development. According to Sass, "The alphabet is easy to learn and to use, and for this reason it has been almost universally adopted. Nevertheless, the earlier writing systems were no less capable of recording their languages, and in this crucial aspect, the alphabet is not superior" (1988, 168).

Gelb (1952) actually tried to deny the Eastern roots of the alphabet altogether by increasing the criteria for what constitutes the "true alphabet" (for example, vowels), thus arguing that it was a Western innovation. However, one of the great intellectual achievements of the Canaanite alphabet was that it demonstrated an understanding of phonemic theory—the notion that any human language can be broken down into a limited and relatively small number of sounds, the phonemes. Where Western modes of writing are concerned, the efficacy of the alphabet as a tool for conveying information, a vital social development, is clear.

MONOTHEISM

Reconstructing ancient ideology from archaeological remains, even with the help of text, can often be quite difficult. The history of an idea must examine both the birth of that idea and the process of its widespread adoption. In most cases, it is virtually impossible to pinpoint the moment when an idea was born, though archaeologists and historians may, and indeed must, consider the sociopolitical context in which it emerged. The same is true for the diffusion of that idea—at what point did the majority of people accept that idea or adopt that belief? When it comes to religion, scholars must also try to distinguish between official religion as it is codified and "popular" religion as it is practiced by the masses.

Attempting to reconstruct the history of monotheism, archaeologists must rely on the same sources of evidence that are important to other developments: archaeological and glyptic evidence; extra-biblical texts; and, in this case, a heavy reliance on the biblical sources. However, several key issues must be considered. One aspect of this problem, discussed at length in the following chapter, concerns the historicity of the Hebrew Bible, for many biblical scholars now agree that the narratives relating to the time of the United Monarchy were not actually written down until some centuries later. The Hebrew Bible, being a product of the very ideology that historians of monotheism wish to reconstruct, is obviously a vital source of information. But if it is history that they seek, then this source must also be treated with circumspection. One reason for this is the tendency within any ideological doctrine for its authors and promoters to reinforce and enhance its authority by giving it an air of historical legitimacy. If the Hebrew Bible was, indeed, first codified centuries after the events described therein, this could explain why some themes—for example, the warnings of the prophets—resonate throughout the text. William G. Dever has argued that many modern biblical scholars tend, unwittingly or not, to appropriate the biases of the Bible's authors, the "minority, ultra-orthodox, nationalistic parties who finally shaped the tradition after the fall of Israel and Judah" (1996, 87).

The notion of monotheism in ancient Israel is generally associated with the worship of a single god named YHWH (often spelled "Yahweh," with the vowels inserted for pronunciation). YHWH is the God of the Hebrew Bible, and the name actually appears in extra-biblical inscriptions found at Arad, Diban, Ein Gedi, Khirbet Beit Lei, Kuntillet 'Ajrud, Jerusalem, and Lachish. Other versions of the name YHWH also appear in antiquity, for instance, theoforic elements of the name are preserved in personal names found in inscriptions from Dan, Dor, and Samaria, among other places (see Chapter 9 sidebar, "Bullae"). It should be noted that the Egyptian pharaoh Akhenaten, with his Amarna Revolution, implemented new forms of religious belief that have been likened to monotheism because he enforced the sole worship of the Aten, the Solar Disc, at the expense of the other Egyptian gods. Yet this movement at most represents a form of monolatry and is something quite different from the concept at issue here. It is not impossible, however, that these ideas had some influence on later theological thought.

Of course, most references to YHWH or God in the Hebrew Bible denote a singular being or force, hence the basic idea behind monotheism. Yet there is also a mounting body of evidence that YHWH as a divinity was not alone. In addition to passages in the Hebrew Bible that refer to Baal, Anat, and El, archaeological discoveries also suggest that YHWH may have had a consort, Asherah, who, as late as the seventh century B.C.E., was alive and well in the minds of many Israelites. In fact, a number of scholars have argued that this

Canaanite goddess was often worshipped alongside YHWH (Albertz 1994; Dever 1996).

The religion of Israel for much of the Iron Age was actually syncretistic; in other words, it combined ideas and practices from several different traditions, and this is true even of the "official" religion (see Albertz 1994). Asherah was not the only Canaanite deity to retain some recognition in the Israelite religion; for example, in the north, there was "ditheism," where both YHWH and Baal were juxtaposed. The name Elohim, sometimes used for the Israelite God, surely echoes the name El; in fact, the word "Elohim" is actually a plural form for the word "El," reflecting the idea that all gods were subsumed by the one.

The fact that other gods were even acknowledged, if not worshipped, raises questions about the origins of "Yahwism"; for instance, was this deity originally conceived as a solitary god, or did he begin as one among a few, in time edging out the others? The earliest known reference to YHWH is in the Meshe Stele, where YHWH is called "the Israelite god." To a certain extent, the problem may be construed as a matter of the degree to which control of religious practice was centralized. For example, it appears that both YHWH and El were recognized in the southern kingdom, where there was even greater control over religion than in the north. As "official Yahwism" emerged, many popular practices, such as the Cult of the Dead and belief in omens, as well as the worship of Asherah, came under attack by central authorities, at least according to the "Deuteronomistic history." It is possible that many people disregarded certain "Yahwist" reforms, such as the mandated worship in Jerusalem alone. It is also possible that many of the commoners, even if devoted to YHWH, failed to see the wrong in maintaining the image of the Asherah or the Sacred Tree in tandem with YHWH, despite the reformists' misgivings (Dijkstra 2002a).

The evolution of monotheism as an idea, therefore, entailed the expulsion of other deities that had been worshipped by Canaanites and Israelites alike, and thus it was a gradual process, not a single event. Both El and Baal seem to have held out for some time, but by far the most persistent and controversial of the Canaanite deities was Asherah, for she was the last to go and seemed rather reluctant to leave. Although many biblical scholars have tended to believe the Deuteronomist claims favoring a single god early on, there is now evidence for alternative forms of religious practice that cannot be ignored (Dever 1996).

Archaeological and Glyptic Evidence

There is a range of archaeological evidence indicating that alternative forms of religion were practiced among the Israelites right through much of the Iron Age. Scholars often speak in terms of "popular religion" practiced by the masses as opposed to the canonized version promulgated in the central temple. According to John S. Holladay Jr. (1987), the practice of popular religion can be identified in the archaeological record by the following artifacts: figurines, such as the horse-and-rider, small animals, and female figurines; a large number of vessels associated with feasting or food offerings; and fenestrated cult stands (as opposed to limestone altars). At both Samaria (E 207) and Jerusalem (Cave 1), shrines located on the outskirts of the main city contained some 165 and 84 figurines, respectively. Another form of evidence representing

10.2   Painted ewer from the Fosse Temple at Lachish depicting a seven-branched tree flanked by an ibex on both sides (Drawing by J. Golden; after Ruth Hestrin. 1987. "Religion in Israel and Judah under the Monarchy: An Explicitly Archaeological Approach." In *Ancient Israelite Religion*, edited by P. Miller, P. Hanson, and S. McBride, 249–299. Philadelphia: Fortress.)

popular religion is cultic installations such as those found at Tel el-Far'ah North, Lachish, Megiddo, Tel el-Mazar, Tel Qiri, and Ta'anach. It is interesting to note that these local and household shrines were in use at a time when the Deuteronomists were busy promoting centralized worship at the Solomonic Temple in Jerusalem.

The most intriguing evidence for religious practice outside of the codified religion concerns the ubiquitous representations of females, leading many scholars to believe that a female deity, probably Asherah, was worshipped quite late into Israelite history. One outstanding example of this phenomenon is the ewer from the Fosse Temple at Lachish, which depicts a seven-branched tree flanked by an ibex on both sides (Fig. 10.2). Above the tree appears an in-

10.3   Representation of the goddess Asherah, holding branches, Samaria, 10–8th century B.C.E. (Photo courtesy of Zev Radovan, Land of the Bible Picture Archive)

scription that reads: "A gift. An offering to my Lady Elat." Elat is understood to mean the feminine word for El, the main god, thus Elat as the female consort of El, or Asherah. The seven-branched tree also suggests Asherah, though Ugaritic texts equate Elath with Anat and Ashtarte, in which case this could simply be a generic word for goddess (Vriezen 2002; Korpel 2002). Another notable representation of the female deity is found on the Ta'anach cult stand, which depicts the "Lion Lady," who should probably also be equated with Asherah, as there is a recurrence of striding lion and procession scenes.

The most common manifestations of this deity, however, are the statuettes known as the "Asherah figurines." These are small statues of a female, though many are of the "pillar-shaped" type. In many cases, the hands are placed immediately below the breasts as if to support them. Some 3,000 examples of these figurines, also referred to as "prayers in clay," have been found in eighth- to seventh-century-B.C.E. contexts. In most cases, the figurines appear in domestic settings. For example, in roughly one-third of the houses excavated at Beer Sheva female figurines were unearthed (Holladay 1987). This points not only to widespread recognition of the female deity but to the fact that she was probably associated with some form of household cult and/or private rituals.

Extra-Biblical Textual Sources

Much of the debate concerning the status of Asherah centers on evidence derived from a handful of extra-biblical texts. This name is mentioned in inscriptions from the ninth- to eighth-century-B.C.E. sanctuary at the desert caravanserai site of Kuntillet 'Ajrud and in an eighth- to seventh-century-B.C.E. inscription from Khirbet el-Qom written on a pillar separating two graves. (See sidebar, "Kuntillet 'Ajrud.")

Goddess or Symbol?

Although many scholars have interpreted references to "YHWH and his Asherah" found on sherds of large store jars in Kuntillet 'Ajrud as evidence that Asherah was indeed considered YHWH's consort (Dever 1984; Freedman 1987), others draw a distinction between the asherah as a cultic symbol such as the sacred pole or sacred tree and Asherah the goddess. Some scholars have argued that the references to "his Asherah" from Kuntillet 'Ajrud and Khirbet el-Qom may refer to "his symbol, Asherah," and not his consort (Smith 2002). According to Othmar Keel and Christoph Uehlinger (1992), by the eighth century B.C.E. the asherah was largely conceived of as a symbol and not an actual goddess, but by the latter part of the seventh century B.C.E., she had regained some of her previous status as a real deity. In either event, the use of figurines raises doubts about the adherence to bans on idolatry.

Who Were the Polytheists?

Another problem concerns the question of who would have worshipped Asherah and/or other deities. Some theories have portrayed Asherah's worshippers as part of a subversive cult rivaling mainstream practice or as practitioners of popular religion or a house or local cult. However, archaeological discoveries and textual evidence have forced many scholars to reconsider her standing within whatever "official" religion existed in the eighth and seventh centuries B.C.E. (Dever 1996; Binger 1997): Although "popular" implies that it varied from "official" religion, a "popular religion" cannot be regarded as truly subversive if a large portion of the population worshipped in this way. It

Kuntillet 'Ajrud

Some of the most important discoveries concerning early Israelite religion come from a series of inscriptions discovered at the site of Kuntillet 'Ajrud, a station, or caravanserai, in the eastern Sinai, dating to the ninth and eighth centuries B.C.E. (Meshel and Meyers 1976; Meshel 1978). Archaeologists found a number of inscribed vessels as well as inscriptions in red and black written directly onto the plaster walls of a small shrine. Much of this text was religious in nature, and several of the inscriptions were benedictions that included the names of the deity in whose honor the blessing was being made, thus providing vital information regarding the god(s) worshipped by guests of the caravanserai.

One of these inscriptions, probably a poem or psalm, includes both El and Baal as venerated gods (Dijkstra 2002a). The most well known of the Kuntillet 'Ajrud inscriptions—those pertaining to Asherah—come from the sherds of large store jars. In these examples, the phrase "YHWH and . . . his a/Asherah" appears no less than three times, once as ". . . I have blessed you by YHWH of Samaria and by his a/Asherah" and twice as ". . . I have blessed you by YHWH of (the) Teman and by his a/Asherah." It has been suggested that the "Asherah" here refers not to the goddess but to a cult figure or symbol. The possibility has also been raised that the *th* ending that appears in the name was not intended as the possessive form but rather represents an archaic spelling of the name. This latter point is significant in that many scholars have understood this phrase to mean that the goddess Asherah belongs to YHWH, that is, she is his consort (Albertz 1994; Dever 1996), an interpretation that relies on the use of the possessive form.

The references to specific places, especially Samaria, the capital and seat of power for the Northern Kingdom, are also highly significant. Both this and the reference to Teman imply localized worship; in other words, the local expression of a national deity, worshipped in various ways in each respective region, with local shrines or temples (McCarter 1987). In addition, researchers cannot exclude the possibility that there were others elsewhere, not mentioned in the Kuntillet 'Ajrud texts.

Figural representations appear on two of the pithoi sherds, but the relationship between the words and images is not clear, and thus the common assumption that the seated female harp player is Asherah is not reliable. However, it is all but certain that one of the other figures represents the Egyptian god Bes, reflecting religious syncretism at the time.

is possible that there were different communities of religious adherents at the various levels of political organization (McCarter 1987, 267).

It has also been suggested that Asherah worship may have been connected with popular women's cults (Albertz 1994). It appears that women suffered a diminution of status during the eighth century B.C.E. (Faust 2001) that was expressed, in part, by their relegation to the domestic sphere, and in this context the idea that they sought solace in a female deity worshipped in the household seems plausible. It is also possible that a number of dispossessed social groups, such as the poor and foreigners, along with women, practiced alternative or "nonconformist" forms of religion (Holladay 1987; McCarter 1987). This may also represent a version of the religion more accessible to the commoners, that is, a "folk religion." A feminist critique of this problem (Frymer-Kensky 1992) has raised questions about why Asherah was seemingly banished but offers an interesting view of the matter, suggesting that it was the strict division between male and female deities emphasized in polytheistic religion that served to reinforce the subordinate roles proscribed for women, while the monotheistic conception tended to reduce this dualism. Though monotheistic society was decidedly patriarchal, women were not necessarily considered to be inherently inferior.

Biblical Sources

In addition to these extra-biblical texts, Asherah's status is betrayed by her strong, and usually conflicting, presence in the Hebrew Bible itself. Prior to even entering Canaan, the Israelites are instructed, in Exodus 34:13–14, to "cut down the Asherim" lest they bow down to some other god. By the days of Judges 3:7, they had succumbed to the worship of both Baal and Asherah, neglecting YHWH. During the time of the monarchy, King Asa of Judah would depose the queen mother, Maacah, because she had made an image in service of Asherah (1 Kings 15:13), which the king duly destroyed. In 2 Kings 21:2–9, Manasseh is condemned as an evil ruler for placing the "graven image of Asherah" in the temple, setting the stage for Josiah's dramatic expulsion of the goddess (2 Kings 23). The defamation campaign against the goddess often involved the association between her and Baal, another outcast Canaanite deity, as in 2 Kings 21:3 and 23:4.

Reformist Campaigns

Evidence for diverse forms of practice comes from the scripture itself, as seen in the pedagogic polemics against such practices. According to the Hebrew Bible, prophets such as Hosea and Amos raged against the worship of other gods, particularly Baal, and were unequivocal in their condemnation of what they viewed as unacceptable practices in the temples of YHWH at Beer Sheva, Bethel, and Gilgal (Amos 4, 5; Hosea 4). Josiah shared these sentiments and acted on them, shutting down these sanctuaries and demanding that all worship be focused on the newly purified temple of Jerusalem (2 Kings 15, 23). In fact, idolatry among the Israelites is a major theme of the entire Hebrew Bible, not only in 1 and 2 Kings but also, for example, in Jeremiah.

According to some scholars, certain reformist acts can be documented archaeologically. For instance, it has been argued that at Arad, and perhaps Beer Sheva, sanctuaries dating to the ninth century B.C.E. were destroyed as part of Hezekiah's reformist campaign (for example, see Herzog 1977). There was also Josiah's movement in the eighth and seventh centuries B.C.E. This campaign may have come after Israel fell to Sennacherib in 701 B.C.E. The Bible also relates that Hezekiah, in hope of getting all of Israel to worship at Jerusalem, abolished the auxiliary temples of Judah (Rainey 1994). But a problem similar to the one archaeologists encounter when considering the conquests of Joshua arises: Destruction levels, even in the unlikely event that a perfect chronological fit can be documented, still do not allow researchers to ascribe the deed to a particular individual.

Social Context for a New Religion

It is certainly worthwhile to consider the social and political circumstances under which monotheism evolved. What were the unique social and cultural needs of this people with their new identity? Several leading archaeologists have suggested that it arose largely out of a socioeconomic movement with reformist tendencies (Dever 1992a, 1996; Stager 1985). Ranier Albertz has described the "Exodus group" as "an oppressed outsider group of Egyptian society" (1994, 47) that met with a mountain deity named YHWH in southern Transjordan in the thirteenth century B.C.E. According to this scenario, many of the important traditions, such as sacred meals and institutionalized priesthood, had evolved by this time. Albertz even suggested there may have already been something of an "incipient monotheism," related, in his view, to a "predisposition for monotheism" because it was founded as a religion of resistance. In other words, monotheism at first was not so much a devotion to a theological doctrine as it was an ideology of unity and separatism from oppressive neighbors (1994, 51–63).

Distinguishing themselves from their neighbors was an important consideration for the early Israelites, the best evidence for this being strict adherence to dietary restrictions (the taboo against pig consumption). Another example is the switch to marital descent, which took place at a time when populations were intermingling, and it became increasingly important to track direct lineage. A number of scholars have pointed out that religious practices may have varied not only in time but across the land as well. For instance, both textual and archaeological data reflect different religious traditions in Israel and Judah, and customs may have varied between town and country (Albertz 1994). There is also a political dimension to the problem, for the nation of Israel, like any nation, required a story about its origins, and thus came the tales of Israelite conquest.

Conclusions

Although there is compelling evidence that for much of the Iron Age more than one deity was recognized, historians must accept that at some point in time a fully developed concept of monotheism emerged. It is useful at this juncture to ask precisely what is meant by monotheism and to consider a set of important issues concerning the level of abstraction with regard to worship. As part of the now legendary Ayers Lectures, William Foxwell Albright defined Israelite monotheism in this way: "Belief in the existence of only one God, who is the creator of the whole world and the giver of all life; the belief that God is holy and just, without sexuality or mythology; the belief that God is invisible to man except under special conditions and that no graphic or plastic representation of Him is permissible; the belief that God is not restricted to any part of his creation, but is equally at home in heaven, in the desert, or in Palestine; the belief that God is so far superior to all created beings . . . that he remains absolutely unique . . . the belief that he has chosen Israel [to be] guided exclusively by laws imposed by Him" (1969, 112–13).

The question of whether YHWH was worshipped in ancient times to the complete exclusion of all other deities is quite complicated. There is certainly some archaeological evidence that suggests this was not the case, and much of the relevant textual evidence corroborates these findings. This is also true of texts from outside the region. For example, Bob Becking (2002) has pointed to a Neo-Assyrian text from the time of Sargon II that indicates polytheistic worship in Samaria. The Canaanite god Baal remained for some time as well, and thus it appears that the story of monotheism's emergence involves the temptation to revert to the polytheistic ways of the Israelites' neighbors. The Hebrew Bible conveys a sense that this was a process whereby the followers of "YHWH alone" sometimes lapsed into polytheism and idolatry. These lapses were followed by episodes of harsh admonition and reform. Initially, YHWH may have subsumed some of Baal's functions. For instance, in Deuteronomy 33:26, YHWH bears the epithet "Rider of the Heavens." However, by the time of Hosea 2:18, there is some indication, in the form of a prophecy, that the eradication of Baal from association with YHWH was under way, for the text reads, "And no more will you call Me Baali."

Among the biblical scholars, there is no consensus. Some seem to have fully accepted the idea that Asherah enjoyed status as a deity during the monarchic period (Binger 1997; Keel and Uehlinger 1998; Olyan 1988), while others reject the idea that Asherah had any real place whatsoever in the official religion of the Israelites (Frevel 1995; Korpel 2001). Others remain circumspect, arguing that although archaeologists cannot completely rule out the possibility of the existence of an Asherah cult during the monarchic period, the evidence cited in support of Asherah worship may be overstated (Wiggins 1993; Smith 2002).

As noted already, some scholars have argued that the references to "his Asherah" allude not to YHWH's consort but literally to his asherah symbol or sacred tree. The pillar-female figurines therefore represent ritual paraphernalia, but no more than this. In other words, even if it were the case that the asherah was, in fact, a symbolic object and not a deity, there remains the problem of whether the symbol itself was the object of veneration. Of course, virtually all religions have certain symbols associated with them, but this does not mean that people worship the object itself, nor even that they believe the deity could sometimes inhabit the symbol. For instance, some symbols may be associated with specific practices (for example, the menorah), and others are used to represent religious identity (for example, the crescent moon).

This raises other questions regarding the level of abstraction in the conception of the deity, and to two issues in particular: aniconic religion and the worship of a nonanthropomorphic Yahweh in the temple of Jerusalem (Na'aman 1999). Although some scholars have argued that aniconism was the general rule in the cults of Judah and Jerusalem (Holladay 1987; Mettinger 1997), others counter that this was not the case until the seventh century B.C.E. The same

Neo-Assyrian text noted above also indicates iconism in Samaria in the eighth century B.C.E., as the Assyrians are said to have carried off as spoils the icons worshipped by the people of Israel (Becking 2002). As the Hebrew Bible tells it, it was the bad ways (that is, polytheism and idolatry) of the Northern Kingdom that brought its demise, the fury of God manifest in the Assyrian conqueror. This was an event that emboldened the religious leaders of Judah, who had been clamoring for a rejection of icons and for trust in one god (Becking 2002). A similar paradox arises with the question of iconism, for banning the worship and use of icons does not alone equate with the conception of an amorphous deity.

The localized worship of YHWH, as indicated by the Kuntillet 'Ajrud inscriptions, raises questions about the nature of monotheism itself; that is, does conceiving of YHWH in localized manifestations preclude the understanding of an abstract being? For while it is one thing to imply that the people of Samaria and Teman alike worshipped YHWH, this is quite different from saying that the deity "hailed from there." Herbert Donner (1959) has termed this "poly-Yahwism." At the same time, researchers must be cautious not to read too literally, for indeed, one of the places where YHWH was first recognized as a warrior-god, distinct from El, was at Teman, and thus YHWH of Teman could be a poetic device alluding to YHWH's place of origin.

There is also the distinction between monotheism and monolatry. This is a complex problem in that deeming worship of only one god as acceptable is not tantamount to arguing that only one god exists. In addition to the archaeological and glyptic evidence, the Hebrew Bible makes clear that most people acknowledged the existence of other gods, even if they were resigned not to worship them. "Who is like you, O Yahweh, among the gods?" sang Moses and the people of Israel in Exodus (15:11). In Exodus 34:13, YHWH commands, "You shall worship no other god, for YHWH whose name is jealous, is a jealous God," which again does little to create an impression that only one god was thought to exist, implying instead that devotion to YHWH was largely a matter of fidelity. It appears that at the time, many people subscribed to a more territorial view of religion, as there are instances of an apparent association between a certain god and certain lands. In some cases, such as Assur and Athena, "the name of the state and the name of a deity are linguistically identical" (Mendenhall 1973, 191; see also Sassoon 2001, 278–281).

It is clear then that two different questions are at stake: When did monotheism as an intellectual idea develop? And when did it become current as the basis of a theological belief system? It is entirely possible, and indeed likely, that the idea developed rather early, but it is also now apparent that it took some time—and perhaps until the Babylonian destruction and exile—to gain widespread acceptance.

Indeed, it appears that Yahwism began as an intellectual idea that circulated among the elite and well-educated members of society. The "high language" used by prophets such as Isaiah reveals the intellectual character of early Israelite religion and suggests this ideology was not readily available to all. According to William Dever, "much of the Hebrew Bible . . . must have circulated, and been edited and preserved, only among the intelligentsia" (2003b, 426). Others have suggested that early Yahwism developed among people of the large administrative centers and society's elite members. In fact, it was the elite who were exiled by the Babylonians while many of the commoners remained (Dijkstra 2002a). Still others argue, however, that such a class did not emerge until the Persian period (Davies 1992; Thompson 1992).

Of course, the doctrine of monotheism was ultimately accepted by the masses. Some may have embraced monotheism believing, as the prophets said, that this national disaster came to pass because of their evil ways, particularly the proclivity toward polytheism and idolatry. In the face of the Babylonian forces, the words of the prophets appeared ever more prescient. Anthropologists, sociologists, and political scientists have demonstrated that a strengthening of ethnic identity is a common response among people whose identity is in jeopardy. To some extent, this new ideology was a religion of resistance, and the threatened group, in this case the Israelites, rallied around the idea that they were one people worshipping one supreme God.

Yet another paradox arises, that is, the need to distinguish between religion as pragmatism and religion as true belief—something difficult to discern in any time period, including the present—but that, of course, is beyond the scope of this discussion. Regardless, it is certainly feasible that the devastation brought by the Babylonian exile convinced many people that salvation could be found in monotheism, and rallying behind a common ideology may have helped to solidify Israelite identity. Many questions about the development of monotheism will never be resolved, for although archaeologists may document campaigns to spread its tenets, they can never know what was in the hearts and minds of the people who lived in the southern Levant more than 2,000 years ago.

NOTES

1. To the Egyptians, the written word was sacred, and the point of writing was not necessarily a matter of pragmatism but was deeply rooted in religion and ideology.

2. A late example of the Biblite script appears on a gold ring found in a tomb at Megiddo.

3. The date of the statue is still uncertain, and some have proposed that it dates to about 1800 B.C.E.

4. One exception may be an inscription from Shechem on a small stone plaque, but it is not clear if this dates to the fourteenth or fifteenth century B.C.E.

5. As in Egypt, literacy at the time was not widespread but remained largely in the hands of official scribes.

SUGGESTED READING

Albertz, Ranier. 1994. *A History of Israelite Religion in the Old Testament Period.* Vol. 1, *From the Beginnings to the End of the Monarchy.* Louisville, KY: Westminster/John Knox Press.

Albright, William F. 1966. *The Proto-Sinaitic Inscriptions and Their Decipherment.* Cambridge, MA: American Schools of Oriental Research.

———. 1969. *Archaeology and the Religion of Israel.* Garden City, NY: Anchor.

Becking, Bob. 2002. "The Gods in Whom They Trusted . . . Assyrian Evidence for Iconic Polytheism in Ancient Israel?" In *Only One God? Monotheism in Ancient Israel and the Veneration of the Goddess Asherah,* edited by B. Becking, M. Dijkstra, M. Korpel, and K. Vriezen, 151–163. London: Sheffield Academic Press.

Borowski, Oded. 1997. "Harvests, Harvesting." In *The Anchor Bible Dictionary.* Bantam: Doubleday Dell, CD-ROM.

Cross, Frank M. 1954. "The Evolution of the Proto-Canaanite Alphabet." *Bulletin of the American Schools of Oriental Research* 134: 15–24.

———. 1967. "The Origin and Evolution of the Early Alphabet." *Eretz Israel* 8: 8–24.

———. 1979. "Early Alphabetic Scripts." In *Symposia Celebrating the 75th Anniversary of the Founding of the American Schools of Oriental Research,* edited by F. Cross, 105–111. Cambridge, MA: American Schools of Oriental Research.

Dever, William. 1984. "Asherah, Consort of Yahweh? New Evidence from Kuntillet 'Ajrud." *Bulletin of the American Schools of Oriental Research* 255: 21–37.

Dijkstra, Meindert. 2002a. "El, the God of Israel—Israel, the People of YHWH: On the Origins of Ancient Israelite Yahwism." In *Only One God? Monotheism in Ancient Israel and the Veneration of the Goddess Asherah,* edited by B. Becking, M. Dijkstra, M. Korpel, and K. Vriezen, 81–126. London: Sheffield Academic Press

———. 2002b. "Women and Religion in the Old Testament." In *Only One God? Monotheism in Ancient Israel and the Veneration of the Goddess Asherah,* edited by B. Becking, M. Dijkstra, M. Korpel, and K. Vriezen, 164–188. London: Sheffield Academic Press.

Freeman, David N. 1987. "Yahweh of Samaria and His Asherah." *Biblical Archaeologist* 50: 241–249.

Frymer-Kensky, Tikva. 1992. *In the Wake of the Goddesses: Women, Culture, and the Biblical Transformation of Pagan Myth.* New York: Free Press.

Garbini, Giovanni. 1988. "The Question of the Alphabet." In *The Phoenicians,* edited by S. Moscati, 101–119. New York: Rizzoli.

Hestrin, Ruth. 1987. "Religion in Israel and Judah under the Monarchy: An Explicitly Archaeological Approach." In *Ancient Israelite Religion,* edited by P. Miller, P. Hanson, and S. McBride, 249–299. Philadelphia: Fortress.

———. 1991. "Understanding Asherah: Exploring Semitic Iconography." *Biblical Archaeology Review* 17: 50–59.

Keel, Othmar, and Christoph Uehlinger. 1998. *Gods, Goddesses, and Images of God in Ancient Israel.* Translated by T. Trapp. Minneapolis: Fortress.

Lemaire, André. 1984. "Who or What was Yahweh's Asherah?" *Biblical Archaeology Review* 10: 42–51.

McCarter, P. Kyle, Jr. 1974. "The Early Diffusion of the Alphabet." *Biblical Archaeologist* 37: 54–68.

Mendenhall, George E. 1993. "The Northern Origins of Old South Arabic Literacy." *Yemen Update* 33: 15–19.

Mettinger, Tryggve. 1995. *No Graven Image? Israelite Aniconism in Its Near Eastern Context.* Stockholm: Almqvist and Wiksell.

Naveh, Joseph. 1982. *The Early History of the Alphabet: An Introduction to West Semitic Epigraphy and Palaeography.* Jerusalem: Magnes Press, Hebrew University.

Olyan, Saul. 1988. *Asherah and the Cult of Yahweh in Israel.* Atlanta: Scholars Press.

Sass, Benjamin. 1988. *The Genesis of the Alphabet and Its Development in the Second Millennium B.C.E.* Wiesbaden: Otto Harrassowitz.

Vriezen, Karel, J. H. 2002. "Archaeological Traces of Cult in Israel." In *Only One God? Monotheism in Ancient Israel and the Veneration of the Goddess Asherah,* edited by B. Becking, M. Dijkstra, M. Korpel, and K. Vriezen, 45–80. London: Sheffield Academic Press.

Wiggins, Steve. 1993. *A Reassessment of "Asherah": A Study according to the Textual Sources of the First Two Millenia* B.C.E. Kevelaer: Verlag Butzon and Bercker.

PART 3

Current Assessments

CHAPTER 11

Major Controversies
and Future Directions

CONTROVERSIES IN CHALCOLITHIC ARCHAEOLOGY

The Chalcolithic period represents a pivotal period in the southern Levant when the transition from simple farming communities to more complex, economically varied, and prestige-driven sociopolitical structures took place. In the past, it has generally been treated as a "monolithic" entity, in the sense that there was no real subchronology for the period. This omission is due in part to the fact that many of the key Chalcolithic sites were of single-period occupation, and at stratified sites, they are at the basal levels, yielding data insufficient to identify the minutiae of slow cultural change. The subject of Chalcolithic chronology, however, has received more attention lately. Interpretations of radiocarbon date sequences have been offered by a number of scholars (Burton and Levy 2001; Bourke 2002; Lovell 2001; Gilead 1993; Levy 1992; Joffe; and Dessel 1995). There have also been numerous studies devoted to understanding the roots of this culture based on ceramics from late Neolithic- and early Chalcolithic-site levels (Bourke 1997; Lovell 2001; Commenge forthcoming; Gilead 1988). The apparent import of metal technology prompted early researchers to speculate about a migration into the region (for example, de Vaux 1971), though recent study of the material culture from early Chalcolithic sites reflects an indigenous culture.

Metal technology provides the basis for most southern Levantine chronologies, yet there are several glaring problems with regard to nomenclature. To begin with, during the first 500 years of the Chalcolithic period, or Copper Age, no copper has been observed. Although this can be misleading, archaeologists could use this fact to their advantage when attempting to subdivide the period by designating the first half of the period as a "pre-metallic" phase (Golden forthcoming). One of the outstanding questions for Chalcolithic archaeology concerns the origins of metallurgical technology as well as the source of the exotic metals used to cast elaborate prestige goods, such as those from the Nahal Mishmar hoard (Key 1980; Moorey 1988; Levy and Shalev 1989; Tadmor et al. 1995).

ARCHAEOLOGICAL ISSUES CONCERNING THE EARLY BRONZE AGE

The chronology for the Early Bronze Age has also been debated. Questions about the beginning of the period, in particular, require further clarification, for recent dates from Ashqelon-Afridar seem to push back the beginning of the EB1 by as much as several centuries. Much of the Early Bronze Age chronology is, in fact, based on correlations between materials found in the southern Levant and securely dated Egyptian finds. Though not easy to reconcile with the figure named in the Egyptian King List, the name of Narmer appears in multiple contexts both in Egypt and southern Canaan, all of which have produced or fit comfortably with the date of 3050 B.C.E. There is now a consensus that Narmer's reign was part of Dynasty 0.[1] Although evidence for contact between Egypt and Canaan is abundant, the nature of these relations has been the subject of long-standing debate (Yadin 1955; Yeivin 1960; Ben-Tor 1992; Gophna 2002; van den Brink and Levy 2002).

BRONZE AGE CHRONOLOGIES AND THE INTERMEDIATE BRONZE AGE

The collapse of Early Bronze Age society toward the end of the third millennium B.C.E. marks the beginning of a sustained period of urban decline and social change. Although there is a general consent that these changes were profound, there is no agreement on what to call this period that spans some two centuries. There is a notable break between the end of the EB3 and the rise of the great city-states of the Middle Bronze Age, and many scholars now lean toward calling this the Intermediate Bronze Age (for example, Gophna 1992). A number of researchers do not distinguish an Intermediate Bronze Age, however, but consider this 200-year period a terminal phase of the Early Bronze Age, or EB4 (Dever 2003a).

PROBLEMS IN THE ARCHAEOLOGY OF THE MIDDLE BRONZE AGE

The debate regarding the nomenclature inevitably carries over into the Middle Bronze Age and the subphases of this period, for when William Foxwell Albright (1966) set out his chronology for the Bronze Age, no intermediate period had yet been recognized. Thus what he called the Middle Bronze 1 (treated here as the Intermediate Bronze Age) had little in common with the urban culture that emerged toward the beginning of the second millennium B.C.E. Following Albright, many scholars referred to the earliest phase of the developed Middle Bronze Age culture as the MB2a, leaving many a novice to wonder what had happened to the MB1. Since there is now some level of general agreement regarding the dates used to subdivide the Middle Bronze Age, there seems to be no reason to prolong the use of the older, less accurate terminology. Thus, many discussions concerning this era, including the present one, follow Patricia Gerstenblith (1983) and William G. Dever (1987) in employing the MB1–3 terminology for this subperiodization (for a brief summary of this topic, see Ilan 2003). Another crucial issue regarding Middle Bronze Age chronology relates to the fact that the local Levantine chronology relies heavily on cross-dating with the contemporary cultures of Egypt and Syro-Mesopotamia (Dever 1992a; Bietak 1991, 1984). Nevertheless, there are several key dates on which all of these chronologies hinge that remain controversial, thus the debates concerning the High, Middle, and Low Chronologies.

Another topic in Middle Bronze Age archaeology that has received considerable attention concerns the function of the earthen ramparts (Bunimovitz 1992; Finkelstein 1992a; Gophna 1992; Kaplan 1975). On the one hand, they appear to represent fortification systems indicative of conflict in the region; on the other, they may have also served as "prestige architecture" in a race for rival city-states to emulate one another. Scholars have also disagreed on the factors that precipitated the decline of the Middle Bronze Age culture, with a number of theories involving a combination of external influences (for example, Egyptians and Hurrians) and internal processes proposed (Ilan 2003; Na'aman 1994; Dever 1990b). Egyptian texts, for instance, describe a series of military campaigns against the cities of Canaan, but it is doubtful that the impact of this would have been felt equally throughout the region, and it is also apparent that certain internal crises were well under way.

One intriguing problem concerning the Middle Bronze Age is the question of whether this was the age of the biblical patriarchs. In recent decades, the patriarchal tradition and the veracity of Genesis altogether have faced great scrutiny. For instance, Albright (1973) associated the story of Abraham and his departure from the Mesopotamian city of Ur with the migration of the Amorites, a process believed to have occurred during the early Middle Bronze Age, sometime between 2100 and 1800 B.C.E. However, subsequent research has resulted in some serious challenges to this reconstruction. Archaeological evidence has revealed that many of the cities mentioned in Genesis did not actually exist at that time. For instance, the frequent appearance of camels in Genesis is clearly problematic, as dromedaries were not domesticated until late in the second millennium B.C.E. and not widely used until after 1000 B.C.E. (Finkelstein and Silberman 2001; Wapnish 1984; Lambert 1960). Another outstanding anachronism is the presence of the Philistines in Genesis, when archaeologists now know that they did not populate the Levantine shores in appreciable numbers prior to the twelfth century B.C.E. Of course, these examples prove only that Genesis was not written at the time in which it is believed to have occurred; it could still represent the canonization of an earlier oral tradition. In other words, someone writing during the first half of the first millennium B.C.E. might have taken for granted that both camels and Philistines had always been around.

Late Bronze Age

The beginning of the Late Bronze Age generally coincides with the reunification of Egypt and the establishment of the Eighteenth Dynasty by Ahmose in about 1550 B.C.E. These events in Egypt are directly related to the periodization of the southern Levant, because Ahmose himself would cross into Canaan and

11.1   A chain of camels climbing a hill in the Judean Desert (J. Golden)

lead the siege of Sharuhen, but, as for all of these periods, there is debate concerning subdivision. According to Albright (1960), the LB1 runs from 1550 to 1400 B.C.E. and the Iron 2 from 1400 to 1200 B.C.E., with two further subdivisions for each of these two phases (that is, LB1a and b; LB2a and b). Several scholars, such as Olga Tufnell (1958) and Ruth Amiran (1969), have proposed dividing the Late Bronze Age into three subphases with the following approximate dates: LB1, 1600/1550–1450 B.C.E.; LB2, 1450–1350 B.C.E.; and LB3, 1350–1200 B.C.E. Mazar, preferring to follow the "precise" dates of historical events in Egypt, has suggested that when employing the three-phase chronology researchers should use the date of Thutmose III's forays (1470 B.C.E.) to divide the LB1 and LB2, and that the LB3 should correspond with the Egyptian Nineteenth Dynasty (c. 1300–1200 B.C.E.).

At least two other major debates in Late Bronze Age archaeology also concern the influence of outside people. The first debate surrounds the Egyptian presence in the region for the duration of the period and the nature of that presence. Although it is clear that Egypt dominated large portions of Canaan (Bunimovitz 2003; McGovern 1993; Mazar 1990), parts of the country were less directly affected than others. Another major topic of discussion concerns the identity of the Sea Peoples and their impact on the region. For example, was their arrival a gradual and relatively peaceful process, or did they appear en masse, bringing violence to Canaanite cities of the coast (Stager 2003; Dothan 2002b; Gitin, Mazar, and Stern 1998; Dothan and Dothan 1992; Stern 1990)?

"BIBLICAL ARCHAEOLOGY" AND THE IRON AGE

From the end of the Late Bronze Age on, many of the most heated debates in the archaeology of the southern Levant relate to one essential question: To what extent can the people, places, and events described in the Hebrew Bible be treated as historical fact? The early years of research and exploration in the region worked under the assumption that much of the biblical account was true and that the spade could be used to confirm scripture. Decades of subsequent archaeological research, however, including settlement surveys, have provided evidence that at times directly contradicts the ancient narrative.

Iron Age Chronology and "Periodization"

Most researchers place the beginning of the period known as the Iron Age with the arrival of the Sea Peoples at around 1200 B.C.E. and its ending with the fall of Jerusalem in 586 B.C.E. Within these general brackets, however, there is considerable debate concerning the subchronology of the Iron Age. David Ussishkin (1985) has suggested that the first half of the twelfth century represents a transitional phase that could be lumped with the end of the Late Bronze Age. Much of the early Iron Age chronology actually hinges on dates from the reigns of Rameses III and IV. There is also debate over the final date of the Iron Age, as scholars disagree on whether Nebuchadnezzar's destruction of Jerusalem occurred in 587 or 586 B.C.E. One year, of course, cannot make or break a historical reconstruction, and issues such as these are of secondary importance to the social archaeologist who takes the long-view approach. The end of the Iron Age 2 is also problematic because of the continuity in the material culture and the difficulties in identifying a distinct material culture of the Babylonian period.

G. Ernest Wright (1961), following Albright, suggested that the Iron Age be divided into Iron 1 from about 1200 to 900 B.C.E. and Iron 2 from 900 to 587 B.C.E. Based on excavations at Hazor, Yohanan Aharoni and Ruth Amiran (1958) suggested that the Iron 1 ended in about 1000 B.C.E., corresponding to the time of David's ascension. Amihai Mazar (1990) generally accepts the latter chronology, though he prefers to subdivide the Iron 2 according to the dates of specific events, such as the dissolution of the United Monarchy in 925 B.C.E. for the end of Iron 2a and the Assyrian conquest of the northern Kingdom of Israel in 720 B.C.E. for the Iron 2b–2c transition.

Though the term "Israelite Period" is often used in reference to the Iron Age of the region as a whole, this terminology, when applied too broadly, takes the risk of grossly oversimplifying the situation that existed at the time. As noted earlier, the archaeological record reflects a strong Egyptian, Canaanite, and Philistine presence in the region during much of the Iron 1. The Hebrew Bible (for example, the Book of Judges) mentions all three of these groups, noting clashes with the Midianites as well. It has been argued, however, that these texts were not actually written until some time after the period they describe, and thus, that some of the "geopolitical" data may be highly questionable. According to Israel Finkelstein (1999, 36), there are no secure chronological anchors relating to the period between the time of the Egyptian Twentieth Dynasty rule in Canaan during the twelfth century B.C.E. and the late eighth-century-B.C.E. Assyrian campaigns.

Exodus, Conquest, and the Rise of the Israelites

The Hebrew Bible, of course, describes a great exodus when over half a million people are said to have left Egypt en masse. Following 1 Kings (6:1), which states that Exodus took place 480 years prior to the construction of Solomon's temple, we may add this figure to the date of around 960 B.C.E. for the temple, thus arriving at a mid-fifteenth-century date for the Exodus. It is, of course, quite difficult to document an ancient migration archaeologically and there are no Egyptian references to an exodus of any sort.

Some scholars have read the Merenptah Stele (the first time the term "Israel" appears in the historical record) as an indication that a tribal group named Israel was one of many already in the hill country at the time. It has also been argued that these early "Proto-Canaanites" could have been Canaanites who were displaced by the incursion of Sea Peoples and forced to move into less desirable places, such as the hill country, which was but sparsely populated at the time (Dever 2003b; Matthews 2002). Another theory, advanced by Kurt Noll (2001), suggests that the Exodus story may combine elements of different traditions, including cultural memories of Merenptah's campaign and conscripted labor in the eastern Delta that may have followed, resulting in a composite myth of liberation. Noll (2001) has also proposed that the story of Exodus may represent a form of revisionist history created in the eighth century B.C.E., perhaps during the reign of Hezekiah, in order to legitimize the new religious and nationalist beliefs.

It is also believed that the people of the Exodus may be related to the Shasu (also Shosu), a nomadic people who appear several times in Egyptian texts (Rainey 1991; Redford 1992). The Papyrus Anastasi and other Egyptian texts dating to the time of Rameses II refer to the Shasu as troublemakers from the Egyptian standpoint. According to one theory, at the end of the Late Bronze Age some of the Shasu migrated north, thereafter taking on a new ethnic identity. However, some of the Shasu may have gone on to become Amalekites, Amonites, and Moabites (Rainey 1991), and thus the one-to-one correlation seems unlikely.

The Emergence of Israel

Although the Merenptah inscription more or less confirms that some entity called Israel existed in Canaan as early as the thirteenth century B.C.E., it does not reveal who these people were. For a long time, the conquest narrative dominated discussions about the emergence of Israel (for example, Lapp 1967; Fritz 1981). According to this model, the Israelites were supposed to have entered Canaan from the east, via Jericho. Eventually, over a five-year period, they fanned out northward and southward and in a short while conquered virtually the entire population of Canaan, then apportioned the land among the various tribes. Archaeologists have questioned the veracity of this account, noting that the Hebrew Bible itself makes it difficult to accept fully a literal reading since it gives two somewhat differing accounts of how the Israelites took possession of the "Promised Land."[2] The scientific data, unfortunately, do little to clarify matters.

Early generations of archaeologists working in the region (for example, Albright 1939, Wright 1961; Yadin 1979) expressed confidence that they could identify destruction layers at various sites dating to the presumed time of Joshua's campaign, thereby corroborating the biblical account of the conquest of Canaan. Yet subsequent archaeological research, including extensive surveys in the region, has rendered many of these claims untenable. As for survey data, the correlation between this evidence and a specific people—the Israelites—has been seriously questioned. More than 300 sites dating to the late thirteenth and early twelfth centuries B.C.E. have been recorded in the central hill country; however, few of these have been excavated—thus making the identification of a specific ethno-cultural group rather difficult.

Although the Bible describes a swift and bloody conquest of virtually the entire region, more recently a number of theories have been advanced relating gradual and peaceful infiltration of Israelites interspersed among surviving Canaanite enclaves. One of the first direct challenges to the biblical account of the Israelite conquest came from Israeli archaeologist Yohanan Aharoni (1957), who conducted pioneering survey work in the Galilee. Aharoni observed a number of unwalled settlements in the Upper Galilee dating to the early Iron Age that, in many cases, were established in places where there had been no previous Late Bronze Age settlement. Based on this evidence, coupled with the redating of pottery from Hazor, he proposed that the Israelite people may have infiltrated the region in a more gradual and unobtrusive manner.

George E. Mendenhall (1962), in contrast, has proposed the "Peasant Revolt Model," which conceives of the emergence of the Israelites as an internal development with little external influence. He suggested that the Exodus from Egypt, if it occurred at all, was less than the grand migration described in the Bible. Furthermore, the people who came to be known as Israelites were originally peasants who revolted against their urban overlords at the end of the Late Bronze Age, subsequently taking flight to the central highlands. It was there, he said, that they developed new ideologies and began to form a coherent group. Norman Gottwald (1979) elaborated on Mendenhall's model, arguing that the Israelites emerged from within Canaanite society, but that the reasons for the split were economic and not theological.

Surely, the Israelite phenomenon must be understood against the backdrop of major sociopolitical upheavals of the late thirteenth century B.C.E., yet, appealing as these theories may seem, it is difficult to find archaeological evidence in support of them. Israel Finkelstein and Neil Asher Silberman (2001) have pointed out that even greater similarity between the material culture of the new highland culture and that of the lowland Canaanites ought to be expected. Furthermore, the Canaanite culture was in a period of decline at the end of the Late Bronze Age and was unlikely to be expanding into new territory at the time. Alternative models focus on the fact that the newcomers were mainly pastoralists who migrated into the region, interacting and intermixing with the local Canaanite population (Dever 1993, 1992a; Finkelstein 2003, 1999). Moreover, the early Iron Age population of the hill country reflects an agrarian and herder background, and there is no indication that its inhabitants were originally desert peoples as described in the Hebrew Bible (Matthews 2002; Ahlstöm 1993). One model widely discussed in the discipline today is that proposed by Finkelstein (2003, 1999, 1988). Based on a conception of the history of settlement in the southern Levant as a series of cycles that shifted between demographic expansion and decline, Finkelstein (1988) has argued that

11.2   Example of modern Bedouins in the Judean Desert (J. Golden)

settlement in the highlands during the Iron Age 1 represents one of several peaks or plateaus in this cycle. This phase culminates with the rise of the national territorial states of the Iron 2.

The Israelite Monarchy

Despite the confusion surrounding the origins of the Israelite people, it is relatively clear that by the tenth century B.C.E., such a group was firmly established in the highlands. As for the Israelite Kingdom itself, and particularly the storied "United Monarchy" of Saul, David, and Solomon, there are a number of hotly debated issues. "Biblical minimalists" have argued that David did not even exist as a historical figure. To be sure, some scholars have searched for evidence reflecting the celebrated deeds of this king. Megiddo, which had remained a Canaanite city during the eleventh century B.C.E. (Str. VIa), was destroyed in a conflagration at the beginning of the tenth century B.C.E. A number of scholars (Rainey 2001; Mazar 1990) have suggested that this could have been the city that was destroyed either by Shishak, a king of Egypt who invaded the region in the late tenth century B.C.E., or by David. (See sidebar, "Who Was King David?")

Who Was King David?

King David is one of the most famous of all the figures of the Hebrew Bible. Large portions of the text are dedicated to his life and storied career. As a young shepherd, he is said to have slain the Philistine giant, Goliath, with a mere sling and stone. David would then be the anointed king of Israel, and under his leadership the armies of Israel would conquer most of the southern Levant and beyond, pushing his kingdom to the shores of the Euphrates. Most important, he would bring all the peoples of Israel together under the rule of one United Monarchy. He was also known as the lover of women and the writer of psalms.

Indeed, King David, at least according to the Hebrew Bible, was nothing less than a legend. However, one of the most fascinating debates in the archaeology of the southern Levant today concerns whether any of his tale is actually more than legend. In recent years, a new generation of minimalist scholars who regard very little of the biblical accounts as reflecting historical reality has emerged (Gabrini 1988; Davies 1992; Thompson 1992; Lemche 1994). It has been argued, for instance, that the narratives concerning David were not written until the Persian period, after the fall of Judah, at the very earliest, and that David may not have even existed as a historical figure.

One may begin by examining the Hebrew Bible itself in search of clues. Although the Bible's authors made use of hyperbole and metaphor, a close reading of the text reveals certain passages that seem to reflect a more pedestrian source. One example comes from 2 Samuel, where the officials of David's court and lists of David's wives and sons are recorded in great detail. It is believed that this may represent lists of real individuals grafted directly into the body of the narrative and that these passages should thus be treated as realistic and fairly accurate historical documents (Hess 1997).

Several biblical scholars have suggested that 1 and 2 Chronicles and Deuteronomy were actually historical works in themselves (Brettler 1995; Halpern 1988). One must, however, bear in mind that each scholar's sense of what constitutes "history" may vary. George A. Smith has argued that even the "historical looking work of Chronicles seems to lack some assessment of sources and it shows a deeply commemorative function in its narrative of the past" (2002, xxviii). He also pointed out that the sources used in Chronicles may themselves have derived from religious traditions designed to celebrate the past.

However, there is now at least one extra-biblical source dating to the Iron Age that refers directly to a royal house associated with David, and possibly two, thus providing the most compelling evidence yet that King David was an actual historical figure.

(continues)

Who Was King David? *(continued)*

The Dan Inscription

Perhaps the most significant archaeological find concerning the historicity of the Israelite monarchy is an inscription from Tel Dan discovered in 1993. The inscription was found on the underside of a paving slab reused in a later structure, but after some initial questions arose regarding its context (Lemche and Thompson 1994; Halpern 1994), it has now been securely dated to about 800 B.C.E., and it is theorized that the stele was on display from perhaps 796 to 791 B.C.E. (Athas 2003). This stone was, in fact, part of a broken basalt stele (32 cm [about 12.5 in.] high and 22 cm [about 8.5 in.] wide) dated to the ninth century B.C.E.; thirteen rows of text remain intact. Written in Aramaic, the stele commemorates historic events and battles between kingdoms to the north of Israel (Aram) and the kings of Israel and Judea. The key phrase in question (Line A9) reads: "I killed Jehoram, son of Ahab, king of Israel, and I killed Ahaziahu, son of Jehoram, king of the house of David" (Biran and Naveh 1995).

These words provide, for the first time, what most scholars now accept as a clear reference to King David and his dynasty (Rainey 2001; Levine 2001; Biran and Naveh 1995). This inscription, therefore, is significant in that it implies the existence of David as a real figure and refers to a dynasty that ruled Judea for more than 400 years. Of course, all archaeological finds are subject to interpretation, and this artifact is not without detractors. Criticisms of the Dan inscription include assertions that the name in question should be read not as David, but rather as Dod, and other scholars have taken issue with the use of the term "House of David" as opposed to the more explicit term "King of Judah." Still others who would prefer to deny David's existence altogether have taken the rather extreme position of alleging that the artifact is a forgery (Thompson 1999).

The "Meshe Stele"

The second inscription that may shed light on the life of David is the "Meshe Stele" commemorating the deeds of the ninth-century-B.C.E. Moabite King Meshe. In this inscription, written in a script similar to the one from Dan (Moabite–Northwest Semitic), Meshe claims victory over an Israelite king east of the Jordan, specifically referring to the tribe of Gad. This stele was actually discovered in 1868, over a century before the Dan inscription was unearthed, but has received renewed attention since the discovery of the latter. Based on careful reexamination of the text, André Lemaire (1994) has suggested that it, too, refers directly to the "House of David." The stele clearly refers to the Kingdom of Israel no less than three times, in addition to specific mention of the Israelite King Omri. This was no doubt Meshe's primary adversary in the military campaign that is the subject of the stele. Toward the end of the inscription (Line 31), there is a reference that is difficult to translate as a result of damage to the stele. Although the translation of the letters *bt wd* has been generally accepted by scholars, Lemaire has suggested inserting a d, which brings the whole phrase to *bt dwd* (Bayt Dawid, or House of David).

According to Lemaire, the use of the term "House of David," as opposed to "King of Judah," to denote the ruler of the southern Judean Kingdom is not surprising, since it is used in several instances in the Hebrew Bible, as well as in the Dan inscription, as a parallel term for "King of Israel." There are other precedents for this convention of using the king's name to refer to his dynasty, for example, in the Annals of Assyrian kings (c. 744–727 B.C.E.), which refers to Israel as Bit Humria, or the "House of Omri" (Matthew 2001; Kitchen 1997). This reading of the Meshe Stele is also supported by the fact that the lands held by the Northern Kingdom in Transjordan were north of the Arnon River, while areas south of the Arnon were part of Judea prior to the rise of Edom in the mid–ninth century B.C.E. As Jan Wim Wesselius (1999), has explained, the Dan inscription thus provides a clear link between the dynastic family of David and a geographic entity. George Athas (2003), however, has argued that the dynastic name and toponym do not go hand in hand, and that the Dan inscription does not refer to a political entity. Rather, he suggested that both the context and the syntax of Bayt Dawid as used in the inscription indicate a geographical location, namely, Jerusalem. As with the Dan Inscription, the validity of the Meshe Stele as evidence for King David has also been questioned.

Archaeological Evidence?

These instances of linguistic evidence aside, definitive proof for the City of David in Jerusalem of the tenth century B.C.E. is lacking. Despite the earnest efforts of archaeologists such as Benjamin Mazar, Yihal Shiloh, and others, material evidence for this "Golden City," including the extensive building projects of David's son and successor Solomon as described in great detail in the Hebrew Bible, has not been forthcoming.

If David was, in fact, a historical figure who lived during the tenth century B.C.E., who was he? His exploits as a warrior-king are described in the Hebrew Bible but are not always easy to accept as fact. The victory of an unarmed shepherd in single combat over the greatest fighter that Philistia had to offer is probably intended as a metaphor, and the record of his territories must be something of a "maximalist" hyperbole. As for his role in religious affairs, David is attributed with having been a key figure in the founding of the "Yahwist" tradition, yet this, too, remains unclear. Several scholars have attempted to understand David's role in the emergence of the state (Matthew 2001; Master 2001; Flanagan 1988).

According to Paula McNutt, "If stripped of the Yahwist roles imposed by the biblical writers, the core image of David in the text is that of paramount

(continues)

> ### Who Was King David? *(continued)*
>
> chief, not a king, a mediator who would have been acceptable as a leader to most of the varied social groups of the time" (1999, 131).
>
> Clearly, it is difficult to separate fact from myth where King David is concerned. Undeniably, he has emerged from the biblical texts as a cultural hero for all of "Western civilization," a role no doubt enhanced by the Renaissance rediscovery of him, epitomized by Michelangelo's widely celebrated sculpture. Although the actual life of this figure may always elude historical proof, archaeologists now seem considerably closer to establishing that, at the very least, David was real.

Again, the anachronisms persist. In 1 Kings (9:15, 17–18) Solomon, the master builder, is credited with having undertaken major building projects at a number of sites outside of Jerusalem, including Baalath, Beth Horon (lower), Gezer, Hazor (Fig. 11.3), Megiddo, and Palmyra (Tadmor). Yet the archaeological evidence, including radiocarbon dates from some of these sites, suggests that several of the structures on Solomon's list of achievements did not exist until at least 100 years after his presumed time of death. Perhaps the most glaring example of this phenomenon is the absence of archaeological evidence for the Temple of Solomon in Jerusalem. A lively debate has revolved for decades around what are thought to be either storage units or the royal stables of Solomon mentioned multiple times in the Hebrew Bible.

Finkelstein (2001), reexamining the survey data from Judea, has argued that there was no kingdom in the region until considerably later than is commonly held. Responding to this argument, Anson Rainey (2001) has taken Finkelstein to task on several points. To begin, he argues that this is but one interpretation of the survey data, and that while the population was still largely agrarian, evidence for demographic change by the Iron 2a cannot be ignored. Rainey points to Aharon Ofer's survey data, which show that during the Iron 2a (mid-eleventh to tenth centuries B.C.E.), "settlement in the Judean hill country almost doubled, compared to the preceding period" (1994, 102). The survey data also indicate that there was some form of settlement hierarchy at the time.

Despite all of the contradictions that arise when researchers scrutinize the Hebrew Bible against the archaeological evidence, one must not lose sight of the fact that a good deal of the archaeological evidence actually supports, if only obliquely, a large portion of the biblical account. For example, massive city gates, oft mentioned as the scene of social activity in the Bible, have been found at a number of sites, including Gezer, Megiddo, and Hazor. Moreover, some of the architectural projects undertaken by various kings do seem to be in evidence in the archaeological record. The construction of a great tunnel by King Hezekiah seems to have a direct archaeological correlate in the tunnel of

11.3   The "Pillared Building" of the Iron 2 city at Hazor (J. Golden)

Siloam, often a highlight of tours of the Old City today. Evidence for the existence of the Israelite monarchy can be seen in the thousand-plus ceramic jars bearing the stamp of *la-melekh* ("belonging to the king") on the handles. There are also direct references to specific Israelite kings, especially Ahab, whose name appears in an inscription from Shalmanseser III (853 B.C.E.) as well as on the "Kurkh Monolith." The latter inscription also mentions Omri, who is named on the Meshe Stele as well. Yehu is mentioned in the inscription on the "Black Obelisk" (841 B.C.E.) (Grayson 1996). Finally, there is David, the founder of a dynasty, whose name, "Bayt David," is directly referred to by an outside source in the Dan inscription.

So although much of the archaeological evidence demonstrates that the Hebrew Bible cannot in most cases be taken literally, many of the people, places, and things probably did exist at some time or another. A number of scholars have raised a new issue in recent years, namely, the undeniable interplay between the formation of cultural identity and nationalism in the present and in representations of the past (Silberman 1982; Zerubavel 1995; Abu el-Haj 1998; Baram 2000). Danielle Steen (2002), for instance, has discussed the relationship between the modern state of Israel and Biblical Archaeology, pointing to the emphasis placed on the Iron Age and support for projects related to this era because of the way it plays into Israeli nationalist ideologies. At two sites loosely linked with events described in Genesis, the "Tomb of the Patriarchs" and "Joseph's Tomb," violence has erupted in recent years. Above all, though, one thing is clear: Whether proving or disproving the veracity of the Bible, a better part of the archaeological research conducted in the southern Levant revolves around this text. It is indeed appropriate to refer to "Biblical Archaeology" as a paradigm, for it not only influences the answers to many of the questions asked, but also frames those questions in the first place.

11.4 The inscription from Tel Dan which refers to the "House of David" (highlighted) (Photo courtesy of Zev Radovan, Land of the Bible Picture Archive)

NOTES

1. The fact that a Dynasty 0 is now recognized reflects the fact that earlier archaeologists had insufficient information for sorting out these most ancient chronologies.

2. The first account is found in the last part of the Book of Numbers and in the Book of Joshua, and the second account is found in the Book of Judges.

SUGGESTED READING

Ahituv, Shmuel. 1993. "Suzerain or Vassal? Notes on the Aramaic Inscription from Tel Dan." *Israel Exploration Journal* 43: 246–247.

Athas, George. 2003. *The Tel Dan Inscription: A Reappraisal and a New Interpretation.* London: Sheffield Academic Press.

Benvenisti, Meron. 2000. *Sacred Landscape: The Buried History of the Holy Land since 1948.* Berkeley: University of California Press.

Biran, Avraham, and Joseph Naveh. 1993. "Aramaic Stele Fragment from Tel Dan." *Israel Exploration Journal* 43: 81–98.

Dever, William G. 1992. "The Chronology of Syria-Palestine in the Second Millennium B.C.E.: A Review of Current Issues." *Bulletin of the American Schools of Oriental Research* 288: 1–25.

———. 2001. "Excavating the Hebrew Bible, or Bury It Again?" *Bulletin of the American Schools of Oriental Research* 322: 67–77.

Finkelstein, Israel. 1992. "Middle Bronze Age 'Fortifications': A Reflection of Social Organization and Political Formations." *Tel Aviv* 19: 201–220.

———. 1998. "Bible Archaeology or Archaeology of Palestine in the Iron Age? A Rejoinder." *Levant* 30: 167–174.

Finkelstein, Israel, and Neil Asher Silberman. 2001. *The Bible Unearthed: Archaeology's New Vision of Ancient Israel and the Origin of Its Sacred Texts.* New York: Free Press.

Flanagan, James W. 1988. *David's Social Drama: A Hologram of Israel's Early Iron Age.* Sheffield, England: Almond Press.

Fritz, Volkmar. 1987. "Conquest or Settlement? The Early Iron Age in Palestine." *Biblical Archaeologist* 50: 84–100.

Levy, Thomas E. 2002. "The Chalcolithic Period." In *Encyclopedia of Prehistory.* Vol. 8, *South and Southwest Asia,* edited by P. Peregrine and M. Ember, 56–74. New York: Kluwer/Plenum.

McNutt, Paula. 1999. *Reconstructing the Society of Ancient Israel.* Louisville, KY: Westminster/John Knox Press.

Muraoka, Takamitsu. 1995. "Linguistic Notes on the Aramaic Inscription from Tel Dan." *Israel Exploration Journal* 45: 19–21.

Rainey, A. 2001. "Stones for Bread: Archaeology versus History." *Near Eastern Archaeology* 64: 140–149.

Routledge, Bruce. 1995. "'For the Sake of Argument': Reflections on the Structure of Argumentation in Syro-Palestinian Archaeology." *Palestine Exploration Quarterly* 127: 41–49.

Shiloh, Y. 1980. "Excavating Jerusalem: The City of David." *Archaeology* 33: 8–17.

Silberman, Neil Asher. 1982. *Digging for God and Country: Exploration, Archeology, and the Secret Struggle for the Holy Land, 1799–1917.* New York: Knopf/Random House.

Silberman, Neil Asher, and David Small, eds. 1997. *The Archaeology of Israel: Constructing the Past, Interpreting the Present.* Sheffield, England: Sheffield Academic Press.

Steen, Danielle. 2002. "Nation Building and Archaeological Narratives in the West Bank." *Stanford Journal of Archaeology* 1: 1–13.

Thompson, Thomas L. 1974. *The Historicity of the Patriarchal Narratives: The Quest for the Historical Abraham.* Berlin: W. de Gruyter.

van den Brink, Edwin C. M., and Thomas E. Levy, eds. 2002. *Egyptian and Canaanite Interaction during the Fourth–Third Millennium B.C.E.* London: Leicester University Press.

Glossary

ABYDOS Site located near the bend in the Nile in Middle Egypt, though traditionally it was an important component in the Upper Egypt kingdom. Abydos was the site of several of Egypt's earliest royal cemeteries, including Cemetery U-J and Umm el-Qab, and was associated with the royal city of Thinis. There is also an important Seti temple at the site.

ABYDOS WARE Style of high-quality, high-fired pottery made on a wheel and decorated with painted bands filled with geometric shapes, such as triangles, often on the vessel shoulder or above. The entire pottery was coated with a burnished red slip. Examples, mostly jugs, juglets, and storage jars, were discovered at Abydos as well as other Egyptian sites. The style originated in Canaan during the second and third periods of the Early Bronze Age (EB2–3).

AHMOSE Egyptian pharaoh (r. 1550–1525 B.C.E.) credited with the "Expulsion of the Hyksos" from the Delta and establishing the Eighteenth Dynasty.

AKHZIV WARE Phoenician-style pottery, mainly jugs, distributed throughout the Mediterranean during the tenth and ninth centuries B.C.E. Examples are covered with a fine red slip—hence they are also called Red Slip Ware—and often have ornate necks with either flaring, pinched, or trefoil rims. This is a diagnostic type for Phoenician "colonies" as far away as Spain, the North African coast, Sicily, and Sardinia.

AKKADIAN An early Semitic language that appears in cuneiform script in the third millennium B.C.E. and that became the lingua franca of the Near East during most of the second millennium B.C.E. The term also refers to the people who spoke this language.

ALABASTER A variety of hard calcite that is translucent and sometimes banded. It can be polished down to a fine surface and was thus used to make a variety of fancy vessels and sculptures in ancient times.

ALALAKH An ancient city located in the Amuq Valley of Syria at present-day Tel Atchana. A city of the kingdom of Yahmad, it was taken by the Hittites in the mid-seventeenth century B.C.E. An important archive of cuneiform tablets was found there.

ALASHIYA A region commonly identified as present-day Cyprus that is mentioned in the main inscription at Medinat Habu and elsewhere.

AMARNA, EL The new (and short-lived) capital founded by the Egyptian pharaoh Akhenaten in about 1350 B.C.E. as part of a religious and cultural revolution; also the cultural phase associated with this ruler (as in "the Amarna Revolution"). The site contained one of the most important archives ever discovered.

AMARNA LETTERS An archive of 336 tablets discovered at the Egyptian New Kingdom capitol of Amarna in 1887 C.E. The letters, written mainly in Akkadian cuneiform, date to the fourteenth century B.C.E. and mention prominent cities in Canaan such as Megiddo and Lachish.

AMON Land east of the Jordan River in modern-day Jordan. Adversaries of Saul and David, the Amonites thrived in the seventh century B.C.E. under Assyrian protection.

AMORITE Probably the primary language spoken throughout most of Canaan during the third millennium B.C.E.; also the West Semitic people who spoke it.

AMPHORA Two-handled vase used for storage of liquids, usually wine. The term comes from the Greek but today is used broadly to refer to all such vessels.

AMPHORISKOS A smaller version of an amphora.

ANNEALING Process of heating and slowly cooling metal (and glass) in order to toughen it and reduce brittleness; frequently employed when hammering metals to soften the material so that it may be more easily shaped.

ANTHROPOMORPHIC Attribution of human characteristics or behavior to nonhuman entities, including animals, inanimate objects, or natural phenomena; also, something made in human form, such as an anthropomorphic figurine.

'APIRU Seminomadic tribes of central Canaan whose main territory was probably in the countryside surrounding Shechem. The 'Apiru are mentioned as mercenaries and laborers in texts from the Late Bronze Age. Also called Hapiru or Habiru.

ARAMAIC Ancient Semitic language preceding biblical Hebrew, which developed in the land of Aram (Syria and Southeast Turkey) probably during the ninth century, becoming the lingua franca in the Levant during the seventh century B.C.E. Several important inscriptions (for example, the Dan inscription) were written in Aramaic.

ARCHAEOLOGY The scientific study of past cultures through examination of their material remains.

ARID ZONE Region characterized by little rainfall (less than 200 mm [7.88 in.] annually), typically insufficient to support most trees or woody plants and dry farming.

ARISTOCRACY A ruling or noble class where status is passed by heredity.

ARTIFACT A portable object modified, made, and/or used by humans.

ASHDODA Name given to a style of ceramic figurine where a female torso is incorporated into the form of a chair or table, commonly found at early Philistine sites.

ASHERAH Canaanite mother goddess associated with a "Sacred Tree" or pole. Various symbols and pillar figurines suggest that worship of this goddess was widespread well into the Iron Age, though this was explicitly condemned in the Hebrew Bible.

ASHLAR Form of masonry using large blocks cut to even faces and square edges that fit snugly together when laid in horizontal courses; often used for the facing of buildings. The style was characteristic of Israelite royal structures, though it probably derived from Phoenician architecture.

ASSYRIA Northern Mesopotamia; also all the lands subsumed into the Assyrian Empire of the ninth to seventh centuries B.C.E., including portions of the southern Levant.

ASTARTE Canaanite goddess of love, fertility, and war; the consort and sister of Baal.

AVARIS Ancient city in the eastern Egyptian Delta (present-day Tel el-Dab'a); capital of the Hyksos dynasty during the Middle Bronze Age. The city had close affinities in material culture with cities of southern Canaan.

BAAL A principal Canaanite god associated with fertility and war. Also known as Hadaad, he is often depicted with weaponry, and the bull is his main symbol. Baal is mentioned many times in the Ugaritic texts and bears the titles "bringer of storms" and "rider of clouds." He was also worshipped by the Phoenicians and recognized by the Israelites, though he ultimately takes on an evil persona among the latter.

BAAL ZEBUB Canaanite god popular among the Philistines during the second period of the Iron Age (Iron 2). He is known from Ugaritic texts as well as the Hebrew Bible (2 Kings 1:2–3, 6, 16), which connects him to the city of Ekron.

BAMAH (SING.)/BAMOT (PL.) Commonly translated as "high place(s)." Bamot probably served as ritual platforms at open-air cult sites. There are more than 100 references to them in the Hebrew Bible.

BASALT Hard igneous rock, often fine-grained, usually dark gray or black, often used to make fancy vessels and sculptures. Sources are known throughout northern Israel and Jordan.

BEER SHEVA Modern town of the northern Negev that was host to a cluster of Chalcolithic sites and an Iron Age tell; the name literally means "well of the oath," and it is here, according to Genesis, where Abraham dug seven wells and made a covenant with God.

BEIT-YERAH WARE *See* Khirbet Kerak Ware.

BET 'AB The extended family, headed by a partriarch; literally, "house of the father." The bet 'ab served as the basic social and economic unit in ancient Israel.

BICHROME WARE Form of pottery named for its decorative motifs painted in two colors, usually black and red. The style emerged late in the Middle Bronze Age and appeared with increasing frequency in the fifteenth century B.C.E. Bichrome Wares from the early Late Bronze Age are similar to Cypriote examples of Bichrome Ware (also known as the Late Cypriote I style). Common motifs include birds, fish, and bulls.

BILIBIL Base ring jugs with a high ring-base, a bulbous body, and a long, slender neck with a handle attached or inserted into it. The style was common in imported Cypriote Ware of the Late Bronze Age.

BUCHERO Imported Cypriote vessels with a "ribbed" form during the Late Bronze Age.

BURNISH A method of treating the surface of a vessel to make it smooth and/or glossy by or as if by polishing it.

BUTO-MAADI CULTURE Chalcolithic culture in the Egyptian Delta in the mid- to late fourth millennium B.C.E.

CANAANEAN BLADE Specialized blade tool, usually trapezoidal in cross section and retouched for smoothness, diagnostic of the Early Bronze Age, though protoforms appeared in Chalcolithic times. A typical blade is 10–15 cm (about 4–6 in.) long and 3 cm (a little over 1 in.) wide and made of high-quality, fine-grained flint.

CANAANITES People inhabiting the land of Canaan, as it is known from the Hebrew Bible as well as extra-biblical texts, especially those dating to the Late Bronze Age.

CARTOUCHE An oval-shaped symbol bearing the name of an Egyptian king's or queen's name, written in hieroglyphics. Because the specific years of most pharaohs' reigns are known, cartouches provide relatively secure absolute dates when founding outside of Egypt.

CHAFF The straw used to temper clay, as in "chaff-temper."

CHALCOLITHIC Period spanning the early fifth through the mid-fourth millennia B.C.E. in the southern Levant, with well-represented cultures in the Negev and Golan regions. The name derives from the Greek term for copper, *chalkos*, although copper does not actually appear in the archaeological record until midway through the period.

CHARIOT A two-wheeled vehicle drawn by horses, used for transportation or in battle. The term "light chariot" refers to those models with spoked wheels that evolved with the coming of iron and were faster and lighter than their predecessors.

CHURN Chalcolithic form of oblong pot with handles on both ends, designed to be suspended so that it could be rocked back and forth. It was used to process dairy goods, especially to separate curds from whey. The oblong shape probably mimics that of churns made from animal hide.

CITADEL Part of a town or fortress, often walled, located atop the highest point of a city. In some cases, citadels functioned as government districts, sometimes with palatial structures, and/or as elite neighborhoods and religious centers.

CORNET Form of cone-shaped drinking cup from the Chalcolithic period, sometimes decorated with geometric designs painted in red, that may have been used for ritual purposes. They may be a chronological indicator for the early Chalcolithic era, as they are quite rare at the latest sites.

CORVÉE LABOR A civilian workforce employed by a central government for public works; in ancient Egypt, a periodic, seasonal workforce engaged in construction or other work for the government made up of citizens who would otherwise be idle or underemployed during the nonagricultural season.

CRESCENTIC AXES Crescent or "epsilon"-shaped axe heads made of copper during the Early Bronze Age. The type evolved into "fenestrated axes" during the Intermediate Bronze Age.

CUBIT Unit of measurement approximately equal to the length of the forearm. One royal cubit is equivalent to 0.5231 m and is divided into seven palms or twenty-eight digits.

CUNEIFORM System of writing developed in Mesopotamia by 3000 B.C.E. and widely used throughout the Near East for millennia. It consists of wedge-shaped strokes derived from writing on soft clay with a triangular stylus as a "pen." Cuneiform developed from pictograms that came to serve as an alphabet, eventually consisting of more than 500 characters. Most stood for words, but there were also some that stood for syllables or speech-sounds.

CYLINDER SEAL Seal in the form of a cylinder made of a stone, a gem, or ceramics, with an engraved design that would leave an impression when rolled over wet clay.

CYPRO-AEGEAN The cultural traditions of mainland Greece (Mycenae), Cyprus, and the Aegean Islands, especially during the Late Bronze and early Iron Ages.

DAGON Originally a god of northern Canaan, especially the ancient city of Ugarit, then the principal deity of the Philistines. The Hebrew Bible mentions Dagon temples at Gaza (Judg. 16:23) and Ashdod (1 Sam. 5), though these have not been identified archaeologically. In the Ugaritic tablets, Baal is often referred to as "son of Dagan."

DARK-FACED BURNISHED WARE Mainly open vessels with a thick dark gray, highly burnished slip, and sometimes a "grain wash" or "band slip." Bowls were usually carinated, often decorated with a rope design and knobs of varying shapes. Also called Gray Burnished Ware.

DAVID King of the United Monarchy (1005–970 B.C.E.). One of the most celebrated figures in the Hebrew Bible, David is said to have greatly expanded the limits of the kingdom, establishing Jerusalem as its capital. One or two extra-biblical inscriptions indicate that David was a real, historical person, though some have tried to dispute this.

DEAD SEA Salt lake in the Jordan Valley near the modern Jordan-Israel border. The surface is some 400 m (1320 ft.) below sea level, forming the lowest continental depression on Earth. The sea and its immediate surroundings offer a number of resources that were vital in ancient times, including salt and bitumen, but it supports no fish or other life forms.

DEIR EL-BALAH Site on the southern Mediterranean coast of Canaan that served as a way station on the "Way of Horus" during the Late Bronze Age.

DIMORPHIC MODEL Economic model proposed by Michael B. Rowton (1976), based on ethnographic research, describing economies with two basic complementary components: agriculturally based sedentism and pastoral nomadism.

DIVIDED MONARCHY The period (c. 925–586 B.C.E.) beginning with the death of Solomon, when the United Kingdom split into the northern Kingdom of Israel and the southern Kingdom of Judah, and the Babylonian conquest of Judah.

DJED PILLAR Egyptian symbol resembling a squat pillar with cross bars, a symbol of stability originally associated with the gods Ptah, Sokar, and later with Osiris. It was often used as an amulet and appears on decorative friezes in Egypt, and rarely, in Canaan.

DJER Egyptian king of the late First Dynasty (c. 2800 B.C.E.); also Palestinian pottery found in his tomb dating to the second part of the Early Bronze Age (EB2).

DOLMEN Megalithic tomb structure made up of a large flat stone laid across upright ones. Thousands of these tombs have been found in the Golan, Galilee, and Transjordan regions. The term comes from French but may originally derive from the Cornish (Celtic) word *tolmen,* which means "hole of stone."

DROMOS A style of domed tomb entrance originally from Mycenae; in some cases, natural caves were transformed into dromos tombs.

DUCKBILL AXE HEAD Distinctive form of bronze axe head, resembling an elongated "beak" in shape, with two "windows" and a small, central rib, common during the Middle Bronze Age.

DUMUZI Near Eastern deity associated with the cycle of birth, death, and renewal, fertility, and the agricultural cycle.

DUMUZI STELE An engraved stone from the Early Bronze Age site of Arad depicting one figure laying in what may be a grave and another figure rising above it, perhaps from the dead. The image is thought to represent the fertility god Dumuzi.

DYNASTY Royal "house" with a line of hereditary rulers. In Egypt, dynasties are based on the priest Manetho's system of dividing the history of ancient Egypt into thirty successive chronological units. *See also* Manetho.

EARLY BRONZE AGE (EBA) Era spanning the end of the fourth and most of the third millennium B.C.E., subdivided into EB1, 2, and 3. Sometimes referred to as the Proto-Canaanite or Proto-Urban period, it is characterized by the earliest cities in the southern Levant.

EARTHEN RAMPART A sloping structure built primarily of earth and rubble, sometimes with a stone core. Earthen ramparts, also called *glacis,* surrounded a number of Canaanite cities during the Middle Bronze Age. They were used to demarcate and protect the city.

EBLA Syrian city excavated in the 1970s. Occupied for much of the Bronze Age, the site had a major archive containing thousands of cuneiform texts that provide important information regarding trade and politics throughout much of the Near East around the years 2400–2250 B.C.E.

EDOM Land neighboring Judah on its southeastern border during the Iron Age. The Kingdom of Edom encompassed the area between the Wadi Hesa in the north to the Gulf of Aqaba, including the area known as Seir. In addition to archaeological research, much of what we know about Edom comes from the Hebrew Bible, along with Assyrian records and a few seals and ostraca.

EGYPTIAN DELTA The Nile River Delta, where the Nile splits into several different branches, all spilling into the Mediterranean. The Delta forms the better part of Lower Egypt.

ELITE A select or superior group with greater wealth and/or status than the masses, usually associated with powerful lineages, and often with control over community resources. This term is frequently used to refer to people, as in "elites," as well as their trappings, as in "elite tombs."

EXCAVATION The systematic removal of sediment from a site in order to search for evidence of past use or occupation.

"EXECRATION TEXTS" Egyptian inscriptions dating to Dynasty 12, roughly the first two centuries of the second millennium B.C.E., so named because they refer to foreign places and/or peoples considered hostile toward Egypt. The texts, which contain lists of proper names, provide the equivalent of rough geopolitical maps of Canaan during this period of more than 100 years.

EXPERIMENTAL ARCHAEOLOGY Method of doing archaeology that includes conducting experiments aimed at reconstructing and/or reenacting ancient behaviors and processes.

FAIENCE Glazed earthenware often used to make amulets and sometimes vessels. Faience was made by combining quartz sand with a solution of natron, which, once heated, can be molded like clay; a copper-rich glaze was then applied to the surface, giving the material its distinctive blue-green color.

FAYNAN *See* Wadi Faynan.

FENESTRATED AXE Axe head with a distinctive shape, characterized by a bowlike form pierced by two large openings, or "windows," and a shaft hole. It was the predominant style during the Intermediate Bronze Age.

FENESTRATED INCENSE STAND A type of bowl on top of a cylindrical base, usually made of basalt or ceramic, dating from the Chalcolithic period. "Windows" were carved into the hollow cylinder supporting the bowl, creating, in the "high-footed" varieties, long, narrow legs attached to a ring-base.

FIBULA Clasp or brooch used in ancient times to fasten clothing, often ornamental. The word is of Greek origin.

FILIGREE Intricate ornamental metalwork, often in gold or silver, made by manipulating finely twisted wire.

FIRST INTERMEDIATE PERIOD Period of political decentralization in Egypt (c. 2180–2050 B.C.E.) following the collapse of the Old Kingdom's Sixth Dynasty. It was characterized by a reversion to regional power structures and rivalries between local dynasties.

FLAX A fine, light-colored textile fiber obtained from the stem of the linseed plant (genus Linum). Along with wool, it constituted one of the primary forms of textile in the ancient world.

FOSSE TEMPLE A form of temple or religious architecture located just outside the city wall in the moat surrounding an earthen rampart. Examples have been found at Middle Bronze Age sites such as Lachish.

FOUNDATION DEPOSIT Small cache of ritual objects (sometimes symbolic tools), buried at critical intervals during the construction of temples and tombs, intended to ensure the durability and longevity of the structure.

GALILEE, SEA OF Relatively large lake formed by a basin in the center of the Jordan Valley just south of the Golan; also known as Lake (Yam) Kinneret and Lake Tiberias. The name also refers to the lush, well-watered region surrounding the lake.

GARRISON A military outpost or fortress-town; also the troops stationed there.

GAZELLE Small species of ungulate, related to the antelope and deer, found in a variety of habitats in the southern Levant, including the arid zones.

GHASSULIAN A culture of the Chalcolithic period taking its name from the type-site of Teleilat Ghassul in Jordan. Recent research indicates that the term "Ghassulian" may be used to refer to an early-middle phase of the Chalcolithic culture, as distinct from a slightly later Beer Sheva culture.

GOLAN The highland region beginning at the northern shore of the Sea of Galilee.

GOVERNORS' RESIDENCES Elaborate structures, including palaces and private houses, built toward the end of the Late Bronze Age and through the early Iron Age. At sites such as Tel el-Far'ah South, this style of building displays an Egyptian influence.

HADAAD *See* Baal.

HAMMEMIAH KNIVES Egyptian form of stone tool; also known as a "razor." Though many examples found in the southern Levant were probably local imitations, some were Egyptian imports; in some cases, they are made from a pink-colored flint that probably came from Egypt itself.

HAPIRU *See* 'Apiru.

HATHOR Egyptian goddess often represented as a cow or as a woman with bovine ears. The wife of Horus; the wife, sister, or daughter of Ra; and the pharaoh's divine mother, she was associated with music, dance, and mortuary ritual. One of her titles was "Lady of Turquoise," and she was worshipped at the copper mines of Timna during the Late Bronze Age.

HATTUSAS Capital of the Hittite Empire located near Boghazköy, about 210 kilometers east of the modern Turkish city of Ankara.

HAZOR One of the most important sites in ancient Canaan throughout both the Bronze and Iron Ages. Situated in the Huleh Basin of the northern Jordan Valley, Hazor played a central role in networks of trade and communication and served as southern Canaan's gateway to the north and to the cities of Syro-Mesopotamia.

HEBREW Semitic language closely related to Aramaic. The ancient language of the Bible, it was modernized in the early twentieth century and is spoken in Jewish communities throughout the world today. The term also refers to the (ancient) speakers of this language.

HEBREW BIBLE The central religious scripture of the Jewish people. As the Old Testament, it also forms part of the Christian scriptures, and some of its accounts are incorporated into the Islamic Koran. This collection of thirty-nine books is often divided into three groups—the Torah, the Prophets, and the Writings—and relates the story of the Israelite people and the evolution of their relationship with their God, YHWH, from creation through the destruction of the temple in Jerusalem and into the early exilic period.

HEZEKIAH Thirteenth king of Judah (727–698 B.C.E.) who is known for instituting "YHWH-alone" religious reforms and challenging Assyrian power.

HIERAKONPOLIS City of Upper Egypt that may have served as an early capital prior to the ascendance of Abydos and Memphis as the primary political centers of Upper and Lower Egypt, respectively.

HIERATIC Cursive form of hieroglyphic writing usually used on papyrus and ostraca as well as in graffiti.

HIEROGLYPHICS System of writing developed in ancient Egypt toward the end of the fourth millennium B.C.E. in which pictorial symbols (pictographs) were used to represent direct meaning. Pictographs also had some sound value. *See also* Phonemic, Pictograph.

HITTITE Oldest known Indo-European language and its speakers. The Hittites occupied Asia Minor and Syria for much of the second millennium B.C.E. From approximately 1650 to 1200 B.C.E., they established an empire, stretching from east of modern Ankara west to the Mediterranean coast and southeast into northern Syria, which often rivaled that of Egypt. By 700 B.C.E., the Hittite culture was in decline.

HOLEMOUTH JAR Neckless vessel, usually round in overall form, with either a flat or a rounded base. The style is diagnostic of the Early Bronze Age, but it also appears both before and after this period.

HOLOCENE Epoch beginning roughly 10,000 years ago with the end of the last Ice Age of the Pleistocene and continuing into the present.

HOR-AHA First king of Egyptian First Dynasty, who followed Narmer. His name appears as a serekh in Early Bronze Age Canaan, and his reign is roughly coterminous with the end of the first part of that age (EB1). *See also* Narmer; Serekh.

HORUS One of the most important Egyptian gods associated with kingship; the son of Isis and Osiris, husband of Hathor. He was represented as a falcon-headed man or a falcon, and his eye was known as the *wudjat* eye, a symbol of great power.

HURRIAN Language and people (the Hurru) of Syria and southern Anatolia in the second millennium B.C.E. The Hurru established the Mitanni state midway through the millennium, vying for power with the Hittites. During the Late Bronze Age, they dominated parts of northern Canaan. Though Hurrian may have been the dominant language after 1500 B.C.E., it was rarely used outside the region. Much of what we know comes from the Nuzi tablets (c. fifteenth century B.C.E.), though Washukanni, the Hurrian capital, has never been found. In Egypt they were called the Naharina.

HYKSOS West Semitic, Asiatic people who settled in the Nile River Delta in Egypt in the nineteenth and eighteenth centuries B.C.E., briefly ruling the region from the city of Avaris. They established Dynasty 15 during what is known as the Second Intermediate Period. Their culture was something of a hybrid because it clearly betrayed its Canaanite origins while incorporating much from Egyptian culture. The name Hyksos comes from the Greek version of the Egyptian term *Hakau Khasut*, which literally means "foreign chiefs" or "foreign rulers."

INGOT A mass of "raw" or unworked metal, often in the form of a bar or block, that is cast as a standardized unit of measure for convenient storage, shipment, exchange, and use.

IRANO-TURANIAN ZONE Semiarid zone in a 30 km–wide band lying between the Mediterranean zone and the arid desert zone to the south, receiving about 150–350 mm (6–14 in.) of rainfall per annum.

IRRIGATION A method of delivering water to dry land via a system of channels dug into the soil, used for the purpose of watering farmland that receives insufficient rainfall for dry farming.

ISRAEL Refers to both a land and its people, the Israelites, during the Iron Age, more specifically, to the Northern Kingdom during the time of the Divided Monarchy (c. 925–586 B.C.E.). The term was revived by the Zionist movement and now refers to the state existing in the region since 1948 C.E. The earliest extra-biblical reference to Israel appears in the inscription of the Merenptah Stele (c. 1200 B.C.E.).

JABAL Arabic term for "mountain," as in Jabal Hamrin. It is sometimes transliterated as "Gebel."

JERICHO Site located in the central Jordan Valley just north of the Dead Sea and northeast of Jerusalem. Among the oldest stratified sites in the region, Jericho was first occupied during the Natufian Neolithic and remained an important city through the Bronze and Iron Ages. Jericho also figures prominently in the Hebrew Bible's Book of Joshua, which describes the Israelite conquest of Canaan, when the walls of the city were famously brought down by the sounding of the horn. The mound of Tel es-Sultan is considered the original site and has been excavated extensively.

JEROBOAM I First king of Israel (931–909 B.C.E.) who led the breakaway Northern Kingdom, dividing the previously united kingdom after Solomon's death.

JUDAH The Southern Kingdom during the time of the Divided Monarchy (c. 925–586 B.C.E.). The Hebrew Bible construes the kings of Judah as less prone to sin than their northern counterparts, but Judah suffered a similar fate nonetheless when the kingdom and its capital, Jerusalem, were devastated by the Babylonians.

KERNOS (SING.)/KERNOI (PL.) Large serving vessel in which fruits were offered, often in the performance of ritual, popular during the Late Bronze Age. Etymologically, the term comes from the Greek.

KHIRBET KERAK WARE Ceramic style recognized as the main "fossil type" for the third stage of the Early Bronze Age (EB3) in the north. This handmade pottery, which includes a range of forms, is best known for its distinctive, highly burnished black slip on the outside, its red interiors, and its geometrical designs. It is also known as Beit-Yerah Ware.

KIBBUTZ (SING.)/KIBBUTZIM (PL.) Type of community or collective in modern-day Israel generally based on socialist values. Locations for kibbutzim are often chosen for the same reasons that attracted people to certain sites in ancient times, such as proximity to water, and therefore many archaeological sites are located on modern kibbutzim and are named after them.

KINNERET, LAKE *See* Galilee, Sea of.

KRATER Form of deep bowl with handles extending from the pot rim to the shoulder. Popular during the Bronze Age, kraters are Aegean inspired, if not imported from that region, and were probably used as wine containers that were elaborately decorated.

KURKAR Hard, calcareous sandstone ridge formations along the northern portion of the Mediterranean coast.

KYLIX Tall, stemmed, shallow drinking cup, probably used for imbibing wine.

LA-MELEKH JAR Narrow-necked, wide-shouldered ceramic storage jar bearing a royal stamp on the handles indicative of royal trade. In early Hebrew, the word stamped on the jars, *lmlk*, meant "belonging to the king." Many of the jars can be dated to around the time of Hezekiah (c. 700 B.C.E.).

LAPIS LAZULI A blue precious stone with speckles of gold often used in decorative items. Lapis lazuli deposits such as that at Badakshan in northeastern Afghanistan probably supplied much of the Near East throughout ancient times.

LIBATION The religious practice of pouring some liquid, usually wine, as a ritual offering to a deity.

LINE GROUP PAINTED WARE Pottery noted for its style of decoration, painted vertical bands of reddish brown against the background of a white slip, typically diagnostic of the first stage of the Early Bronze Age (EB1).

LISSAN BASIN The lowest continental depression on Earth (398 meters below sea level) and host to the Dead Sea, which was originally a lake. It is located near the center of the Jordan Rift Valley.

LOWER EGYPT Northern Egypt, primarily the Delta region and points south of there. This region saw a generally distinct line of cultural development prior to the late Nagada and was overtaken by the Hyksos during the first half of the second millennium B.C.E.

MANETHO Egyptian priest who wrote a history of Egypt in Greek in the third century B.C.E., devising the basic scheme of kingdoms and dynasties still in use today.

MARI City of Syria that figured prominently in international commercial and political relations during the Bronze Age. It is noted for an important archive, the "Mari Letters," discovered there (c. 1800–1750 B.C.E.), as well as for the Palace of Zimri Lim with its vivid wall paintings.

MASSEBAH (SING.)/MASSEBOT (PL.) Standing stone, or stele (though rarely inscribed). Massebot, often appearing in groups, were probably used in religious practices. They are found both in temples and at open-air worship sites.

MASTABA Arabic word literally meaning "bench." The term is used to refer to early tombs (especially from the First and Second Dynasties) that consist of a rectangular structure above the ground with a flat roof.

MEDITERRANEAN ECONOMY As used here, production and trade surrounding "cash crops," particularly grapes and olives, cultivated in the Mediterranean zone.

MEDITERRANEAN HUMID ZONE Ecological zone in the northern part of Canaan receiving 350–1000 mm (about 14–40 in.) of annual rainfall on average and generally characterized by denser vegetation than the more arid areas.

MEGIDDO Important site located along trade routes running though the fertile Jezreel Valley. Occupied during the Bronze and Iron Ages, Megiddo was host to important royal and religious institutions. It is mentioned in biblical and extra-biblical texts and was the scene of an important battle between Canaanites and Egyptians (c. 1450 B.C.E.).

MERENPTAH Pharaoh who succeeded Rameses II. He was Rameses' thirteenth son and succeeded him to the throne at the age of sixty, reigning for but ten years (c. 1212–1202 B.C.E.). Merenptah is said to have led expeditions into Nubia and Libya and sent food to the Hittites during a famine. In an inscription from his temple at Thebes, there is written the first known reference to the people of Israel, whom he attacked.

MESHE STELE *See* Moabite Stone.

METALLIC WARE Form of high-fired and high-quality ceramics popular in Canaan, particularly the north, during the second part of the Early Bronze Age (EB2).

METOPE Element of decoration where rectangular registers are used to divide the space in which other decorative motifs appear.

MIDIANITE WARE A class of ceramics originating from northwestern Arabia and the Hejaz and found at Iron Age sites in Syro-Palestine, especially the northern Negev sites (for example, Tel Masos).

MITANNI Hurru kingdom of the mid-second millennium B.C.E. established in the highlands between the Tigris and the Euphrates rivers. The capital, Washukanni, has not been identified, but Mitanni apparently traded on near equal terms with Egypt and the Hittite empire for more than a century, until it was overthrown by the Hittites in the mid-fourteenth century B.C.E.

MOAB Kingdom located on the highland plateau east of the Dead Sea, with its capital at Dibon (Dhiban). Moab is mentioned numerous times in the Hebrew Bible, both as a rival and as a vassal state of Israel. North Moab, which covered an area from just northeast of the Dead Sea to the Arnon, was at one point under direct Israelite control. David had Moabite connections.

MOABITE The language of Moab and its speakers, closely related to Hebrew.

MOABITE STONE Stele discovered at the Moabite capital of Dibon (Dhiban) in 1868. The long inscription, written in the Moabite language, commemorates King Meshe's liberation of Moab from Israelite control (mid-ninth century B.C.E.) and provides information about building projects and slave labor as well as foreign relations and geopolitics. It is also known as the Meshe Stele.

MONOCHROME WARE Pottery with designs painted in one color, specifically a form of painted ware from Philistia during the early Iron Age representing either Cypro-Aegean imports or, more often, local copies of this style.

MONOLATRY The worship of a single god while acknowledging the existence of other deities.

MONOTHEISM The worship of a single god accompanied by the belief or doctrine that only one God exists.

MUD BRICK Square or rectangular building bricks made from mud mixed with straw, usually sun-dried. This was the primary building material in the ancient Near East.

MUWATALLIS Hittite king who fought against Rameses II in the Battle of Qadesh (c. 1275 B.C.E.).

MYCENAE Important Bronze Age city of mainland Greece and type-site for the Mycenaean culture that spread throughout the Aegean. It featured monumental architecture, including the famous Lion Gate (c. mid-thirteenth century B.C.E.).

MYCENAEAN IIIC Specific pottery horizon first identified in the Aegean at the beginning of the twelfth century B.C.E. Though invariably made in local workshops, pottery made in this style signals the arrival of the Sea Peoples in Cyprus and the Levant at this time.

NAHAL *See* Wadi.

NARMER Egyptian King of Dynasty 0 credited with unifying Upper and Lower Egypt (c. 3050 B.C.E.), though this may be more myth than historical reality. His serekh appears at sites throughout Canaan in the Early Bronze Age (EB1b) horizon. *See* Serekh.

NARMER PALETTE A slate plaque discovered at Hierakonpolis in the Great Deposit that bears inscriptions and bas-relief indicating Narmer as the unifier of Upper and Lower Egypt, and apparently an aggressor against peoples of Canaan.

NAWAMI Circular stone-built burial chambers, common in arid areas during the Early Bronze Age, probably used by transhumant populations.

NEBUCHADNEZZAR Ruler of the Neo-Babylonian Empire (605–555 B.C.E.) whose conquest of Judea culminated with the destruction of Jerusalem in 586 B.C.E.

NEOLITHIC Period spanning the ninth through sixth millennia B.C.E., characterized by the earliest appearance of settled communities, the domestication of plants and animals, and the first fired ceramics.

NINEVEH Assyrian city, site of Sennacherib's "Palace without a Rival," adorned with bas-relief panels. The panels, among other things, recount the story of the fall of Lachish, the city beloved of the goddess Ishtar.

NOMADISM *See* Pastoral nomadism.

NUZI Important Hurrian city in what is today northern Iraq. Numerous inscribed tablets dating to the fifteenth century B.C.E. were found at the site.

OLD KINGDOM Period in ancient Egypt subsuming Dynasties 3–6 (c. 2700–2150 B.C.E.). This was a time of great cultural achievement, highlighted by the Djoser complex at Saqqara (D3) and the Great Pyramids of Giza (D4).

ORTHOSTAT Large upstanding stone, often carved in the form of a lion or some mythical beast (for example, a griffin). Orthostats were used in constructing the walls of monumental buildings and as architectural features, especially to flank the sides of an entrance.

OSSUARY Receptacle, usually of ceramic, though sometimes limestone, used to hold the bones of deceased individuals. Also known as "bone boxes" or "charnel houses," ossuaries were often house-shaped and sometimes decorated with both painted and/or applied designs in anthropomorphic forms.

OSTRACON (SING.)/OSTRACA (PL.) Pottery fragment used as a writing surface, sometimes for short notes or for scribal practice.

OX-HIDE INGOTS Copper ingots named for their shape, which resembles a hide. The ingots were transported throughout the eastern Mediterranean during the Late Bronze Age.

PANTHEON The suite of deities worshipped by polytheistic peoples. Although the term originally referred to the Greek panel of gods, it now is often applied more generally to all polytheistic religions.

PAPYRUS A water reed once abundant in Egypt. It was processed into a form of paper used for important records. The term is used in reference to specific documents, as in Papyrus Anastasi.

PASTORAL NOMADISM Of or relating to shepherds or herders, that is, a group of people who have no fixed home and move according to the seasons from place to place in search of food, water, and grazing land for flocks of animals.

PATRIARCH Term used to refer Abraham, Isaac, and Jacob of the Hebrew Bible (Genesis). It also applies to the time when they are thought to have lived, usually presumed to be the Middle Bronze Age.

PATRIARCHAL A social system where men are the dominant members of society.

PATRICIAN HOUSE Canaanite luxury homes that typically included an open courtyard or atrium, storage rooms, and, in some cases, a pillared hall and staircase leading to a second floor.

PATRILINEAL Term usually referring to descent, where kinship is traced through the male lineage.

PENTAPOLIS Five principal cities of Philistia described in the Hebrew Bible—Gath, Gaza, Ashqelon, Ekron (Tel Miqne), and Ashdod.

PHARAOHS Kings of ancient Egypt, usually traced through male heredity, with one or two rare female exceptions. The earliest use of this term, which literally means "Great House," within Egypt is found in the New Kingdom, though it is applied retroactively by modern scholars to earlier rulers.

PHILISTIA The land of the Philistines, mainly on the southern Levant coast during the Iron Age. It has been documented through the distinctive Philistine material culture (such as Bichrome Ware) and figures prominently in the Hebrew Bible,

PHILISTINES Ethnic/cultural group inhabiting the southern Levantine coast during the Iron Age. The Philistines are known from biblical narratives and extra-biblical texts, where they are rivals of the Israelites, and identified archaeologically by their pottery and other aspects of material culture. The origin of the Philistines is uncertain, though it is thought that they derive from the Aegean.

PHOENICIA The land of the Phoenicians on the strip of Lebanese and Syrian coast running parallel to the Lebanon Mountains, between Arvad in the north and the Carmel ridge in the south. Its main cities were Tyre, Sidon and Byblos, with important strongholds in northern Canaan, including Tel Dor, Akhziv, and Acre.

PHOENICIAN BICHROME WARE Style of pottery, often painted with banded designs, first appearing on the Lebanese coast in the mid-eleventh century B.C.E.

PHONEMIC System of writing that uses arbitrary symbols to represent speech sounds.

PICTOGRAPH Sign in a written script that uses pictures to represent words and objects.

PILGRIM FLASK Ceramic type, with a rounded, flattened body and small neck with handles on each side, appearing in the Late Bronze Age.

PITHOS (SING.)/PITHOI (PL.) Large storage vessel with a narrow mouth at the top that was used to hold liquids. Pithoi are often cited as a diagnostic feature of Israelite culture, though they are found before the Iron Age and outside the Israelite region. The term comes from the Greek language.

POLYMETALLIC Refers to both the materials and technique employed when two metals are used in the manufacture of a single artifact (for example, one base metal and one inset metal), as opposed to an alloy, where two or more metals are combined at the chemical level.

POLYTHEISM Worship of or belief in more than one god.

POPPY CAPSULE Specialized form of base-ring juglet, possibly originating in Cyprus, that resembles the head of a poppy plant, thus giving rise to speculation that they at some point contained opium.

PROTO-AEOLIC Refers to a style of architecture, especially a form of column capitol elaborating on the "palmette" form, used in monumental (royal) buildings of the second part of the Iron Age (Iron 2). It is connected with a style also known from Phoenicia, though it is not clear where the proto-Aeolic style originated.

PYLOS Town on the west coast of the Peloponnese in Greece that was prominent during the time of the spread of Mycenaean culture (c. late second millennium B.C.E.); also the name of the adjoining bay (Bay of Pylos).

PYXIDES Aegean-style ornamental box, often cylindrical in form, common during the Late Bronze Age as imports and among the Philistines, who developed local versions. These are often made of ivory and probably precious woods that do not survive.

QADESH, BATTLE OF Great battle fought between the Egyptians and Hittites in approximately 1275 B.C.E. near Qadesh in a part of northern Canaan. According to "historical" texts, Rameses II led an army of 20,000 men against 37,000 troops of Muwatallis. The outcome of the battle was indecisive, though Rameses II boasted of brilliant victory in accounts of the battle inscribed on temple walls back home in Egypt.

QANAH, NAHAL Site of a Chalcolithic cave tomb containing the earliest known appearance of gold in the southern Levant.

QATIFIAN A style of ceramics, known from the Besor/Gerar area, associated with what is probably a subregional variant of the late Neolithic (Wadi Rabah) and early Chalcolithic periods.

QUERN Stone appliance, often made of basalt, used for rolling grains into flour. It was used in conjunction with a pestle or handstone.

RAMESES II Egyptian New Kingdom pharaoh who ruled for sixty-seven years (c. 1279–1212 B.C.E.). Rameses II was one of Egypt's most accomplished kings, especially in terms of his resumé as a builder, which included temples at Luxor and Karnak, the great rock-cut temple at Abu Simbel, and the Ramesseum Temple at Thebes. He also founded the eastern Delta city of Pr-Ramesse. Shortly after he ascended the throne (regnal year 5, c. 1275 B.C.E.) at the age of twenty, he led Egyptian troops against the Hittites in the battle of Kadesh. According to the Hebrew Bible, and in light of chronological data, some have speculated that Rameses II was the pharaoh of Exodus.

RAMESSEUM Vast memorial temple at Thebes built by Rameses II.

RAMPART *See* Earthen rampart.

REHOBOAM First king of Judah (931–914 B.C.E.), Solomon's son, who held the southern portion of the kingdom while the northern half split off to become Israel.

REPOUSSÉ Technique of hammering sheet metal from the inside, especially to create decorative motifs in relief on jewelry (such as gold earrings) and luxury wares (such as bronze bowls).

RHYTON Specialized horn-shaped drinking vessel, usually used for wine, often incorporating the form of an animal, especially a lion.

RIFT VALLEY Massive rift system running from the Gulf of Aqaba northward into Syria. It features the Lissan/Dead Sea basin and constitutes the northern extension of the bigger African Rift system.

SACRED TREE Religious symbol with variations found throughout the ancient Near East, normally associated with the goddess Asherah. Sometimes the tree is flanked by animals (such as antelopes). This motif is fairly common in the glyptic art of Canaan and Hurru.

SAHARO-ARABIAN ARID DESERT ZONE Arid desert zone receiving less than 125 mm (about 4 in.) and as little as 25 mm (1 in.) of rainfall annually, with limited vegetation.

SARCOPHAGUS Receptacle for a coffin (though sometimes referring to the coffin itself), known particularly in Egypt, often inscribed or decorated. Sarcophagi were usually made of stone, though ceramic examples are found in the southern Levant.

SAUL In the Hebrew Bible, first king of the United Monarchy, ruling 1025–1005 B.C.E. He was portrayed as a flawed ruler who lost a key battle to the Philistines at Gilboa and lost the throne to David.

SCARAB Beetle considered sacred by the Egyptians. Ceramic, stone, or cut gem sculptures in the form of this beetle were used as amulets and often bore an owner's name on the bottom.

SCRIBE Clerk or secretary, keeper of records, possessing skills in literacy, which were rare prior to the Iron Age. Scribes were often employed by the palace and temple.

SEA PEOPLES A variety of peoples from Cyprus and the Aegean, noted for having challenged the Mycenaeans, Hittites, and Egyptians. They destroyed numerous cities in around 1200 B.C.E. and had an impact on virtually all the lands of the eastern Mediterranean.

SECONDARY PRODUCTS REVOLUTION A significant shift in the focus of pastoral production emphasizing secondary products such as dairy goods and wool.

SENNACHERIB Assyrian king who ruled over large parts of the Near East at the end of the eighth and the beginning of the seventh centuries B.C.E. He campaigned into the southern Levant, laying siege to the city of Lachish in approximately 701 B.C.E., and recorded these events on the walls of his palace at Nineveh.

SEREKH Royal insignia bearing a royal name. Serekhs were used by Egypt's earliest kings and were forerunners of the cartouche. A number of Egyptian serekhs, especially that of Narmer, were found at sites representing the first part of the Early Bronze Age (EB1) in southern Canaan.

SHARUHEN Asiatic (Canaanite) city said to have been destroyed by Ahmose as part of the campaign against the Hyksos in the mid-sixteenth century B.C.E.

There is evidence for mass burning and destruction at the site of Tel el-Ajjul, and most scholars now accept this as Sharuhen, though others have identified it as Tel el-Far'ah South.

SHASU Pastoral-nomadic population living in the Canaanite countryside, highlands, and desert fringes during the Late Bronze Age. Known at times to have caused trouble with the settled peoples through raiding, the Shasu may have been ancestral to early Israelite culture.

SHEKEL Basic unit of weight equaling roughly 11.4 grams; also the coins, usually gold or silver, equal in weight to this unit, which were used as the basic unit of currency in ancient Israel.

SHEPHELAH Transitional ecological zone characterized by foothills rising between 100 and 400 m above sea level, lying in a narrow strip between the coastal plain and central highlands zone, with rainfall patterns similar to those of the coastal plain.

SISTRUM Rattle used as a musical instrument, with discs threaded onto bars across a fork. Sistrums were often used by women in religious ceremonies, especially in association with the goddess Hathor.

SOLOMON In the Hebrew Bible, king of the United Monarchy (970–931 B.C.E.), son of David and Bathsheba. Solomon is credited with carrying out monumental building projects in multiple cities, including the capital, Jerusalem (for example, the first Temple), and Hazor.

SPINDLE WHORL Small disc, usually stone or ceramic, used in conjunction with a rod on which fibers can be spun by hand into thread and wound.

STAMP SEAL A seal used to designate ownership and for official transactions. It is impressed into soft clay, not rolled like a cylinder seal.

STELE Upright stone or slab usually bearing an inscription and/or sculpted bas-relief and displayed as a monument or commemorative tablet in a building, or sometimes as a boundary marker. Stelae often functioned as a way to relate stories or convey information, particularly of a political or religious nature, to a broader public, as in a tool of propaganda.

STRATIGRAPHY Major methodological tool of scientific archaeology dealing with the deposition of layers of debris, or strata, over time, and the technique of interpreting this record in an effort to reconstruct the sequence of events at a site. Archaeologists attempt to explain how each layer accumulated, and the relationship of each layer to each other layer, following the basic law of superposition, where the lowest level is the earliest, moving forward in time with each successive layer.

STYLUS Writing implement made out of reed, wood, metal, bone, or other materials and used to inscribe soft clay tablets; also a wedge-shaped stick often associated with cuneiform writing.

SUDANIAN TROPICAL DESERT ZONES Small oases characterized by pockets of relatively dense vegetation, especially reeds and date palms, usually created by natural springs (such as at Jericho).

SUPPILULIUMAS I Hittite king who ruled in about 1380–1340 B.C.E. He is credited with bringing the Hittite Empire back to glory and expanding its territory by attacking the Mittani and taking a number of Syrian city-states as vassals, pushing southward into lands held by Egypt, thus ushering in a period of superpower rivalry.

SYRIAN STYLE Refers to a hybrid style of glyptic art used on cylinder seals combining Mesopotamian and Egyptian motifs with local motifs. The style was popular during the eighteenth century B.C.E.

TABULAR FLINT High-quality, fine-grained flint, chocolate brown in color, used to make "fan-shaped" Chalcolithic and Canaanean blades in the Early Bronze Age. Sources for this material are known in the western Negev and Sinai. The soft white cortex was usually left on the flint but ground down.

TABUN Small oven, often of clay and usually domed, used primarily for baking bread.

TALE OF SINUHE Egyptian text, dating to the Middle Bronze Age (c. twentieth century B.C.E.), recounting the tale of an expatriate who sojourns in Canaan-Syria.

TEL Mound site built up by the accumulation of successive occupation levels over time; *tell* in Arabic.

TELEILAT GHASSUL Archaeological site in Jordan, roughly 10 km (6 mi.) northeast of the Dead Sea, settled at the end of the Neolithic and occupied through the mid-Chalcolithic period (mid-sixth to late fifth millennium B.C.E.). The site served as an important cult center, with a temple complex that featured vivid wall paintings, and is the type-site for the Ghassulian culture.

TEL MIQNE-EKRON Important Philistine site located some 20 km (12.5 mi.) inland from the coast and roughly 40 km (25 mi.) from Jerusalem. The site was occupied for the duration of the Iron Age. Originally excavated as Tel Miqne, it was subsequently identified as the Philistine Pentapolis city of Ekron.

THEOPHORIC An element in a personal name that incorporates the name of a deity.

THUTMOSE III Egyptian pharaoh (c. 1479–1425 B.C.E.) who led a series of brutal military campaigns into Canaan during the Late Bronze Age, following in the tradition of his predecessors, beginning with Ahmose and the "Expulsion of the Hyksos."

TIMNA Mining region with copper-bearing deposits located just north of modern Eilat and the Gulf of Aqaba. It is an offshoot of the Wadi-Aravah system. Timna mines were exploited as early as the Chalcolithic period and the Early Bronze Age but became the site of extensive activity, under Egyptian control, during the Late Bronze Age.

TOGGLE PIN Pin, usually made of copper or bronze, used to fasten together garments; also used as a fashion accessory.

TOURNETTE "Slow wheel" used to throw pottery prior to the invention of the full-blown potter's wheel. It was used to make pot rims as early as the Chalcolithic period.

TRIPARTITE Composed of or divided into three parts. The term often refers to a specific mode in architectural design common in the Levant and elsewhere in the Near East throughout the Bronze and Iron Ages.

TUMULUS Burial structure, often composed of a cist grave covered with mounds of earth and stone.

TUYÉRE Clay nozzle tool placed at the end of blowpipes during metal production in order to direct a blast into a furnace or crucible as a means of raising the temperature.

UGARIT Important ancient city located just inland from the Syrian coast. Settlement at the site, located at present-day Ras Shamra, began during the pre-...ed throughout the second millennium ...and Hittites vied for control of the city. ...guages (Akkadian, Hurrian, Hittite hi-...ound at Ugarit. The city's prominence ...ie Minet el-Beida harbor, and it is men-...extra-biblical texts.

...of Ugarit and its surroundings, written

...gypt, centered along both banks of the ...such as Hierakonpolis, Abydos, and ...d the religious precincts of Luxor and

...e pharaoh as part of his headdress that

...pulation becomes increasingly concen-...ed largely on cities.

...pied throughout the history of ancient Mesopotamia. The term also refers to the period (c. 3500–3000 B.C.E.) when Uruk became the type-site for a culture that spread throughout Mesopotamia and beyond as part of a system of commercial expansion (called the "Uruk Expansion").

V-SHAPED BOWLS Form of shallow, thin-walled, buff-colored bowl made of fine clay, with a red band on the rim, that was popular during the Chalcolithic period.

VIZIER Chief minister of Egypt, second only to the pharaoh, responsible for affairs of state. Upper Egypt and Lower Egypt each had a separate vizier during the New Kingdom.

VOTIVE A gift or token given, offered, or dedicated in fulfillment of a vow.

WADI Dry watercourse, part of a seasonal drainage system, usually characterized by steep walls created by alluvial erosion and denser vegetation than the rest of its surroundings (*nahal* in Hebrew). In more humid times, some wadis may have had standing water for much of the year.

WADI FAYNAN Mining region with copper-bearing deposits, part of the Wadi-Aravah system, exploited for "geenstones" in the Neolithic period; also the scene of mining activity during the Chalcolithic period and Early Bronze Age and again during the Late Bronze and Iron Ages.

WADI RABAH An archaeological horizon or culture of the late Neolithic period characterized by painted pottery similar to that of the Halaf. Residual features of the Wadi Rabah appear in the earliest levels of some Chalcolithic sites.

WARRIOR BURIAL A tradition of burial, exclusive to adult males, often with weapons (for example, iron daggers) and sometimes a horse, though it is not always clear whether the interred individual was actually a warrior or a wealthy person adopting military trappings for style.

WAY OF HORUS Coastal route for trade between Egypt and Asia, with stations, such as Deir el-Balah, along the way.

YARMUKIAN Pottery-bearing culture of the Neolithic period named for the type-site Yarmuk.

YHWH Monotheistic deity of the Israelites in the Hebrew Bible. The tetragrammaton YHWH is often spelled "Yahweh," with the vowels inserted for pronunciation. The name also appears in a number of extra-biblical texts. In some inscriptions, YHWH may be represented as having a consort in Asherah, though interpretation of these is uncertain.

ZOAN *See* Avaris.

Chronology

Note: All dates in the Chronology are B.C.E.

10,500–8500	*Natufian Epi-Paleolithic*
8500–4500	*Neolithic*
8500–7500	Pre-Pottery Neolithic A (PPNA)
7500–6500	Pre-Pottery Neolithic B (PPNB)
6500–6000	Pre-Pottery Neolithic C (PPNC)
6000–5000	Pottery Neolithic A (PNA)
5000–4500	Pottery Neolithic B (PNB)
4500–3500	*Chalcolithic*
4500–4200	Pre-metallic Chalcolithic (Transitional-Ghassulian)
4200–3800	Developed Chalcolithic (Beer-Sheba)
3800–3500	Terminal Chalcolithic
3500–2200	*Early Bronze Age (EBA)*
3500–3050	Early Bronze Age 1 (EB1)
3050–2650	Early Bronze Age 2 (EB2)
2650–2200	Early Bronze Age 3 (EB3)
2200–2000	*Intermediate Bronze Age (EB4)*
2000–1550	*Middle Bronze Age (MBA)*
2000–1800	Middle Bronze Age 1 (MB1)
c. 1800–1550	Middle Bronze Age 2/3 (MB2/3)
1550–1200	*Late Bronze Age (LBA)*
1550–1400	Late Bronze Age 1 (LB1)
c. 1400–1300	Late Bronze Age 2a (LB2a)
c. 1300–1200	Late Bronze Age 2b (LB2b)
1200–586	*Iron Age*
1200–1000	Iron 1
c. 1000–900	Iron 2a
c. 900–700	Iron 2b
c. 700–586	Iron 2c

EGYPTIAN DYNASTIC CHRONOLOGY

c. 1550–1292	*Dynasty 18*
1550–1525	Ahmose Nebpehtire
1525–1504	Amenhotep I Djeserkare
1504–1492	Thutmose I Aakheperkare

1492–1479	Thutmose II Aakheperenre
1479/1473–1458/1457	Hatshepsut Maatkare
1479–1425	Thutmose III Menkheperre
1428–1397	Amenhotep II Aakheperrure
1397–1388	Thutmose IV Menkheperure
1388–1351/1350	Amenhotep III Nebmaatre
1351–1334	Akhenaten (Amenhotep IV) Neferkheperure-waenre
1337–1334	Semenkhkare Ankhkheperure
1333–1323	Tutankhamun Nebkheperure
1323–1319	Ay Kheperkheperure
1319–1292	Horemheb Djeserkheperure-setpenre
c. 1292–1185	*Dynasty 19*
1292–1290	Rameses I Menpehtire
1290–1279/1278	Seti I Menmaatre
1279/1278–1213	Rameses II Usermaatre-setpenre
1213–1203	Merenptah Banenre
1200/1199–1194/1193	Seti II Userkheperure
1203–1200/1199	Amenmesse Menmire-setpenre
1194/1193–1186/1185	Siptah Sekhaenre/Akhenre
1194/1193–1186/1185	Tausret Satre-merenamun
c. 1186–1069	*Dynasty 20*
1186/1185–1183/1182	Setnakht Userkhaure
1183/1182–1152/1151	Rameses III Usermaatre-meryamun
1152/1151–1145/1144	Rameses IV User/Heqamaatre-setpenamun
1145/1144–1142/1140	Rameses V Usermaatre-sekheperenre
1142/1140–1134/1132	Rameses VI Nebmaatre-meryamun
1134/1132–1126/1123	Rameses VII Usermaatre-setpenre-meryamun
1126/1123–1125/1121	Rameses VIII Usermaatre-akhenamun
1125/1121–1107/1103	Rameses IX Neferkare-setpenre
1107/1103–1103/1099	Rameses X Khepermaatre-setpenptah
1103/1099–1070/1069	Rameses XI Menmaatre-setpenptah

THE UNITED MONARCHY

1020–922	*Kingdom of the Israelites*
1020–1000	Saul
1000–961	David
961–922	Solomon

THE DIVIDED KINGDOMS

Dates (B.C.E.) Israel (Northern) | Dates (B.C.E.) Judah (Southern)

922–901	Jeroboam I	922–915	Rehoboam
915–913	Abijah		
913–873	Asa		
901–900	Nadab		

900–877	Baasha |
877–876	Elah | 873–849 Jehoshaphat
876	Zimri Tibni |
876–869	Omri |
869–850	Ahab |
850–849	Ahaziah | 849–843 Jehoram
849–843 Joram (Jehoram) | 843	Ahaziah
843–815 Jehu | 843–837 Athaliah (non-Davidic Queen)	
815–802 Jehoahaz | Joash 837–800	
802–786 Jehoash (Joash) | 800–783	Amaziah
786–746 Jeroboam II | 783–742	Uzziah (Azariah)
746–745 Zachariah | 750–742	Jotham (co-regent)
745 Shallum | 742–735	Jotham (king)
745–737 Menahem |	
737–736 Pekahiah |	
736–732 Pekah | 735–715	Ahaz
732–724 Hoshea |	
721 Fall of Samaria |	
| 715–687	Hezekiah
| 687–642	Manasseh
| 642–640	Amon
| 640–609	Josiah
| 609	Jehoahaz
| 609–598	Jehoikim (Eliakim)
| 598–597	Jehoiachin (Jeconiah)
| 597–587	Zedekiah (Mattaniah)
| 587	Fall of Jerusalem

Kings of Judah

931–914	Rehoboam
914–911	Abijah/Abijam
911–870	Asa
870–846	Jehoshaphat
851–843 (co-regency)	Jehoram/Joram
843–842	Ahaziah
842–836	Athaliah
836–798	Joash/Jehoash
798–769	Amaziah
785–733	Azariah (co-regency)
758–743	Jotham (co-regency)
743–727	Ahaz (co-regency)
727–698	Hezekiah
698–642	Manasseh
642–640	Amon
639–609	Josiah
609–608	Jehoahaz
608–598	Jehoiakim

597	Jehoiachin
597–586	Zedekiah

Kings of Israel

931–909	Jeroboam I
909–908	Nadab
908–885	Baasha
885–884	Ela
884	Zimri
884–873	Omri
884–880	Tibni (rival kingship)
873–852	Ahab
852–851	Ahaziah
851–842	Jehoram/Joram
842–814	Jehu
817–800	Jehoahaz (co-regency)
800–785	Joash/Jehoash
788–747	Jeroboam II (co-regency)
747	Zechariah
747	Shallum
747–737	Menahem
737–735	Pekahiah
735–732	Pekah
732–722	Hoshea

Resources for Further Study

Abu el-Haj, Nadia. 1998. "Translating Truths: Nationalism, the Practice of Archaeology, and the Remaking of Past and Present in Contemporary Jerusalem." *American Ethnologist* 25 (2): 166–188.

Commentary on the role of nationalism in archaeological research design and interpretation in Israel.

Adams, Robert McC., and Theodore Downing. 1972. "Demography and the 'Urban Revolution' in Lowland Mesopotamia." In *Population Growth: Anthropological Implications,* edited by B. Spooner, 60–63. Cambridge, MA: MIT Press.

Discussion of the rise of urbanism in ancient Mesopotamia, with an emphasis on settlement patterns.

———. 1974. "Historic Patterns of Mesopotamian Agriculture." In *Irrigation's Impact on Society,* edited by T. E. Downing and M. Gibson, 1–6. Tucson: University of Arizona Press.

Landmark work on the role of hydraulic farming systems on cultural development.

———. 1978. *Strategies of Maximization, Stability, and Resilience in Mesopotamian Society, Settlement, and Agriculture.* Philadelphia: American Philosophical Society.

Discussion of subsistence strategies and their relation to the development of social complexity in ancient Mesopotamia.

Adams, Russell. 1991. "Archaeological Notes: The Wadi Fidan Project. Jordan, 1989." *Levant* 23: 181–183.

Brief summary of evidence from archaeological research in the Faynan mining region.

———. 1995. "Excavations at Wadi Fidan 4: A Chalcolithic Village Complex in the Copper Ore District of Feinan, Southern Jordan." *Palestine Exploration Quarterly* 127: 8–20.

Summary of archaeological evidence from excavations in the Faynan mining region, especially a small village that may have been used by miners.

Aharoni, Yohanan. 1957. "Problems of the Israelite Conquest in the Light of Archaeological Discoveries." *Antiquity and Survival* 2: 1–150.

Landmark article raising questions about the historicity of the Hebrew Bible's version of the Israelite conquest story in light of archaeological evidence, especially the data from archaeological survey.

———. 1967. "Arad: Its Inscriptions and Temple." *Biblical Archaeologist* 31: 2–32.

Discussion of archaeological evidence from excavations at Iron Age Arad in the northern Negev.

———. 1971. "A 40-Shekel Weight with a Hieratic Numeral." *Bulletin of the American Schools of Oriental Research* 201: 35–36.

Examination of an artifact used as a monetary measure, with a focus on the significance of a number inscribed on it.

———. 1972. "Excavations at Tel Beer-Sheba." *Biblical Archaeologist* 35: 111–127.

Report on the archaeological findings from the excavation of Beer Sheva with an emphasis on the Iron Age.

———. 1974. "The Horned Altar of Beer-Sheba." *Biblical Archaeologist* 37: 2–6.

Analysis of a cultic "four-horned" altar discovered at Beer Sheva and its relation to similar artifacts.

———. 1976. "Nothing Early and Nothing Late: Re-Writing Israel's Conquest." *Biblical Archaeologist* 39: 55–76.

Discussion of archaeological and survey evidence as it relates to the story of the Israelite conquest as described in the Hebrew Bible.

———. 1982. *The Archaeology of the Land of Israel: From the Prehistoric Beginnings to the End of the First Temple Period.* Translated by Anson F. Rainey. Philadelphia: Westminster.

Aharoni, Yohanan, and Ruth Amiran. 1958. "New Scheme for the Subdivision of the Iron Age in Palestine." *Israel Exploration Journal* 8: 171–184.

Description of chronological problems associated with the Iron Age, with a proposed revised subchronology.

Ahituv, Shmuel. 1978. "Economic Factors in the Egyptian Conquest of Canaan." *Israel Exploration Journal* 28: 93–105.

An examination of the reasons behind the apparent disparities in wealth held by some cities of the Late Bronze Age, with a focus on the impact of Egyptian imperial demands.

———. 1993. "Suzerain or Vassal? Notes on the Aramaic Inscription from Tel Dan." *Israel Exploration Journal* 43: 246–247.

Commentary on the so-called Tel Dan inscription, with a focus on the reading of the term *bat dawd* and its interpretation and significance.

Ahlström, Gösta W. 1991. "The Role of Archaeological and Literary Remains in Reconstructing Israel's History." In *The Fabric of History (Journal for the Study of the Old Testament)*, edited by Diana Vikander Edelman, 116–142. Supplement Series 127. Sheffield, England: Sheffield Academic Press.

Discussion about the study of the history of Israel, with a focus on methodological problems associated with the use of archaeological and textual evidence.

————. 1993. *The History of Ancient Palestine from the Palaeolithic Period to Alexander's Conquest*. With a contribution by Gary O. Rollefson. Edited by Diana Edelman. Sheffield, England: Journal for the Study of the Old Testament (JSOT) Press.

A social and political history of ancient Israel based on textual, epigraphic, and archaeological evidence through the time of Alexander the Great.

Albertz, Ranier. 1994. *A History of Israelite Religion in the Old Testament Period*. Vol. 1, *From the Beginnings to the End of the Monarchy*. Louisville, KY: Westminster/John Knox Press.

A reconstruction of the history of both Israelite and Canaanite religious practice in the southern Levant.

Albright, William Foxwell. 1939. "Ceramics and Chronology in the Near East." In *So Live the Works of Men: Seventieth Anniversary Volume Honoring Edgar Lee Hewett*, edited by Donald B. Brand and Fred E. Harvey, 49–63. Albuquerque: University of New Mexico Press.

Landmark study outlining the method of using ceramics to formulate chronologies for the ancient Near East, particularly the southern Levant.

————. 1950. *The Biblical Period*. Pittsburgh: Pittsburgh Press.

Discussion of archaeological evidence available in 1950 and its relation to the "history" as outlined in the Hebrew Bible.

————. 1960. *The Archaeology of Palestine*. Baltimore: Penguin.

Classic overview and summary of the archaeological evidence found in Syro-Palestine prior to the 1960s by the field's leading scholar at the time.

————. 1966. *The Proto-Sinaitic Inscriptions and Their Decipherment*. Cambridge, MA: American Schools of Oriental Research.

Analysis of evidence for the development of the early Canaanite script.

————. 1969. *Archaeology and the Religion of Israel*. Garden City, NY: Anchor.

Discussion of religion in ancient Israel, with an emphasis on archaeological and glyptic evidence and its relation to religion in adjacent areas.

————. 1973. "The Historical Framework of Palestinian Archaeology between 2100 and 1600 B.C." *Bulletin of the American Schools of Oriental Research* 209: 12–18.

Examination of the archaeological evidence in relation to the biblical narrative, with an emphasis on the correspondences between the Middle Bronze Age and the time of the patriarchs.

Allen, James. 2000. *Middle Egyptian: An Introduction to the Language and Culture of Hieroglyphics*. Cambridge: Cambridge University Press.

Overview of the Middle Egyptian language and script, explaining hieroglyphics and the basic elements of the language and its structure.

Alon, David. 1977. "A Chalcolithic Temple at Gilat." *Biblical Archaeologist* 40: 63–65.

Report on the earliest archaeological research at the Chalcolithic site in the northern Negev, with an emphasis on the evidence for cultic practice.

Alon, David, and Thomas E. Levy. 1989. "The Cult Sanctuary at Gilat." *Journal of Mediterranean Archaeology* 2: 163–221.

Discussion of the archaeological evidence from the Chalcolithic shrine, with an extended discussion on the archaeology of cult.

Alt, Albrecht. 1925. *Die Landnahme der Israeliten in Palästina: Territorialgeschichtliche Studien.* Leipzig: Druckerei der Werkgemeinschaft.

Landmark study in early biblical scholarship with a focus on ancient geopolitics.

Amiran, Ruth. 1969. *Ancient Pottery of the Holy Land: From Its Beginnings in the Neolithic Period to the End of the Iron Age.* With the assistance of Purhiya Beck and Uzza Zevulun. Jerusalem: Massada Press.

Landmark study of the ceramics from the southern Levant from late prehistoric periods through the Iron Age.

———. 1970. "Beginnings of Urbanization in Canaan." In *Near Eastern Archaeology in the Twentieth Century: Essays in Honor of Nelson Glueck,* edited by James A. Sanders, 83–100. Garden City, NY: Doubleday.

Discussion of the archaeological evidence from the excavation of Early Bronze Age sites.

———. 1972. "A Cult Stele from Arad." *Israel Exploration Journal* 22: 86–88.

Report on the discovery of the so-called Dumuzi Stele, an inscribed standing stone bearing anthropomorphic imagery.

———. 1984. "Basalt Vessels of the Chalcolithic Period and Early Bronze Age I." *Tel Aviv* 11: 11–19.

A review of ground stone bowls and fenestrated stands from late prehistoric periods.

———. 1989. "Urban Canaan in the Early Bronze II and III Periods: Emergence and Structure." In *Urbanisation de la Palestine à l'âge du Bronze Ancien,* edited by Ruth Amiran and Ram Gophna, 109–116. Oxford: British Archaeological Reports.

Discussion of the emergence of urbanism during the second and third parts of the Early Bronze Age (EB2–3) with an emphasis on specific developments at Arad.

Amiran, Ruth, and Ornit Ilan. 1992. *Arad, eine 5000 Jahre Stadt in der Wüste Negev, Israel.* mit einem Beitrag von Wolfgang Helck. Neumünster: K. Wachholtz.

———. 1993. "Malhata, Tel (Small)." In *The New Encyclopedia of Archaeological Excavations in the Holy Land,* edited by Ephraim Stern, 3: 937–939. New York: Simon and Schuster.

Brief report on the archaeological finds from a satellite settlement of Arad, including a summary of evidence for contact with Egypt.

———. 1996. *Early Arad II.* Jerusalem: Israel Museum.

Description of the archaeological evidence from an Early Bronze Age site.

Amiran, Ruth, and Naomi Porat. 1984. "Basalt Vessels of the Chalcolithic Period and Early Bronze Age I." *Tel Aviv* 11: 11–19.

Examination of evidence for the use of basalt bowls and of how this tradition changes from the Chalcolithic period to the Early Bronze Age.

Amiran, R., U. Puran, Y. Shiloh, R. Brown, Y. Tsafir, and A. Ben-Tor. 1978. *Early Arad: Chalcolithic Settlement and the Early Bronze Age City I. First–Fifth Seasons of Excavations, 1962–1966.* Jerusalem: Israel Exploration Society.

Report on the archaeological discoveries from excavations at Tel Arad, with a discussion of the rise of urbanism and social complexity at the site.

Atzy, Michal, and Ezra Marcus. 1995. "Loom Weight from Tel Nami with a Scarab Seal Impression." *Israel Exploration Journal* 45: 136–149.

Discusses evidence for the import of food, reflecting maritime contact in the eastern Mediterranean during the first quarter of the second millennium B.C.E.

Ash, Paul S. 1995. "Solomon's District List." *Journal for the Study of the Old Testament* 67: 67–86.

———. 1999. *David, Solomon and Egypt: A Reassessment.* Sheffield, England: Sheffield Academic Press.

Discussion of archaeological and textual/historical evidence relating to the time of the United Monarchy.

Athas, George. 2003. *The Tel Dan Inscription: A Reappraisal and a New Interpretation.* London: Sheffield Academic Press.

Thorough discussion of the Tel Dan inscription, including a study of the stele's manufacture and commentary on the script and historical significance of the inscription.

Avigad, Nahman. 1978. "Baruch the Scribe and Yerahme'el the King's Son." *Israel Exploration Journal* 28:52–56.

———. 1983. *Discovering Jerusalem.* Nashville: Thomas Nelson.

Summary of archaeological findings from excavations in the Old City of Jerusalem.

———. 1986. *Hebrew Bullae from the Time of Jeremiah: Remnants of a Burnt Archive.* Jerusalem: Israel Exploration Society.

Examination of inscribed bullae from the Late Iron Age and discussion of the identification of historical figures mentioned in the Hebrew Bible.

Avner, Uzi. 1984. "Ancient Cult Sites in the Negev and Sinai Deserts." *Tel Aviv* 11: 115–131.

Investigation of massebot, "open sancturaries," and cairn lines near settlements of fourth to third millennium B.C.E. reflecting the relationship between religion and desertic elements.

Baird, Douglas, and Graham Philip. 1994. "Preliminary Report on the Third Season of Excavations at Tel es-Shuna North." *Levant* 26: 111–133.

Report on the archaeological research at the late prehistoric site in Jordan.

Balensi, Jacqueline, M. Herrera, and Michal Artzy. 1993. "Tell Abu-Hawam." In *New Encyclopedia of Archaeological Excavations in the Holy Land*, edited by E. Stern, 3: 7–14. New York: Simon and Schuster.

Banning, Edward, and Ilse Köhler-Rollefson. 1992. "Ethnographic Lessons for the Pastoral Past: Camp Locations and Material Remains Near Beidha, Southern Jordan" In *Pastoralism in the Levant: Archaeological Materials in Anthropological Perspectives,* edited by Ofer Bar-Yosef and Anatoly Khazanov, 181–204. Madison, WI: Prehistory Press.

Discussion of pastoral nomadism and transhumant strategies, especially how to study such activity through archaeological remains in conjunction with ethnographic observations.

Bar-Adon, Pesach. 1980. *The Cave of the Treasure.* Jerusalem: Israel Exploration Society.

Book devoted to the archaeological finds from the Nahal Mishmar Cave, especially the spectacular hoard of cast metal goods.

Bar-Yosef, Ofer, and Anna Belfer-Cohen. 1989. "The Origins of Sedentism and Farming Communities in the Levant." *Journal of World Prehistory* 3: 447–498.

Discussion of the origins of settled life and agriculture in the southern Levant by two of Israel's preeminent prehistorians.

Bar-Yosef, Ofer, and Anatoly Khazanov, eds. 1992. *Pastoralism in the Levant: Archaeological Materials in Anthropological Perspectives.* Madison, WI: Prehistory Press.

Edited volume devoted to the study of pastoralism in antiquity, with contributions from some of the field's top researchers.

Baram, Uzi. 2000. "Entangled Objects from the Palestinian Past: Archaeological Perspectives for the Ottoman Period, 1500–1900." In *Historical Archaeology of the Ottoman Empire: Breaking New Ground,* edited by U. Baram and L. Carroll, 137–160. New York: Kluwer/Plenum.

Critique of cultural heritage management in modern-day Israel, with an emphasis on attitudes toward the Ottomon past.

Barnett, Richard D. 1982. *Ancient Ivories in the Middle East.* Qedem 14. Jerusalem: Hebrew University.

Examination of carved ivory objects from the Iron Age, with a discussion about their significance as luxury goods.

Bass, George. 1967. *Cape Gelidonya: A Bronze Age Shipwreck.* Philadelphia: American Philosophical Society.

Report on the archaeological finds from the underwater site off the coast of Turkey, with a discussion of their wider significance with regard to international trade.

Beck, Pirhiya. 1982. "Drawings from Horvat Teiman (Kuntillet 'Ajrud)." *Tel Aviv* 9: 13–15.

Discussion of symbolic imagery from artifacts found at Kuntillet 'Ajrud, with an emphasis on representations of Asherah.

———. 1983. "Bronze Plaque from Hazor." *Israel Exploration Journal* 33: 78–80.

Detailed study of an artifact from Hazor that probably functioned as a ritual item, with a discussion of the object's symbolic meaning.

———. 1985. "Middle Bronze Age IIA Pottery from Aphek, 1972–1984: First Summary." *Tel Aviv* 12: 181–203.

Preliminary report on the ceramic evidence and its chronological implications.

———. 1990. "Note on the 'Schematic Statues' from the Stelae Temple at Hazor." *Tel Aviv* 17: 91–95.

Commentary on the artistic style and iconography of cultic artifacts from Hazor.

———. 1993. "Transjordanian and Levantine Elements in the Iconography of Qitmit." In *Biblical Archaeology Today, 1990, Pre-congress Symposium: Population, Production and Power (Proceedings of the Second International Congress on Biblical Archaeology)*, edited by A. Biran and J. Aviram, 231–236. Jerusalem: Israel Exploration Society.

Discussion of cultic elements at a seventh- to sixth-century site in the northern Negev.

Beck, Pirhiya, and Moshe Kochavi. 1985. "A Dated Assemblage of the Late 13th Century B.C.E. from the Egyptian Residency at Aphek." *Tel Aviv* 12: 29–42.

Examination of evidence from Aphek at the end of the Late Bronze Age, including the names of two governors mentioned in cuneiform tablets.

Becking, Bob. 2002. "The Gods in Whom They Trusted . . . Assyrian Evidence for Iconic Polytheism in Ancient Israel?" In *Only One God? Monotheism in Ancient Israel and the Veneration of the Goddess Asherah,* edited by B. Becking, M. Dijkstra, M. Korpel, and K. Vriezen, 151–163. London: Sheffield Academic Press.

Discussion of religious practice in ancient Israel in light of an Assyrian inscription from Sargon II, arguing that monotheism and aniconism were not widespread until after the fall of the Northern Kingdom.

Beit-Arieh, Israel, and Ram Gophna. 1999. "Egyptian Protodynastic (Late EB I) Site at Tel Ma'ahaz: A Reassessment." *Tel Aviv* 26: 191–207.

Review of archaeological evidence from the site of Tel Ma'ahaz, with a focus on the Egyptian material and its significance.

Ben-Tor, Amnon. 1978. "Cylinder Seals of Third Millennium Palestine." *BASOR Supplemen Series* 22. Cambridge: American School of Oriental Research.

Comprehensive look at seal impressions from the Early Bronze Age, specifically as evidence for contact with Egypt and Syro-Mesopotamia.

———. 1979. "Tell Qiri: A Look at Village Life." *Biblical Archaeologist* 42: 105–113.

Brief report on the archaeological finds from excavations at the Middle Bronze and Iron Ages site in the Jezreel Valley.

———. 1991. "New Light on the Relations between Egypt and Southern Palestine during the Early Bronze Age." *Bulletin of the American Schools of Oriental Research* 281: 3–10.

Discussion of evidence for contact between the two culture areas, with an emphasis on the Egyptian presence at En Besor, especially the assemblage of clay sealings.

———. 1992. *The Archaeology of Ancient Israel.* New Haven, CT: Yale University Press.

Edited volume with a chapter on each of the main periods, from the Neolithic to the Iron Age, contributed by leading scholars in the field.

———. 2000. "Hazor and the Chronology of Northern Israel: A Reply to Israel Finkelstein." *Bulletin of the American Schools of Oriental Research* 317: 9–15.

Commentary on new data from recent excavations at Hazor as they pertain to chronology.

Ben-Tor, Amnon, and Doron Ben-Ami. 1998. "Hazor and the Archaeology of the Tenth Century B.C.E." *Israel Exploration Journal* 48: 1–37.

Discussion of the archaeological evidence from Hazor during the second part of the early Iron Age (Iron 2).

Ben-Tor, Daphna. 1988. "Scarabs Bearing Titles and Private Names of Officials from the Middle Kingdom and the Second Intermediate Period (c. 2050–1550 B.C.E.)." *Israel Museum Journal* 7: 35–46.

Reconstruction of sociopolitical organization based on names and titles found on scarabs.

———. 1994. "The Historical Implications of Middle Kingdom Scarabs Found in Palestine Bearing Private Names and Titles of Officials." *Bulletin of the American Schools of Oriental Research* 294: 7–22.

Study of the names and titles found on scarabs as historical evidence, especially with regard to the Egyptian account of the Hyksos interlude.

———. 1997. "The Relations between Egypt and Palestine in the Middle Kingdom as Reflected by Contemporary Canaanite Scarabs." *Israel Exploration Journal* 47: 162–189.

———. 1999. "Seals and Kings." *Bulletin of the American Schools of Oriental Research* 315: 47–74.

Benenson, Itshak. 1997. "The Sites." In *Highlands of Many Cultures: The Southern Samaria Survey—The Sites,* edited by Israel Finkelstein, Zvi Lederman, and Shlomo Bunimovitz, 131–484. Tel Aviv: Institute of Archaeology of Tel Aviv University.

Benvenisti, Meron. 2000. *Sacred Landscape: The Buried History of the Holy Land since 1948.* Berkeley: University of California Press.

A journalist and former deputy mayor of Jerusalem (1971–1978) examines the problem of cultural heritage, geopolitics, and the impact of the Zionist movement in the modern state of Israel.

Bienkowski, Piotr. 1986. *Jericho in the Late Bronze Age.* Warminster, England: Aris and Phillips.

Bietak, Manfred. 1984. "Problems of Middle Bronze Age Chronology: New Evidence from Egypt." *American Journal of Archaeology* 88: 471–485.

———. 1991. "Egypt and Canaan during the Middle Bronze Age." *Bulletin of the American Schools of Oriental Research* 281: 27–72.

Discussion of relations between the two regions during the Middle Bronze Age, with a specific focus on the Hyksos problem and evidence from Tel el-Daba (Avaris).

Binger, Tilde. 1997. *Asherah: Goddesses in Ugarit, Israel and the Old Testament.* Sheffield, England: Sheffield Academic Press.

Biran, Avraham. 1989. "Collared-Rim Jars and the Settlement of the Tribe of Dan." In *Recent Excavations in Israel: Studies in Iron Age Archaeology,* edited by Seymour Gitin and William G. Dever, 71–96. Annual of the American Schools of Oriental Research, 49. Winona Lake, IN: Eisenbrauns.

Examination of evidence for Israelite material culture during the early Iron Age at Tel Dan.

———. 1994. *Biblical Dan.* Jerusalem: Israel Exploration Society.

Book for a popular audience summarizing some of the key archaeological discoveries at Tel Dan from the Neolithic period through the Iron Age, including one of the earliest arched gates in the region, the Iron Age high place, and the long-standing tradition of metal production.

Biran, Avraham, and Ram Gophna. 1970. "Iron Age Burial Cave at Tel Halif." *Israel Exploration Journal* 20: 151–169.

Report on the archaeological finds from excavation of a burial cave.

Biran, Avraham, David Ilan, and Raphael Greenberg. 1996. *Dan I: A Chronicle of the Excavations, the Pottery Neolithic, the Early Bronze Age and the Middle Bronze Age Tombs.* Jerusalem: Hebrew Union College–Jewish Institute of Religion.

Archaeological site report on the early periods of occupation at Tel Dan.

Biran, Avraham, and Joseph Naveh. 1993. "Aramaic Stele Fragment from Tel Dan." *Israel Exploration Journal* 43: 81–98.

> Discussion of the significance of a stele inscribed in Aramaic with what is widely interpreted as a rare direct reference to the Davidic Dynasty, by an archaeologist and an epigrapher.

———. 1995. "Tel Dan Inscription: A New Fragment." *Israel Exploration Journal* 45: 1–18.

Bird-David, Nurit. 1992. "Beyond 'The Original Affluent Society': A Culturalist Reformulation." *Current Anthropology* 33: 25–47.

Blanton, Richard, Stephen Kowalewski, Gary Feinman, and Laura Finsten. 1993. *Ancient Mesoamerica: A Comparison of Change in Three Regions,* 2d ed. Cambridge: Cambridge University Press.

> Theoretical models for the rise of the state and social complexity in Mesoamerica.

Bloch-Smith, Elizabeth. 1992. *Judahite Burial Practices and Beliefs about the Dead.* Sheffield, England: Sheffield Academic Press.

> Summary of mortuary evidence from the late Iron Age and discussion of social organization and religious beliefs.

Bloch-Smith, Elizabeth, and Beth Alpert-Nakhai. 1999. "A Landscape Comes to Life: The Iron I Period." *Near Eastern Archaeology* 62: 62–92, 101–127.

Borowski, Oded. 1997. "Harvests, Harvesting." In *The Anchor Bible Dictionary.* Bantam Doubleday Dell, CD-ROM.

> Dictionary entry discussing the importance of harvest and community events planned around the agricultural cycle.

Bourke, Stephen J. 1997. "Pre-Classical Pella in Jordan: A Conspectus of Ten Years' Work (1985–1995)." *Palestine Exploration Quarterly* 129: 94–115.

> Summary of important archaeological data from the early periods through the Iron Age.

———. 2002. "The Origins of Social Complexity in the South Jordan Valley: New Evidence from Teleilat Ghassul, Jordan." *Palestine Exploration Quarterly* 134:2–27.

> Review of data from renewed excavations at the Chalcolithic site in Jordan, with an emphasis on evidence for social complexity.

Brandl, Baruch. 1986–1987. "Two Scarabs and a Trapezoidal Seal from Mount Ebal." *Tel Aviv* 13–14: 166–172.

> Examination of archaeological remains found at the controversial Mt. Ebal site. The pieces were dated to the second half of the thirteenth century B.C.E. based on parallels from Egypt, Cyprus, and Transjordan.

Braun, Eliot. 1989. "The Problem of the Apsidal House: New Aspects of Early Bronze

Domestic Architecture in Israel, Jordan and Lebanon." *Palestine Exploration Quarterly* 121: 1–43.

Discussion of trends in architecture as a reflection of social change.

———. 1990. "Basalt Bowls of the EBI Horizon in the Southern Levant." *Paleorient* 16: 87–96.

Study of an artifact type, with a discussion of material sources and methods of manufacture and use.

Brettler, Marc. 1995. *The Creation of History in Ancient Israel*. London/New York: Routledge.

Commentary on questions about the historicity of the Hebrew Bible, exploring alternative ways of reading the biblical texts in conjunction with other literary and archaeological evidence.

Briend, Jacques. 1993. *Actes du IIe Colloque International La Syrie–Palestine a l'Époque Perse: Continuités et Ruptures à la Lumi Ere des Périodes Néo-Assyrienne et Hellénistique. Institut Catholique de Paris, 3–5 Octobre 1991*. Paris: Gabalda.

Broshi, Magen. 1984. "Settlements and Population of Palestine during the Early Bronze Age II-III." *Bulletin of the American Schools of Oriental Research* 253: 41–53.

Reconstruction of Canaanite population and settlement patterns during the Early Bronze Age, based largely on survey data.

———. 1986. "Middle Bronze Age II Palestine: Its Settlements and Population." *Bulletin of the American Schools of Oriental Research* 261: 73–90.

Reconstruction of Canaanite population and settlement patterns during the Middle Bronze Age, based largely on survey data.

Broshi, Magen, and Israel Finkelstein. 1992. "Population of Palestine in Iron Age II." *Bulletin of the American Schools of Oriental Research* 287: 47–60.

Study attempting to reconstruct the population of the southern Levant based on settlement data.

Bunimovitz, Shlomo. 1990. "Problems in the 'Ethnic' Identification of the Philistine Material Culture." *Tel Aviv* 17: 210–222.

Discussion of the various artifact types that have been used as criteria for identifying Philistine material culture.

———. 1992. "Middle Bronze Age Fortifications in Palestine as a Social Phenomenon." *Tel Aviv* 19: 221–234.

Survey of earthen ramparts at Middle Bronze Age sites with a discussion of their possible functions.

———. 1994. "Socio-Political Transformations in the Central Hill Country in the Late

Bronze Iron I Transition." In *From Nomadism to Monarchy: Archaeological and Historical Aspects of Early Israel,* edited by I. Finkelstein and N. Na'aman. Jerusalem: Israel Exploration Society.

> Study of the central hill country population at the end of the second millennium B.C.E., with a focus on nomadic peoples and settlement patterns.

———. 1998–1999. "Egyptian 'Governor's Residency' at Gezer? Another Suggestion." *Tel Aviv* 15–16: 68–76.

> Examination of an Egyptian-style building at Gezer and its possible function.

———. 2003. "On the Edge of Empires—Late Bronze Age (1500–1200 B.C.E.)." In *The Archaeology of the Holy Land,* 3d ed., edited by T. E. Levy, 320–331. New York: Facts on File.

> Summary of archaeological evidence from excavations in the southern Levant pertaining to the MBA.

Bunimovitz, Shlomo, and Avraham Faust. 2001. "Chronological Separation, Geographical Segregation, or Ethnic Demarcation? Ethnography and the Iron Age Low Chronology." *Bulletin of the American Schools of Oriental Research* 322: 1–10.

> Examination of archaeological evidence from the Iron Age in light of ethnographic research on ethnicity, with a discussion of ways to interpret material culture.

Bunimovitz, Shlomo, and Asaf Yasur-Landau. 1996. "Philistine and Israelite Pottery: A Comparative Approach to the Question of Pots and People." *Tel Aviv* 23: 88–101.

> Analysis of ceramic evidence from the Iron Age and how this relates to culture groups.

Burdjewicz, Mariusz. 2002. "New Evidence from the Old Excavations: Iron Age I Pottery from Tell Keisan (Israel)." Paper presented at the Third International Conference on the Archaeology of the Ancient Near East, April 16, Paris.

> Reexamination of archaeological material from the Iron Age Phoenician site near the northern coast.

Burton, Margie, and Thomas E. Levy. 2001. "The Chalcolithic Radiocarbon Record and Its Use in Southern Levantine Archaeology." *Radiocarbon* 43: 1223–1246.

> Summary of radiocarbon data from late Neolithic times to the end of the Chalcolithic period, with a discussion of chronology and the origins of Chalcolithic cultures of the southern Levant.

Callaway, Joseph A. 1978. "New Perspectives on Early Bronze III in Canaan." In *Archaeology in the Levant: Essays for Kathleen Kenyon,* edited by Roger Moorey and Peter Parr. Warminster, England: Aris and Phillips.

———. 1980. *The Early Bronze Age Citadel and Lower City at Ai (et-Tell).* With the assistance of Kermit Schoonover and William W. Ellinger III. Cambridge, MA: American Schools of Oriental Research.

Report of the archaeological findings from excavations of Early Bronze Age levels at Ai.

———. 1985. "New Perspective on the Hill Country Settlement of Canaan in Iron Age I." Occasional publication no. 11. London: Institute of Archaeology, 31–49.

Cameron, Dorothy O. 1981. *The Ghassulian Wall Paintings.* London: Kenyon-Deane.

Discussion and interpretation of the famous wall paintings in the Chalcolithic shrine at Ghassul.

Carniero, Robert. 1970. "A Theory of the Origin of the State." *Science* 169: 733–738.

Landmark article outlining a model where "environmental circumscription" and competition for land are factors in the rise of state structures.

———. 1981. "The Chiefdom as a Precursor to the State." In *The Transition to Statehood in the New World,* edited by G. Jones and R. Krautz, 37–79. Cambridge: Cambridge University Press.

Description of the ethnographic evidence for competition over land in South American chiefdoms as a model for explaining the rise of the state.

Carter, Charles, and Carol Meyers, eds. 1996. *Community, Identity, and Ideology: Social Science Approaches to the Hebrew Bible.* Winona Lake, IN: Eisenbrauns.

Chapman, Rupert. 1990. "Pioneers of Biblical Archaeology." In *Archaeology and the Bible,* edited by J. Tubb and R. Chapman, 9–37. London: British Museum Publications.

Examination of the history of archaeological discovery in the southern Levant, with a focus on the early years.

Clamer, Christa, and Benjamin Sass. 1977. "Middle Bronze I." In *Prehistoric Investigations in Gebel Meghara, Northern Sinai,* edited by O. Bar-Yosef and J. Philips, 245–254. Jerusalem: Institute of Archaeology, Hebrew University.

Discussion of evidence from the Intermediate Bronze Age (Middle Bronze Age 1) discovered in the Sinai.

Clarke, Edward D. 1817. *Travels in the Holy Land.* Philadelphia: David Brown.

Classic "traveler's log" recounting the Cambridge scholar's expedition to the southern Levant in an effort to relate tangible features on the landscape to those described in the Hebrew Bible.

Cohen, Rudolph. 1992. "Nomadic or Seminomadic Middle Bronze Age I Settlements in the Central Negev." In *Pastoralism in the Levant: Archaeological Materials in Anthropological Perspectives,* edited by Ofer Bar-Yosef and Anatoly Khazanov, 105–131. Madison, WI: Prehistory Press.

Discussion of the evidence for mobile populations of the Negev.

Cohen, Rudolph, and William G. Dever. 1978. "Preliminary Report of the Pilot Season of the 'Central Negev Highlands Project.'" *Bulletin of the American Schools of Oriental Research* 232: 29–45.

Report on the archaeological discoveries from research in the Negev.

Commenge, Catherine, David Alon, Thomas E. Levy, and Eric Kansa. Forthcoming. "Gilat Ceramics: Cognitive Dimensions of Pottery Production." In *Archaeology, Anthropology and Cult: The Sanctuary at Gilat (Israel)*, edited by D. Alon and T. E. Levy. London: Cassell.

Examination of the ceramics from Gilat, especially from the earliest levels, where the material displays elements from the Late Neolithic.

Commenge-Pellerin, Catherine. 1987. *La Poterie d'Abou Matar et de l'Ouadi Zoumeili (Beershéva) au IVe millénaire avant 1Ère Chretienne*. Paris: Association Paleorient.

Description of ceramics from two Chalcolithic settlements in the northern Negev.

———. 1990. *La Poterie de Safadi (Beershéva) au IVe millénaire avant lÈre Chretienne*. Paris: Association Paleorient.

Report on the ceramics from Beer es-Safadi, a Chalcolithic site in the northern Negev.

Costin, Cathy. 1991. "Craft Specialization: Issues in Defining, Documenting, and Exploring the Organization of Production." In *Archaeological Method and Theory*, edited by M. Schiffer, 3: 1–56. Tucson: University Of Arizona Press.

Landmark article outlining the forms of archaeological evidence that correlate with different levels of craft production activities.

Cross, Frank M. 1954. "The Evolution of the Proto-Canaanite Alphabet." *Bulletin of the American Schools of Oriental Research* 134: 15–24.

———. 1967. "The Origin and Evolution of the Early Alphabet." *Eretz Israel* 8: 8–24.

———. 1979a. "Early Alphabetic Scripts." In *Symposia Celebrating the 75th Anniversary of the Founding of the American Schools of Oriental Research*, edited by F. Cross, 105–111. Cambridge, MA: American Schools of Oriental Research.

———. 1979b. "Two Offering Dishes with Phoenician Inscriptions from the Sanctuary of 'Arad." *Bulletin of the American Schools of Oriental Research* 235: 75–78.

———. 1980. "Newly Found Inscriptions of Old Canaanite and Early Phoenician Scripts." *Bulletin of the American Schools of Oriental Research* 238: 1–20.

Series of articles discussing the earliest examples of the use of alphabetic scripts during the late Middle Bronze Age and how they changed over the succeeding centuries.

Cross, Frank M., and J. T. Milik. 1956. "A Typological Study of the El Khadr Javelin- and Arrow-Heads." *Annual of the Department of Antiquities of Jordan* 3: 15–23.

Discussion of metal artifacts bearing some of the earliest inscriptions using the Canaanite script.

Crowfoot, John Winter, and Grace M. Crowfoot. 1938. *Early Ivories from Samaria.* London: Palestine Exploration Fund.

Report and analysis of the ivory artifacts found during excavations at Samaria.

Crowfoot, John Winter, Joan Crowfoot, and Kathleen Kenyon. 1957: *The Objects from Samaria.* London: Palestine Exploration Fund.

Report on the archaeological finds from excavations at Samaria.

Crowfoot, Joan, Kathleen Kenyon, and Eliezar Sukenik. 1942. *The Buildings at Samaria.* London: Palestine Exploration Fund.

Report on the architectural remains from excavations at Samaria.

Danin, Avinoam. 2003. "Man and the Natural Environment." In *The Archaeology of Society in the Holy Land,* 3d ed., edited by T. E. Levy, 24–37. New York: Facts on File.

Discussion of ecology and land use in the southern Levant.

Davey, Christopher J. 1980. "Temples of the Levant and the Buildings of Solomon." *Tyndale Bulletin* 31: 107–146.

Discussion of temple architecture in light of the Hebrew Bible's descriptions of King Solomon's building projects.

Davies, Phillip. 1992. *In Search of Ancient Israel.* Sheffield, England: Journal for the Study of the Old Testament (JSOT) Press.

A biblical scholar discusses problems associated with the relationship between archaeology, history, and the biblical tradition.

Dayton, John E. 1971. "The Problem of Tin in the Ancient World." *World Archaeology* 3: 49–70.

A pioneer work focused on the search for tin, one of the most valuable commodities in the ancient Near East.

Demsky, Aaron. 1997. "The Name of the Goddess of Ekron: A New Reading." *Journal of the Ancient Near Eastern Society* 25: 1–5.

Interpretation of an inscription from the Philistine city of Tel Miqne–Ekron.

Dessel, J. P. 1991. "Ceramic Production and Social Complexity in Fourth Millennium Canaan: A Case Study from Halif Terrace." Ph.D. dissertation, University of Arizona.

Dissertation based on the study of ceramics from the Early Bronze Age settlement at Tel Halif, with a discussion of typology and production techniques.

Dever, William G. 1980. "Archaeological Method in Israel: A Continuing Revolution." *Biblical Archaeology* 43: 40–48.

Landmark study discussing methodology in Israeli archaeology in light of the so-called New Archaeology.

———. 1981a. "Cave G26 at Jebel Qa'aqir: A Domestic Assemblage of Middle Bronze I." *Eretz-Israel* 15: 22–32.

Report on the archaeological discoveries from an Intermediate Bronze Age (Middle Bronze Age 1) cave site.

———. 1981b. "The Impact of the 'New Archaeology' on Syro-Palestinian Archaeology." *Bulletin of the American Schools of Oriental Research* 242: 15–29.

Comparison of Biblical Archaeology with research elsewhere in the field in the context of archaeological method and theory.

———. 1982. "Recent Archaeological Confirmation for the Cult of Asherah in Ancient Israel." *Hebrew Studies* 23: 37–43.

Discussion of the archaeological finds from Kuntillet Ashrud, with a focus on the evidence for worship of Asherah.

———. 1984a. "Asherah, Consort of Yahweh? New Evidence from Kuntillet Ajrud." *Bulletin of the American Schools of Oriental Research* 255: 21–37.

———. 1984b. "Gezer Revisited: New Excavations of the Solomonic and Assyrian Period Defenses." *Biblical Archaeologist* 47: 206–218.

———. 1984c. "Yigael Yadin (1917–1984): In Memoriam." *Bulletin of the American Schools of Oriental Research* 256: 3–5.

———. 1985a. "Relations between Syria-Palestine and Egypt in the 'Hyksos' Period." *Occasional Publication—Institute of Archaeology* 11: 69–87.

———. 1985b. "Solomonic and Assyrian Period 'Palaces' at Gezer." *Israel Exploration Journal* 35: 217–230.

———. 1986. "Late Bronze Age and Solomonic Defenses at Gezer: New Evidence." *Bulletin of the American Schools of Oriental Research* 262: 9–34.

———. 1987. "The Middle Bronze Age: The Zenith of the Urban Canaanite Era." *Biblical Archaeologist* 50: 148–177.

———. 1989a. "Archaeology in Israel Today: A Summation and Critique." In *Recent Excavations in Israel: Studies in Iron Age Archaeology,* edited by Seymour Gitin and William G. Dever, 143–152. Annual of the American Schools of Oriental Research, 49. Winona Lake, IN: Eisenbrauns.

———. 1989b. "Collapse of the Urban Early Bronze Age in Palestine: Toward a Systemic Analysis." In *Urbanisation de la Palestine à l'âge du Bronze Ancien,* edited by Ruth Amiran and Ram Gophna, 255–246. Oxford: British Archaeological Reports.

———. 1990a. "Archaeology and Israelite Origins." *Bulletin of the American Schools of Oriental Research* 279: 89–95.

————. 1990b. "'Hyksos,' Egyptian Destructions, and the End of the Palestinian Middle Bronze Age." *Levant* 22: 75–81.

————. 1990c. "Of Myths and Methods." *Bulletin of the American Schools of Oriental Research* 277–278: 121–130.

————. 1991. "Tell el-Dab'a and Levantine Middle Bronze Age Chronology: A Rejoinder to Manfred Bietak." *Bulletin of the American Schools of Oriental Research* 281: 73–79.

————. 1992a. "The Chronology of Syria-Palestine in the Second Millennium B.C.E.: A Review of Current Issues." *Bulletin of the American Schools of Oriental Research* 288: 1–25.

Discussion of archaeological evidence from the Middle and Late Bronze Ages, with a special focus on diagnostic chronological indicators.

————. 1992b. "Pastoralism and the End of the Urban Early Bronze Age in Palestine." In *Pastoralism in the Levant: Archaeological Materials in Anthropological Perspectives,* edited by Ofer Bar-Yosef and Anatoly Khazanov, 83–92. Madison, WI: Prehistory Press.

Examination of the evidence for a trend away from urbanism toward increased pastoral nomadism at the end of the Early Bronze Age.

————. 1993. "Further Evidence on the Date of the Outer Wall at Gezer." *Bulletin of the American Schools of Oriental Research* 289: 33–54.

Analysis of specific architectural features at Gezer and their dating.

————. 1995a. "The Death of a Discipline." *Biblical Archaeology Review* (September): 54–58.

Polemical article challenging the field to reconsider its theoretical underpinnings.

————. 1995b. "Orienting the Study of Trade in Near Eastern Archaeology." In *Recent Excavations in Israel: A View to the West,* edited by S. Gitin, 41–60. Dubuque, IA: Kendall Hunt.

————. 1995c. "'Will the Real Israel Please Stand Up?': Archaeology and Israelite Historiography—Part I." *Bulletin of the American Schools of Oriental Research* 297: 61–80.

A reconsideration of aspects of material culture traditionally associated with the Israelite people.

————. 1996. *Preliminary Excavation Reports—Sardis, Idalion, and Tell el-Handaquq North.* Cambridge, MA: American Schools of Oriental Research.

————. 1997. "Is There Any Archaeological Evidence for the Exodus?" In *Exodus: The Egyptian Evidence,* edited by Ernest S. Frerichs and Leonard H. Lesko, 67–86. Winona Lake, IN: Eisenbrauns.

————. 1998. "What Did the Biblical Writers Know, and When Did They Know It?" In *Hesed ve-Emet: Studies in Honor of Ernest S. Frerichs,* edited by J. Magness and S. Gitin, 241–257. Atlanta: Scholars Press.

Discussion of the authorship of the Hebrew Bible and its chronological relation to archaeological evidence.

———. 1999. "Histories and Nonhistories of Ancient Israel." *Bulletin of the American Schools of Oriental Research* 316: 89–105.

———. 2001. "Excavating the Hebrew Bible, or Bury It Again?" *Bulletin of the American Schools of Oriental Research* 322: 67–77.

———. 2003a. "Social Structure in the Early Bronze IV Period in Palestine." In *The Archaeology of Society in the Holy Land*, 3d ed., edited by T. E. Levy, 282–296. New York: Facts on File.

———. 2003b. "Social Structure in Palestine in the Iron II Period on the Eve of Destruction." In *The Archaeology of Society in the Holy Land*, 3d ed., edited by T. E. Levy. New York: Facts on File.

Dever, William G., and Suzanne Richard. 1977. "A Reevaluation of Tell Beit Mirsim Stratum J." *Bulletin of the American Schools of Oriental Research* 226: 1–14.

Explanation of archaeological evidence from the site's early occupation.

Dever, William G., and Miriam Tadmor. 1976. "A Copper Hoard of the Middle Bronze Age I." *Israel Exploration Journal* 26: 163–169.

Report on the artifacts from a rare Intermediate Bronze Age (Middle Bronze Age 1) copper hoard.

Devries, Lamoine F. 1987. "Cult Stands: A Bewildering Variety of Shapes and Sizes." *Biblical Archaeology Review* 13: 26–37.

Dijkstra, Meindert. 2002a. "El, the God of Israel—Israel, the People of YHWH: On the Origins of Ancient Israelite Yahwism." In *Only One God? Monotheism in Ancient Israel and the Veneration of the Goddess Asherah*, edited by B. Becking, M. Dijkstra, M. Korpel, and K. Vriezen, 81–126. London: Sheffield Academic Press.

A study on the evolution of "Yahwism" as the worship of one god exclusively, with a focus on the role of the Canaanite god El.

———. 2002b. "I Have Blessed You by YHWH of Samaria and His Asherah: Texts with Religious Elements from the Soil Archive of Ancient Israel." In *Only One God? Monotheism in Ancient Israel and the Veneration of the Goddess Asherah*, edited by B. Becking, M. Dijkstra, M. Korpel, and K. Vriezen, 17–44. London: Sheffield Academic Press.

Discussion of texts found in ancient Israel, mainly from the seventh to third centuries B.C.E., that indicate that the goddess Asherah continued to be associated with the cult of YHWH later than previously thought.

———. 2002c. "Women and Religion in the Old Testament." In *Only One God? Monotheism in Ancient Israel and the Veneration of the Goddess Asherah*, edited by B. Becking, M. Dijkstra, M. Korpel, and K. Vriezen, 164–188. London: Sheffield Academic Press.

Examination of the role of women in early Israelite religion.

Dikaios, Porphyrios. 1969. *Enkomi Excavations, 1948–1959 III.* Mainz am Rhein: Ph. von Zabern.

Report on the archaeological finds from Enkomi in western Cyprus.

Donner, Herbert. 1959. "Art und Herkunft des Amtes der Königinmutter im Alten Testament." In *Fs. Johannes Friedrich,* edited by R. von Kienle, A. Moortgat, H. Otten, E. von Schuler, and W. Zaumsell, 111–119. Heidelberg: Universitätsverlag.

———. 1967. "Review of Albright 1966." *Journal of Semitic Studies* 12: 272–281.

Dothan, Moshe. 1965. "The Fortress at Kadesh-Barnea." *Israel Exploration Journal* 15: 134–151.

Report on archaeological discoveries during excavations at the site of Kadesh-Barnea near the Wilderness of Zin, with a discussion of its role as an Israelite encampment in the Hebrew Bible.

———. 1978. *Deir el-Balah.* Qedem 10. Jerusalem: Hebrew University.

Monograph on archaeological findings from excavations at the coastal site of Deir el-Balah, including a discussion of evidence for contact with Egypt.

———. 1981. "Sanctuaries along the Coast of Canaan in the MB Period: Nahariyah." In *Temples and High Places in Biblical Times: Proceedings of the Colloquium in Honor of the Centennial of Hebrew Union College–Jewish Institute of Religion, Jerusalem, 14–16 March 1977,* edited by Avraham Biran, 74–81. Jerusalem: Nelson Glueck School of Biblical Archaeology of Hebrew Union College–Jewish Institute of Religion.

Discussion of the evidence for cultic architecture at the coastal city of Nahariyah.

Dothan, Moshe, and Yehoshuah Porat. 1993. *Ashdod V.* 'Atiqot, 23. Jerusalem: Israel Antiquities Authority.

Report on archaeological findings from excavations at the Philistine city of Ashdod.

Dothan, Trude. 1978. *Deir el-Balah.* Qedem 10. Jerusalem: Hebrew University.

Archaeological site report for a city that served as an outpost along the coastal trade routes used by Egyptians.

———. 1995. "Tel Miqne–Ekron: The Aegean Affinities of the Sea Peoples' (Philistines') Settlement in Canaan in the Iron 1." In *Recent Excavations Israel: A View to the West,* edited by S. Gitin, 41–60. Dubuque, IA: Kendall Hunt.

Discussion of the cultural parallels between Philistines who settled on the Levantine coast and those of their place of probable origin in the Aegean, with particular focus on evidence for religious practice.

———. 2002a. "Bronze and Iron Objects with Cultic Connotations from Philistine Temple Building 350 at Ekron." *Israel Exploration Journal* 52: 1–25.

Analysis of the evidence for cultic activity at Tel Miqne–Ekron.

———. 2002b. "Reflections on the Initial Phase of Philistine Settlement." In *The Sea Peoples and Their World: A Reassessment*, edited by Eliezer D. Oren and Donald W. Jones, 145–158. University Museum Monograph, 108. Philadelphia: Museum of Archaeology and Anthropology, University of Pennsylvania.

Examination of evidence from the earliest waves of Philistine settlement on the coastal plain.

Dothan, Trude, and Moshe Dothan. 1992. *People of the Sea: In Search for the Philistines.* New York: Macmillan.

Book on the Philistines written for a popular audience by Israeli archaeology's best-known couple, who interweave a history of archaeological discovery with current evidence regarding the origins and development of Philistine culture on the coastal plain.

Dothan, Trude, and Seymour Gitin. 1990. "Ekron of the Philistines." *Biblical Archaeology Review* 16: 20–36.

Doumani, Beshara. 1995. *Rediscovering Palestine: Merchants and Peasants in Jabal Nablus, 1700–1900.* Los Angeles: University of California Press.

Dreyer, Gunter. 1992. "Recent Discoveries at Abydos Cemetery U." In *The Nile Delta in Transition: 4th–3rd Millennium B.C.*, edited by E. van den Brink, 293–299. Tel Aviv: Edwin C. M. van den Brink.

Report on archaeological findings from the royal cemetery of the earliest Egyptian rulers.

Dunayevsky, Imanuel, and Aharon Kempinski. 1973. "The Megiddo Temples." *Zeitschrift des Deutschen Palästina Verieins* 89: 161–187.

Review of archaeological findings from the cultic area at Megiddo.

Edelman, Diana. 1985. "The 'Ashurites' of Eshbaal's State (2 Sam. 2.9)." *Palestine Exploration Quarterly* 175: 85–91.

Eisenberg, Emmanuel. 1985. "A Burial Cave of the Early Bronze Age IV (MB I) Near 'Enan." *Átiqot* 17: 59–74.

Report on the archaeological findings from a burial cave from the Intermediate Bronze Age (Early Bronze Age 4–Middle Bronze Age 1).

———. 1998. "Khirbet et-Tuwal: Salvage Excavations at an EB1B Settlement in the Beth She'an Valley." *Átiqot* 35: 1–7.

Description of archaeological findings from an Early Bronze Age site.

Epstein, Claire. 1993. "Golan, Chalcolithic Period to the Iron Age." In *New Encyclopedia of Archaeological Research*, 2: 529–534. New York: Simon and Schuster.

————. 1998. *The Chalcolithic Culture of the Golan*. Jerusalem: Israel Antiquities Authority.

The culmination of years of research on a regional variant of Chalcolithic culture observed in the Golan region, combining previously unpublished data with a summary of the extant data.

Esse, Douglas. 1989. "Secondary State Formation and Collapse in Early Bronze Age Palestine." In *L'Urbanization du Palestine à la Âge du Bronze Ancien,* edited by P. de Miroschedji, 81–96. Oxford: British Archaeological Reports.

Discussion of the evolution of social complexity as a secondary development with the rise of states in adjacent areas.

Evenari, Michael. 1961. "Ancient Agriculture in the Negev." *Science* 133: 979–996.

Study of agro-technological innovations used for farming in the arid zone in antiquity.

Falconer, Steven E. 1987. "Village Pottery Production and Exchange: A Jordan Valley Perspective." In *Studies in the History and Archaeology of Jordan,* edited by A. Hadidi, 251–259. Amman, Jordan: Department of Antiquities.

Faltings, Dina. 2002. "An Early Egyptian City at Tell es-Sakan near Gaza." Paper presented at the Third International Conference on the Archaeology of the Ancient Near East, April 16, Paris.

Report on the archaeological findings from an Egyptian coastal city of the Early Bronze Age.

Faust, Avraham. 1999a. "Differences in Family Structure between Cities and Villages in Iron Age II." *Tel Aviv* 26: 233–252.

Study of family structure during the Iron Age comparing evidence from urban and rural communities.

————. 1999b. "Socioeconomic Stratification in an Israelite City: Hazor VI as a Test Case." *Levant* 31: 179–190.

Examination of the evidence for social structure at Iron Age Hazor.

————. 2000a. "Ethnic Complexity in Northern Israel during Iron Age II." *Palestine Exploration Quarterly* 132: 2–27.

Study on the evidence for ethnicity in the Northern Kingdom during the Iron Age, with a focus on the question of Israelite identity.

————. 2000b. "The Rural Community in Ancient Israel during Iron Age II." *Bulletin of the American Schools of Oriental Research* 317: 17–39.

A refreshing perspective on Iron Age 2 examining evidence from outside the large urban centers to reconstruct rural life.

————. 2001. "Doorway Orientation, Settlement Planning and Cosmology in Ancient Israel during Iron Age II." *Oxford Journal of Archaeology* 20: 129–155.

Examination of house design and town planning during the time of the rise of the state.

————. 2002a. "Abandonment, Urbanization, Resettlement and the Formation of the Israelite State." *Near Eastern Archaeology.*

————. 2002b. "Burnished Pottery and Gender Hierarchy in Iron Age Israelite Society." *Journal of Mediterranean Archaeology* 15: 53–73.

Discussion of evidence for domestic activities (such as food preparation) and the sexual division of labor.

————. 2003a. "Judah in the Sixth Century B.C.E.: A Rural Perspective." *Palestine Exploration Quarterly* 135: 37–53.

————. 2003b. "Residential Patterns in the Ancient Israelite City." *Levant* 35: 123–138.

Examination of evidence for social organization during the second part of the Iron Age (Iron 2).

Feldman Marian. 2002. "Visual Hybridity and International Kingship in the Late Bronze Age." Paper presented at the Third International Conference on the Archaeology of the Ancient Near East, April 18, Paris.

Review of evidence for iconography related to kingship, arguing that a common hybrid style may have been shared in part by various peoples throughout the broader region.

Finkelstein, Israel. 1985. "A Group of Metal Objects from Shiloh." *Israel Museum Journal:* 17–26.

Report on a cache of metal artifacts from Shiloh.

————. 1986. *Izbet Sartah: An Early Iron Age Site near Rosh Ha'ayin, Israel.* Oxford, England: British Archaeological Reports.

Summary of the archaeological findings from excavations at the Izbet Sartah site, with a focus on the question of highland settlement at the beginning of the Iron Age.

————. 1988. "Arabian Trade and Socio-Political Conditions in the Negev in the Twelfth–Eleventh Centuries B.C.E." *Journal of Near Eastern Studies* 47: 241–252.

Discussion of trade routes and contact between Arabia and the southern Levant in the early Iron Age.

————. 1989. "Further Observations on the Socio-Demographic Structure of the Intermediate Bronze Age." *Levant* 21: 129–140.

Review of evidence for settlement patterns during the Intermediate Bronze Age, with a focus on pastoral nomadism.

————. 1990a. "Excavations at Khirbet ed-Dawwara: An Iron Age Site Northeast of Jerusalem." *Tel Aviv* 17: 163–208.

Report on the archaeological findings from excavations at the highland site.

———. 1990b. "Processes of Sedentarization and Nomadization in the History of Sinai and the Negev." *Bulletin of the American Schools of Oriental Research* 279: 67–88.

Discussion of settlement patterns and ecology in the arid zones, populating a cyclical model of shifts between urbanism and "ruralism."

———. 1991. "Central Hill Country in the Intermediate Bronze Age." *Israel Exploration Journal* 41: 19–45.

Summary of archaeological evidence and survey data from the central highlands during the Intermediate Bronze Age.

———. 1992a. "Middle Bronze Age 'Fortifications': A Reflection of Social Organization and Political Formations." *Tel Aviv* 19: 201–220.

Review of evidence for earthen ramparts, with commentary on their possible function, especially whether they served as functional fortifications or prestige architecture.

———. 1992b. "Pastoralism in the Highlands of Canaan in the Third and Second Millennia B.C.E." In *Pastoralism in the Levant: Archaeological Materials in Anthropological Perspectives*, edited by Ofer Bar-Yosef and Anatoly Khazanov, 133–142. Madison, WI: Prehistory Press.

Discussion of the evidence for the shifting emphasis on transhumance over time.

———. 1993. "Settlement, Demographic, and Economic Patterns in the Highlands of Palestine in the Chalcolithic and Early Bronze Periods and the Beginning of Urbanism." *Bulletin of the American Schools of Oriental Research* 289: 1–22.

A look at the rise of urbanism during the Early Bronze Age, with a focus on settlement patterns and ecology.

———. 1995. *Living on the Fringe: The Archaeology and History of the Negev, Sinai and Neighbouring Regions in the Bronze and Iron Ages.* Sheffield, England: Sheffield Academic Press.

Review of archaeological evidence from the arid zones, with a focus on cultural ecology.

———. 1996a. "Ethnicity and the Origin of Iron I Settlers in the Highlands of Canaan: Can the Real Israel Stand Up? *Biblical Archaeologist* 59: 198–212.

Reexamination of what is traditionally accepted as evidence for Israelite material culture during the early phase of settlement.

———. 1996b. "The Stratigraphy and Chronology of Megiddo and Beth-Shan in the 11th–12th Centuries B.C.E." *Tel Aviv* 23: 170–184.

Report on the archaeological evidence for settlement in Israel's inland valleys.

———. 1997. "Ethno-Historical Background: Land Use and Demography in Recent Generations." In *Highlands of Many Cultures: The Southern Samaria Survey—The Sites,* edited by Israel Finkelstein, Zvi Lederman, and Shlomo Bunimovitz, 109–130. Tel Aviv: Institute of Archaeology of Tel Aviv University.

Review of ethno-historical evidence for the purpose of understanding the cultural ecology of the past.

————. 1998. "Bible Archaeology or Archaeology of Palestine in the Iron Age? A Rejoinder." *Levant* 30: 167–174.

Commentary on the problem of the Hebrew Bible and its relation to archaeology in the southern Levant.

————. 1999. "State Formation in Israel and Judah: A Contrast in Context, a Contrast in Trajectory." *Near Eastern Archaeology* 62: 35–52.

Discussion of the rise of the state in both the Northern and Southern Kingdoms, arguing that Judah was not a state and Jerusalem was not the capital prior to the eighth century B.C.E.

————. 2001. "The Rise of Jerusalem and Judah: The Missing Link." *Levant* 33: 105–115.

An essay arguing that the establishment of Jerusalem as the capital of Judah did not occur until later than traditionally thought.

————. 2003. "The Great Transformation: The Conquest of the Highlands Frontiers and the Rise of the Territorial States." In *The Archaeology of the Holy Land,* 3d ed., edited by T. E. Levy, 349–367. New York: Facts on File.

Finkelstein, Israel, Shlomo Bunimovitz, and Zvi Lederman. 1993. *Shiloh: The Archaeology of a Biblical Site.* Tel Aviv: Tel Aviv University.

Book devoted to the study of Shiloh, with primary evidence and commentary.

Finkelstein, Israel, and Ram Gophna. 1993. "Settlement, Demographic, and Economic Patterns in the Highlands of Palestine in the Chalcolithic and Early Bronze Periods and the Beginning of Urbanism." *Bulletin of the American Schools of Oriental Research* 289: 1–22.

An attempt to use evidence from survey research to reconstruct settlement patterns and the process of urban development in the highlands in later prehistory.

Finkelstein, Israel, and Zvi Lederman. 1997. "Introduction." In *Highlands of Many Cultures: The Southern Samaria Survey—The Sites,* edited by Israel Finkelstein, Zvi Lederman, and Shlomo Bunimovitz, 1–7. Tel Aviv: Institute of Archaeology of Tel Aviv University.

Discussion of settlement survey methodology as applied to the study of settlement patterns in the past.

Finkelstein, Israel, and Neil Asher Silberman. 2001. *The Bible Unearthed: Archaeology's New Vision of Ancient Israel and the Origin of Its Sacred Texts.* New York: Free Press.

A consideration of the problem of archaeological evidence in relation to biblical narrative and how the two do and do not fit, by an archaeologist and a historian of the discipline.

Fischer, Peter. 2002. "Tel el-Ajjul: Stratigraphy and Imports. Results from the New Excavations." Unpublished paper.

Report on the archaeological finds from excavations at the coastal city of Tel el-Ajjul.

Flanagan, James W. 1988. *David's Social Drama: A Hologram of Israel's Early Iron Age.* Sheffield, England: Almond Press.

Discussion of the time of the United Monarchy in terms of social evolution.

Forstner-Müller, Irene. 2002. "House or Temple—A Typical Egyptian Architectural Feature in a Sacral Area at Tell el-Dab'a." Paper presented at the Third International Conference on the Archaeology of the Ancient Near East, April 16, Paris.

Examination of architectural features found at Avaris and interpretations of them.

Fowler, Mervyn D. 1985. "Excavated Incense Burners: A Case for Identifying a Site as Sacred." *Palestine Exploration Quarterly* 117: 25–29.

Commentary on evidence for cultic paraphernalia and religious practices.

Frankenstein, Susan. 1979. "The Phoenicians in the Far West: A Function of Neo-Assyrian Imperialism." In *Power and Propaganda,* edited by M. Larsen, 263–294. Copenhagen: Akademisk.

Analysis of the role of seafaring Phoenicians in the expansion of the Assyrian Empire.

Frankenstein, Susan, and Michael J. Rowlands. 1978. "The Internal Structure and Regional Context of Early Iron Age Society in South-Western Germany." *Institute of Archaeology Bulletin (London University)* 15: 73–112.

Reconstruction of the social system in ancient Europe, with an emphasis on prestige goods exchange.

Franklin, Norma. 2002. "The Tombs of the Kings of Israel." Paper presented at the Third International Conference on the Archaeology of the Ancient Near East, April 16, Paris.

Discussion of the archaeological evidence for royal tombs of the Northern Kingdom in light of textual evidence for the kings of Israel.

Freedman, David N. 1987. "Yahweh of Samaria and His Asherah." *Biblical Archaeologist* 50: 241–249.

Comments on the evidence for the presence of the goddess in the northern Kingdom of Israel.

Frevel, Christian. 1995. *Aschera und der Ausschliesslichkeitsanspruch YHWHs: Beiträge zu Literarischen, Religionsgeschichtlichen und Ikonographischen Aspekten der Ascheradiskussion.* Weinheim: Germany, Beltz Athenäum.

Frick, Frank S. 1985. *The Formation of the State in Ancient Israel: A Survey of Models and Theories*. Sheffield, England: Almond Press.

Review of the various theories that have been proposed for explaining the rise of the Israelite monarchy.

Fritz, Volkmar. 1981. "Israelite 'Conquest' in the Light of Recent Excavations at Khirbet el-Meshash." *Bulletin of the American Schools of Oriental Research* 241: 61–73.

Examination of the evidence for Israelite settlement in the northern Negev based on excavations at Khirbet el-Meshash (Tel Masos).

———. 1982. "The 'List of Rehoboam's Fortresses' in 2 Chr. 11:5–12: A Document from the Time of Josiah." *Eretz-Israel* 15: 46–53.

Discussion of the evidence for "fortresses" in the northern Negev and the relation to biblical descriptions.

———. 1983. "Tel Masos: A Biblical Site in the Negev." *Archaeology* 36: 30–37, 54.

Presentation of archaeological discoveries at the northern Negev tell site written for a popular audience.

———. 1987. "Conquest or Settlement? The Early Iron Age in Palestine." *Biblical Archaeologist* 50: 84–100.

Examination of the processes of Israelite settlement during the Iron Age, particularly the question of how well archaeological findings correspond with the biblical narrative.

Fritz, Volkmar, and Aharaon Kempinski. 1983. *Ergebnisse der Ausgrabungen auf der Hirbet el-Masos (1972–75)*. Wiesbaden, Germany: Harrassowitz.

Report on the archaeological finds from excavations at Tel Masos.

Frumkin, Amos. 1997. "Middle Holocene Environmental Change." In *Late Quaternary Chronology and Paleoclimates of the Eastern Mediterranean*, edited by O. Bar Yosef and R. Kra, 314–331. Madison, WI: Prehistory Press.

Reconstruction of the ancient environment based on paleobotanical remains.

Frymer-Kensky, Tikva. 1992. *In the Wake of the Goddesses: Women, Culture, and the Biblical Transformation of Pagan Myth*. New York: Free Press.

Discussion of the role played by religion in the creation of gender relations, arguing that polytheistic religions tend to emphasize dualism, thereby reinforcing a strict division of gender roles, much of which is mitigated in monotheistic religion.

Gal, Zvi, Howard Smithline, and Dina Shalem. 1997. "A Chalcolithic Burial Cave in Peqi'in, Upper Galilee." *Israel Exploration Journal* 47: 145–154.

Report on the archaeological discoveries from this Chalcolithic burial cave, including an extensive assemblage of ossuaries from the period.

Galil, Gershon. 1996. *The Chronology of the Kings of Israel and Judah.* Leiden and New York: E. J. Brill.

Book devoted to reconstructing the dynasties of Judahite and Israelite kings.

———. 2001. "A Re-Arrangement of the Fragments of the Tel Dan Inscription and the Relations between Israel and Aram." *Palestine Exploration Quarterly* 133: 16–21.

Discussion proposing an alternative repositioning of the two fragments from the Tel Dan inscription that affect the historical context of the king's name.

Galili, E. Ehud. 1985. "Group of Stone Anchors from Newe-Yam." *International Journal of Nautical Archaeology and Underwater Exploration* 14: 143–153.

Examination of evidence for maritime activity on the Mediterranean coast.

———. 1986. "Metal from the Depths of the Sea." *IAMS Newsletter* 9: 4–6.

Discussion of metal artifacts, especially ingots, from a Mediterranean shipwreck.

Garbini, Giovanni. 1988. "The Question of the Alphabet." In *The Phoenicians,* edited by S. Moscati, 101–119. New York: Rizzoli.

Analysis of the emergence of the Canaanite alphabet and its relation to Ugaritic and Phoenician scripts.

Gardiner, Alan H. 1916. "The Egyptian Origin of the Semitic Alphabet." *Journal of Egyptian Archaeology* 3: 1–16.

Commentary on the influence of the Egyptian language on the origins of the Canaanite alphabet by one of the foremost authorities on the subject.

———. 1957. *Egyptian Grammar Being an Introduction to the Study of Hieroglyphs.* Oxford: Oxford University Press.

———. 1962. "Once Again, the Proto-Sinaitic Inscriptions." *Journal of Egyptian Archaeology* 48: 45–48.

A renewed look at questions concerning the development the Canaanite script in light of more recent evidence.

Garstang, John, and J. B. E. Garstang. 1948. *The Story of Jericho,* rev. ed. London, Marshall, Morgan and Scott.

Narrative account of excavations at the multiperiod tell site.

Gelb, Ignace J. 1952. *A Study of Writing: The Foundations of Grammatology.* Chicago: University of Chicago Press.

Discussion of the origins of the Canaanite script in the context of the structure of language.

Gerstenblith, Patricia. 1983. *The Levant at the Beginning of the Middle Bronze Age.* Philadelphia: American Schools of Oriental Research.

Analysis of the archaeological evidence for the resurgence of urbanism in the early second millennium B.C.E.

Gilead, Isaac. 1988. "The Chalcolithic Period in the Levant." *Journal of World Prehistory* 2: 397–443.

Overview of archaeological evidence for the Chalcolithic period, with commentary on the question of social organization.

———. 1989. "Grar: A Chalcolithic Site in the Northern Negev, Israel." *Journal of Field Archaeology* 16: 377–394.

Report on archaeological discoveries at the early Chalcolithic site in the Besor area.

———. 1993. "Sociopolitical Organization in the Northern Negev at the End of the Chalcolithic Period." In *Biblical Archaeology Today 1990, Pre-congress Symposium: Population, Production and Power (Proceedings of the Second International Congress on Biblical Archaeology)*, edited by A. Biran and J. Aviram, 82–97. Jerusalem: Israel Exploration Society.

Review of evidence from the Chalcolithic period, arguing that social organization was not particularly complex.

———. 1994. "The History of the Chalcolithic Settlement in the Nahal Beer Sheva Area: The Radiocarbon Aspect." *Bulletin of the American Schools of Oriental Research* 296: 1–13.

An attempt to reconstruct the history of settlement in the Besor region, comparing radiocarbon dates from several sites.

Gilead, Isaac, Steven Rosen, and Peder Fabian. 1991. "Excavations at Tell Abu–Matar (the Hatzerim Neighborhood), Beer Sheva." *Mitekufat Haeven—Journal of the Israel Prehistoric Society* 24: 173–179.

Report on the archaeological findings from renewed excavations in the northern Negev settlement.

Gitin, Seymour. 1990. "Ekron of the Philistines, Part II: Olive Oil Suppliers to the World." *Biblical Archaeology Review* 16: 32–42, 59.

Discussion of the archaeological evidence from Tel Miqne–Ekron for olive production, with a discussion of the regional economy.

———. 1993. "Seventh Century B.C.E. Cultic Elements at Ekron." In *Biblical Archaeology Today, 1990, Pre-congress Symposium: Population, Production and Power (Proceedings of the Second International Congress on Biblical Archaeology)*, edited by A. Biran and J. Aviram, 248–258. Jerusalem: Israel Exploration Society.

Commentary on the relationship between Philistine material culture and religious practice.

———. 1995. *Recent Excavations in Israel: A View to the West*. Dubuque, IA: Kendall Hunt.

Edited volume with contributions from some of the field's top scholars on archaeological finds from Iron Age sites, with an emphasis on the appearance of Cypro-Aegean elements.

———. 1997. "The Neo-Assyrian Empire and Its Western Periphery: The Levant with a Focus on Philistine Ekron." In *Assyria 1995: Proceedings of the 10th Anniversary Symposium of the Neo-Assyrian Text Corpus Project, Helsinki,* edited by S. Parpola and R. M. Whiting, 77–103. Helsinki: University of Helsinki.

Discussion of the archaeological and textual evidence pertaining to Ekron's role as a vassal city-state in the Assyrian Empire.

———. 2002. "The Four-Horned Altar and Sacred Space: An Archaeological Perspective." In *Sacred Time, Sacred Place: Archaeology and the Religion of Israel,* edited by B. Gittlen, 95–123. Winona Lake, IN: Eisenbrauns.

Examination of the form and function of four-horned altars used for burning incense and the broader context in time and space, suggesting that these altars can be used to identify ritual activities in places not normally associated with cultic activity.

Gitin, Seymour, and Trude Dothan. 1987. "The Rise and Fall of Ekron of the Philistines." *Biblical Archaeologist* 50: 197–199.

Brief overview of the evidence for the Philistine occupation of the Pentapolis city, Ekron, examining cultural evolution over time.

Gitin, Seymour, Trude Dothan, and Joseph Naveh. 1997. "Royal Dedicatory Inscription from Ekron." *Israel Exploration Journal* 47: 1–16.

Report on a royal inscription discovered at Tel Miqne, including a proposed translation and interpretation of the text confirming the site's identification as the Philistine city of Ekron, in addition to providing clues about the origins of the city and its rulers.

Gitin, Seymour, and Amir Golani. 2001. "The Tel Miqne–Ekron Silver Hoards: The Assyrian and Phoenician Connections." In *Hacksilber to Coinage: New Insights into the Monetary History of the Near East and Greece,* edited by Miriam S. Balmuth, 27–48. New York: American Numismatic Society.

Gitin, Seymour, Amihai Mazar, and Ephraim Stern. 1998. "Mediterranean Peoples in Transition: Thirteenth to Early Tenth Centuries B.C.E. In Honor of Trude Dothan." Jerusalem: Israel Exploration Society.

Volume dedicated to the study of the Philistines and their "Sea Peoples" origins in the early Iron Age, in honor of one of the great contributors to this topic.

Glueck, Nelson. 1959. *Rivers in the Desert: A History of the Negev.* Philadelphia: Jewish Publication Society of America.

Classic narrative account of the rabbi/archaeologist's exploration of the Negev.

Golani, Amir. 1999. "New Perspectives on Domestic Architecture and the Initial Stages of Urbanization in Canaan." *Levant* 31: 123–133.

Examination of the archaeological evidence for house design across the landscape and over time, suggesting these changes come in relation to spatial needs associated with the development of urbanism.

Golani, Amir, and Benjamin Sass. 1998. "Three Seventh-Century B.C.E. Hoards of Silver Jewelry from Tel Miqne–Ekron." *Bulletin of the American Schools of Oriental Research* 311: 57–81.

Discussion of silver artifacts from Philistine Ekron, including evidence for the Assyrian influence.

Golani, Amir, and Dror Segal. 2002. "Redefining the Onset of the EBA in Southern Canaan: New Evidence of C14 Dating from Ashkelon-Afridar." In *Quest of Ancient Settlements and Landscapes: Archaeological Studies in Honour of Ram Gophna,* edited by E. C. M. van den Brink and E. Yannai. Tel Aviv: Ramot.

Goldberg, Paul. 1986. "Late Quaternary Environmental History of the Southern Levant." *Geoarchaeology* 3: 225–244.

A geologist uses a variety of data to reconstruct changes in the ancient environment.

———. 2003. "The Changing Landscape." In *The Archaeology of Society in the Holy Land,* 3d ed., edited by T. E. Levy, 40–57. New York: Facts on File.

Examination, by a geologist, of the evidence for a shifting landscape from antiquity through the present and discussion of its significance with regard to human land use in the past and archaeological interpretation in the present.

Goldberg, Paul, and Arlene Rosen. 1987. "Early Holocene Paleoenvironments of Israel." In *Shiqmim I,* edited by T. Levy, 35–43. Oxford: British Archaeological Reports.

A reconstruction of the southern Levantine environment in late prehistoric times by a geologist-paleobotanist team.

Golden, Jonathan. 2002a. "The Early Bronze Age." In *Encyclopedia of Prehistory.* Vol. 8, *South and Southwest Asia,* edited by P. Peregrine and M. Ember, 86–111. New York: Kluwer/Plenum.

Encyclopedia entry summarizing the archaeological evidence from the Early Bronze Age in the southern Levant.

———. 2002b. "The Middle Bronze Age." In *Encyclopedia of Prehistory.* Vol. 8, *South and Southwest Asia,* edited by P. Peregrine and M. Ember, 293–304. New York: Kluwer/Plenum.

Encyclopedia entry summarizing the archaeological evidence from the Middle Bronze Age in the southern Levant.

———. 2002c. "The Origins of the Copper Trade in the Eastern Mediterranean during the Early Bronze Age." In *Egyptian and Canaanite Interaction during the Fourth–Third Millennium B.C.E.,* edited by E. van den Brink and T. Levy, 225–238. London: Leicester University Press.

Discussion of archaeological evidence for the early metals trade, including ore sources and copper workshops in the southern Levant and copper artifacts from the tombs of Egypt's earliest kings.

————. Forthcoming. *The Dawn of the Metal Age.* London: Continuum.

Analysis of the relationship between the advent of metallurgy and the rise of social complexity in the southern Levant, including an extended discussion of the evidence for wealthy cave tombs and a reconstruction of metal production and use within the context of a Chalcolithic village.

Golden, Jonathan, Thomas E. Levy, and Andreas Hauptmann. 2001. "Recent Discoveries Concerning Ancient Metallurgy at the Chalcolithic (ca. 4000 B.C.) Village of Shiqmim, Israel." *Journal of Archaeological Science* 9: 951–963.

Summary of archaeometallurgical evidence from Chalcolithic Shiqmim, including data on both technical and social aspects of copper production.

————. 2004. "Targeting Heritage: The Abuse of the Past in Conflicts of the Present." In *Marketing Heritage: The Consumption of the Past,* edited by Y. Rowan and U. Baram. Walnut Creek, CA: Alta Mira.

Examination of recent events regarding the destruction of heritage sites as part of modern ethnopolitical conflicts and the broader significance of this problem.

Gonen, Rivka. 1984. "Urban Canaan in the Late Bronze Period." *Bulletin of the American Schools of Oriental Research* 253: 61–73.

Brief summary of archaeological evidence for urbanism during the Late Bronze Age.

————. 1992. "The Late Bronze Age." In *The Archaeology of Ancient Israel,* edited by A. Ben-Tor, 211–257. New Haven, CT: Yale University Press.

Overview of the Late Bronze Age, with a discussion of the archaeological and textual/historical evidence.

Gopher, Avi, and Tzvika Tsuk. 1991. *Ancient Gold: Rare Finds from the Nahal Qanah Cave.* Jerusalem: Israel Museum.

————. 1996. *The Nahal Qanah Cave: Earliest Gold in the Southern Levant.* Monograph Series of the Institute of Archaeology. Tel Aviv: Tel Aviv University.

Small monograph on the archaeological finds from a Chalcolithic burial cave.

Gophna, Ram. 1974. "The Settlement of the Coastal Plain of Eretz Israel during the Early Bronze Age." Ph.D. dissertation, Tel Aviv University.

Discussion, in Hebrew, of the archaeological evidence for the initial wave of settlement on the Mediterranean coastal plain.

————. 1984. "Settlement Landscape of Palestine in the Early Bronze Age II–III and Middle Bronze Age II." *Israel Exploration Journal* 34: 24–31.

Examination of the changing demographics in the southern Levant during the third and second millennia B.C.E.

———. 1992. "Early Bronze Age Fortification Wall and Middle Bronze Age Rampart at Tel Poran." *Tel Aviv* 19: 267–273.

Discussion of Bronze Age architecture at Tel Poran, proposing use of the term "rampart settlement" to describe Middle Bronze Age sites with earthen enclosures.

———. 2002. "Elusive Anchorage Points along the Israel Littoral and the Egyptian-Canaanite Maritime Route during the Early Bronze Age I." In *Egyptian and Canaanite Interaction during the Fourth–Third Millennium B.C.E.*, edited by E. van den Brink and T. Levy, 418–421. London: Leicester University Press.

A search for tangible archaeological evidence relating to maritime activities during the Early Bronze Age, with a discussion of possible routes taken.

Gophna, Ram, and Yuval Portugali. 1988. "Settlement and Demographic Process in Israel's Coastal Plain from the Chalcolithic to the Middle Bronze Age." *Bulletin of the American Schools of Oriental Research* 269: 11–28.

Summary of survey data in an attempt to reconstruct the settlement landscape from the fourth through the second millennia B.C.E.

Goren, Yuval. 1995. "Shrines and Ceramics in Chalcolithic Israel: The View through the Petrographic Microscope." *Archaeometry* 37: 287–306.

An attempt to identify evidence for the import of ceramics, possibly through pilgrimage, to Chalcolithic cult centers through petrographic analysis of ceramics.

Gottwald, Norman K. 1979. *The Tribes of Yahweh: A Sociology of the Religion of Liberated Israel, 1250–1050 B.C.E.* Maryknoll, NY: Orbis.

Study on social structure in the early Iron Age, based mainly on the examination of texts.

———. 1983. *The Bible and Liberation: Political and Social Hermeneutics.* Maryknoll, NY: Orbis.

Volume dedicated to the study of social and political organization in ancient Israel through the interpretation of the Hebrew Bible.

Grayson, A. Kirk. 1975. "Two Fragmentary Assyrian Royal Inscriptions." *Iraq* 37: 69–74.

A translation of two royal Assyrian inscriptions, written by an Assyriologist.

———. 1996. *Assyrian Rulers of the First Millennium BC, II (858–745 B.C.).* Toronto: University of Toronto Press.

A look at the evidence, mainly textual, for Assyrian kings of the later Iron Age.

Greenberg, Raphael. 1990. "The Settlement of the Hula Valley in the Urban Phase of the Early Bronze Age." *Eretz Israel* 21: 127–131.

Discussion, in Hebrew, of the archaeological evidence for early urbanism in the north of Israel.

————. 1992. "Ramat ha-Nadiv Tumulus Field: Preliminary Report." *Israel Exploration Journal* 42: 129–152.

Report on the investigation of ancient tumuli in the Mount Carmel region.

————. 1996. "Third Millennium Levantine Pottery Production Center: Typology, Petrography, and Provenance of the Metallic Ware of Northern Israel and Adjacent Regions." *Bulletin of the American Schools of Oriental Research* 301: 5–24.

Examination of evidence for pottery production and use, including petrographic provenance studies, in an attempt to identify the locus of production for the high-quality northern pottery type known as Metallic Ware.

Grigson, Carolyn. 2003. "Plough and Pasture in the Early Economy of the Southern Levant." In *The Archaeology of Society in the Holy Land*, 3d ed., edited by T. E. Levy, 226–244. New York: Facts on File.

Discussion of evidence for secondary uses of pastoral animals in the late prehistory of the southern Levant, based on analysis of faunal assemblages and representations of animals.

Gruenwald, Ithamar. 2003. *Rituals and Ritual Theory in Ancient Israel*. Boston: Brill.

A consideration of the evidence for religious practice in ancient Israel, especially during the Iron Age.

Halpern, Baruch. 1988. *The First Historians: The Hebrew Bible and History*. San Francisco: Harper and Row.

Analysis of issues related to the historicity of the Hebrew Bible, suggesting that Chronicles and Deuteronomy may represent actual historical works.

————. 1994. "Stelae from Dan: Epigraphic and Historical Considerations." *Bulletin of the American Schools of Oriental Research* 296: 63–80.

Discussion of the Tel Dan inscription, with a focus on the historical context and the specific people and places mentioned.

Hauptmann, Andreas. 1989. "The Earliest Periods of Copper Metallurgy in Feinan, Jordan." In *Old World Archaeometallurgy*, edited by A. Hauptmann, E. Pernicka, and G. A. Wagner, 119–36. Bochum: Selbstverlag des Deutsches Bergbau-Museum.

An archaeometallurgist dicusses the evidence, including scientific analyses of archaeometallurgical remains, for early mining and metal production in the Faynan region.

Hein, Irmgard. 2002. "A New Class of Pottery Ware from New Kingdom Egypt—Metallic Ware. Tel el-Daba 18th Dynasty Pottery (First Half)." Paper presented at the Third International Conference on the Archaeology of the Ancient Near East, April 16, Paris.

Analysis identifying a distinct style of pottery from Egypt during the early Late Bronze Age.

Helms, Svend W. 1987. "Jawa, Umm Hammad, and the EB I/Late Chalcolithic Landscape." *Levant* 19: 49–81.

Report on the archaeological findings from excavations of Jawa in Jordan.

Hendrickx, Stan, and Bavay Laurent. 2002. "The Relative Chronological Position of Egyptian Predynastic and Early Dynastic Tombs with Objects Imported from the Near East and the Nature of Interregional Contacts." In *Egyptian and Canaanite Interaction during the Fourth–Third Millennium B.C.E.*, edited by E. van den Brink and T. Levy, 58–82. London: Leicester University Press.

Reexamination of the evidence for interregional trade during the Early Bronze Age, with a focus on both economic activity and chronology.

Hennessy, John Basil. 1982. "Teleilat Ghassul: Its Place in the Archaeology of Jordan." In *Studies in the History and Archaeology of Jordan*, edited by A. Hadidi, 55–88. Amman, Jordan: Department of Antiquities.

Discussion of the archaeological evidence from the Chalcolithic center at Ghassul and its broader significance.

Henry, Donald O. 1996. "Middle Paleolithic Behavioral Organization: 1993 Excavation of Tor Faraj, Southern Jordan." *Journal of Field Archaeology* 23: 31–53.

Herdner, Andree. 1963. *Corpus des tablettes en cunéiformes alphabétiques découvertes à Ras Shamra-Ugarit de 1929 à 1939.* Paris: P. Geuthner.

Herzog, Zeev. 1978. "Tel Michal: A Coastal Site in the Sharon Plain." *Expedition* 20: 44–49.

Brief report on the archaeological findings from excavations at Tel Michal, with a focus on the evidence for cultic activity during the Middle Bronze Age.

———. 1984. "Tel Michal: A Coastal Site in the Sharon Plain." *Expedition* 20: 44–49.

Brief overview of archaeological research at Tel Michal.

———. 2001. "The Date of the Temple at Arad: Reassessment of the Stratigraphy and the Implications for the History of Religion in Judah." In *Studies in the Archaeology of the Iron Age in Israel and Jordan*, edited by A. Mazar, 156–178. Sheffield, England: Sheffield Academic Press.

Reexamination of the archaeological evidence from Arad, suggesting a shorter period of use for the temple than previously thought and questioning certain assumptions about the site that follow the biblical tradition.

Herzog, Zeev, Miriam Aharoni, Anson Rainey, and Schmuel Moshkovitz. 1984. "Israelite Fortress at Arad." *Bulletin of the American Schools of Oriental Research* 254: 1–34.

Report on the excavations of a northern Negev Iron Age site.

Herzog, Zeev, Anson Rainey, and Schmuel Moshkovitz. 1977. "Stratigraphy at Beer-Sheba and the Location of the Sanctuary." *Bulletin of the American Schools of Oriental Research* 225: 49–58.

Archaeological site report, with a specific focus on the Iron Age sanctuary as described in the Hebrew Bible.

Hess, Richard S. 1997. "The Form and Structure of the Solomonic District List in 1 Kings 4:7–19." In *Crossing Borders and Linking Horizons: Studies in Honor of Michal C. Astour on his 80th Birthday*, edited by G. Young, M. Chavalas, and R. Averbeck, 279–292. Bethesda, MD: CDL Press.

Analysis of a list included in the Hebrew Bible, with a discussion of whether it represents part of a historical document.

Hesse, Brian. 1986. "Animal Use at Tel Miqne–Ekron in the Bronze Age and Iron Age." *Bulletin of the American Schools of Oriental Research* 264: 17–27.

Report on the faunal remains from Ekron, with a discussion of animal use and diet.

Hesse, Brian, and Paula Wapnish. 1998. "Pig Use and Abuse in the Ancient Levant: Ethno-Religious Boundary-Building with Swine." In *Ancestors for the Pigs: Pigs in Prehistory*, edited by Sarah M. Nelson, 123–135. MASCA Research Papers in Science and Archaeology, 15. Philadelphia: Museum Applied Science Center for Archaeology.

Examination of the faunal remains from southern Levantine sites and their significance for questions concerning dietary restrictions among cultural groups.

Hestrin, Ruth. 1987a. "The Lachish Ewer and the 'Asherah.'" *Israel Exploration Journal* 37: 222–223.

Discussion focused on an inscription and accompanying image relating to the goddess Asherah.

———. 1987b. "Religion in Israel and Judah under the Monarchy: An Explicitly Archaeological Approach." In *Ancient Israelite Religion*, edited by P. Miller, P. Hanson, and S. McBride, 249–299. Philadelphia: Fortress.

A look at Israelite religion focusing on the archaeological evidence, as opposed to practice as described in the Hebrew Bible.

———. 1991. "Understanding Asherah: Exploring Semitic Iconography." *Biblical Archaeology Review* 17: 50–59.

A review of the archaeological evidence for the worship of Asherah in ancient Canaan and Israel.

Hestrin, Ruth, and Michal Dayagi-Mendels. 1979. *Inscribed Seals: First Temple Period, Hebrew, Ammonite, Moabite, Phoenician and Aramaic, from the Collections of the Israel Museum and the Israel Department of Antiquities and Museums.* Jerusalem: Israel Museum.

Examination of the linguistic aspects of the different seals and their historical significance.

Hestrin, Ruth, and Miriam Tadmor. 1963. "A Hoard of Tools and Weapons from Kfar Monash." *Israel Exploration Journal* 13: 265–288.

Report on the discovery of a hoard of copper goods, with a discussion of the cultural context and date pointing to a possible Egyptian origin.

Hocking, Nancy. 2001. "Lessons from the Kiln: Reduction Firing in Cypriot Iron Age Pottery." *Near Eastern Archaeology* 64: 132–149.

Analysis of the effects of firing techniques on Cypriote ceramics and how manufacturing techniques reflect the overall dynamics of pottery production.

Hoffman, Michael. 1979. "Egypt before the Pharaohs: The Prehistoric Foundations of Egyptian Civilization." Austin: University of Texas Press.

Comprehensive discussion of cultural evolution in Upper and Lower Egypt during prehistoric times, including the Fayum Neolithic, and the Nagada and Maadi cultures, with an emphasis on the history of discovery.

Holladay, John S., Jr. 1987. "Religion in Israel and Judah under the Monarchy: An Explicitly Archaeological Approach." In *Ancient Israelite Religion,* edited by P. Miller, P. Hanson, and S. McBride, 249–299. Philadelphia: Fortress.

Review of the archaeological evidence for religious practice during the later Iron Age.

———. 1990. "Red Slip, Burnish, and the Solomonic Gateway at Gezer." *Bulletin of the American Schools of Oriental Research* 277: 23–70, 121–130.

———. 1992. "Israelite House." In *Anchor Bible Dictionary,* 3: 308–318. Garden City, NY: Doubleday.

———. 1997. "Four-Room House." In *Oxford Encyclopedia of Archaeology in the Near East,* 2: 337–342. New York: Oxford University Press

Article on the evidence for domestic architecture, with a focus on questions about the "four-room house."

———. 2003. "The Kingdoms of Israel and Judah: Political and Economic Centralization in the Iron IIA-B (ca. 1000–750 B.C.E.)." In *The Archaeology of Society in the Holy Land,* 3d ed., edited by T. E. Levy, 368–398. New York: Facts on File.

Discussion of the archaeological and historical evidence from the second part of the Iron Age (Iron Age 2) concerning the rise of urbanism, examining the impact of nationhood and individual rulers, with a focus on the relationship between economic and political developments.

Hopkins, David C. 1985. *The Highlands of Canaan: Agricultural Life in the Early Iron Age.* Decatur, IL: Almond Press.

Discussion of archaeological and botanical evidence for agriculture and rural life at the beginning of the Iron Age.

————. 1987. "Life on the Land: The Subsistence Struggles of Early Israel." *Biblical Archaeologist* 50.

> Examination of archaeological evidence indicating that individuals and extended families were the primary units of production during the early Iron Age.

Horwitz, Liora Kolska, and Daphna Ben-Tor. 1997. "The Relations between Egypt and Palestine in the Middle Kingdom as Reflected by Contemporary Canaanite Scarabs." *Israel Exploration Journal* 47: 162–189.

> Analysis of the evidence for interrelations between Canaanites and Egyptians during the Middle Bronze Age, with a focus on the adoption of Egyptian conventions by Canaanite elites.

————. 1998. "Faunal Remains from Middle Bronze Age Tel Te'enim." *Tel Aviv* 5: 105–109.

> Report on faunal assemblage from a Middle Bronze Age site.

Horowitz, Wayne, and Aaron Shaffer. 1992. "Fragment of a Letter from Hazor." *Israel Exploration Journal* 42: 165–167.

> Commentary on a letter from Hazor, with a focus on its implications for understanding international relations.

Ilan, David. 1991. "'Stepped-rim' Juglets from Tel Dan and the 'MBA I-II (MB IIA-B) Transitional Period.'" *Israel Exploration Journal* 41: 229–238.

> Examination of Middle Bronze Age pottery from Tel Dan, with a discussion of the evidence for contact with the people of Syria and southwestern Anatolia.

————. 1992. "Middle Bronze Age Offering Deposit from Tel Dan and the Politics of Cultic Gifting." *Tel Aviv* 19: 247–266.

> Review of the evidence for small artifact caches found at Tel Dan, arguing that they may represent deliberate deposits related to social and religious tradition.

————. 1995. "Mortuary Practices at Tel Dan in the Middle Bronze Age: A Reflection of Canaanite Society and Ideology." In *Archaeology of Death in the Ancient Near East,* edited by Stuart Campbell, 117–139. Oxford: Oxbow.

> Summary of archaeological evidence for burial practices during the Middle Bronze Age and their significance for understanding Canaanite social structure.

————. 1996. "Middle Bronze Age Painted Pottery from Tel Dan." *Levant* 28: 157–172.

> Examination of the Canaanite pottery of the second part of the Middle Bronze Age (MB2), with a focus on evidence for contact with the Khabur region in Syria.

————. 2003. "The Dawn of Internationalism: The Middle Bronze Age." In *The Archaeology of Society in the Holy Land,* 3d ed., edited by T. E. Levy, 297–319. New York: Facts on File.

> Discussion of archaeological evidence from the Middle Bronze Age, with a focus on

evidence for exchange systems, suggesting that foreign contacts during this period set the stage for the widespread networks of the Late Bronze Age.

Ilan, David, Pamela Vandiver, and Maud Spaer. 1993. "Early Glass Bead from Tel Dan." *Israel Exploration Journal* 43: 230–234.

Archaeological report on glass found at Dan, with a discussion of its manufacture and place of origin, and implications for understanding trade relations.

Ilan, Ornit, and Michael Sebbane. 1989. "Copper Metallurgy, Trade, and the Urbanization of Southern Canaan in the Chalcolithic and Early Bronze Age." In *L'Urbanization du Palestine à la Âge du Bronze Ancien,* edited by P. de Miroschedji, 139–162. Oxford: British Archaeological Reports.

Discussion of the Early Bronze Age copper industry, with a focus on the production and use of metal at the northern Negev site of Arad and the potential sources of ore.

James, Thomas Garnet Henry. 1988. *Ancient Egypt: The Land and Its Legacy.* Austin, TX: University of Texas Press.

Joffe, Alexander. 1991. "Early Bronze I and the Evolution of Social Complexity in the Southern Levant." *Journal of Mediterranean Archaeology* 4: 3–58.

Examination of the processes of social evolution during the Early Bronze Age applying models of society derived from anthropological theory.

Joffe, Alexander, and J. P. Dessel. 1995. "Redefining Chronology and Terminology for the Chalcolithic of the Southern Levant." *Current Anthropology* 36: 507–518.

Summary of radiocarbon dates for the Chalcolithic period, with a proposed subchronology of Early, Developed, and Terminal Chalcolithic.

Kaplan, Joseph. 1975. "Further Aspects of Middle Bronze Age II Fortifications in Palestine." *Zeitschrift des Deutschen Palästina Verieins* 91: 1–17.

Discussion of earthen ramparts surrounding Middle Bronze Age sites, suggesting they functioned primarily for defensive purposes.

Kaplony, Peter. 2002. "The Bet Yerah Jar Inscription and the Annals of King Dewen—Dewen as 'King Narmer Redivivus.'" In *Egyptian and Canaanite Interaction during the Fourth–Third Millennium B.C.E.,* edited by E. van den Brink and T. Levy, 487–498. London: Leicester University Press.

Interpretation of an Early Bronze Age inscription in light of related Egyptian inscriptions, including the Narmer Palette, and in the context of Egyptian foreign policy during the First Dynasty.

Kassis, Hanna E. 1965. "Gath and the Structure of the 'Philistine' Society." *Journal of Biblical Literature* 84: 259–271.

Examination of evidence from Gath, including inscriptions, suggesting that at least one ruler of the site may not have been of Philistine background.

Keel, Othmar. 1993. "Hyksos Horses or Hippopotamus Deities?" *Levant* 25: 208–212.

Keel, Othmar, and Christoph Uehlinger. 1992. *Göttinnen, Götter, and Gottessymbole: Neue Erkenntinisse zur Religiongeschichte Kanaans und Israel aufgrund bislang unnerschlossener ikonographischer Quellen.* Freiburg: Herder.

————. 1998. *Gods, Goddesses, and Images of God in Ancient Israel.* Translated by T. Trapp. Minneapolis: Fortress.

Discussion of the various forms of religious iconography in ancient Israel.

Kelm, George L. 1984. "Timnah: A Biblical City in the Sorek Valley." *Archaeology* 37: 52–59.

Brief overview of excavations at Tel Batash and its identification as Timnah of the Hebrew Bible.

Kelm, George L., and Amihai Mazar. 1982. "Three Seasons of Excavations at Tel Batash—Biblical Timnah." *Bulletin of the American Schools of Oriental Research* 248: 1–36.

Report on the archaeological discoveries from excavations at Tel Batash (Timnah) focusing on the Iron Age, especially the Iron 2 city-fortress.

————. 1985. "Tel Batash (Timnah) Excavations: Second Preliminary Report (1981–1983)." *BASOR Supplement* 23: 94–100.

Update on archaeological findings from excavations at Tel Batash, identified as the biblical city of Timnah.

Kempinski, Aharon. 1976. "Tel Masos (Khirbet El-Meshesh)." In *Encyclopedia of Archaeological Excavations in the Holy Land 3,* edited by M. Avi-Yonah and E. Stern, 816–818. New York: Simon and Schuster.

Brief summary of archaeological discoveries at the site of Tel Masos.

————. 1978. *The Rise of an Urban Culture: The Urbanization of Palestine in the Early Bronze Age, 300–2150 B.C.* Israel Ethnographic Society Studies, 4. Jerusalem: Israel Ethnographic Society.

Review of the archaeological evidence related to the rise of urbanism in the southern Levant during the Early Bronze Age.

————. 1989. *Megiddo: A City-State and Royal Centre in North Israel.* Munich: C. H. Beck.

Comprehensive overview of evidence from research at Megiddo and its significance as a major center in the northern Kingdom of Israel.

————. 1992a. "Fortifications, Public Buildings, and Town Planning in the Early Bronze Age." In *The Architecture of Ancient Israel,* edited by A. Kempinski and R. Reich, 68–80. Jerusalem: Israel Exploration Society.

Discussion of the archaeological evidence from the Early Bronze Age, with a focus on architecture and how it reflects the development of social and political complexity.

———. 1992b. "The Middle Bronze Age." In *The Archaeology of Ancient Israel,* edited by A. Ben-Tor, 159–210. New Haven, CT: Yale University Press.

Comprehensive overview of the Middle Bronze Age in the southern Levant.

Kempinski, Aharon, and Isaac Gilead. 1991. "New Excavations at Tel Erani: A Preliminary Report of the 1985–1988 Seasons." *Tel Aviv* 18: 164–191.

Report on the archaeological discoveries from excavations at the Early Bronze Age city of Tel Erani.

Kempinski, Aharon, and Joseph Naveh. 1991. "Phoenician Seal Impression on a Jar Handle from Tel Kabri." *Tel Aviv* 18: 244–247.

Discussion of a seal impression from the Phoenician site of Tel Kabri and its significance in terms of political organization and interregional trade.

Kenyon, Kathleen. 1958. "Some Notes of the Early and Middle Bronze Age Strata of Megiddo." *Eretz Israel* 5: 51–60.

Report on the archaeological finds from excavation of the early levels at Megiddo.

———. 1979. *Archaeology in the Holy Land,* 4th ed. New York: W. W. Norton.

Summary of archaeological finds from the Neolithic period through the Iron Age from throughout the southern Levant, with a view largely from Jericho.

Key, C. A. 1980. "Trace Element Composition of the Copper and Copper Alloys of the Nahal Mishmar Hoard." In *The Cave of the Treasure,* edited by P. Bar-Adon, 238–243. Jerusalem: Israel Exploration Society.

Landmark report analyzing the chemical composition of the metals from the famous Nahal Mishmar Hoard indicating that a range of copper "alloys" were used prior to the use of bronze.

Khalil, Lutfi. 1984. "Metallurgical Analyses of Some Weapons from Tell El-'Ajjul." *Levant* 16: 167–170.

Report on the chemical composition of metal artifacts from the Middle Bronze Age.

Killebrew, Ann E. 1996. *Tel Miqne–Ekron: Report of the 1985–1987 Excavations in Field INE: Areas 5, 6, 7—The Bronze and Iron Ages.* Jerusalem: W. F. Albright Institute of Archaeological Research.

Review of archaeological findings from Bronze and Iron age occupation levels at Tel Miqne–Ekron, including a detailed discussion of evidence for ceramic production.

———. 2000. "Aegean-Style Early Philistine Pottery in Canaan during the Iron I Age: A Stylistic Analysis of Mycenaean IIIC:1b Pottery and Its Associated Wares." In *The Sea Peoples and Their World: A Reassessment,* edited by Eliezer D. Oren, 233–253. Philadelphia: Museum of Archaeology and Anthropology, University of Pennsylvania.

Discussion of imported and local pottery of the twelfth and eleventh centuries B.C.E. in an attempt to understand early Philistine settlement in the southern Levant.

King, Leonard W., and A. Kirk Grayson. 2001. "The Palace of Ashur-Resha-Ishi I at Nineveh." *Iraq* 63: 169–170.

Description of inscriptions from the Assyrian Royal Palace at Nineveh.

King, Philip J. 1985. "Archaeology, History and the Bible." In *Harper's Bible Dictionary*, edited by P. J. Achtemeier, 44–52. San Francisco: Harper and Row.

Discussion of the various issues concerning the historical value of the Hebrew Bible in light of archaeological knowledge.

———. 1987. "The Influence of G. Earnest Wright on the Archaeology of Palestine." In *Archaeology and Biblical Interpretation*, edited by L. Purdue, L. Tombs, and G. Johnson, 15–30. Atlanta: Scholars Press.

History of archaeological discovery in the southern Levant, specifically the contribution of G. E. Wright and the first generation of Albright students.

King, Philip J., and Lawrence E. Stager. 2001. *Life in Biblical Israel.* Louisville, KY: Westminster/John Knox Press.

A reconstruction of daily life in ancient Israel based on archaeological and textual evidence.

Kislev, Mordechai, Michal Artzy, and Ezra Marcus. 1993. "Import of an Aegean Food Plant to a Middle Bronze IIA Coastal Site in Israel." *Levant* 25: 145–154.

Kitchen, Kenneth A. 1997. "Three Old-South-Arabian Fragments in the Wellcome Collection, University of Wales, Swansea." *Arabian Archaeology and Epigraphy* 8: 241–244.

Kletter, Raz. 1998. *Economic Keystones: The Weight System of the Kingdom of Judah.* Sheffield, England: Sheffield Academic Press.

Analysis of the ancient system of weights and measures based on archaeological and textual evidence.

———. 2001. "Between Archaeology and Theology: The Pillar Figurines from Judah and the Asherah." In *Studies in the Archaeology of the Iron Age in Israel and Jordan*, edited by A. Mazar, 179–216. Sheffield, England: Sheffield Academic Press.

Discussion of evidence relating to the use of pillar figurines (from, for example, breakage patterns) and how this relates to interpretations of them.

———. 2002. "Israeli Archaeologists Find Cache of Philistine Vessels." Http://www.ananova.com/news/story/sm_707926.html.

Brief news item reporting on archaeological discoveries from excavations near Tel Aviv, including Philistine material from the ninth and tenth centuries B.C.E.

Kletter, Raz, and Amir Gorzalczany. 2001. "Middle Bronze Age II Type of Pottery Kiln from the Coastal Plain of Israel." *Levant* 33: 95–104.

Examination of evidence for Middle Bronze Age ceramic production, especially the multiple kilns and ceramic slag found at the coastal site of Tel Michal.

Knapp, A. Bernard. 1989. "Complexity and Collapse in the North Jordan Valley: Archaeometry and Society in the Middle-Late Bronze Age." *Israel Exploration Journal* 39: 129–148.

Discussion of the archaeological evidence for crafts production in Jordan during the Middle to Late Bronze Age and its relation to social complexity.

———. 1992. "Independence and Imperialism: Politico-Economic Structures in the Bronze Age Levant." In *Archaeology, Annales, and Ethnohistory,* edited by A. Bernard Knapp, 83–98. Cambridge: Cambridge University Press.

Knauf, Ernst Axel. 2000. "Jerusalem in the Late Bronze and Early Iron Ages: A Proposal." *Tel Aviv* 27: 75–90.

Knauf, Ernst Axel, and Manfred Lindner. 1997. "Between the Plateau and the Rocks: Edomite Economic and Social Structure." *Studies in the History and Archaeology of Jordan* 6: 261–264.

Kochavi, Moshe. 1969. "Excavations at Tel Esdar." *Átiqot* 5: 14–48.

Report on the archaeological findings from excavations at Tel Esdar.

———. 1978. "Canaanite Aphek: Its Acropolis and Inscriptions." *Expedition* 20: 12–17.

Discussion of the archaeological evidence from Aphek, with an emphasis on royal architecture and texts.

———. 1989. "Urbanization and Re-Urbanization: Early Bronze Age, Middle Bronze Age and the Period In-Between Them." In *Urbanisation de la Palestine à l'âge du Bronze Ancien,* edited by Ruth Amiran and Ram Gophna, 257–259. Oxford: British Archaeological Reports.

Examination of the processes of urban development and decline during the third to second millennium B.C.E.

Köhler, E. Christiana. 1995. "The State of Research on Late Predynastic Egypt: New Evidence for the Development of the Pharaonic State?" *Göttinger Miszellen* 147: 79–92.

Reevaluation of the archaeological evidence from the late prehistory of Egypt, challenging several traditional views while offering new insight on the problem of state formation.

Korpel, Marjo. 2001. *The Structure of the Book of Ruth.* Assen, Netherlands: Van Gorcum.

Commentary and critique on the Book of Ruth, analyzing the antiquity of the Hebrew text among other ancient languages while advocating the use of ancient reading conventions in literary analysis.

———. 2002. "Asherah outside Israel." In *Only One God? Monotheism in Ancient Israel and the Veneration of the Goddess Asherah,* edited by B. Becking, M. Dijkstra, M. Korpel, and K. Vriezen, 127–150. London: Sheffield Academic Press.

Examination of the evidence, both textual and artistic, for Asherah and related goddesses in the lands of Israel's neighbors, especially Ugarit.

LaBianca, Oystein Sakala. 1990. "Sedentarization and Nomadization: Food System Cycles at Hesban and Vicinity in Transjordan." Berrien Springs, MI: Andrews University Press.

Report on archaeological discoveries from research in Jordan, with a focus on the evidence for transhumance and shifting settlement patterns.

Lambert, Wilfred George. 1960. "The Domesticated Camel in the Second Millennium— Evidence from Alalakh and Ugarit." *Bulletin of the American Schools of Oriental Research* 160: 42–43.

Discussion of the archaeological evidence for the domestication of the camel from two of the most important cities in Syria.

Lang, Bernhard. 1983. *Monotheism and the Prophetic Minority: An Essay in Biblical History and Sociology.* Sheffield, England: Almond Press.

Examination of the role of prophets in the development of monotheism as described in the Hebrew Bible, and to what extent this reflects the social history of the Iron Age.

Lapp, Paul. 1967. "The 1966 Excavations at Tell Ta'annek." *Bulletin of the American Schools of Oriental Research* 185: 2–39.

Report on archaeological findings from excavations at the site of Tel Ta'anak.

———. 1969. *Biblical Archaeology and History.* New York: World Publishing.

Discussion about the historical value of the Hebrew Bible and its influence on archaeological research in the southern Levant.

———. 1970. "Palestine in the Early Bronze Age." In *Near Eastern Archaeology in the Twentieth Century,* edited by James A. Sanders, 101–131. Garden City, NY: Doubleday.

Larsen, Mogens Trolle. 1987. "Commercial Networks in the Ancient Near East." In *Centre and Periphery in the Ancient World,* edited by Michael Rowlands, Mogens Larsen, and Kristian Kristiansen, 47–56. Cambridge: Cambridge University Press.

A consideration of the archaeological evidence for exchange systems between the southern Levant and surrounding regions.

Lattimore, Owen. 1940. *Inner Asian Frontiers of China.* New York, American Geographical Society.

Study of Asian society presenting the classic model of desert and sown regions based on interaction between settled and transhumant populations.

Laughlin, John C. H. 1999. *Archaeology and the Bible.* London and New York: Routledge.

Description of the most recent evidence from surveys and excavations around the ancient Near East and the implications for understanding the Hebrew Bible.

Lemaire, André. 1984. "Who or What Was Yahweh's Asherah?" *Biblical Archaeology Review* 10: 42–51.

A synthesis of the earliest archaeological evidence suggesting that YHWH had a consort.

————. 1994. "'House of David' Restored in Moabite Inscription." *Biblical Archaeology Review* 20: 30–37.

Reevaluation of the famous Moabite Stone and a new interpretation suggesting a direct historical reference to the Davidic Dynasty of the Judean Kingdom.

Lemche, Niels Peter. 1991. *The Canaanites and Their Land: The Tradition of the Canaanites.* Sheffield: Journal for the Study of the Old Testament (JSOT) Press.

————. 1998. *The Israelites in History and Tradition.* Louisville, KY: Westminster/John Knox Press.

A "minimalist" approach to the study of ancient Israel, arguing that the Hebrew Bible should not be read as a historical text.

Lemche, Niels Peter, and Thomas L. Thompson. 1994. "Did Biran Kill David? The Bible in the Light of Archaeology." *Journal for the Study of the Old Testament* 64: 3–22.

Discussion of the "Bet Dwd" inscription from Tel Dan proposing an alternative interpretation of the text.

Leonard, Albert, and Eric H. Cline. 1998. "The Aegean Pottery at Megiddo: An Appraisal and Analysis." *Bulletin of the American Schools of Oriental Research* 309: 3–39.

Examination of the pottery from Megiddo, with a discussion of evidence for Aegean contact with the people of the Jezreel Valley.

Levine, Lee, I. 2001. "Biblical Archaeology." In *Etz Hayim: Torah and Commentary,* edited by D. Lieber, 1339–1344. New York: Rabbinical Assembly/Jewish Publication Society.

A perspective on the relationship between the biblical narrative and the archaeological evidence from excavations in the southern Levant.

Levy, Thomas E. 1983. "The Emergence of Specialized Pastoralism in the Southern Levant." *World Archaeology* 15: 15–36.

Examination of the evidence for pastoral nomadism and the production of secondary goods.

————. 1985. "Shiqmim: A Chalcolithic Village and Mortuary Center in the Northern Negev." *Paléorient* 11: 17–83.

Discussion of pastoral nomadism as a means of subsistence and its impact on social organization.

————. 1986. "The Chalcolithic Period." *Biblical Archaeologist* 49: 83–106.

————. 1987. *Shiqmim I: Studies Concerning Chalcolithic Societies in the Northern Negev Desert, Israel (1982–1984).* Oxford: British Archaeological Reports.

Report on the archaeological findings from excavations at the Chalcolithic village in the northern Negev.

———. 1992. "Transhumance, Subsistence, and Social Evolution." In *Pastoralism in the Levant,* edited by O. Bar-Yosef and A. Khazanov, 65–82. Madison, WI: Prehistory Press.

Discussion of socioeconomic organization during the Chalcolithic period and the impact of the secondary products revolution.

———. 1996. "Anthropological Approaches to Protohistoric Palestine: A Case Study from the Negev Desert." In *Retrieving the Past,* edited by J. D. Seger, 163–178. Winona Lake, IN: Eisenbrauns.

A look at the evidence from late prehistory in the southern Levant in the context of social models derived from ethnographic research.

———. 2002a. "The Chalcolithic Period." In *Encyclopedia of Prehistory.* Vol. 8, *South and Southwest Asia,* edited by P. Peregrine and M. Ember, 56–74. New York: Kluwer/ Plenum.

An up-to-date overview of the Chalcolithic period written as a reference tool.

———. 2002b. "New Light on Iron Age Nomads in the Faynan District, Jordan." Unpublished paper.

Discussion of mobile populations in the Faynan area based on archaeological discoveries from an Iron Age cemetery.

———. 2003a. *The Archaeology of Society in the Holy Land,* 3d ed. New York: Facts on File.

Edited volume covering the archaeology and social history of the southern Levant from the Paleolithic through the modern era with contributions from the field's leading experts.

———. 2003b. "Cult, Metallurgy and Rank Societies—Chalcolithic Period (ca. 4500–3500 B.C.E.)." In *The Archaeology of Society in the Holy Land,* 3d ed., edited by T. E. Levy, 226–244. New York: Facts on File.

Description of social, economic, and political organizations during the Chalcolithic period, with a focus on the influence of cult and the development of metallurgy.

Levy, Thomas E., Russel B. Adams, Andreas Hauptmann, Michael Prange, S. Schmitt-Strecker, and Mohammed Najjar. 2002. "Early Bronze Age Metallugy: A Newly Discovered Copper Manufactory in Southern Jordan." *Antiquity* 76: 425–427.

Examination of the archaeological evidence from a copper production site in the Faynan region, with a discussion of the application of Global Positioning System (GPS) technology for the study of artifact distribution.

Levy, Thomas E., and David Alon. 1985. "Shiqmim: A Chalcolithic Village and Mortuary Center in the Northern Negev." *Paléorient* 11: 17–83.

Preliminary report on the first seasons of excavation at the northern Negev site.

Levy, Thomas E., and Jonathan Golden. 1996. "Syncrestic and Mnemonic Dimensions of

Chalcolithic Art: A New Human Figurine from Shiqmim." *Biblical Archaeologist* 59: 150–159.

> Examination of a bone figurine from Shiqmim, with a broader discussion of the Chalcolithic tradition of figurative art.

Levy, Thomas E., and Sariel Shalev. 1989. "Prehistoric Metalworking in the Southern Levant: Archaeo-Metallurgical and Social Perspectives." *World Archaeology* 20: 352–372.

> Study on the archaeometallurgical evidence from Shiqmim within the context of the village in order to understand social aspects of production and use.

Levy, Thomas E., et al. 1991. "Protohistoric Investigations at the Shiqmim Chalcolithic Village and Cemetery: Interim Report on the 1987 Season." *BASOR Supplement* 27: 29–45.

> Interim report on the archaeological finds from Shiqmim.

———. 1997. "Egyptian-Canaanite Interaction at Nahal Tillah, Israel (ca. 4500–3000 B.C.E.): An Interim Report on the 1994–95 Excavations." *Bulletin of the American Schools of Oriental Research* 308: 1–51.

> Interim report on archaeological discoveries at the Early Bronze Age site at Halif Terrace, with a focus on evidence for the Egyptian presence.

Lichtheim, Miriam, trans. 1973. "Story of Sinuhe." In *Ancient Egyptian Literature.* Vol. 1, *The Old and Middle Kingdoms,* 223–233. Berkeley: University of California Press.

> Translation and discussion of an ancient Egyptian tale of an expatriate sojourning in Canaan that provides information about societies of the Middle Bronze Age.

Liphschitz, Nili, Ram Gophna, Moshe Hartman, and Gideon Biger. 1991. "Beginning of Olive (*Olea europaea*) Cultivation in the Old World: A Reassessment." *Journal of Archaeological Science* 18: 441–453.

> Discussion of cultural ecology and land use during the third millennium B.C.E., with an examination of evidence for the clearing of wooded areas for agriculture.

Liphschitz, Nili, Ram Gopha, and Simcha Lev-Yadun. 1989. "Man's Impact on the Vegetational Landscape of Israel in the Early Bronze Age II–III." In *Urbanisation de la Palestine à l'âge du Bronze Ancien,* edited by Ruth Amiran and Ram Gophna, 263–268. Oxford: British Archaeological Reports.

> A look at cultural ecology and land use during the third millennium B.C.E., with an examination of evidence for the clearing of wooded areas for agriculture.

Loud, Gordon. 1948. *Megiddo II Seasons, 1935–1939.* Chicago: University of Chicago Press.

> Report on the archaeological findings from early excavations at Megiddo.

Lovell, Jaimie. 2001. *The Late Neolithic and Chalcolithic Periods in the Southern Levant: New Data from the Site of Teleilat Ghassul, Jordan.* Oxford: Archaeopress/Hadrian Books.

Discussion of the Neolithic-Chalcolithic transition in the southern Levant, based on the study of the ceramic assemblage from Ghassul.

———. 2002. "Shifting Subsistence Patterns: Some Ideas about the End of the Chalcolithic in the Southern Levant." *Paleorient* 28: 89–102.

Examination of the floral and faunal remains from the Chalcolithic, especially at the site of Teleilat Ghassul, and their implication for understanding socioeconomic life.

Machinist, Peter. 1982. "Assyrians and Hittites in the Late Bronze Age." In *Mesopotamien und seine Nachbarn*, edited by Hans J. Nissen and Johannes Renger, 265–267. Berlin: Reimer.

Discussion of the Canaanites' neighbors, based largely on the examination of textual evidence.

———. 2000. "Biblical Traditions: The Philistines and Israelite History." In *The Sea Peoples and Their World: A Reassessment*, edited by Eliezer D. Oren and Donald W. Jones, 53–83. University Museum Monograph, 108. Philadelphia: Museum of Archaeology and Anthropology, University of Pennsylvania.

Analysis of Philistine social, economic, and political organization as well as the issue of relations between the Philistines and Israelites of the Iron Age based on textual evidence, including the Hebrew Bible.

Maddin, Robert. 1989 "The Copper and Tin Ingots from the Kas Shipwreck." In *Old World Archaeometallurgy*, edited by A. Hauptmann, E. Pernicka, and G. A. Wagner, 99–106. Bochum: Selbstverlag des Deutsches Bergbau-Museum

One of the pioneers in archaeometallurgical studies examines metal finds from the Late Bronze Age shipwreck.

Maeir, Aren. 2000. "The Political and Economic Status of MB II Hazor and the MB II Trade: An Inter- and Intra-Regional View." *Palestine Exploration Quarterly* 132: 37–57.

Examination of Hazor's role in "international" politics and trade during the Middle Bronze Age, with an emphasis on Hazor's relation to the cities of Syria.

———. 2002. "Canaanite and Philistines: Recent Excavations at Tel-es-Safi/Gath." Paper presented at the Third International Conference on the Archaeology of the Ancient Near East, April 16, Paris.

Evaluation of archaeological evidence from Tel el-Safi, arguing that the site should be identified as the Philistine Pentapolis city of Gath.

Maeir, Aren, and Carl S. Ehrlich. 2001. "Excavating Philistine Gath: Have We Found Goliath's Hometown?" *Biblical Archaeology Review* 27: 22–31.

Brief overview of archaeological findings from Tel el-Safi with a focus on the site's identification as the Philistine city of Gath.

Magness-Gardiner, Bonnie, and Steven Falconer. 1994. "Community, Polity, and Temple in a Middle Bronze Age Levantine Village." *Journal of Mediterranean Archaeology* 7: 127–164.

> Discussion of the archaeological evidence from the Middle Bronze Age farming hamlet of Tel el-Hayyat, Jordan, along with related textual evidence, with a focus on the relationship between socioeconomic activity and the temple.

Mairs, Lachan D. 1997. *Ghassul Archaeozoological Report: 1995–1997 Seasons.* Sydney: Teleilat Ghassul Project.

> Summary of the faunal remains from the Chalcolithic center near the Dead Sea.

Maisler, Benjamin, Moshe Stekelis, and Michael Avi-Yonah. 1952. "The Excavations at Beit-Yerah (Khirbet el-Kerak), 1944–1946." *Israel Exploration Journal* 2: 165–173.

> Report on the archaeological findings from excavations at the northern Early Bronze Age center of Beit Yerah.

Marcus, Ezra. 2002. "Early Seafaring and Maritime Activity in the Southern Levant from Prehistory through the Third Millennium B.C.E." In *Egyptian and Canaanite Interaction during the Fourth–Third Millennium B.C.E.*, edited by E. van den Brink and T. Levy, 403–417. London: Leicester University Press.

> Discussion of the evidence for maritime transport and seafaring technology during the Early Bronze Age and its possible impact on peoples of the southern Levant.

Marfoe, Leon. 1979. "The Integrative Transformation: Patterns of Sociopolitical Organization in Southern Syria." *Bulletin of the American Schools of Oriental Research* 234: 1–42.

Master, Daniel M. 2001. "State Formation and the Kingdom of Ancient Israel." *Journal of Near Eastern Studies* 60: 117–131.

> Analysis of the rise of the United Monarchy as a process of state formation.

Matthews, Victor Harold. 2002. *A Brief History of Ancient Israel.* Louisville, KY: Westminster/John Knox Press.

> Reconstruction of late Canaanite and early Israelite history, with an emphasis on the interpretation of the biblical narrative in light of social theory.

May, Herbert, G. 1935. *Material Remains of the Megiddo Cult.* Chicago: Oriental Institute.

> Examination of the archaeological remains pertaining to religious practice at Iron Age Megiddo, offering an interpretation of how various cultic paraphernalia, such as stands, were used for burning incense.

Mazar, Amihai. 1973. "A Philistine Temple at Tell Qasile." *Biblical Archaeologist* 36: 42–18.

> Brief summary of archaeological evidence from excavations at Tel Qasile, focusing on remains from the temple.

———. 1982. "The 'Bull Site': An Iron Age I Open Cult Place." *Bulletin of the American Schools of Oriental Research* 247: 27–42.

Report on archaeological discoveries at an open-air site in the central hill country, arguing that the site functioned as a shrine during the Iron Age.

————. 1985. "Emergence of the Philistine Material Culture." *Israel Exploration Journal* 35: 95–107.

Discussion of material culture and the identity of Sea Peoples and Philistines.

————. 1986. "On the Israelite Fortress at Arad." *Bulletin of the American Schools of Oriental Research* 263: 87–91.

Examination of archaeological evidence from excavations at Iron Age Arad, including a discussion of its relation to the Hebrew Bible.

————. 1990. *Archaeology of the Land of the Bible, 10,000–586 B.C.E.* New York: Doubleday.

Comprehensive overview of the archaeological evidence from the Neolithic period through the Iron Age.

————. 1993. "Beth Shean in the Iron Age: Preliminary Report and Conclusions of the 1990–1991 Excavations." *Israel Exploration Journal* 43: 201–229.

————. 1994. "The 11th Century B.C.E. in Palestine." In *Proceedings of the International Colloquium: Cyprus in the 11th Century B.C.,* edited by V. Karageorghis, 39–58. Nicosia: University of Cyprus.

A look at cultural and political developments in the southern Levant during the early Iron Age, with a focus on relations with Cyprus.

————. 1996. "Hartuv, an Aspect of the Early Bronze I Culture of Southern Israel." *Bulletin of the American Schools of Oriental Research* 302: 1–40.

Report on archaeological findings from excavations at the single period (Early Bronze Age 1) site in the southern Shephelah, proposing that the material culture represents a regional variant.

————. 1997a. "Four Thousand Years of History at Tel Beth-Shean: An Account of the Renewed Excavations." *Biblical Archaeologist* 60: 62–76.

————. 1997b. "Iron Age Chronology: A Reply to I. Finkelstein." *Levant* 29: 157–167.

————. 1999a. "The 'Bull Site' and the 'Einun Pottery' Reconsidered." *Palestine Exploration Quarterly* 131: 144–148.

————. 1999b. "The 1997–1998 Excavations at Tel Rehov: Preliminary Report." *Israel Exploration Journal* 49: 1–42.

————. 2000. "The Temples and Cult of the Philistines." In *The Sea Peoples and Their World: A Reassessment,* edited by Eliezer D. Oren and Donald W. Jones, 213–232. University Museum Monograph, 108. Philadelphia: Museum of Archaeology and Anthropology, University of Pennsylvania.

————. 2001. "Beth Shean during the Iron Age II: Stratigraphy, Chronology and Hebrew Ostraca." In *Studies in the Archaeology of the Iron Age in Israel and Jordan,* edited by A. Mazar, 289–309. Sheffield, England: Sheffield Academic Press.

> Discussion of archaeological evidence from the 1989–1996 excavation of Beth Shean, as well as textual material (ostraca) from the second part of the Iron Age (Iron 2), that points to occupation of the site from the tenth to the eighth centuries B.C.E.

———. 2002. "An Early Bronze I Public Building and EbII–III Rampart Fortifications in the Beth Shean Valley, Israel." Unpublished paper.

Mazar, Amihai, and Carmi, Israel. 2001. "Radiocarbon Dates from Iron Age Strata at Tel Beth Shean and Tel Rehov." *Radiocarbon* 43: 1333–1342.

> Examination of the radiocarbon data from two Iron Age sites in an attempt to reconstruct the chronology of settlement in the Beth Shean Valley.

Mazar, Amihai, et al. 1999. "The 1997–1998 Excavations at Tel Rehov: Preliminary Report." *Israel Exploration Journal* 49: 1–42.

Mazar, Benjamin. 1952. "The Excavations at Beth Yerah (Khirbet el-Kerak), 1944–1946, by B. Maisler, M. Stekelis and M. Avi-Yonah." *Israel Exploration Journal* 2: 165–173.

> Report on the archaeological findings from research at Beit Yerah, focused on occupation during the third part of the Early Bronze Age (EB3) (levels I–IV).

———. 1981. "The Early Israelite Settlement in the Hill Country." *Bulletin of the American Schools of Oriental Research* 241: 75–85.

> Discussion about the early settlement of Israelite tribes in the central highlands, comparing the available archaeological evidence with the biblical narrative

———. 1992. *Biblical Israel: State and People.* Jerusalem: Israel Exploration Society.

Mazar, Benjamin, and Hanan Eshel. 1988. "Who Built the First Wall of Jerusalem?" *Israel Exploration Journal* 48: 265–268.

> An attempt to date the construction of a massive wall found during excavations in Jerusalem's Old City.

McCarter, P. Kyle, Jr. 1974. "The Early Diffusion of the Alphabet." *Biblical Archaeologist* 37: 54–68.

> Examination of the evidence for the earliest use of the Canaanite script and its possible influence on the development of other scripts.

———. 1987. "Aspects of the Religion of the Israelite Monarchy: Biblical and Epigraphic Data." In *Ancient Israelite Religion,* edited by P. Miller, P. Hanson and S. McBride, 137–155. Philadelphia: Fortress.

> Discussion of religious practice during the second and third parts of the Iron Age (Iron 2–3), based on the interpretation of references in the Hebrew Bible as well as extra-biblical texts and inscriptions.

McGovern, Patrick E. 1993. "The Late Bronze Egyptian Garrison at Beth Shan: Glass and Faience Production and Importation in the Late New Kingdom." *Bulletin of the American Schools of Oriental Research* 290: 1–27.

An evaluation of the evidence for the production of glass and faience at Beth Shean during the Late Bronze Age, via the use of microscopy and chemical analysis, by one of the leading researchers in the field of archaeometry.

McNutt, Paula. 1991. *The Forging of Israel: Iron Technology, Symbolism and Tradition in Ancient Society.* Sheffield: Journal for the Study of the Old Testament (JSOT) Press.

Extended discussion of iron production in ancient Israel, applying perspectives gained from ethnographic studies of African production in modern times.

———. 1999. *Reconstructing the Society of Ancient Israel.* Louisville, KY: Westminster/ John Knox Press.

Reconstruction of social and political organization during the Iron Age, with an emphasis on social class and gender, and an attempt to assess the historical value of archaeological and textual evidence.

Mendenhall, George E. 1962. "The Hebrew Conquest of Palestine." *Biblical Archaeologist* 25: 66–87.

Landmark article in which the author outlines the "Peasant Revolt Model" as an explanation for Israelite settlement in the central highlands.

———. 1973. *The Tenth Generation: The Origins of the Biblical Tradition.* Baltimore: Johns Hopkins University Press.

A study on the role of Yahwism in the formation of Israelite identity and the rise of the state, the 'Apiru, and the impact of the Sea Peoples.

———. 1985. *The Syllabic Inscriptions from Byblos.* Beirut, Lebanon: American University of Beirut.

Discussion of textual evidence from excavations at Byblos and its significance for understanding the evolution of the alphabet.

———. 1993. "The Northern Origins of Old South Arabic Literacy." *Yemen Update* 33: 15–19.

Discussion of the emergence of the Old Arabic script and its relation to the Byblite and Canaanite scripts.

Merkel, John, and William Dever. 1989. "Metalworking Technology at the End of the Early Bronze Age in the Southern Levant." Newsletter, Institute for Archaeo-Metallurgical Studies 14: 1–4.

A consideration of the archaeometallurgical evidence from the end of the third millennium B.C.E., including some of the region's first bronze artifacts.

Meshel, Zeev. 1978. *Kuntillet 'Ajrud: A Religious Centre from the Time of the Judean Monarchy on the Border of Sinai.* Jerusalem: Israel Museum.

Archaeological site report, with a focus on the site's function as a religious center, especially for pilgrims and caravans to and from the Sinai.

Meshel, Zeev, and Carol L. Meyers. 1976. "The Name of God in the Wilderness of Zin." *Biblical Archaeologist* 39: 6–10.

Brief discussion of religious inscriptions from the Iron Age, including references to Yahweh.

Mettinger, Tryggve. 1995. *No Graven Image? Israelite Aniconism in Its Near Eastern Context.* Stockholm: Almqvist and Wiksell.

Analysis of the evidence for aniconism both inside and outside Israel.

———. 1997. "The Roots of Aniconsim: An Israelite Phenomenon in Comparative Perspective." In *Congress Volume Cambridge 1995,* edited by J. Emerton, 219–233. Leiden: E. J. Brill.

Examination of the origins of the prohibitions against idol worship as part of the development of monotheism.

Meyers, Carol. 1988. *Discovering Eve: Ancient Israelite Women in Context.* New York: Oxford University Press.

An attempt to reconstruct the everyday lives of women in ancient Israel and their role in society, challenging some of the traditionally held notions.

———. 1997. "The Family in Ancient Israel." In *Families in Ancient Israel,* edited by L. Perdue, J. Blenkinsopp, J. Collins, and C. Meyers, 1–47. Louisville, KY: Westminster/John Knox Press.

Discussion of the evidence for family structure in ancient Israel and the role of family in broader socioeconomic organization.

Milevski, Ianir. 2002. "The Quleh Figurine: A New Aspect of Cultic Beliefs during the Chalcolithic of the Southern Levant." Paper presented at the Third International Conference on the Archaeology of the Ancient Near East, April 16, Paris.

Report on a carved figurine from the Chalcolithic and its wider cultural context.

Millard, Alan Ralph. 1972. "The Practice of Writing in Ancient Israel." *Biblical Archaeologist* 35: 98–111.

Analysis of evidence for the early development and spread of literacy, with a discussion of the origins of the Canaanite script.

———. 1979. "The Ugaritic and Canaanite Alphabets, Some Notes." *Ugarit-Forschung* 11: 613–616.

Examination of the evidence for these two early scripts, arguing that the Ugaritic alphabet may have borrowed the order of its letters and other aspects from the Canaanite alphabet.

Miroschedji, Pierre de. 1989. *L'urbanisation de la Palestine à l'âge du Bronze Ancien.* International Series. Oxford: British Archaeological Reports.

> Edited volume devoted to studying the process of urbanization and the development of social complexity during the Early Bronze Age, with contributions from many of the field's leading scholars.

———. 1993. "Jarmuth, Tel." In *New Encyclopedia of Archaeological Excavations in the Holy Land,* 2: 661–665. New York: Simon and Schuster.

> Brief summary of archaeological research at Tel Yarmuth.

Misch-Brandl, Osnat. 1984. "A Silver Figurine from Megiddo—Fifty Years Later." *Israel Museum Journal:* 46–51.

> Reexamination of a silver figurine in light of more recent discoveries, with a discussion of its function and wider significance.

Moorey, Peter R. S. 1988. "The Chalcolithic Hoard from Nahal Mishmar, Israel, in Context." *World Archaeology* 20: 171–189.

> Review of the metal assemblage from Nahal Mishmar, focused on explaining the origins of the hoard.

———. 1992. "British Women in Near Eastern Archaeology: Kathleen Kenyon and the Pioneers." *Palestine Exploration Quarterly* 124: 91–100.

Moorey, Peter R.S., and Schweizer, F. 1972. "Copper and Copper Alloys in Ancient Iraq, Syria, and Palestine: Some New Analyses." *Archaeometry* 14:177–98.

> A landmark study in the application of scientific analyses to ancient metals.

Moran, William L. 1992. *The Amarna Letters.* Baltimore: Johns Hopkins University Press.

> Translation and discussion of the famous archive from New Kingdom Egypt (el Amarna), contemporary with the Canaanite Late Bronze Age.

Moscrop, John James. 2000. *Measuring Jerusalem: The Palestine Exploration Fund and British Interest in the Holy Land.* London: Leicester University Press.

> History of archaeological discovery in the southern Levant, with a focus on the early years of the Palestine Exploration Fund (PEF) and the British researchers who explored beneath the modern city of Jerusalem.

Muhly, James, D. 1993. "Early Bronze Age Tin and the Taurus." *American Journal of Archaeology* 97:239–254.

> One of the leading experts on Old World metallurgy refutes assertions made by Yener and Vandiver (1993) with regard to tin sources.

———. 1999. "Copper and Bronze in Cyprus and the Eastern Mediterranean." In *The Archaeometallurgy of the Asian Old World,* edited by V. C. Pigott, 15–26. Philadelphia: University Museum, University of Pennsylvania.

Discussion of metal production and trade based on a reassessment of material from the eastern Mediterranean.

Muraoka, Takamitsu. 1995. "Linguistic Notes on the Aramaic Inscription from Tel Dan." *Israel Exploration Journal* 45: 19–21.

Commentary on the Tel Dan inscription, with a focus on specific aspects of the early Aramaic language.

Na'aman, Nadav. 1975. "The Political Disposition and Historical Development of Eretz-Israel according to the Amarna Letters." Ph.D. dissertation, Tel-Aviv University.

Doctoral dissertation, in Hebrew with an English summary, devoted to the examination of the Amarna Letters, with a focus on what can be learned about ethnicity and the political situation during the Late Bronze Age.

———. 1981. "Economic Aspects of the Egyptian Occupation of Canaan." *Israel Exploration Journal* 31: 172–185.

Comparison of the economic impact of Egyptian imperialism on cities and rural areas in Canaan.

———. 1984. "Statements of Time-Spans by Babylonian and Assyrian Kings and Mesopotamian Chronology." *Iraq* 46: 115–123.

———. 1986. "Habiru and Hebrews: The Transfer of a Social Term to the Literary Sphere." *Journal of Near Eastern Studies* 45: 271 *ff.*

———. 1994. "Hurrians and the End of the Middle Bronze Age in Palestine." *Levant* 26: 175–187.

Discussion about the presence of Hurrian peoples in Canaan via examination of Hurrian names and linguistic elements appearing in texts from the Middle and Late Bronze Ages.

———. 1996. "The Contribution of the Amarna Letters to the Debate on Jerusalem's Political Position in the Tenth Century B.C.E." *Bulletin of the American Schools of Oriental Research* 304: 17–27.

Reconstruction of political organization during the Iron Age based on references to the region found in the Amarna Letters.

Na'aman, Zeev. 1999. "No Anthropomorphic Graven Image: Notes on the Assumed Anthropomorphic Cult Statues in the Temples of YHWH in the Pre-Exilic Period." *Ugarit-Forshungen* 31: 391–415.

Discussion of the development of aniconic religion and the nature of Yahweh worship in the temple of Jerusalem.

Najjar, Mohammad. 1992. "Jordan Valley (East Bank) during the Middle Bronze Age in the Light of New Excavations." *Studies in the History and Archaeology of Jordan* 4: 149–153.

Nakhai, Beth A. 1993. "Religion in Canaan and Israel: An Archaeological Perspective." Ph.D. dissertation, University of Arizona.

———. 1994. "What's a Bamah? How Sacred Space Functioned in Ancient Israel." *Biblical Archaeology Review* 20: 18–29.

Naveh, Danny. 2003. "PPNA Jericho: A Socio-Political Perspective." *Cambridge Archaeological Journal* 13: 83–96.

Naveh, Joseph. 1970. "The Scripts in Palestine and Trans Jordan in the Iron Age." In *Near Eastern Archaeology in the Twentieth Century: Essays in Honor of Nelson Glueck,* edited by James A. Sanders, 277–283. Garden City, NY: Doubleday.

———. 1973. "Some Semitic Epigraphical Considerations on the Antiquity of the Greek Alphabet." *American Journal of Archaeology* 77: 1–8.

———. 1978. "Some Considerations on the Ostracon from 'Izbet Sartah." *Israel Exploration Journal* 28: 31–35.

———. 1980. "The Greek Alphabet: New Evidence." *Biblical Archaeologist* 43: 22–25.

———. 1982. *The Early History of the Alphabet: An Introduction to West Semitic Epigraphy and Palaeography.* Jerusalem: Magnes Press, Hebrew University.

———. 1985. "Writing and Scripts in Seventh-Century B.C.E. Philistia: The New Evidence from Tell Jemmeh." *Israel Exploration Journal* 35: 8–21.

———. 1987. "Unpublished Phoenician Inscriptions from Palestine." *Israel Exploration Journal* 37: 25–30.

———. 1990. "Nameless People." *Israel Exploration Journal* 40: 108–123.

———. 1998a. "Achish-Ikausu in the Light of the Ekron Dedication." *Bulletin of the American Schools of Oriental Research* 310: 35–37.

———. 1998b. "Scripts and Inscriptions in Ancient Samaria." *Israel Exploration Journal* 48: 91–100.

Negbi, Ora. 1966. "The 'Foundation Deposits' or 'Offering Deposits' of Byblos." *Bulletin of the American Schools of Oriental Research* 184: 21–26.

———. 1968. "Dating Some Groups of Canaanite Bronze Figurines." *Palestine Exploration Quarterly* 100: 45–55.

———. 1976. *Canaanite Gods in Metal: An Archaeological Study of Ancient Syro-Palestinian Figurines.* Tel Aviv: Tel Aviv University, Institute of Archaeology.

———. 1993. "Israelite Cult Elements in Secular Contexts of the Tenth Century B.C.E." In *Biblical Archaeology Today, 1990, Pre-congress Symposium: Population, Production and*

Power (Proceedings of the Second International Congress on Biblical Archaeology), edited by A. Biran and J. Aviram, 221–230. Jerusalem: Israel Exploration Society.

   Examination of the context in which cultic artifacts are found, with a focus on Megiddo and Lachish.

Netzer, Ehud. 1992. "Domestic Architecture in the Iron Age." In *The Architecture of Ancient Israel: From the Prehistoric to the Persian Periods,* edited by Reich Aharon and Ronny Kempinski, 193–201. Jerusalem: Israel Exploration Society.

   Overview of the archaeological evidence for houses and domestic life during the Iron Age, with a discussion of family and community socioeconomic organization.

Niemann, Hermann Michael. 1997. "The Socio-Political Shadow Cast by the Biblical Solomon." In *The Age of Solomon,* edited by L. K. Handy, 252–299. Leiden: E. J. Brill.

   Discussion of archaeological evidence for the biblical King Solomon, revisiting debates concerning the city gate systems and so-called "stables."

Noll, Kurt Lesher. 1997. *The Faces of David.* Sheffield, England: Sheffield Academic Press.

———. 2001. *Canaan and Israel in Antiquity: An Introduction.* London: Sheffield Academic Press.

North, Robert G. 1989. "Yahweh's Asherah." In *To Touch the Text: Biblical and Related Studies in Honor of Joseph A. Fitzmyer, S. J.,* edited by M. Morgan and P. Kobelski, 118–137. New York: Crossroad.

   A look at the evidence concerning the question of Asherah and whether she was considered a consort of Yahweh.

Northover, Peter. 1998. "Exotic Alloys in Antiquity" In *Metallurgica Antiqua: In Honor of Hans-Gert Bachmann and Robert Maddin,* edited by T. Rehren, A. Hauptmann, and J. Muhly, 113–122. Bochum: Dt. Bergbau Museum.

   An archaeometallurgist discusses the evidence for changes in the use of various copper-based alloys throughout the ancient Old World.

Nur el-Din, Hani. 2002. "Underground Water Systems in Palestine: A Reinterpretation." Paper presented at the Third International Conference on the Archaeology of the Ancient Near East, April 16, Paris.

   A reexamination of the water systems of Jerusalem, revealing what may be a much earlier date for them than was earlier thought.

Ofer, Aharon R. 1994. "All the Hill Country of Judah: From a Settlement Fringe to a Prosperous Monarchy." In *From Nomadism to Monarchy: Archaeological and Historical Aspects of Early Israel,* edited by I. Finkelstein and N. Na'aman, 92–121. Washington, DC: Biblical Archaeology Society.

Olyan, Saul. 1988. *Asherah and the Cult of Yahweh in Israel.* Atlanta: Scholars Press.

Oren, Eliezer D. 1971. "A Middle Bronze Age Warrior Tomb at Beth-Shan." *Zeitschrift des deutschen Palästine-Vereins* 87: 109–139.

Oren, Eliezer D., and Donald W. Jones, eds. 2000. *The Sea Peoples and Their World: A Reassessment.* University Museum Monograph, 108. Philadelphia: Museum of Archaeology and Anthropology, University of Pennsylvania.

Oren, Eliezer D., and Yuval Yekutiele. 1990. "North Sinai during the MB I Period—Pastoral Nomadism and Sedentary Settlement." *Eretz Israel* 21: 6–22, 101.

Discussion of the evidence for pastoral nomadism and its impact on shifting settlement patterns during the Middle Bronze Age, in Hebrew, with a summary in English.

Ornan, Tallay. 2001. "Isˇtar as Depicted on Finds from Israel." In *Studies in the Archaeology of the Iron Age in Israel and Jordan,* edited by A. Mazar, 179–216. Sheffield, England: Sheffield Academic Press.

Discussion of the appearance of the Near Eastern goddess Isˇtar and her relation to Asherah.

Ottosson, Magnus. 1980. *Temples and Cult Places in Palestine.* Stockholm: Almqvist and Wiksell.

General overview of religious architecture in the southern Levant.

Ovadia, Eran. 1992. "The Domestication of the Ass and Pack Transport by Animals: A Case of Technological Change." In *Pastoralism in the Levant: Archaeological Materials in Anthropological Perspective,* edited by O. Bar-Yosef and A. Khazanov, 19–28. Madison, WI: Prehistory Press.

A look at the evidence for the domestication of the ass and its impact on overland trade.

Palumbo, Gaetano. 1987. "'Egalitarian' or 'Stratified' Society? Some Notes on Mortuary Practices and Social Structure at Jericho in EB IV." *Bulletin of the American Schools of Oriental Research* 267: 43–59.

Examination of mortuary evidence from Jericho during the Intermediate Bronze Age (EB4), with a discussion of how it reflects social organization.

———. 1991. *The Early Bronze Age IV in the Southern Levant: Settlement Patterns, Economy, and Material Culture of a 'Dark Age.'* Roma: Università degli studi Roma "La Sapienza."

Monograph devoted to the study of social and economic life during the Intermediate Bronze Age (EB4).

Peilstöcker, Martin. 2002. "Excavations at the Bronze Age Cemetery of Shuni." Paper presented at the Third International Conference on the Archaeology of the Ancient Near East, April 16, Paris.

Discussion of mortuary evidence from the cemetery at Shuni, with a focus on burials from the Intermediate and Middle Bronze Ages, in addition to some from the Late Bronze, Iron, and Chalcolithic Ages.

Peltenburg, E. J. 1987. "Lemba Archaeological Project, Cyprus, 1985." *Levant* 19: 221–224.

Perrot, Jean. 1955. The Excavations at Abu Matar, near Beersheva. *Israel Exploration Journal* 5:17–41, 73–84, 167–89.

Report on the archaeological findings from excavations at the Chalcolithic site of Abu Matar.

———. 1968. "Préhistoire Palestinienne." In *Supplément au Dictionaire de la Bible*, 286–466. Paris: Letouzey et Ané.

Summary of evidence from the Neolithic through Chalcolithic periods in the southern Levant.

———. 1984. Structures d'Habitat: Mode de Vie et Environnement: Les Villages Souterrains des pasteurs de Beershéva dans la Sud'Israël au IVe Millénaire avant l'Ère Chrétienne. *Paléorient* 10/1: 75–96.

Discussion of evidence from the Beer Sheva Chalcolithic, with a special focus on architecture and its function.

Petrie, W. M. Flinders. 1906. *Researches in Sinai*. London: J. Murray.

Philip, Graham. 2003. "Copper Metallurgy in the Jordan Valley from the Third to First Millennia B.C.: Chemical, Metallographic and Lead Isotope Analyses of Artifacts from Pella." *Levant* 35: 71–100.

Examination of copper goods and metallurgical remains, including scientific analysis of the material and a discussion of their broader significance.

Philip, Graham, and Olwen Williams-Thorpe. 1993. "A Provenance Study of Jordanian Basalt Vessels of the Chalcolithic and Early Bronze I Periods." *Paléorient* 19: 51–63.

Report on scientific analyses of basalt artifacts from the southern Levant in an attempt to determine the source of the material.

Piggot, Vincent C., ed. 1999. *The Archaeometallurgy of the Asian Old World*. Philadelphia: University Museum, University of Pennsylvania.

Edited volume devoted to the study of metal production and use throughout the ancient Near East and Aegean, Iran, and South Asia, with contributions from a number of leading scholars.

Portugali, Yuval, and Ram Gophna. 1993. "Crisis, Progress and Urbanization: The Transition from the Early Bronze I to the Early Bronze II in Palestine." *Tel Aviv* 20: 164–186.

Discussion of Early Bronze Age settlement patterns and the rise of urbanism during the Early Bronze Age 2, based largely on survey data.

Pritchard, James Bennett. 1985. *Tell es-Saidiyeh: Excavations on the Tell, 1964–1966.* Philadelphia: University Museum, University of Pennsylvania.

Report on archaeological discoveries from excavations at Tell es-Saidiyeh in the Jordan Valley.

Rainey, Anson. 1991. "Rainey's Challenge." *Biblical Archaeology Review* 17: 56–60.

A challenge to Frank Yurco's interpretation of Egyptian representations of the various Asian peoples, suggesting that the Israelites can be identified on the basis of their kilts and turbans.

———. 1994. "Hezekiah's Reform and the Altars at Beer-Sheba and Arad." In *Scripture and Other Artifacts: Essays on the Bible and Archaeology in Honor of Philip J. King,* edited by M. Coogan, C. Exum and L. Stager, 344–354. Louisville, KY: Westminster/John Knox Press.

Discussion of the archaeological evidence for King Hezekiah's religious reforms as recounted in the Hebrew Bible.

———. 1996. "Who Is a Canaanite? A Review of the Textual Evidence." *Bulletin of the American Schools of Oriental Research* 304: 1–15.

Study of ethnicity and society during the Middle and Late Bronze Ages based on textual evidence, primarily names, and certain aspects of social and political organization.

———. 2001. "Stones for Bread: Archaeology versus History." *Near Eastern Archaeology* 64: 140–149.

Examination of the relationship between material culture and text, suggesting that the linguistic and philological studies on ancient inscriptions should be considered at least as important as archaeological evidence.

Redford, Donald B. 1992. *Egypt, Canaan, and Israel in Ancient Times.* Princeton, NJ: Princeton University Press.

Overview of the history of interaction between the southern Levant and Egypt from late prehistoric times through the Iron Age, written for a popular audience.

Rehren, Thilo, Karsten Hess, and Graham Philip. 1997. "Fourth Millennium B.C. Copper Metallurgy in Northern Jordan: The Evidence from Tell es-Shuna." In *The Prehistory of Jordan II: Perspectives from 1997,* edited by H.-G. Gebel, Z. Kafafi, and G. Rollefson, 625–640. Berlin: Ex Oriente.

Examination of archaeometallurgical remains from the Early Bronze Age site of Shuna, with a discussion of systems of production and exchange.

Renfrew, Colin. 1971. "Carbon 14 and the Prehistory of Europe." *Scientific American* 225: 63–70.

———. 1986. "Introduction: Peer Polity Interaction and Socio-Political Change." In *Peer Polity Interaction and Socio-Political Change,* edited by Colin Renfrew and John F. Cherry, 1–19. Cambridge: Cambridge University Press.

Richard, Suzanne. 1990. "The 1987 Expedition to Khirbet Iskander and Its Vicinity: Fourth Preliminary Report." In *Preliminary Reports of ASOR-Sponsored Excavations 1983–87,* edited by Walter Rast, 33–58. BASOR Supplement 26. Baltimore: Johns Hopkins University Press.

Report on the archaeological findings from excavations at the early Iron Age site, with a discussion of settlement and ecological adaptation.

Robinson, Edward, G. 1841. *Biblical Researches in Palestine, Mount Sinai, and Arabia Petraea.* 2 vols. London: John Murray.

Landmark work from the era of pre-excavation research on Palestine's ancient past by the leading scholar of the day, who established the precedent for combining biblical scholarship with the exploration of the physical remains of the past.

Rosen, Arlene M. 1986. "Environmental Change and Settlement at Tel Lachish, Israel." *Bulletin of the American Schools of Oriental Research* 263, 55–60.

Examination of the floral assemblage, by a paleobotanist, in order to study long-term environmental change at Lachish.

———. 1993. "Phytolith Evidence for Early Cereal Exploitation in the Levant." In *Current Research in Phytolith Analysis: Applications in Archaeology and Paleoecology,* edited by D. Pearsall and D. Piperno, 160–171. MASCA Research Papers in Science and Archaeology, 10. Philadelphia: University of Pennsylvania.

Report on the paleobotanical evidence from the Levant in an attempt to reconstruct the ancient environment and early agricultural strategies.

———. 1995. "The Social Response to Environmental Change in Early Bronze Age Canaan." *Journal of Anthropological Archaeology* 14: 26–46.

Discussion of economic organization and social change in the Early Bronze Age from the perspective of shifts in climate and environmental factors.

Rosen, Arlene Miller, and Stephen Weiner. 1994. "Identifying Ancient Irrigation: A New Method Using Opaline Phytoliths from Emmer Wheat." *Journal of Archaeological Science* 21: 125–132.

Explanation of the use of phytolith analysis studies to determine whether plants were grown under irrigation conditions.

Rosen, Baruch. 1986–1987. "Wine and Oil Allocations in the Samaria Ostraca." *Tel Aviv* 13–14: 39–45.

Study of Iron Age inscriptions pertaining to the production of wine and oil in the northern Kingdom of Israel.

Rosen, Steven A. 1983. "Canaanean Blades and the Early Bronze Age." *Israel Exploration Journal* 33: 15–29.

Examination of the evidence for the production and use of Canaanean blades during the Early Bronze Age, by one of the field's leading lithic analysts.

———. 1984. "The Adoption of Metallurgy in the Levant: A Lithic Perspective." *Current Anthropology* 25: 504–505.

Comparison of the lithic and copper assemblages of the Chalcolithic period and Early Bronze Age, focusing on the relative frequency of different types in order to understand the patterns of usage and thereby some of the reasons for the adoption of metal.

———. 1987. "The Potentials of Lithic Analysis in the Chalcolithic of the Northern Negev." In *Shiqmim I,* edited by T. Levy, 295–312. Oxford: British Archaeological Reports.

Report on the chipped stone artifacts from the Chalcolithic village of Shiqmim in the northern Negev.

———. 1993. "The Edge of the Empire: The Archaeology of Pastoral Nomads in the Southern Negev Highlands in Late Antiquity." *Biblical Archaeology* 56: 189–199.

Discussion of pastoral nomadism as a means of subsistence in the arid zone and the archaeological evidence for mobile populations and their activities.

Rosenfeld, Amnon, Shimon Ilani, and Michael Dvorachek. 1997. "Bronze Alloys from Canaan during the Middle Bronze Age." *Journal of Archaeological Science* 24: 857–864.

Review of archaeometallurgical evidence for bronze alloys of the Middle Bronze Age.

Rothenberg, Beno. 1998. "Who Were the 'Midianite' Copper Miners of the Arabah?" In *Metallurgica Antiqua: In Honor of Hans-Gert Bachmann and Robert Maddin,* edited by T. Rehren, A. Hauptmann, and J. Muhly, 197–212. Bochum: Deutsches Bargbau-Musum.

A suggestion, based on an examination of ceramics and other archaeological evidence found in mining regions of the Arabah, that immigrants of Aegean/Anatolian origin came to the area to collaborate with Egyptians in their mining operations.

Rothenberg, Beno, and Jonathan Glass. 1983. "Midianite Pottery." In *Midian, Moab and Edom,* edited by John F. A. Sawyer and David J. A. Clines, 65–124. Sheffield, England: Journal for the Study of the Old Testament (JSOT) Press.

Report on ceramics from the Timna site.

———. 1992. "Beginnings and the Development of Early Metallurgy and the Settlement and Chronology of the Western Arabah, from the Chalcolithic Period to Early Bronze Age." *Levant* 24: 141–157.

Examination of the archaeological evidence for early metal production at the Negev site of Timnah, with a discussion of early metallurgical technology.

Routledge, Bruce. 1995. "'For the Sake of Argument': Reflections on the Structure of Argumentation in Syro-Palestinian Archaeology." *Palestine Exploration Quarterly* 127: 41–49.

Commentary on the nature of debate in Iron Age archaeology using the history of scholarship on architectural features that have been interpreted by some as representing royal stables as described in the Hebrew Bible.

Rowan, Yorke. 1998. "Ancient Distribution and Deposition of Prestige Objects: Basalt Vessels during Late Prehistory in the Southern Levant." Ph.D. dissertation, University of Texas, Austin.

Examination of the production and use of basalt during the Neolithic and Chalcolithic periods, with a focus on craft specialization.

Rowan, Yorke, and Thomas E. Levy. 1994. "Proto-Canaanean Blades from the Chalcolithic Site of Gilat." *Levant* 26: 167–174.

Examination of the stone tool assemblage from Gilat, revealing a Chalcolithic forerunner of the Canaanean blades known from the Early Bronze Age.

Rowton, Michael B. 1976. "Dimorphic Structure and the Tribal Elite." In *Al Bahit: Festschrift Joseph Henniger.* St. Augustin bei Bonn, Germany: Studia Instituti Anthropos.

Model for subsistence systems where agriculturally based sedentism and pastoral nomadism form the two basic components of the economy.

Sass, Benjamin. 1988. *The Genesis of the Alphabet and Its Development in the Second Millennium B.C.E.* Wiesbaden: Otto Harrassowitz.

Discussion on the origins of the Proto-Canaanite and Proto-Sinaitic alphabets, with a summary of evidence from the Middle and Late Bronze Ages.

Sassoon, Isaac S. D. 2001. "Destination Torah: Notes and Reflections on Selected Verses from the Weekly Torah Readings." Hoboken, NJ: KTAV Publishing.

Examination of a selection of verses from the Hebrew Bible in search of deeper meaning, including a look at passages that allow for inferences about social and religious life in ancient times.

Scheftelowitz, Na'ama, and Ronit Oren. 1997. "Givat Ha'oranim (Nahal Barequet)." In *New Antiquities: Recent Discoveries from Archaeological Excavations in Israel,* 20. Jerusalem: Israel Museum.

Brief preliminary report on archaeological findings from the Chalcolithic burial cave of Givat Ha'oranim.

Schneider, T. 1991. "Six Biblical Signatures: Seals and Seal Impressions of the Six Biblical Personages Recovered." *Biblical Archaeology Review* 17: 26–33.

Schniedewind, William M. 1996. "Tel Dan Stela: New Light on Aramaic and Jehu's Revolt." *Bulletin of the American Schools of Oriental Research* 302: 75–90.

Analysis of the Tel Dan inscription, incorporating both the linguistic aspects of early Aramaic and the historical information concerning King Jehu.

———. 1998. "The Geopolitical History of Philistine Gath." *Bulletin of the American Schools of Oriental Research* 309: 69–77.

Discussion of the textual and archaeological evidence pertaining to the Philistine Pentapolis city of Gath.

Schniedwind, William M., and Bruce Zuckerman. 2001. "A Possible Reconstruction of the Name of Haza'el's Father in the Tel Dan Inscription." *Israel Exploration Journal* 51: 88–91.

An attempt to extrapolate additional evidence for the Judean Dynasty based on examination of the Tel Dan inscription.

Schulman, Alan R., and Ram Gophna. 1981. "An Archaic Egyptian Serekh from Tel Ma'ahaz." *Israel Exploration Journal* 31: 165–167.

Report on the discovery of the serekh of an early Egyptian king at the Early Bronze Age site of Tel Ma'ahaz.

Seger, Joseph, Brent Baum, Oded Borowski, Donald Powell Cole, Harold Forshey, Eugene Futato, Mark Laustrap, Pattio O'Connor Seger, and Melinde Zeder. 1990. "The Bronze Age Settlements at Tel Halif: Phase II Excavations, 1983–1987." In *Preliminary Report of ASOR-Sponsored Excavations, 1983–1987*, edited by W. Rast, 1–32. BASOR Supplement 26. Baltimore: Johns Hopkins University Press.

Report on the archaeological findings from excavations at Bronze Age Tel Halif, in the southern Shephelah.

Shaffer, Aaron. 1970. "Fragment of an Inscribed Envelope." In *Gezer I: Preliminary Report of the 1966–64 Seasons*, edited by W. Dever and G. Wright, 111–114. Jerusalem: Hebrew Union College Biblical and Archaeological School.

Analysis of an inscribed envelope fragment from Gezer bearing Hurrian names and representing some of the first evidence for the appearance of Hurrians in the southern Levant.

———. 1988. "Cuneiform Tablets from Palestine I: The Letter from Shechem." In *Linguistic Studies in Memory of Moshe Held*, edited by M. Cogan, 163–169. Beer-Sheva and Jerusalem: Ben-Gurion University of the Negev Press/Magnes Press, Hebrew University.

Examination of cuneiform tablets from Shechem, specifically one bearing a Hurrian name, with a discussion of the evidence for the arrival of a Hurrian element south of Syria.

Shalev, Sariel. 1994. "Change in Metal Production from the Chalcolithic Period to the Early Bronze Age in Israel and Jordan." *Antiquity* 68: 630–637.

Evaluation of the archaeomatallurgical evidence for copper in the Chalcolithic period and Early Bronze Age, comparing material from the two periods to examine patterns of change in production and use.

Shanks, Hershel. 1987. "Jeremiah's Scribe and Confidant Speaks from a Hoard of Clay Bullae." *Biblical Archaeology Review* 13: 58–65.

Shay, Talia. 1983. "Burial Customs at Jericho in the Intermediate Bronze Age: A Componential Analysis." *Tel Aviv* 10: 26–37.

Analysis of evidence for grave inclusions from the tombs of Jericho during the Intermediate Bronze Age, inferring from the lack of evidence for pronounced social gaps that Jericho was essentially an egalitarian society at the time.

Sherratt, Andrew. 1981. "Plough and Pastoralism: Aspects of the Secondary Products Revolution." In *Patterns of the Past: Essays in Honour of David Clark,* edited by I. Hodder, G. Isaac, and N. Hammond, 261–305. Cambridge: Cambridge University Press.

Discussion of subsistence patterns involving pastoral nomadism with a focus on the production of secondary goods, that is, the shift from meat and hides to dairy products and wool.

Shiloh, Yigal. 1970. "The Four-Room House—Its Situation and Function in the Israelite City." *Israel Exploration Journal* 20: 180–190.

Review of the archaeological evidence for four-room houses during the Iron Age, with a focus on this style as an Israelite characteristic.

———. 1977. "The Proto-Aeolic Capita—the Israelite 'Timorah' (Palmette) Capital." *Palestine Exploration Quarterly* 109: 39–52.

Examination of the "Proto-Aeolic" capital as part of royal Israelite architecture and its possible origins.

———. 1978. "Elements in the Development of Town Planning in the Israelite City." *Israel Exploration Journal* 28: 36–51.

Analysis of evidence for urbanism during the Iron Age, with a focus on Israelite cities.

———. 1979. "Iron Age Sanctuaries and Cult Elements in Palestine." In *Symposia Celebrating the 75th Anniversary of the Founding of the American Schools of Oriental Research (1900–1975),* edited by F. Cross, 147–157. Cambridge, MA: American Schools of Oriental Research.

Survey of evidence for religious practice and cultic activities during the Iron Age.

———. 1980. "Excavating Jerusalem: The City of David." *Archaeology* 33: 8–17.

Summary of archaeological research on the Iron Age in the Old City of Jerusalem, written for a popular audience.

———. 1993. *The New Encyclopedia of Archaeological Excavations in the Holy Land,* edited by Ephraim Stern, 2: 198–172. New York: Simon and Schuster.

Shiloh, Yigal, and David Tarler. 1986. "Bullae from the City of David: A Hoard of Seal Impressions from the Israelite Period." *Biblical Archaeologist* 49: 196–209.

Examination of inscribed bullae from late Iron Age Jerusalem and a discussion of their significance for understanding socioeconomic and political orgnaziation.

Shugar, Aaron N. 2000. "Archaeometallurgical Investigation of the Chalcolithic Site of Abu Matar, Israel: A Reassessment of Technology and Its Implications for the Ghassulian Culture." Ph.D. dissertation, University College London.

Study of early copper production technology based on the examination and analysis of archaeometallurgical remains from the Chalcolithic village of Abu Matar discovered during salvage excavations during the 1990s.

Silberman, Neil Asher. 1982. *Digging for God and Country: Exploration, Archeology, and the Secret Struggle for the Holy Land, 1799–1917.* New York: Knopf/Random House.

A landmark history of discovery for archaeological research in the southern Levant, set within the broader context of the national politics over the past century.

———. 1990. *Between Past and Present: Archaeology, Ideology, and Nationalism in the Modern Middle East.* New York: Anchor.

A history of important discoveries in Near Eastern archaeology, with a focus on the role of nationalism in this field.

———. 1993. *A Prophet from Amongst You: The Life of Yigael Yadin, Soldier, Scholar, and Mythmaker of Modern Israel.* Reading, MA: Addison-Wesley.

A study of the life and career of one of Israel's most famous archaeologists and his influence on the discipline, with a focus on the nationalist agenda evident in Yadin's research.

———. 1999. "Digging at Armageddon: A New Expedition Tackles One of the Near East's Most Famous Tels and Legends." *Archaeology* 52: 32–39.

———. 2003. "Power, Politics, and the Past: The Social Construction of Antiquity in the Holy Land." In *The Archaeology of Society in the Holy Land,* 3d ed., edited by T. Levy, 9–23. New York: Facts on File.

A brief history of archaeological research in the southern Levant, with a focus on the influence of international politics during each of the major phases.

Silberman, Neil Asher, and David Small, eds. 1997. *The Archaeology of Israel: Constructing the Past, Interpreting the Present.* Sheffield, England: Sheffield Academic Press.

Simkins, Ronald. 1999. "Patronage and the Political Economy of Monarchic Israel." In *The Social World of the Hebrew Bible: Twenty-Five Years of the Social Sciences in the Academy,* edited by R. Simkins and S. Cook, 123–144. Semeia 87. Atlanta: Society of Biblical Literature.

Discussion of political and socioeconomic organization during the later Iron Age, including issues concerning the role of gender hierarchies.

Singer, Itamar. 1983. *The Hittite KI.LAM Festival.* Wiesbaden: Harrassowitz.

Study of a Hittite festival, reconstructed primarily from inscribed tablet fragments.

———. 1988. "The Origin of the Sea Peoples and Their Settlement on the Coast of Canaan." In *Society and Economy in the Eastern Mediterranean,* edited by M. Heltzer and E. Lipinski, 239–250. Leuven, Belgium: Peeters.

Summary of the evidence for Philistine settlement on the coastal plain during the early Iron Age, with a discussion of both archaeological and textual evidence.

Smith, George A. 1894. *The Historical Geography of the Holy Land.* London: Hodder and Stoughton.

Smith, Mark S. 2002. *The Early History of God: Yahweh and Other Deities in Ancient Israel,* 2d ed. Grand Rapids, MI: William B. Eerdmans.

Detailed study of the evidence for religious practice, with a focus on the Iron Age and the deities Yahweh and Asherah.

Spooner, Brian. 1972. "The Iranian Deserts." In *Population Growth: Anthropological Implications,* edited by B. Spooner, 245–268. Cambridge, MA: MIT Press.

Discussion of cultural ecology and subsistence practices in the arid zones of Iran, based on ethnohistorical evidence.

Stager, Lawrence. 1982. "The Archaeology of the East Slope of Jerusalem and the Terraces of the Kidron." *Journal of Near Eastern Studies* 41: 111–121.

———. 1985. "The Archaeology of the Family in Ancient Israel." *Bulletin of the American Schools of Oriental Research* 260: 1–35.

Extended discussion of the evidence for family and domestic life in ancient times, with a focus on the archaeological data.

———. 1991. *Ashkelon Discovered: From Canaanites and Philistines to Romans and Moslems.* Washington, DC: Biblical Archaeology Society.

———. 1992. "The Periodization of Palestine from Neolithic through Early Bronze Times." In *Chronologies in Old World Archaeology,* edited by R. Ehrich, 22–41. Chicago: University of Chicago Press.

Analysis of the evidence for interregional trade as well as "local" material culture that reflects culture change, focusing on the late prehistory of Palestine, in an edited volume devoted to Old World chronologies.

———. 1996. "The Fury of Babylon: Ashkelon and the Archaeology of Destruction." *Biblical Archaeology Review* 22: 57–69, 76–77.

Review of archaeological discoveries from the late Iron Age at the Philistine site of Ashqelon, with a focus on evidence related to the historical Babylonian attack on the city.

———. 2003. "The Impact of the Sea Peoples." In *The Archaeology of Society in the Holy Land,* 3d ed., edited by T. Levy, 332–348. New York: Facts on File.

Summary of evidence from a Sea Peoples settlement along the coastal plain, with a focus on the origins and development of key Philistine cities.

Starkey, James Leslie. 1934. "Excavations at Tel el-Duweir, 1933–1934." *Palestine Exploration Quarterly* 67: 164–175.

Report on the archaeological finds from excavations at Lachish.

Stech, Tamara, James Muhly, and Robert Maddin. 1985. "Metallurgical Studies on Artifacts from the Tomb near 'Enan." 'Atiqot 17: 75–82.

Examination of some of the earliest evidence for tin bronze in the ancient Near East, suggesting an origin from the end of the Early Bronze Age to the early Intermediate Bronze Age, including a discussion of Cypriote artifacts.

Stech, Tamara, and Vincent Pigott. 1986. "The Metals Trade in Southwest Asia in the Third Millennium B.C." Iraq 48: 39–64.

Two leading scholars on ancient metallurgy examine a range of artifacts from around the Near East and address broad issues concerning the ancient metals trade.

Steel, Louise. 2002. "Consuming Passions: A Contextual Study of the Local Consumption of Mycenaean Pottery at Tell el-'Ajjul." Journal of Mediterranean Archaeology 15: 25–51.

Discussion of pottery use as a reflection of domestic roles and social organization.

Steen, Danielle. 2002. "Nation Building and Archaeological Narratives in the West Bank." Stanford Journal of Archaeology 1: 1–13.

Article, written for an online journal, examining the role of nationalism and modern politics in the definition of an approach to the past.

Steiner, Margaret. 2001. "Jerusalem in the Tenth and Seventh Centuries B.C.E.: From Administrative Town to Commercial City." In Studies in the Archaeology of the Iron Age in Israel and Jordan, edited by A. Mazar, 310–325. Sheffield, England: Sheffield Academic Press.

Examination of evidence, some of it unpublished, from excavations in Jerusalem, especially those conducted by Kathleen Kenyon in the 1960s, with a focus on the question of when the city rose to prominence.

———. 2002. "Jerusalem in the Middle Bronze Age." Paper presented at the Third International Conference on the Archaeology of the Ancient Near East, April 16, Paris.

Stern, Ephraim. 1990. "New Evidence from Dor for the First Appearance of the Phoenicians along the Northern Coast of Israel." Bulletin of the American Schools of Oriental Research 279: 27–34.

A look at the archaeological evidence for a Phoenician presence at the port city of Tel Dor.

———. 1993. "Tel Dor." In New Encyclopedia of Archaeological Excavations in the Holy Land, edited by Ephraim Stern, 3: 357–372. New York: Simon and Schuster.

Brief summary of archaeological discoveries at the site of Tel Dor through all phases of occupation in ancient times.

———. 1995. Excavations at Dor: Final Report. Jerusalem: Institute of Archaeology, Hebrew University.

Report on the final seasons of excavation at Tel Dor, with a summary of research conducted at the site.

Stern, Ephraim, and Diane Lynn Saltz. 1978. "Cypriote Pottery from the Middle Bronze Age Strata of Tel Mevorakh." *Israel Exploration Journal* 28: 137–145.

Discussion of some of the earliest evidence for Cypriote ceramics imported to cities on the Mediterranean coast of the southern Levant.

Stieglitz, Robert. 1977. "Described Seals from Tel Ashdod: The Philistine Script?" *Kadmos* 16.

A study of seals from the Philistine city of Ashdod and evidence for an early Philistine script with Cypro-Aegean roots.

Stos-Gale, Zofia, George Maliotis, and Noel Gale. 1998. "A Preliminary Survey of the Cypriote Slag Heaps and Their Contribution to the Reconstruction of Copper Production on Cyprus." In *Metallurgica Antiqua: In Honor of Hans-Gert Bachmann and Robert Maddin,* edited by T. Rehren, A. Hauptmann, and J. Muhly, 235–262. Bochum, Germany: Deutsches Bargbau-Musum.

Summary of evidence for copper production on Cyprus, including the use of lead-isotope analysis to link slag heaps with known ore deposits.

Stos-Gale, Zofia, George Maliotis, Noel Gale, and Nick Annetts. 1997. "Lead Isotope Characteristics of the Cyprus Copper Ore Deposits Applied to Provenance Studies of Copper Oxhide Ingots." *Archaeometry* 39: 83–124.

Discussion of copper oxhide ingots and their possible place of origin, based on lead-isotope evidence.

Tadmor, Miriam. 2002. "The Kfar Monash Hoard Again: A View from Egypt and Nubia." In *Egyptian and Canaanite Interaction during the Fourth–Third Millennium* B.C.E., edited by E. van den Brink and T. Levy, 239–251. London: Leicester University Press.

A new look at the famed Kfar Monash Hoard of copper goods, this time emphasizing the possible Nubian origins of at least some of the artifacts.

Tadmor, Miriam, Dan Kedem, Friedrich Begemann, Andreas Hauptmann, Ernst Pernicka, and Sigrid Schmitt-Strecker. 1995. "The Nahal Mishmar Hoard from the Judean Desert: Technology, Composition, and Provenance." *'Atiqot* 27: 95–148.

A reexamination of artifacts from the Nahal Mishmar Hoard by a group of leading scholars who apply a variety of analytical techniques in order to understand their production.

Tadmor, Miriam, and Moshe Prausnitz. 1959. "Excavations at Rosh Hanniqra." *Átiqot* 2: 72–88.

Report on archaeological findings from excavations at the site of Rosh Hanniqra.

Tappy, Ron E. 1992. *The Archaeology of Israelite Samaria.* Atlanta: Scholars Press.

Broad summary of archaeological evidence from excavations at Samaria during the Iron Age.

Teissier, Beatrice. 1996. *Egyptian Iconography on Syro-Palestinian Cylinder Seals of the Middle Bronze Age*. Fribourg, Switzerland: University Press.

Epigraphic and iconographic study of Egyptian elements in Middle Bronze Age seal impressions.

Thompson, Thomas J. A. 1982. *The Bible and Archaeology*. Michigan: William B. Eerdmans.

Thompson, Thomas L. 1974. *The Historicity of the Patriarchal Narratives: The Quest for the Historical Abraham*. Berlin: W. de Gruyter.

———. 1992. *Early History of the Israelite People*. Leiden: E. J. Brill.

An interdisciplinary approach to the history of ancient Israel incorporating regional and historical geography with the more traditional field of biblical studies.

Tubb, Jonathan N. 1983. "MBIIA Period in Palestine: Its Relationship with Syria and Its Origin." *Levant* 15: 49–62.

Discussion of evidence from the early Middle Bronze Age, with a focus on new practices and questions about the arrivals of new cultural elements in the region.

———. 2002. *The Canaanites*. London: British Museum.

A study of the history of the Canaanite culture during the Bronze and Early Iron Age, focusing on evidence from the Jordan Valley site of Tel es-Saidiyeh.

Tufnell, Olga. 1953. *The Iron Age: Lachish III (Tell Ed-Duweir)*. 2 vols. New York: Oxford University Press.

Report on the archaeological findings from the Iron Age levels at the biblical/historical site of Lachish.

———. 1958. *Lachish IV: The Bronze Age*. London: Oxford University Press.

Report on the archaeological findings from the Bronze Age levels at the biblical/historical site of Lachish.

Ussishkin, David. 1977. "The Destruction of Lachish by Sennacherib and the Dating of the Royal Judean Storage Jars." *Tel Aviv* 4: 28–60.

Study of the archaeological evidence from Lachish in light of texts referring to the city's destruction.

———. 1980. "The Ghassulian Shrine at En Gedi." *Tel Aviv* 7: 1–44.

Report on the archaeological finds from the cult site overlooking the Dead Sea and its relation to other Chalcolithic shrines.

————. 1985. "Level VII and VI at Tel Lachish and the End of the Late Bronze Age in Canaan." *Occasional Publication, Institute of Archaeology* 11: 213–230.

Discussion of the archaeological findings from excavations at Lachish, with a focus on the first half of the twelfth century B.C.E. as a transitional phase at the end of the Late Bronze Age.

————. 1989. "Schumaker's Shrine in Building 338 at Megiddo." *Israel Exploration Journal* 39: 149–172.

Reexamination of a cultic context at Megiddo in light of more recent research, with a focus on the evidence for ritual paraphernalia.

————. 1993. *The Village of Silwan: The Necropolis from the Period of the Judean Kingdom.* Jerusalem: Israel Exploration Society.

Van Beek, Gus. 1987. "Arches and Vaults in the Ancient Near East." *Scientific American* 257: 96–103.

Review of architectural remains throughout the Near East, including a discussion of an Assyrian building at Tel Jemmeh.

————. 1993. "Jemmeh." In van den Brink, Edwin C. M., ed. 1992. *The Nile Delta in Transition: 4th–3rd Millennium BC.* Proceedings of the seminar held in Cairo, October 21–24, 1990, at the Netherlands Institute of Archaeology and Arabic Studies. Tel-Aviv: Edwin C. M. van den Brink.

Edited volume devoted to the study of late prehsitory in Egypt, with a section focused on evidence for an Egyptian presence in the southern Levant during the Chalcolithic period and Early Bronze Age, including contributions from some of the field's leading scholars.

van den Brink, Edwin C. M., and Thomas E. Levy, eds. 2002. *Egyptian and Canaanite Interaction during the Fourth–Third Millennium B.C.E.* London: Leicester University Press.

Edited volume on contact between the peoples of Egypt and Canaan during the late Chalcolithic period and Early Bronze Age, with contributions from scholars around the world.

van Zeist, Willem, and S. Bottema. 1982. "Vegetational History of the Eastern Mediterranean and the Near East during the Last 20,000 Years." In *Paleoclimates, Paleoenvironments and Human Communities in the Eastern Mediterranean Region in Later Prehistory*, edited by J. Bintliff and W. van Zeist. Oxford: British Archaeological Reports.

Detailed study of paleobotanical remains attempting to reconstruct environments from the late Pleistocene-Holocene eras.

Vaux, Roland de. 1971. "Palestine during the Neolithic and Chalcolithic Periods." In *The Cambridge Ancient History*, 1: 499–538. Cambridge: Cambridge University Press.

Summary of evidence from the late prehistory of the southern Levant, with a discussion of cultural development.

Vriezen, Karel J. H. 2002. "Archaeological Traces of Cult in Israel." In *Only One God? Monotheism in Ancient Israel and the Veneration of the Goddess Asherah,* edited by B. Becking, M. Dijkstra, M. Korpel, and K. Vriezen, 45–80. London: Sheffield Academic Press.

> A study of the material remains representing religious practice during the Bronze and Iron Ages, in an attempt to understand attitudes toward the female deity Asherah.

Waldbaum, Jane C. 1989. "Copper, Iron, Tin, Wood: The Start of the Iron Age in the Eastern Mediterranean." *Archeomaterials* 3: 111–122.

> Analysis of the evidence for shifts in technology within the broader context of culture change throughout the eastern Mediterranean region.

———. 1994. "Early Greek Contacts with the Southern Levant, ca. 1000–600 B.C.: The Eastern Perspective." *Bulletin of the American Schools of Oriental Research* 293: 53–66.

> Discussion of evidence for contact between peoples of the southern Levant and Greece, especially Mycenae, during the later portions of the Iron Age (Iron 2–3).

———. 1997. "Greeks in the East or Greeks and the East? Problems in the Definition and Recognition of Presence." *Bulletin of the American Schools of Oriental Research* 305: 1–17.

> A look at the archaeological evidence for regional interaction in the eastern Mediterranean focusing on the problem of what constitutes the movement of goods and what represents human migration.

———. 1999. "The Coming of Iron in the Eastern Mediterranean: Thirty Years of Archaeological and Technological Research." In *The Archaeometallurgy of the Asian Old World,* edited by V. C. Pigott, 27–58. Philadelphia: University Museum, University of Pennsylvania.

> Review of the earliest evidence for the use of iron in the southern Levant, with a discussion of where the technology came from and how and why it spread throughout the region.

Waldbaum, Jane C., and Jodi Magness. 1997. "Chronology of Early Greek Pottery: New Evidence from Seventh-Century B.C. Destruction Levels in Israel." *American Journal of Archaeology* 101: 23–40.

> Examination of the ceramic evidence for the Greek presence during the late Iron Age and how it correlates with evidence for destruction.

Wapnish, Paula. 1981. "Camel Caravans and Camel Pastoralists at Tell Jemmeh." *Journal of the Ancient Near Eastern Society* 13: 101–121.

> Analysis of some of the earliest evidence for the use of the camel, by a leading zooarchaeologist.

———. 1984. "Dromedary and Bactrian Camel in Levantine Historical Settings: The Evidence from Tell Jemmeh." *BAR International Series* 202: 171–200.

Discussion on the domestication of the camel and its earliest exploitation in the ancient Near East.

Wapnish, Paula, and Brian Hesse. 1988. "Urbanization and the Organization of Animal Production at Tell Jemmeh in the Middle Bronze Age Levant." *Journal of Near Eastern Studies* 47: 81–94.

A study of the evidence for animal husbandry during the Middle Bronze Age, with a focus on how it contributed to the overall economy at Tel Jemmeh, by two zooarchaeologists.

Ward, William A. 1991. "Early Contacts between Egypt, Canaan, and Sinai: Remarks on the Paper by Amnon Ben-Tor." *Bulletin of the American Schools of Oriental Research* 281, 11–26.

Discussion of the nature of economic and political relations between Egypt and Canaan in the Early Bronze Age.

Watrin, Luc. 2002. "Tributes and the Rise of a Predatory Power: Unraveling the Intrigue of EB I Palestinian Jars Found by E. Amélineau at Abydos." In *Egyptian and Canaanite Interaction during the Fourth–Third Millennium B.C.E.*, edited by E. van den Brink and T. Levy, 450–463. London: Leicester University Press.

Reexamination of pottery from Abydos indicating the existence of noble burials.

Watson, Charles M. 1915. *Fifty Years' Work in the Holy Land: A Record and a Summary.* London: Committee of the Palestine Exploration Fund.

Summary of early exploration in Palestine by the Palestine Exploration Fund (PEF), with commentary on knowledge to date and future directions for further research.

Watzinger, Carl. 1933–1935. *Denkmäler Palästinas; eine Einfürung in die Archäologie des Heiligen Landes.* Leipzig: J. C. Hinrichs'sche buchhandlung.

Overview of the early years of archaeological investigation of Palestine, including a discussion of early Canaanite religion.

Webb, Jennifer M. 1985. "The Incised Scapulae." In *Excavations at Kition V: The Pre-Phoenician Levels, Part II*, edited by V. Karageorghis, 317–328. Niscosia, Cyprus: Department of Antiquities, Cyprus.

Examination of the evidence for incised scapulae, with a discussion of their use in ritual practice.

Weinstein, James. 1981. "The Egyptian Empire in Palestine: A Reassessment." *Bulletin of the American Schools of Oriental Research* 241: 1–28.

Analysis of the evidence for an Egyptian presence in Canaan and the validity of traditional models that have the latter as an Egyptian colony.

———. 1992. "The Chronology of Palestine in the Early Second Millennium B.C.E." *Bulletin of the American Schools of Oriental Research* 288: 27–46.

Examination of the archaeological and textual evidence in an attempt to reconstruct the chronology of the Middle Bronze Age, particularly the debate regarding the high and low chronology.

Wesselius, Jan Wim. 1999. "Discontinuity, Congruence and the Making of the Hebrew Bible." *Scandinavian Journal of the Old Testament* 13: 24–77.

An investigation into the historicity of the Hebrew Bible through an examination of the text's own internal structure, by a biblical scholar.

Wiggins, Steve. 1993. *A Reassessment of "Asherah": A Study according to the Textual Sources of the First Two Millennia B.C.E.* Kevelaer: Verlag Butzon and Bercker.

An evaluation of the evidence for the existence of an Asherah cult during the monarchic period concluding that, although such a cult may have existed, the evidence cited in support of Asherah worship may be overstated.

Wilson, John A. 1969. "The Journey of Wen Amon to Phoenicia." In *Ancient Near Eastern Texts Relating to the Old Testament*, edited by J. B. Pritchard, 25–29. Princeton, NJ: Princeton University Press.

Translation of an Egyptian tale recounting the travels of an envoy dispatched to Phoenicia, providing valuable information for the period when Egyptian power in the Levant began to wane (early Twenty-First Dynasty) and the rise of the Sea Peoples in the eastern Mediterranean.

Winter, Urs. 1983. "Frau und Göttin: Exegetische und Ikonographische Studien zum Weiblichen Gottesbild im Alten Israel und in Dessen Umwelt." Freiburg: Universitätsverlag; Göttingen: Vandenhoeck and Ruprecht.

Discussion of religion in ancient Israel and neighboring regions, with a focus on the deities worshipped, via the study of iconography.

Wright, G. Ernest. 1961. *The Bible and the Ancient Near East: Essays in Honor of William Foxwell Albright*. Winona Lake, IN: Eisenbrauns.

A landmark volume in the tradition of Biblical Archaeology, with contributions from some of the great scholars of the day.

Yadin, Yigael. 1955. "The Earliest Record of Egypt's Military Penetration into Asia." *Israel Exploration Journal* 5: 1–16.

One of the first attempts to understand Canaanite-Egyptian interaction during the Early Bronze Age, based largely on an interpretation of the Narmer Palette.

———. 1967. "The Rise and Fall of Hazor." In *Archaeological Discoveries in the Holy Land*, compiled by the Archaeological Institute of America, 57–66. New York: Crowell.

Discussion of cultural development at the major center of the north, based on a summary of findings from Yigael Yadin's excavations at the site.

———. 1970. "Symbols of Deities at Zinjirli, Carthage and Hazor." In *Near Eastern Ar-*

chaeology in the Twentieth Century: Essays in Honor of Nelson Glueck, edited by James A. Sanders, 199–231. Garden City, NY: Doubleday.

Analysis of the evidence for religious representations, with a search for shared themes among ancient peoples.

———. 1972. *Hazor.* London : Oxford University Press, for the British Academy.

A narration of the history of research at the Hazor site and a review of the archaeological evidence for cultural evolution over time, written for a popular audience by the site's long-term excavator.

———. 1979. "The Transition from a Semi-Nomadic to a Sedentary Society in the 12th Century B.C.E." In *Symposia Celebrating the Seventy-Fifth Anniversary of the Founding of the American Schools of Oriental Research (1900–1975),* edited by F. M. Cross, 57–68. Cambridge, MA: American Schools of Oriental Research.

Discussion of the evidence for Israelite settlement during the early Iron Age, with an emphasis on the historicity of the Hebrew Bible's account of the conquest story.

Yannai, Eli. 1997. "A Tomb from the Early Bronze I and Intermediate Bronze Age near Tel Esur (Assawir)." *'Atiqot* 30: 1–15.

Summary, in Hebrew, of archaeological evidence from an Early or Intermediate Bronze Age tomb.

Yee, Gale A. 1999. "Gender, Class, and the Social Scientific Study of Genesis 2–3." In *The Social World of the Hebrew Bible: Twenty-Five Years of the Social Sciences in the Academy,* edited by Ronald A. Simkins and Stephen L. Cook, 177–192. Semeia, 87. Atlanta: Society of Biblical Literature.

An attempt to reconstruct social organization during the time of the patriarchs via an interpretation of the Book of Genesis.

Yeivin, Shemuel. 1960. "Early Contacts between Canaan and Egypt." *Israel Exploration Journal* 10: 193–203.

Yekutieli, Yuval, and Ram Gophna. 1994. "Excavations at an Early Bronze Age Site near Nizzanim." *Tel Aviv* 21: 162–185.

Report on the archaeological finds from excavations at the coastal site of Nizzanim, with a focus on ceramic chronology and evidence for an Egyptian presence.

Yellin, John. 1992. "The Origin of the Pictorial Krater from the 'Mycenaean' Tomb at Tel Dan." *Archaeometry* 34: 31–36.

Detailed study of one of the more outstanding finds from Tel Dan, with an interpretation of iconography and a discussion of the broader implications for understanding the Mycenaean influence in the southern Levant.

Yellin, John, and Jan Gunneweg. 1989. "Instrumental Neutron Activation Analysis and the Origin of Iron Age I Collared-Rim Jars and Pithoi from Tel Dan." *Annual of the American Schools of Oriental Research* 49: 133.

Application of Neutron Activation Analysis (NAA) to the study of Iron Age ceramics in order to answer questions regarding the origins of ceramics traditionally thought to belong to the Israelites.

Yener, K. Aslihan, and Vandiver, Pamela. 1993 "Tin Processing at Göletepe, an Early Bronze Age Site in Anatolia." *American Journal of Archaeology* 97: 207–238.

Discussion of controversial evidence regarding the early processing of tin in Anatolia.

Yurco, Frank J. 1990. "3,200-Year-Old Picture of Israelites Found in Egypt." *Biblical Archaeology Review* 16: 20–33.

A look at Egyptian texts and images from Thebes (Merenptah Stele and the Cour de la Cachette Wall), along with other historical sources, in an attempt to identify representations of Israelite peoples.

———. 1991. "Yurco's Response." *Biblical Archaeology Review* 17: 61.

One-half of a debate between two scholars, in which the interpretation of ethnicity in the southern Levant and Egypt is discussed.

Zertal, Adam. 1988. *The Israelite Settlement in the Hill Country of Manasseh.* Haifa: Haifa University.

Reconstruction of Israelite settlement, in Hebrew, based on an archaeological survey of this portion of the hill country.

———. 1991. "Israel Enters Canaan." *Biblical Archaeology Review* 17: 28–49, 75.

Discussion of the processes of Israelite settlement in the hill country, written for a popular audience.

———. 1994. "'To the Land of the Perizzites and the Giants': On the Israelite Settlement in the Hill Country of Manasseh." In *From Nomadism to Monarchy,* edited by N. Na'aman and I. Finkelstein, 37–70. Jerusalem: Israel Exploration Society.

A study on the role of the tribes of Manasseh in the formation of the Israelite state, including a review of evidence for cultic sites.

———. 1998. "The Iron Age I Culture in the Hill-Country of Canaan: A Manassite Look." In *Mediterranean Peoples in Transition: Thirteenth to Early Tenth Centuries B.C.E.,* edited by S. Gitin, A. Mazar, and E. Stern, 238–251. Jerusalem: Israel Exploration Society.

Discussion of Israelite settlement in the hill country, specifically the land of Manasseh, based on evidence from excavation and survey.

———. 2001. "The Heart of the Monarchy: Patterns of Settlement and Historical Considerations of the Israelite Kingdom of Samaria." In *Studies in the Archaeology of the Iron Age in Israel and Jordan,* edited by Amihai Mazar, 38–64. Sheffield, England: Sheffield Academic Press.

Examination of social and economic organization in the heartland of the Northern Kingdom, with an emphasis on geography as a factor.

Zerubavel, Yael. 1995. *Recovered Roots: Collective Memory and the Making of Israeli National Tradition.* Chicago: University of Chicago Press.

Critique of Biblical Archaeology and the role that Israeli nationalism and identity has played in the history of research.

Zimhoni, Orna. 1997. *Studies in the Iron Age Pottery of Israel: Typological, Archaeological, and Chronological Aspects.* Tel Aviv: Tel Aviv University, Institute of Archaeology.

Examination of ceramic evidence from the Iron Age, finding an increase in slipped and burnished wares during the late eleventh and early tenth centuries B.C.E.

Zohary, Daniel. 1992. "Domestication of the Neolithic Near Eastern Crop Assemblage." In *Prehistoire de l'Agriculture, Nouvelles Approches Experimentales et Ethnographiques,* edited by C. Anderson, 81–86. Paris: CNRS.

An article tracing the roots of the basic Near Eastern crop suite back to its domestication during the Neolithic period, by a leading paleobotanist.

Zorn, Jeffrey R. 2003. "Tell en-Nasbeh and the Problem of the Material Culture of the Sixth Century." In *Judah and the Judeans in the Neo-Babylonian Period,* edited by O. Lipschits and J. Blenkinsopp. Winona Lake, IN: Eisenbrauns.

A review of the architectural remains discovered during excavations at Tel en-Nasbeh.

Index

Loanwords, 242
Lod, 81
Lost wax process, 217
Loud, Gordon, 38
Love, 180, 182
Lower Egypt, 56, 148
Lower Galilee, 17, 19, 80
Lower Paleolithic age, 15
Lsr r, 167
Luxury goods
  bronze as, 218, 232
  burial practices and, 113
  Chalcolithic period and, 47, 109, 139
  Early Bronze Age and, 73
  Intermediate Bronze Age and, 83
  Iron Age and, 131, 133, 234
  Late Bronze Age and, 58, 87, 152, 225
  Middle Bronze Age and, 87
  See also Prestige goods
Lybians, 122
Lynch, William F., 35

Maacah, 253
Macalister, R. A. S., 37, 38
Maceheads
  Chalcolithic period and, 75, 109, 206
  Early Bronze Age and, 80, 213
  as prestige goods, 140
Maddin, 83
Mahaneh Dan, 128
Malhata, 162
Manahat, 245
Manasseh, 61, 253
Mari (Syria)
  archive at, 121
  biblical texts, 31
  Egyptian King List and, 31
  extra-biblical texts from, 43
  king of Hazor and, 7
  Mari Letters, 56
  Middle Bronze Age and, 87
  trade and, 87
Masada, 42
Mass production
  Assyrians and, 106
  of ceramics, 210, 229
  of tool forms, 80
Massebah/massebot
  at Arad, 191
  Bull Site and, 188
  description of, 173
  at Gezer, 178–180, 179(ill.)
  at Hartuv, 176
  at Hazor, 185

  Horvat Qitmit and, 201
  Israelites and, 196
  at Megiddo, 178
  at Tel Rehov, 191
Material culture
  Chalcolithic period, 206–210
  Early Bronze Age, 210–216
  Intermediate Bronze Age, 216–220
  Iron Age, 227–238
  Israelites, 228, 229–234
  Late Bronze Age, 223–227
  Middle Bronze Age, 220–223
  Philistines, 234–238
  Phoenicians, 238–239
  Sea Peoples and, 234
Matres lectionis, 245
Matthews, Victor, 122, 161
Mazar, Amihai
  on Egyptian raids, 52
  on fortifications, 153
  on Iron Age, 267
  as Israeli archaeologist, 43
  on languages, 242
  on Late Bronze Age, 59, 266
  on periods of discovery, 32–33
  on Sea People, 126
Mazar, Benjamin, 43, 273
McNutt, Paula, 273
Mechanot, 197
Medinat Habu, 124, 126, 157, 158
Mediterranean coast
  common belief system and, 180
  exchange in, 7
  oxhide ingots, 219, 225
  Phoenicians and, 71
  topography of, 18
Mediterranean humid zone, 21, 74, 77, 110
Mediterranean Sea, 15, 16, 18
Medum, 37
Megadim, 238
Megaron-style chapels, 178, 179(ill.)
Megiddo
  Aegean pottery at, 126
  Amarna Letters and, 57
  animal motifs at, 177
  animal sacrifices at, 194
  apsidal buildings, 112
  attacks on, 150
  Bichrome Wares and, 224
  Canaanean blades and, 80
  Canaanites and, 60
  capture of, 154
  city gates at, 233(ill.), 274

ABOUT THE AUTHOR

JONATHAN M. GOLDEN teaches anthropology at both Drew University and Fairleigh Dickinson University in Madison, NJ. Golden specializes in the archaeology of the Ancient Near East and Europe; his most recent book, *Dawn of the Metal Age*, focuses on ancient technology. He lives in Philadelphia.

St. Louis

81

LIBRARY

St. Louis Community College
at Meramec
LIBRARY